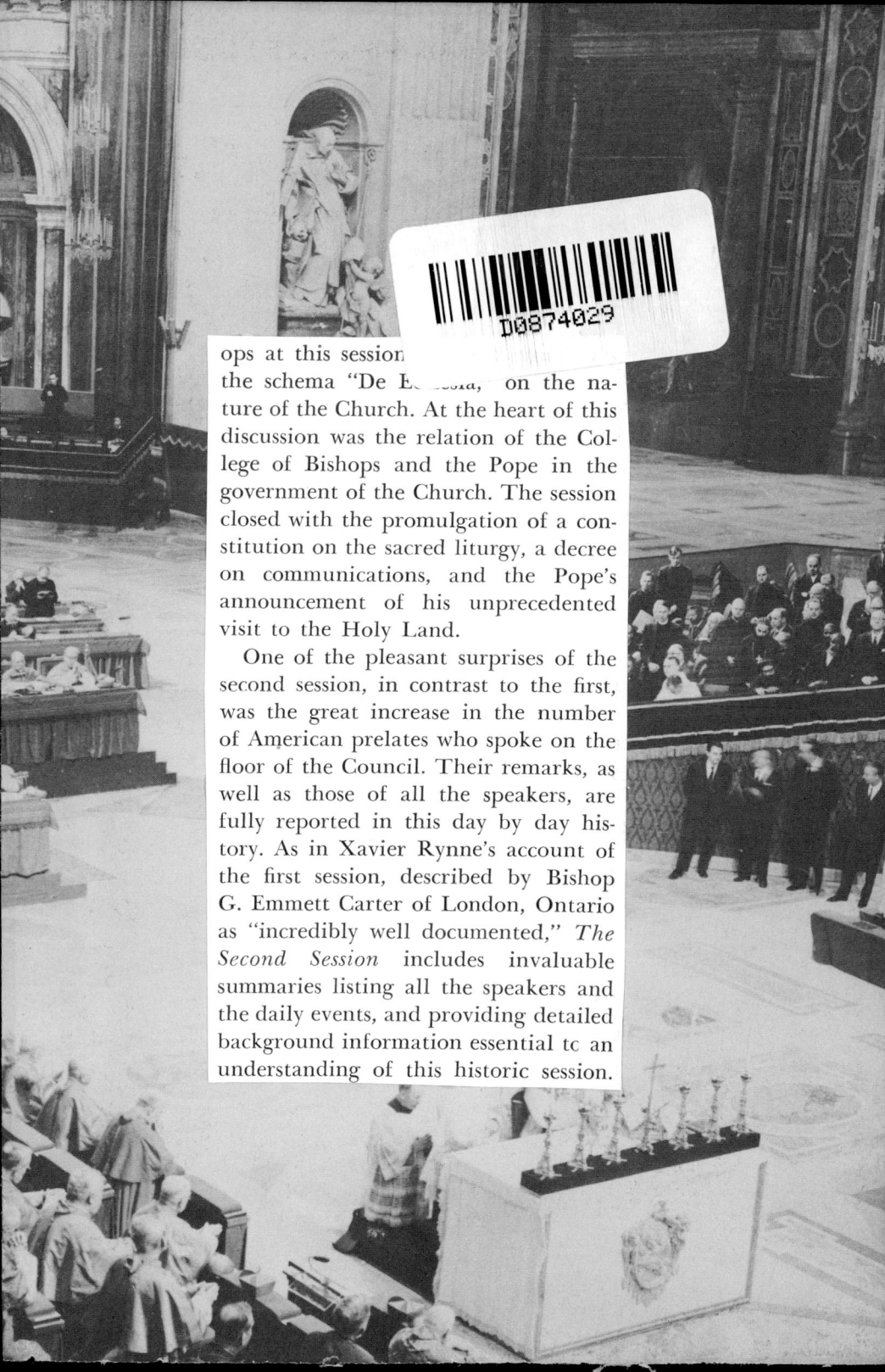

ops at this session [was]
the schema "De E[cclesia," on the nature of the Church. At the heart of this
discussion was the relation of the College of Bishops and the Pope in the
government of the Church. The session
closed with the promulgation of a constitution on the sacred liturgy, a decree
on communications, and the Pope's
announcement of his unprecedented
visit to the Holy Land.

One of the pleasant surprises of the
second session, in contrast to the first,
was the great increase in the number
of American prelates who spoke on the
floor of the Council. Their remarks, as
well as those of all the speakers, are
fully reported in this day by day history. As in Xavier Rynne's account of
the first session, described by Bishop
G. Emmett Carter of London, Ontario
as "incredibly well documented," *The
Second Session* includes invaluable
summaries listing all the speakers and
the daily events, and providing detailed
background information essential tc an
understanding of this historic session.

THE SECOND SESSION

WITHDRAWN

Xavier Rynne

THE
SECOND
SESSION

THE DEBATES AND DECREES OF
VATICAN COUNCIL II,
SEPTEMBER 29 TO DECEMBER 4, 1963

New York
Farrar, Straus & Company

COPYRIGHT © 1963, 1964
BY FARRAR, STRAUS AND COMPANY, INC.

LIBRARY OF CONGRESS CATALOG CARD NUMBER: 64-17875

The authors are grateful to the editors of *The New Yorker,* in whose pages some of the material in this book first appeared in somewhat different form.

MANUFACTURED IN THE UNITED STATES OF AMERICA
BY AMERICAN BOOK–STRATFORD PRESS, INC., NEW YORK

FIRST PRINTING, 1964

. . . History marches on. The Church is obligated to a realistic view of things, and that view imposes on it—at times painfully—the task of selecting from its heritage of institutions and customs all that is essential and vital so as to reinvigorate its true traditional commitments. . . .

Paulus P. P. VI-

Contents

✠

List of Illustrations

*Opening page of "Relatio" by Cardinal Lercaro,
delivered on November 15, 1963 : 202*

*Notification about the election of new members to the
Commissions, November 21, 1963 : 246*

*Circular signed by 25 Council Fathers urging a
"Non Placet" vote on the Communications Schema,
November 25, 1963 : 255*

*Title page and preface of Decree on Communications
Media : 258 and 259*

*Title page and first page of Constitution on
Sacred Liturgy : 294 and 295*

*Notice announcing temporary suspension of the Liturgy
Constitution, L'Osservatore Romano, December 6, 1963 : 301*

FRONT ENDPAPERS

The Moderators presiding over the Second Session.

BACK ENDPAPERS

Left, The Pope at the shore of the River Jordan. *Right,* the historic meeting of Pope Paul VI and Patriarch Athenagoras.

Preface

The Second Session of Vatican II, from September 29 to December 4, 1963, was a religious event of equal, perhaps greater, significance than the First Session. Pope Paul VI not only decided on the early reconvening of the Council, but in his opening address reaffirmed the Council's purpose "to open up new horizons in the Church, and to tap the fresh spring water of the doctrine and grace of Christ our Lord and let it flow over the earth." In the same speech, addressing the spirit of "our most beloved John XXIII" directly, Pope Paul also said:

Penetrating into the dark and tormented needs of the modern age, you have picked up the broken thread of the First Vatican Council, and by that very fact you have banished the fear wrongly deduced from that Council, as if the supreme powers conferred by Christ on the Roman Pontiff to govern and vivify the Church were sufficient, without the assistance of ecumenical councils.*

By this and other actions throughout the ten weeks of the Second Session, the Pauline phase of Vatican II has preserved and extended the revolutionary quality of the Johannine First Session. The authors do not agree with those assessors who have adjudged the Second Session "disappointing." Its shortcomings, fully discussed in this volume, were due in large part to the transitional character of the session. The great achievement of the Liturgical Constitution, promulgated at this session, has already begun to bear fruit throughout the world. Like the First Session, the Second Session was marked by a number of dramatic triumphs and pitfalls, and two important facts were once again demonstrated: the vast majority of the Council Fathers *are* progressive; it is the minority that resists renewal and obstructs *aggiornamento*. The fact that the Second Session ended with the Council's work incomplete is cause not for discouragement, but for renewed determination on the part of the majorty to restore to the Church the lineaments it had when it left the hands of its Founder, Jesus Christ.

The excessively generous attention (39 pages) given our modest report on the First Session by the *American Ecclesiastical Review*** has emboldened the authors to provide a similar service for the Second Session. We were particularly gratified to find in this lengthy article by a spokesman for the minority at the Council an irrefutable confirmation of the factuality of our analysis. We feel, however, that we were given more credit than we deserved for "breaking the secrecy of the Council,"† and making possible the unprecedentedly full coverage of the Second Session.

* Address at St. Peter's, September 29, 1963. See full text in Appendix.
** Issue of December, 1963, pp. 392-430.
† *The Newark Advocate,* book review, June, 1963.

Finally, we admit that Dr. Robert McAfee Brown, in a valiant attempt to satisfy John Cogley's desperate query,

> *I know their habits, their next of kin,*
> *But who the hell is Xavier Rynne?**

has come close to, but not quite on, target with this ingenious bit of sleuthing:

One person . . . fulfills all the qualifications necessary for authorship, i.e. (1) a non-Jesuit, (2) a writer competent enough to produce the flowing style of the "Letters," (3) one aware of the time-zone discrepancies between New York and Rome and therefore previously published in *The New Yorker,* (4) most conclusively, a possessor of the initials "P.M." It is clear that Xavier Rynne is none other than Phyllis McGinley!**

This inspired piece of induction was equalled only by the rumor, first published in the Manchester *Guardian,* that "the Vatican has roped [Xavier Rynne] into some conciliar position so as to hobble him at the next [i.e. the second] session."† This and other reports of our literary demise, we are happy to announce, were premature.

—XAVIER RYNNE.

* "Literary Intelligence," *America,* October 19, 1963.
** *Christian Century,* July 31, 1963, p. 956.
† The *Guardian,* review by Geoffrey Moorhouse, August 30, 1963.

Chronology of the Second Session

✠

FRI.   OCT.   4   41st General Congr.—*De Ecclesia,* Chs. I. & II.
                   Debate on Ch. II begun.
                   Lay Auditors present at sessions.
                   Announcement about new seating on Monday.
                   Conference by Père Yves Congar, O.P., on
                   collegiality.
SAT.   OCT.   5   Press conference of Bishop René Stourm.
                   Letter of Cardinal Tisserant to Holy Father
                   on latter's Curia speech of Sept. 21st.

SECOND WEEK

SUN.   OCT.   6   Mass celebrated by Archbishop O'Connor for
                   journalists at Sant' Ivo.
MON.   OCT.   7   42nd General Congr.—*De Ecclesia,* Ch. II.
TUE.   OCT.   8   43rd General Congr.—*De Ecclesia,* Ch. II.
                   Report of Card. Lercaro on Liturgy amend-
                   ments.
                   Vote on Amendments 1-4 of Liturgy Ch. II.
                   Conference of Cardinal Suenens.
                   V. Veronese and J. Guitton appointed Lay
                   Auditors.
WED.   OCT.   9   44th General Congr.—*De Ecclesia,* Ch. II.
                   Vote on Amendments 5-12 of Liturgy Ch. II.
                   Interview of Patriarch Maximos IV.
THU.   OCT. 10   45th General Congr.—*De Ecclesia,* Ch. II.
                   Vote on Amendments 13-19 of Liturgy Ch. II.
                   Audience to Pastor M. Niemoeller.
FRI.   OCT. 11   46th General Congr.—*De Ecclesia,* Ch. II.
                   Announcement by Card. Lercaro about con-
                   tinuance of debate on *De Ecclesia* Ch. II.
                   Pope at S. Maria Maggiore for commemora-
                   tion of commencement of First Session un-
                   der John XXIII.
SAT.   OCT. 12   Conference by Bishop J. Cirarda.
                   Conference by Archbishop Heenan of West-
                   minster.

THIRD WEEK

SUN.   OCT. 13   Beatification of Bishop John Nepomucene
                   Neumann.

MON. OCT. 14   47th General Congr.—*De Ecclesia,* Ch. II.

Vote on Liturgy Ch. II as whole fails of majority.

Patriarchs occupy new seats opposite cardinals.

TUE. OCT. 15   48th General Congr.—*De Ecclesia,* Ch. II.

Vote on Amendments 1-4 of Liturgy Ch. III.

Vote to close debate on *De Ecclesia,* Ch. II.

Announcement about straw-vote on "four points" on Thursday.

E. Inglesis appointed Lay Auditor.

WED. OCT. 16   49th General Congr.—*De Ecclesia,* Chs. II & III.

Continuance of debate on *De Eccl.* Ch. II.

Debate on *De Ecclesia,* Ch. III begun.

Vote on Amendments 5-8 of Liturgy Ch. III.

THU. OCT. 17   50th General Congr.—*De Ecclesia,* Ch. III.

Vote on Amendments 9-10 of Liturgy Ch. III.

Audience to Observer Delegates.

FRI. OCT. 18   51st General Congr.—*De Ecclesia,* Ch. III.

Vote on Liturgy Ch. III as whole fails of majority.

Announcement about 10-minute limit on debate.

Communiqué of Secretariat for Unity on Jews.

Reception of Cardinal Bea for Observer Delegates.

Audience to Bishop Fred P. Corson of Methodist Church.

SAT. OCT. 19   Conference of Archbishop Grimshaw.

Bach concert for Fathers.

Press conference of Bishop McGrath of Panama.

FOURTH WEEK

SUN. OCT. 20   Mission Sunday: Pope consecrates 14 missionary bishops in St. Peter's.

Mass by Cardinal Silva Henriquez for journalists in Sant' Ivo.

MON. OCT. 21   52nd General Congr.—*De Ecclesia,* Ch. III.
                      Vote on Amendments 1-2 of Liturgy Ch. IV.
TUE. OCT. 22   53rd General Congr.—*De Ecclesia,* Ch. III.
                      Vote on Amendments 3-8 of Liturgy Ch. IV.
                      Press interview of Archbishop Roberts, S.J.
WED. OCT. 23   54th General Congr.—*De Ecclesia,* Ch. III.
                      Vote on Amendments 9-13 of Liturgy Ch. IV.
                      Meeting of Council Presidency and Secretariat.
THU. OCT. 24   55th General Congr.—*De Ecclesia,* Ch. III.
                      Vote on Liturgy Ch. IV as whole.
                      Vote to close debate on *De Eccl.* Ch. III.
                      Vote on Amendments 1-5 of Liturgy Ch. V.
                      "Relationes" of Cardinals Koenig and Santos
                          on incorporation of Mary in schema on
                          Church.
FRI. OCT. 25   56th General Congr.—*De Ecclesia,* Chs. III &
                          IV.
                      Vote on Amendments 6-10 of Liturgy Ch. V.
                      Audience to Council Moderators.
                      Conference of Abbot Butler on Mary.
SAT. OCT. 26   Audience to Archbishop Pietro Parente.
                      Press conference of Bishop H. Wittler.

FIFTH WEEK

SUN. OCT. 27   Beatification of Dominic of the Mother of God.
MON. OCT. 28   Mass celebrated by Pope Paul VI, commemoration of Pope John XXIII, in St. Peter's.
TUE. OCT. 29   57th General Congr.—*De Ecclesia,* Ch. IV.
                      Vote to include Mary in schema on Church.
                      Vote on Liturgy Ch. V. as a whole.
                      Vote on Amendments 1-2 of Liturgy Ch. VII.
WED. OCT. 30   58th General Congr.—*De Ecclesia,* Ch. IV.
                      Vote to close debate on *De Eccl.* Ch. IV.
                      Vote on "Five Propositions."
                      Vote on Amendments 3-6 of Liturgy Ch. VII.
                      Statements of Archbishop Krol and Bishop
                          Wright at American Bishops' Press Panel.

THU.	OCT. 31	59th General Congr.—*De Ecclesia*, Ch. IV continued.
		Vote on combining Liturgy Chs. VI and VIII and approval of same as a whole.
		Announcement of Card. Doepfner about speeding up debates.
		Pope visits Lateran University.
FRI.	NOV. 1	Declaration of Italian Bishops on Communism.
SAT.	NOV. 2	Pope at S. Lorenzo fuori le Mura.
		Audience to Cardinal Frings.

SIXTH WEEK

SUN.	NOV. 3	Beatification of Leonardo Murialdo.
MON.	NOV. 4	Commemoration of centenary of Council of Trent in St. Peter's.
		Apostolic Letter on Seminaries.
		Radio interview of Cardinal Suenens.
TUE.	NOV. 5	60th General Congr.—Bishops in general.
		Debate on Bishops begun.
WED.	NOV. 6	61st General Congr.—Bishops in general.
		Vote to accept Bishops as basis for discussion.
		Audience to Cardinal Ottaviani.
		Statement of Archbishop Alter at American Bishops' Press Panel on schema and Bishop Carli.
THU.	NOV. 7	62nd General Congr.—Bishops, Ch. I.
		Card. Doepfner summarizes remaining speakers on *De Eccl.* Ch. IV.
		Audience to German and Austrian Bishops, and Karl Rahner, S.J.
		Audience to Archbishop Felici, Secretary General.
		Appointment of new Pont. Commission for Revision of Canon Law.
FRI.	NOV. 8	63rd General Congr.—Bishops, Chs. I & II.
		Frings-Ottaviani clash on floor.
		Debate on Bishops Ch. II begun.
		Audience to Council Moderators.

Distribution of Ch. IV of Ecumenism on Jews.

Reception of Observer Delegates for Secretariat for Unity.

SAT. NOV. 9 Audience to Cardinal Siri.

Conference of Archbishop Thiandoum.

SEVENTH WEEK

SUN. NOV. 10 Pope takes possession of Lateran Basilica.

MON. NOV. 11 64th General Congr.—Bishops, Ch. II.

Audience to Patriarch Maximos IV.

Discussion in Theological Commission on Religious Liberty (Ch. V of schema on Ecumenism).

TUE. NOV. 12 65th General Congr.—Bishops, Ch. II.

Vote to refer Ch. V of Bishops to Commission for Revision of Canon Law.

Vote to close debate on Bishops Ch. II.

Vote in Theological Commission on reporting out Religious Liberty.

WED. NOV. 13 66th General Congr.—Bishops, Chs. II & III.

Announcement that debate on Ecumenism will follow that on Bishops.

Interview of Card. Ottaviani on "Five Propositions" (Divine Word Service).

THU. NOV. 14 67th General Congr.—Bishops, Ch. III.

2 votes on text of Communications decree.

Announcement about Eucharistic Congress at Bombay.

Vote to close debate on Bishops Ch. III.

Pope receives relics of St. Clement in Sistine Chapel.

FRI. NOV. 15 68th General Congr.—Bishops, Chs. III & IV.

Debate on Bishops Ch. III continued.

Debate on Bishops Ch. IV begun.

Meeting of Council "Summit" (Moderators, Presidents, Secretariat) presided over by Pope, report of Cardinal Lercaro.

Audience to U.S. Bishops.

SAT. NOV. 16 Interview of Cardinal Koenig.

EIGHTH WEEK

SUN. NOV. 17   Beatification of Vincenzo Romano.
Pope transfers relics of St. Clement to San Clemente.

MON. NOV. 18   69th General Congr.—Ecumenism in general.
Vote on final text of Liturgy Ch. I.
Reports of Card. Cicognani and Archbishop Martin on Ecumenism, Chs. I-III.
Debate on Ecumenism in general begun.
Audience to Cardinal Ottaviani.
Message of Lay Auditors (published 11/21).

TUE. NOV. 19   70th General Congr.—Ecumenism in general.
Reports of Card. Bea and Bishop De Smedt on Chs. IV and V of Ecumenism.
Text of Ch. V of Ecumenism distributed.

WED. NOV. 20   71st General Congr.—Ecumenism in general.
Votes on *Modi* 1-3 of Liturgy Ch. II.
Complaint of Cardinal Bacci.
Announcement about promulgation of Liturgy constitution and Communications decree.

THU. NOV. 21   72nd General Congr.—Ecumenism in general.
Announcement about increase in Commission membership.
Votes on *Modi* to Liturgy Ch. III.
Vote to accept Chs. I-III of Ecumenism as basis for discussion, announcement about voting on Chs. IV and V "at later date."

FRI. NOV. 22   73rd General Congr.—Ecumenism, Ch. I.
Vote on Liturgy Ch. IV.
Vote on Liturgy Chs. V-VII.
Vote on Liturgy schema as a whole.
Assassination of President Kennedy.

SAT. NOV. 23   Requiem for deceased cardinals and bishops.

NINTH WEEK

MON. NOV. 25   74th General Congr.—Ecumenism, Chs. I & II.
Announcement concerning closing ceremony on Dec. 4th.

Vote approving *Modi* and text of Communications decree as a whole.

Announcement of Cardinal Tisserant about distribution of sheets to Fathers.

Requiem for President Kennedy at Lateran Basilica.

TUE. NOV. 26   75th General Congr.—Ecumenism, Chs. I & II.

Press interview of Maximos IV.

WED. NOV. 27   76th General Congr.—Ecumenism, Ch. III.

"Moleben" in honor of St. Josaphat.

THU. NOV. 28   77th General Congr.—Ecumenism, Chs. II & III.

Voting for new Commission members.

Audience to English Bishops.

FRI. NOV. 29   78th General Congr.—Ecumenism, Ch. III

Results of elections to Commissions announced.

Announcement about Third Session.

Announcement about "non-infallibility" of Liturgy and Communications decrees.

Text of a Message to Priests distributed.

Audience to Lay Auditors.

SAT. NOV. 30   Audience to Council *Periti*.

Conference of Oscar Cullmann at St-Louis-des-Français.

Interview of Cardinal Ottaviani.

TENTH WEEK

SUN. DEC. 1   Beatification of Nunzio Sulprizio.

Pope says mass for journalists in Pauline Chapel.

MON. DEC. 2   79th General Congr.—Ecumenism, Ch. III.

Announcement about Intersession period.

Announcement, Message to Priests withdrawn.

Copies of Lercaro Report of Nov. 15th distributed to Fathers.

Speech of Cardinal Bea closing debate on Ecumenism.

Remarks by Bishop Hengsbach on Apostolate of Laity.

TUE. DEC. 3   Commemoration of Council of Trent by Cardinal Urbani, in St. Peter's.

Motu Proprio on Bishops issued.

Speeches by V. Veronese and J. Guitton, Lay Auditors.

WED. DEC. 4   Closing Session in St. Peter's.

Address by Pope, announcement of forthcoming pilgrimage to Holy Land.

I

The Johannine Council becomes the Pauline Council

✠

THE VACANCY OF THE HOLY SEE began on June 3, 1963 at 7:49 A.M. in Rome when, after an agonizing illness, Pope John XXIII died. For the whole world, his death left a big vacancy indeed. Few successors of St. Peter labored as hard as Pope John to achieve Christ's injunction, "May they all be one," and none succeeded so completely in convincing the world of his sincerity. Besides his own flock, non-Catholics and non-Christians turned to him as to a father. Only history can determine how he will rank among the popes, but his largeness of spirit, his wisdom, his goodness, and his actions have already changed the history of the Church, and history itself.

Angelo Roncalli did what he said the Council would do: he opened the windows of the Church and let in fresh air.

At the time of his death, he was eighty-one; yet he was a man of today in every sense. The word *aggiornamento,* with which his reign will always be associated, contains in itself an Italian form of the word *today.* A man of his own times, said Goethe, is of all times.

It was Pope John's human qualities that most endeared him to people. As he lay suffering in his last illness, he demonstrated many of his characteristics—humor, kindness, serenity—in a single remark to his physician: "Don't look so worried. My bags are packed, and I'm ready to go." True humility is a rare quality, but everyone recognized it in him. It was no surprise that after his death this entry was found in his diary, under the date of August 12, 1961: "The Vicar of Christ? Ah, I am not worthy of this title—I, the poor son of Battista and Maria Anna Roncalli, two good Christians, to be sure, but so modest and so humble!" And when one thinks how much he accomplished before his death, this 1929 entry in his diary, on the occasion of his twenty-fifth anniversary as a priest (he was 49 at this time), is unforgettable:

Countless priests already dead or still living after 25 years of priesthood have accomplished wonders in the apostolate and the sanctification of souls. And I, what have I done? My Jesus, mercy! But while I humble myself for the little or nothing I have achieved up to now, I raise my eyes toward the future. There still remains light in front of me; there still remains the hope of doing some good. Therefore, I take up my staff again, which from now on will be the staff of old age, and I go forward to meet whatever the Lord wishes for me.

His three most considerable claims on history's attention are his convocation of the first Council of the Church to be held in one hundred years, and his authorship of two great encyclicals—*Mater et Magistra,* which brought up to date the social teaching of Leo XIII's *Rerum Novarum;* and *Pacem in Terris,* the first encyclical ever addressed not only to the Catholic clergy and laity but to "all men of good will."

In some respects, Pope John seemed as old-fashioned as his most conservative religious advisers. For one thing, he preferred an older fashion in papal dress, choosing to wear the *camauro,* or fur-trimmed cap, associated with Renaissance rather than modern popes (the papal medals and coins struck during his reign show him in profile wearing this cap). For another, the spiritual homilies he delivered during public audiences at St. Peter's were exactly what he might have said if he had been a small-town pastor in his native diocese of Bergamo. He also said his prayers as if he were on familiar terms with the angels and the saints. These old-fashioned qualities disarmed and confused his critics in the Vatican entourage, who could not understand how a man of such spiritual simplicity could be so daring, and even revolutionary, in his approach to age-old Catholic usages. They missed the point that, as he saw it, the mission of the papacy was twofold. "Our sacred obligation is not only to take care of this precious treasure (the deposit of faith) as if we had only to worry about the past," he said in 1962. "We must also devote ourselves, with joy and without fear, to the work of giving this ancient and eternal doctrine a relevancy corresponding to the conditions of our era." This statement is a paradigm of his greatness. Prelates who fear change ("fear," Pope John said, "comes only from a lack of faith") and resist it with denunciations and condemnations, subscribe to the first half only; those who see progress in change alone tend to harp exclusively on the latter half. Pope John believed in both, and acted on both. He was faithful to the past but devoted to the present, and he was wise enough to know that nothing from the past can really be preserved unless it is made meaningful here and now.

"With joy and without fear"—a typical Johannine phrase

—also describes the way he lived. In 1954, shortly after he
was made cardinal by Pius XII and entrusted with the patriarchate of Venice, he introduced himself to his new parish-
ioners in these words:

I wish to speak to you with the utmost frankness. You have
waited impatiently for me; people have told you about me and
written accounts that far surpass my merits. I introduce myself
as I really am. Like every other person who lives here on earth, I
come from a definite family and place. Thank God, I enjoy
bodily health and a little good sense which allows me to see
matters quickly and clearly. Ever ready to love people, I stand by
the law of the Gospel, a respecter of my own rights and of those
of others, a fact that prevents me from doing harm to anybody
and which encourages me to do good to all.

I come of humble stock. I was raised in the kind of poverty
which is confining but beneficial, which demands little, but
which guarantees the development of the noblest and greatest
virtues and which prepares one for the steep ascent of the
mountain of life. Providence drew me out of my native village
and made me traverse the roads of the world in the East and in
the West. The same Providence made me embrace men who were
different both by religion and by ideology. God made me face
acute and threatening social problems, in the presence of which
I kept a calm and balanced judgment and imagination in order
to evaluate matters accurately, ever preoccupied, out of my respect for Catholic doctrinal and moral principles, not with what
separates people and provokes conflicts, but rather with what
unites men.

The Venetians loved their new pastor, who instead of condemning the annual Venice Film Festival, as his predecessors had done, gave it his blessing and acted as host to its
committees and participants—no doubt thereby improving
the general tone of behavior. On the day in 1958 when he
left for Rome as a member of the conclave summoned to
elect a successor to Pius XII, he was correcting proofs of
diocesan regulations and hoped to return quickly to his be-

loved Venice to finish the job. On his election, he chose a papal name unused for centuries. "Nearly all (the pontiffs named John) had a brief pontificate," he said to the cardinals, indicating that he knew full well why some of the electors might have chosen him. In his diary he confessed, in his simple and direct manner, "In the first days of my pontifical service, I did not fully realize what it meant to be Bishop of Rome and therefore the pastor of the universal Church. Then, one week after another, full light spread, and I felt at home, as if I had not done anything else all my life."

The pontificate of John XXIII was brief—four and a half years, the shortest since that of Pius VIII (1829-30)—but no pontificate in our century has had vaster implications for the present and the future. Cardinal Suenens, in his extraordinary address at the special ceremony in St. Peter's during the Second Session's period of crisis (see page 167), reminded his hearers of the intense feelings aroused all over the world by the death of Pope John. "The television, the radio and the press brought his death so close to us that it was like a death in the family. Never has the whole world taken part at such close quarters in the poignant stages of a mortal sickness. . . . The death of John XXIII was precious in the sight of the world. The Pope transformed it into a final proclamation of faith and hope; he made it something like the celebration of an Easter liturgy. . . .

"John XXIII is present in our midst in a mysterious and profound way. He is with us by reason of the sacrifice of his life, which he offered for the happy outcome of the Council's labors. On this point there comes to mind an incident at Castel Gandolfo in July of last year (1962). John XXIII had spent the day, pen in hand, studying the preparatory schemata. In the course of an audience he read aloud some of the notes he had written in the margin. Then suddenly he stopped and said: 'Oh, I know what my personal part in the preparation of the Council will be.' And after a pause he concluded: 'It will be suffering.' "

The peroration of Cardinal Suenens' eulogy of Pope John deserves to be quoted in full:

John XXIII was the pope of dialogue, and this has special reference to the men of our time.

It is not easy to make the world of today hear the voice of the Church. It is drowned by too much noise; there is too much static and interference in the air for the message to get through.

In spite of these obstacles, John XXIII managed to make himself heard: he broke through the sound-barrier.

The words of John awakened a response.

Men recognized his voice, a voice speaking to them of God, but also of human brotherhood, of the re-establishment of social justice, of a peace to be established throughout the whole world.

They heard a challenge addressed to their better selves, and they raised their eyes towards this man whose goodness made them think of God. For men, whether they know it or not, are always in search of God, and it is the reflection of God that they sought in the countenance of this old man who loved them with the very love of Christ.

This is why they wept for him as children for their father, pressing around him to receive his blessing. The poor wept for him; they knew he was one of them and that he was dying poor like them, thanking God for the poverty that for him had been such a grace. The prisoners wept for him: he had visited them and encouraged them with his presence. Who does not remember that visit to the prison of Rome? Among the prisoners were two murderers. After having heard the Holy Father, one of them approached and said: "These words of hope that you have just spoken, do they also apply to me, such a great sinner?" The Pope's only answer was to open his arms and clasp him to his heart.

This prisoner is surely a sort of symbol for the whole of mankind, so close to the heart of John XXIII.

Now that his pontificate has come to an end, how can we without deep emotion reread the words he spoke in 1934 as he was leaving Bulgaria. We recognize John XXIII in this farewell message, a message that has prophetic value.

"Oh my brothers," he said, "do not forget me. Come what may, I will remain always the fervent friend of Bulgaria. According to an old tradition of Catholic Ireland, on Christmas Eve each home puts a lighted candle in the window to show Saint Joseph and the Blessed Mother, searching for a place to stay, that inside there is a family waiting to receive them. Wherever I may be, even at the ends of the earth, any Bulgarian away from his native land passing by my house will find in the window the lighted candle. If he knocks, the door will be opened, whether he be Catholic or Orthodox. A Brother from Bulgaria, this will be title enough. He will be welcome and will find in my house the warmest and the most affectionate hospitality."

This invitation has gone far beyond the borders of Bulgaria; John XXIII addressed it to all men of good will, irrespective of national frontiers.

He will be for history the Pope of Welcome and of Hope. This is the reason his gentle and holy memory will remain in benediction in the centuries to come.

At his departure, he left men closer to God, and the world a better place for men to live.

The news that the Roman Catholic Church—and the world—had a new Pope broke unexpectedly on the morning of Friday, June 21, 1963, at precisely 11:18 A.M. When the tall glass doors behind the balcony above the porch of St. Peter's were opened and the red-bordered white papal tapestry (still bearing the Roncalli arms of a tower topped by the lion of St. Mark) was draped over the balustrade, the crowd roared in anticipation of a great moment. As the procession of ecclesiastics filed onto the balcony and the stocky figure of Cardinal Ottaviani, dean of the cardinal deacons, was ushered to the microphone, silence possessed the multitude of one hundred thousand people. In a clear and slightly tremulous voice, the nearly blind Cardinal chanted, "I announce to you a great joy. We have a Pope!

Eminentissimum ac reverendissimum dominum (pause)—
dominum Joannem Baptistam . . . MONTINI!" Only the rising
burst of the "MON" was heard, but it was sufficient. The
crowd exploded. Ottaviani resumed patiently, ". . . Who has
taken the name . . . PAULUM SEXTUM!" There was another
vocal explosion from below. Surrounded by the red- and pur-
ple-clad retinue, the Cardinal withdrew, leaving the glass
doors ajar. The man who had just become Pope Paul VI
then appeared and advanced firmly to the front of the balcony. With just the slightest indication of a smile—or perhaps a tremor—on his lips, he accepted the tremendous
acclamation of the crowd. He was flanked by two old prac-
ticed masters of ceremonies—Monsignor Salvatore Capoferri
and Archbishop Enrico Dante—who had enacted this unusual ritual three or four times in the last forty years, the
dark-skinned, gentle, and cavernous-eyed Capoferri going
back to the election of Pius XI, in 1922. At a signal from
Dante, the new Holy Father began the formula of his blessing
to the city of Rome and to the world. "Blessed be the name
of the Lord!" The words rang out in the new Pope's clear,
melodious voice. "Now and forever and ever!" came the
response. "Our help is from the Lord," chanted Pope Paul.
"Who has made heaven and earth," answered the crowd.
Then, as the Pope turned slowly and majestically in a three-
quarter circle to cover the whole earth before him with three
stately signs of the Cross, he sang out, clearly and precisely,
"May the blessing of Almighty God, the Father, Son, and
Holy Spirit, descend upon you and remain with you forever."

In his first audience with newspapermen and correspond-
ents, Pope Paul referred ironically to some of the stories
about the conclave as being "unusual," echoing Pope John's
comment on the accounts of his election ("I could not find a
word of truth in them"). Pope Paul was apparently referring

to an article in the Italian picture magazine, *Epoca,* which claimed that he actually received a majority vote on the first day of the conclave but that, "very pale, almost speechless, (he) begged the cardinals to meditate—and to let him meditate—on their decision overnight." In order to accede to this Hamlet-like request, the cardinals would have had to fake a "black" burning on Thursday afternoon—and that, said the *Epoca* story, was what happened: "The crowd was manifestly deceived." Not only is this account patently absurd—implying an invalid election, and failing to reckon with the formidable presence of the ranking member of the conclave, Cardinal Tisserant, Dean of the Sacred College, who would brook no such nonsense—but it is also significant as a reiteration of a charge of indecisiveness from which Cardinal Montini suffered throughout the latter part of his career.

As if to dispel at the very outset of his reign this false interpretation of his character, Paul VI began at once a series of actions that astonished everyone and showed him to be a vigorous man of decision who knows his own mind. After the public blessing from the balcony, it was time for lunch, but instead of eating alone, as formal papal etiquette required, he ate with the cardinals at the big table set up for conclave meals in the Borgia apartments, and he sat not at the head place but in his old seat. At the end of lunch, he indicated that he was reappointing Cardinal Cicognani, Pope John's appointee, as his Secretary of State. Then, instead of waiting the customary few days before moving into the sealed-off private apartments vacated by his predecessor, he insisted on moving in right away. That night, Romans noticed lights behind the third-floor windows that had been dark for eighteen days. Though the formal ceremonies of the conclave are traditionally concluded by a second and third "obedience" of the cardinals, the new Pope, after re-

ceiving all the conclavists in the Hall of Vestments, said
simply, "We will do the rest tomorrow." He seemed anxious
to begin receiving his aides and making decisions, and soon
was at his desk writing out, in his own hand, a draft of the
speech that he would deliver the next day over television—
a speech containing a reassurance that an expectant world-
wide audience was waiting to hear: he would continue the
Ecumenical Council. Not long afterward, he set the date of
the reopening of the Council for Sunday, September 29,
1963—much sooner than had been expected by even the
most optimistic, since all preparations had been brought to
a standstill during the three-week interregnum. Finally, the
first meeting of the Council's all-important Coordinating
Commission since Pope John's death was held on July 3rd,
showing clearly that Pope Paul VI meant business.

In his speech, Pope Paul affirmed that he had no desire
to interfere in the internal affairs of governments, and his
subsequent replies to congratulatory telegrams from Premier
Khrushchev and from President Zawadzki of Poland, indicated his intention of continuing the discussions that were
started by Pope John with some of the Iron Curtain countries. These were not the only politic straws in the wind.
The same afternoon, he left the Vatican—itself a significant
feature on the first day after his election. He was on an
errand of mercy, but this particular errand had overtones.
Before the conclave met, it had been reported that the government of Spain was unhappy with Cardinal Montini.
In 1962, urged on by the students of Milan, the Cardinal
had cabled Generalissimo Franco begging him to remit the
death sentence of a young Spaniard, and Franco had coldly
replied that the sentence was imprisonment, not death. (The
Montini cable was called a "blunder" by some, though it is
difficult to see how a plea for mercy, even when it is mistaken
in detail, can be so regarded.) Thus it was interesting that

the first visit of the new Pope's reign took him to the Spanish College, near the Piazza Navona, to call on the ill and aged Cardinal Enrique Pla y Deniel, Archbishop of Toledo. As Pope Paul arrived to see the Cardinal, he was warmly greeted by the Spanish students, seminarians, faculty, and other personnel, who had gathered in the courtyard to pay him homage and to acknowledge that Spain, even as the rest of the world, had a new Pope. The following day Pope Paul appeared at the window of his papal library to introduce to the cheering crowd Cardinal Suenens who, at Pope John's behest, had presented a copy of his encyclical *Pacem in Terris* to Secretary-General U Thant, of the United Nations. And three days later, in reply to two Protestant ministers who had sent him wishes for the success of his pontificate, Pope Paul wrote, by hand, of his desire to continue friendly relations with non-Catholics. On June 29th, he again left the Vatican, this time for the Roman church of St. Charles Borromeo to celebrate Mass according to the Ambrosian rite for a delegation of pilgrims from his own city of Milan, led by the mayor. They presented him with the new triple tiara that was used to crown him at the coronation ceremony—a tall, rather tapered, and Gothic-looking crown, fashioned according to a design that the new Pope had approved himself. Finally, he announced the resumption of the custom of daily audiences *di tabella* ("by schedule") with heads of the various Congregations and Offices of the Curia.

The election of Cardinal Montini was extremely welcome to the members of the press, if only because he was the man about whom they had the most information. It did not take the public long to learn that the new Pope was sixty-five; that he was born in Concesio, a suburb of Brescia, in northern Italy, of a family belonging to the professional class (his father had edited the local daily, *Il Cittadino,* for twenty-five years, and had served three terms in the Italian Parliament

before the era of Fascism); that he had first undertaken his
studies for the priesthood privately (as Pius XII had), and
then in the Brescian seminary; and that he had been ordained a priest on May 29, 1920. During that summer, young
Don Giambattista Montini served as a parish curate, and in
the fall he went to Rome for graduate work at the Gregorian
University. (He also studied literature at this time at the
University of Rome.) Recommended to Pope Pius XI by
Cardinal (then Monsignor) Pizzardo, who also sponsored his
entrance into the papal foreign-service school for diplomatic
training, Don Montini was sent to Warsaw as a minor official in the Holy See's nunciature. His health failed after
several months there, however, and he was brought back
to Rome, where he was given duties in the Secretariat of
State. In 1930, when Eugenio Cardinal Pacelli became Pius
XI's Secretary of State, he singled out Monsignor Montini for
special training. From the start, Montini had interested himself in Catholic youth organizations, particularly on the university level; as a keen follower of the political theories of
the anti-Fascist priest Luigi Sturzo, whose principal protégé
was Alcide de Gasperi, Italy's great postwar Premier and
founder of the Christian Democratic Party, he had fostered
political-training programs for Catholic students. This had
brought him into contact with such early anti-Fascists as Dr.
Luigi Gedda and Vittorino Veronese, future presidents of
Italy's Catholic Action movement, and also into conflict
with the Fascist organizers, who singled him out as a "dangerous" cleric.

During the first ten years of his Vatican apprenticeship,
he was spiritual adviser to the Federazione Universitarii
Cattolici Italiani, known as Fuci, whose intellectual pursuits
he was able to stimulate by his ability to discuss the writings
of Bergson, Spengler, and Mann, as well as modern theological
writers and early Church Fathers. It was during this period

that he acquired a preference for the *castelli* or little mountain towns south of Rome in the Alban Hills. (The night before the conclave started, he had stayed with Professor Bonomelli, custodian of the papal summer residence, Castel Gandolfo, and told him that one of his fondest wishes was to revisit these picturesque spots he had come to know so well as a young Vatican official.) While serving in the Vatican Secretariat of State, Monsignor Montini made many American friends whose practical mentality, and minimal interest in intramural intrigues, appealed to him. The late Monsignor Walter Carroll of Pittsburgh, who served as a *minutante,* or minor aide, for American affairs, and slow-speaking but efficient Monsignor Joseph McGeough of New York, with whom in 1950 he made the first of his two visits to the United States, were two of his best friends. He was associated in the early years with Monsignor Francis J. Spellman of Boston, and learned to collaborate with him closely later when, as Archbishop of New York, Cardinal Spellman turned out to be one of Pope Pius XII's closest personal friends. Monsignor Montini took a keen interest in the National Catholic Welfare Conference, or NCWC, the organization of the United States bishops. Founded in 1919, this was one of the first effective groupings of bishops on a national scale that was not regarded by the Curia as a threatened revival of anti-Romanism (as with the Gallicanism of the bishops of France before the French Revolution, and the Josephism in Austria prior to World War I). The late Monsignor Howard Carroll, as secretary of the NCWC in Washington, brought promising American clerics to the attention of Monsignor Montini through his brother Walter in the Vatican. All these contacts proved extremely helpful during World War II, when the Vatican was called upon to set up in cooperation with the International Red Cross an organization for the exchange of war-prisoner information.

During the war years Monsignor Montini had become a key figure in the Secretariat of State, and it was assumed that either he or Monsignor Domenico Tardini would succeed the aging Cardinal Maglione as Secretary, on his death in 1944. However, Pope Pius XII decided to function as his own Secretary of State, and named his two chief aides as Sub-Secretaries of State. Monsignor Tardini, who was somewhat senior, was entrusted with Extraordinary Affairs, or dealings with secular governments and their diplomats accredited to the Holy See; Monsignor Montini was put in charge of Ordinary Affairs, or dealings with bishops and the internal affairs of the Church. The outlooks of the two men were almost antithetical, and conflict was inevitable. Tardini, the older man, enjoyed the support of such powerful and ultra-conservative figures as Cardinals Canali and Pizzardo, and Monsignor Ottaviani of the Holy Office. Montini's policy, generally speaking, was in favor of a gradual withdrawal of the Church from the political forum in the postwar era. He had supported the worker-priest movement in France, considering it more spiritually than (as it turned out to be) politically oriented, and had encouraged the leaders of the Italian Catholic Action in their attempt to find a means of influencing the leftist parties, particularly by approaching such groups as the Nenni Socialists. His final objective was to dissociate Catholic Action from the Christian Democratic Party, as Pope John later succeeded in doing with his ordinances spelled out by the synod of Rome, convened in 1959. Monsignor Montini had also encouraged the Holy See's relations with UNESCO, in which he was joined by Archbishop Angelo Roncalli, who was then Apostolic Nuncio to France. They were both overruled by the Canali-Tardini-Ottaviani forces. A final source of disagreement lay in Montini's insistence that representatives of the Holy See, and Catholics generally, should cooperate with organizations throughout the world working for international peace. In July, 1953, writing to the 40th Semaine Sociale de France, he deplored the fact that so many Christians still failed to heed the warnings of the Holy See in this grave period of international relations, just as they had been slow to follow papal encyclicals on the equally important question of social justice; he was saddened, he said, by the narrow nationalism and strange inertia of some Catholics, in view of the repeated appeals of the Holy Father for relations with non-Catholic agencies working on the social aspects of international affairs.

In 1953, Pope Pius XII convened what was to be the final consistory of his reign, and on this occasion two things of historic importance occurred—he made Angelo Roncalli a cardinal, and he revealed that both Monsignor Montini and Monsignor Tardini had declined to accept this supreme papal honor. Pope Pius attributed these refusals to the high virtue and humility of both men, and this was true enough, but Vatican observers felt there was more to it than that. As Robert Neville pointed out:

There was talk around the Vatican that Pope Pius XII was grooming Montini to be his successor, just as Pacelli himself had been groomed to succeed Pius XI. Certainly Montini had built a reputation as a liberal, forward-looking, thoroughly wise prelate who would make the kind of pope the Vatican needed for the quickly changing world.

But [this view] reckoned without Tardini's opposition. When [Pius XII] began thinking of creating new cardinals, he announced his intention of raising both Montini and Tardini to the purple. Tardini, however, declined the honor, thus making it difficult for [Pius XII] to give either of his vice-secretaries the red hat. Vatican insiders concluded that Tardini had reasoned that with the red hat Montini would be named Secretary of State, and thus would become the leading candidate in the next conclave. Tardini knew that with his own generally conservative outlook he had little chance of the Tiara.*

A pasquinade soon became current: "When Tardini would not, Montini could not." The internal crisis within the Secretariat was not long in coming to a head. In 1954, at a time when Pius XII was ill, a section of the Catholic Action group found itself in the position of having helped beat the Christian Democrats in a series of local elections, and it was at this point that the Tardini faction succeeded in convincing the Pope that Montini must go. On August 31st of that year, the day after the death of Ildefonso Cardinal Schuster, Archbishop of Milan, Montini was chosen as his successor. He was given the news of his new post by Pius XII himself, in an hour-long telephone call, although official announcement of the appointment was not made until November 3rd.

In the postwar period, the city of Milan had become a strong Communist center, used by the Party as a model for the other great population centers of Italy. Montini's appointment was therefore a challenge to him, particularly since the final years of Cardinal Schuster's twenty-five-year reign had not kept pace with the social problems resulting from Milan's phenomenal postwar industrial and commercial expansion. It was not difficult for the Tardini faction to convince Pius XII that in removing Montini from the Curia he was giving him a task worthy of his great talents. When Montini left Rome for Milan, it was noted that ninety cases of books were shipped after him. In Milan, however, he acted not as a bookish intellectual but as "the workers' archbishop," and he became a familiar sight in the city, approaching workers with a sad smile and an outstretched hand, despite their hoots and jeers; in the end, they usually shook his hand. He

---

* Robert Neville, *The World of the Vatican*, Harper, 1962, p. 92.

visited the Communist districts of the city, went down into mines, and toured factories, always carrying a portable kit for saying Mass, which he set up and used wherever he went. He preached a message of love to "the unhappy ones who gather behind Marx," and told them that "Jesus still loves you strongly, immensely, divinely," and that the Church works to satisfy "the profound need for a new and worthwhile life that is hidden in your souls." When Pius died, late in 1958, it was said that at the ensuing conclave several voters crossed out the word "Cardinal" printed on the ballots and wrote Montini's name in the blank space that followed. Pope John XXIII called his first consistory immediately after his election, in order to bolster up the depleted College of Cardinals. Not only was the Archbishop of Milan the first prelate he raised to the purple, but Pope John thereafter went out of his way to show the new cardinal special consideration. In 1960, he sent Montini to the United States, where he received an honorary degree from Notre Dame, along with President Eisenhower and the late Dr. Tom Dooley. He afterward went on a mission to South America, and in 1962 he made a visit to Africa, to report to Pope John on the problems that the Church faces on that continent.

When Pope John convened the Council in 1962, Montini was the only cardinal from outside Rome who was invited to use papal apartments during the eight weeks of the First Session, and he was said to have had a hand in the remarkable opening speech that Pope John addressed to the Council. At the Council itself, he spoke twice, and in the debate on "The Church" it was with extraordinary effect. Speaking in support of Cardinal Suenens' statement, he said that the Church was not so much a society founded by Christ as it was Christ Himself using us as instruments to bring salvation to all mankind. He said that it was up to the Fathers of the Council to define the collegial nature of the episcopate, to give a

truly ecumenical outlook to the Church, and to insist that
each bishop was "the image of the Father and the image of
Christ." The less we insisted on the rights of the Church,
he said, the more chance we had of being heard, especially in
those parts of the world suspicious of the Church as a colonial-
minded institution. Then in a letter to the Archdiocese of
Milan, sent from Rome, he laid the blame for the Council's
failure to make greater progress on those members of the
Curia who had prevented cooperation between the various
commissions during the period preceding its opening. Although *L'Osservatore Romano* published excerpts from the
late Pope's diary before the conclave met, it was concealed
from everyone until well after the conclave that the diary
expressed Pope John's hope that Cardinal Montini would be
his successor.

A reminder of Pope Paul's ecumenical hopes was contained
in the special blessing he imparted to non-Catholics during
an audience he granted a group of pilgrims from Philadelphia on June 25, 1963: "We wish our thoughts also to go to
those of our brethren who are not Catholics. On them and
on their dear ones we invoke the abundance of heavenly
grace." The most widely quoted incident of President Kennedy's visit to Pope Paul on July 3rd, was the latter's reference to the fight against racial segregation in the United
States, but many who quoted it failed to make a connection
between Pope Paul's words and the gift that Pope John
XXIII had earmarked for the President when he thought
that he would live to greet him in person. The gift was an
autographed copy of the encyclical *Pacem in Terris,* and
President Kennedy was visibly moved when Cardinal Cushing
presented it to him. Pope Paul made the connection very
clear, however, in the statement he read to President Kennedy
in English:

We find a spontaneous harmony with that which our venerable predecessor, Pope John XXIII, said in his last encyclical letter, *Pacem in Terris,* when he presented anew to the world the Church's constant teaching of dignity of the individual human person, a dignity which the Almighty Creator bestowed in creating man to His own image and likeness. We are ever mindful in our prayers of the efforts to insure to all your citizens the equal benefits of citizenship, which have as their foundation the equality of all men because of their dignity as persons and children of God.

In evaluating the first days of Pope Paul's pontificate, one can see that his most striking single act was his choosing of a name. St. Paul, by following literally the injunction of Christ to "go ye into the whole world, and preach the gospel to every creature," earned the title of Apostle of the Gentiles—that is, of all mankind, and not only a chosen few. In the middle of the twentieth century, a new Paul started his reign by dedicating himself to the same worldwide ecumenical mission.

On the morning of Sunday, August 18th, Pope Paul motored from his *villeggiatura* at Castel Gandolfo in the Alban Hills to the ancient Greek monastery of St. Nilus, at the foot of Monte Cavo, some five miles distant. There he celebrated Mass for a community of Basilian monks who have revitalized the atmosphere and traditions of the Eastern Church, preserved on that spot for close to a thousand years. The Pope took the occasion to comment on a major theme of the Council—the unity of Christians. "I long to make mine the wish that spontaneously and generously welled up in the hearts of my predecessors, especially John XXIII," he said. "Come, let the barriers that separate us fall! Let us explain the points of doctrine that are not common to us but are still subjects of controversy; let us seek to render our creed a joint one and a solid one. . . . We wish neither to absorb nor to detract from the great flowering of Eastern Churches but wish it to be engrafted on the tree of the unity of Christ." He also said that his respect for the Orthodox Churches was motivated by "the same feeling of brotherhood that recently authorized a bishop of the Catholic Church to go to Moscow in honor of the eightieth birthday of Aleksei, the Patriarch of Moscow." He added, "We did this with the intention of paying homage, of showing that there were no motives of rivalry . . . or any desire to perpetuate discords and disagreements that now seem completely anachronistic." Referring to the day's Gospel story of Christ healing the deaf-and-dumb man, Pope Paul said, "We are all a little dumb, we are all a little deaf. May the Lord open our senses to understand the voices of history."

Four days later, the Pope paid a visit to the summer quarters of the English Catholic College at Palazzola, in the same neighborhood, on the slopes of Monte Cavo. He told the rector and students of the ancient college that his visit was informal and unofficial; he came as a neighbor, he said, who breathed the same fresh Lake Albano air, and he commented that their view of the lake was better than that from Castel Gandolfo. He spoke appreciatively of England, saying, "How many people there are who have received from England a message of civilized humanity and courtesy!" When the students sang a hymn by the Elizabethan poet Robert Southwell, author of "The Burning Babe," it so impressed the Pope that he said it ought to be translated into other languages. This visit ended in true English fashion, with the students shouting three cheers for the Pope as he drove off.

At a general audience that summer, Pope Paul made particular mention of the numerous non-Catholics in the gathering. In his greeting, he assured them that his intentions were identical with his predecessor's, and said, "Your coming to the house of the Vicar of Christ is evidence not only of our universal fatherhood but also of your membership in the great and mysterious family of Christ." This statement has been hailed by the newer theologians as another papal confirmation of the view that baptism makes all believers members of Christ's Church—a departure from the juridical definition, formulated by the seventeenth-century Jesuit Cardinal, St. Robert Bellarmin, that insisted on submission to the Holy See as a final requirement for membership in the Church. Modern Catholic ecclesiologists consider the Bellarmin approach defective, because it fails to take into account the mysterious effect of God's grace, granted by Christ to those who sincerely believe in Him. The newer theology finds it difficult to admit that anyone linked to Christ by participating in the supernatural benefits of divine grace should at the same time be excluded from membership in the Church— the extension of Christ's Mystical Body on earth.

During the Council's First Session, in the debate on the nature of the Church, it became clear that the Council Fathers favored the view that not only are all men called to be members but vast numbers of people, even if they do not accept the external bonds of Catholic unity, nevertheless belong to the Church as long as they are baptized and act in accord with the dictates of conscience. Though this view is an abomination to fundamentalist Catholic theologians, the *American Ecclesiastical Review*—widely regarded as the mouthpiece of Catholic theological intransigence in the United States—ran an article in 1963 by the young Dominican Father Colman E. O'Neill, who taught at Lateran University, that must have amazed a number of its readers. Father O'Neill said:

Those who define Church membership in purely juridical terms are forced to the conclusion that [the baptized non-Catholic] cannot be a member . . . since the matter has been settled by *Mystici corporis* (Pius XII's encyclical) and *Suprema haec sacra* (the Holy Office letter). St. Thomas Aquinas, on the contrary, without the slightest hesitation, says that such a person is a member; and the Council of Trent says exactly the same thing. . . .

Monsignor Fenton [formerly of Catholic University] considers that all non-Catholics are positively excluded from any kind of membership. In the case of baptized non-Catholics in good faith, at least, as we have seen, this is not so.

Catholics who have been misled to believe the false notion that the Church never changes—it is the Truth that never changes—find this development in Catholic theology unsettling. On the other hand, Catholics who are shocked when political-sounding labels like "progressive" and "conservative" are applied to individual Council Fathers have been reassured of the validity of these terms by a Council Father himself—Bishop Ernest J. Primeau, of Manchester, New Hampshire, who wrote in *America:*

I agree with the general use of the words "conservative" and "liberal" to express the extreme positions taken by the Fathers of the Council. There was a real cleavage, not just a question of semantics. And these labels serve to express the difference quite well. As a matter of fact, this difference of opinion, since it was not of faith or morals, should cause no scandal. . . . Very few men are conservative or liberal on every question.

That final sentence would certainly not apply to the editors of the Italian rightist magazine *Il Borghese,* who are conservative on all questions, especially those concerning Vatican Council II. They thoroughly disapproved of Pope John's policies and blamed him for the size of the Communist vote in the Italian election. At the First Session of the Council, according to them, it was "almost as if the Church had been transformed into a degenerate democratic assembly." In their view, the "holy liberty" that Pope John allowed the Council Fathers in the debates was a mistake. It would not be repeated in the Second Session, *Il Borghese* felt, because the Curia, "with its humane recourse to logic, good sense, and the light of reason," regained complete control of the Council during the intersession. *Il Borghese* predicted that the Council would quickly conclude its business in the Second Session "with feet firmly on the ground," acting as the "purely consultative organ of the Supreme Pontiff." By "Supreme Pontiff," the editors meant, of course, not the Pope alone but the Pope as represented by their party in the Curia.

However, Pope Paul's actions and utterances indicated to anyone who studied them closely that he was in every sense the heir and continuator of Pope's John's pastoral policies, with a special character of his own. He announced on September 15, 1963 the creation of a Steering Commission of four cardinals with an "executive mandate" to direct the work of this session, and three of its members—Cardinals Suenens, Doepfner, and Lercaro—were known to be progressives. Nor could the fourth member, Cardinal Agagianian, a representative of the Curia who bridges the gap between the Church of Rome and the Eastern Church (he was for many years the Armenian Patriarch), be fully classed as a traditionalist. These four cardinals were also members of the important ten-member Coördinating Commission, the body that gets proposals to the floor and coördinates the work of the various commissions responsible for the Council's agenda. Pope Paul's dissatisfaction with the procedural confusions at the First Session of the Council was made clear even while it was being held. As Archbishop of Milan, he wrote weekly letters to all the faithful of his archdiocese, published in the diocesan paper, revealing a liberal attitude on conciliar secrecy quite unlike that of most Council Fathers.* His final letter, just before the close of the First Session, emphasized the primary importance of the schema "On the Church," which he described as "the foundation of the entire council." It was therefore not surprising when the Vatican announced that the first item on the Council's agenda, after the ceremonial

---

* Collected in book form, these letters were given to the Council Fathers as a gift at the end of the Second Session.

and organizational business of the opening days, would be further debate on "De Ecclesia."

One of the most interesting and controversial topics in this schema was the relationship of the bishops with the Pope and with each other. The very act of calling the Council dramatized this subject, because it made the Fathers more fully aware that they are bishops. There is no higher office, as the Pope's own title, "Bishop of Rome," indicates. The Pope and the bishops of the Church are bound together in collegiality, just as their predecessors, the Apostles, were bound together with Christ. While this fundamental truth has always been formally acknowledged in the Church, it has become obscured in practice. In the last four hundred years, a new entity has intervened between the Pope and the bishops —the Roman Curia. This necessary body, consisting of the various administrative arms with which the Pope governs the Church, became endowed in the course of centuries with super-episcopal powers. As a result of increasing centralization, the Curial officials in Rome claimed to "represent" the Pope, but in practice they arrogated to themselves the papal function of policy-making. Many bishops hesitated to do anything important without first "checking with Rome"—that is, with the Curia. By procrastination in administrative matters and by a close surveillance of what was said and written, the Curia over the years reinforced its undisputed authority. A hundred years ago, an archbishop at Vatican Council I gave utterance to these deeply felt words:

The experience that I have acquired, during many years, of the *personnel* of the Pontifical Curia has produced in me an unconquerable conviction that *never, never,* to the very end of the world, will they consent to renounce Temporal Power. They will utilize every means (at one time public, at another secret; at one time more violent, at another less so) to repossess themselves of that Power. . . .

That there are great churchmen in the Curia today (Cardinal Bea is an outstanding example) is beyond dispute. But the attitude of mind that confuses the Curia with the Church is all too common. A number of articles in the American Catholic press, imputing lack of competence to journalists and authors of books on the Council, have been guilty of this confusion. One American monsignor, a member of the Congregation for Oriental Churches, wrote these warning words: "Let those who, in articles or books, perpetrate false notions about the Roman Curia face their responsibility to present to the world an undistorted image of the Church," thus equating the Curia and the Church in a *latius hos,* or error of logic, in which the part is mistaken for the whole. An article, "Pope, Bishops and Curia," in the German theological magazine, *Wort und Wahrheit,* discussed the problem of this relationship with unusual frankness. It stated that the Curia as a whole has certain necessary functions that ought not to be underestimated nor bypassed, but its role should be strictly executive, and confined to carrying out the directives of the Church's leaders—that is, the Pope *and* the bishops. Giving concrete form to the collegial powers of the bishops is entirely compatible with the papal primacy, the article said, and one way of achieving this would be to have a standing committee of bishops in Rome. The present autonomous role of the Curia, perhaps warranted in an age of nationalism, was no longer desirable. Such a body, appointed by the bishops themselves and functioning as a sort of continuation of the college of Apostles around Peter, would enable the bishops to exercise their responsibility of guiding the whole Church in union with its head. The relationship, the article pointed out, would then be Pope–Bishops–Curia, rather than, as at present, Pope–Curia–Bishops. Under the circumstances, it was no small gesture on the part of Pope Paul to announce that the Fathers could wear the *mozzetta* at the Council. This elbow-length cape, an emblem of episcopal jurisdiction, is never worn outside a bishop's own diocese. To allow its use in Rome was a symbolic and highly significant act of the Pope. It was as if he were saying to the Fathers of the Council, "I am the Bishop of Rome, just as you are the bishop of your diocese."

The general desire to give concrete form to the collegiality of the bishops was seen in a proposal to revitalize the ancient office of patriarch, as an intermediary stage between the Pope and the rest of the episcopate. The Dutch canonist Piet Fransen, S.J., proposed the grouping of the whole Church into patriarchates along regional or continental lines. It is known that the colorful and outspoken Melchite patriarch, His Beatitude Maximos IV Saigh, of Antioch, had long nurtured the hope of one day seeing the Eastern patriarchates enjoy their rightful and historical place in the Church, preceding the cardinalate. (The cardinals, historically the successors of the ancient Roman parish clergy and canonically forming part of the diocese of Rome, are subject to the Pope in his office as Patriarch of Rome.) For this reason, His Beatitude, following the precedent of the former Melchite patriarchs had three times refused a cardinal's hat, offered twice by Pius XII and once by John XXIII; however, the patriarchs Tappouni and Agagianian both accepted, thus breaking the solidarity of the Eastern patriarchs (Alexandria, Antioch and Jerusalem) in their claim to be the equals of the Pope as Patriarch of the West (though not in his primatial authority over the whole Church or primacy). It represented no little compromise therefore when Maximos IV was recently persuaded, along with his eastern colleagues, to accept "associate membership" in the Roman Congregation for the Oriental Churches of which hitherto only cardinals have been members. With the experience of the First Session behind him, and the prospects for change brighter, he felt that he could be more effective in achieving the goals of guarding against Latinization and reforming the Code of Canon Law for the Oriental Churches by having one foot inside the door rather than by remaining entirely outside.

Although it was well known that the First Session had exceeded the hopes of the progressives by revealing that they had an articulate majority among the bishops, it was less well known that the shortcomings of that gathering were subjected to a searching examination during the intersession by those responsible for guiding the Council's work. A highly interesting and authoritative critique—made on the level of the Coördinating Commission, and thus close to the top—pointed out that the chief stumbling block was the rules under which the Council operated. The report said—in tactful terms, of course—that these rules were demonstrably contrived to assure domination of the proceedings at all stages by the Curial party. The critique also said that the rules failed to profit from the experience of other parliaments or international assemblies in expediting the flow of business, and were inadequate for guiding a deliberative assembly of over two thousand bishops. They failed to define clearly the functions of the Council Presidents, with the result that the supreme direction of affairs had to be improvised and was virtually lodged in the Secretariat for Extraordinary Affairs, a subordinate committee not intended to have this role. Perhaps the worst defect was the organization and excessive number of the conciliar Commissions. The Commissions ought to have been both fewer in number and better coordinated, with responsibilities corresponding to the matters likely to come before the Council, not merely slavishly reflecting the divisions of the Curia. Moreover, the cardinals presiding over them had powers that were too vast and arbitrary—again a reflection of the Curia. Not enough use was made, said the critique, of the council experts or *periti* who not infrequently found themselves virtually excluded from any participation in the work. Finally, there were complaints about the system of voting, both in committee and on the floor. Any curialist tempted to conclude that because Pope John had promulgated these rules he, for one, considered them infallible, should have remembered what he told a group of Pakistani bishops: "Nobody around here knows how to run a Council, and the reason is simple— none of us has ever been to one before!"

Though there were hopeful signs in this intersession period of a full-scale liberalization of the Church's policy, the "hardcore" Curia group and their collaborators continued to manifest their obstructionism, particularly in the commissions working on the Council's schemata. The bishops and *periti* on the Liturgical Commissions during the late summer had to fight, word by word, to force the president and secretary of that body to align the document to accord with the mind of the vast majority of the Council Fathers as expressed in their speeches during the First Session and in their voting on the first chapter of the schema. An obvious tactic of the cardinal president was to do all the talking at the meetings, until the day an exasperated Negro bishop, in impeccable French, told him off before the whole group, asking whether he had been brought all the way from his diocese in Africa to listen to cardinalitial lectures. In the joint meetings of the Theological Commission and other Commissions, veiled hints of retribution against *periti* with advanced views were occasionally uttered by representatives of the Holy Office. In the gatherings of the Commission dealing with the schema on the hierarchy, there was so much pandemonium, with everyone talking at cross purposes, that it enabled Bishop Carli of Segni to emerge as secretary of the Commission that put together the worst schema reported on the Council floor. (It was not, in fact, the most retrograde or inadequate of *all* the schemata, however. This distinction belonged to the schema dealing with marriage, which opened with a chapter devoted to "impediments" and continued with solely canonical considerations, the subject of love being mentioned almost accidentally in an appendix. To judge from this schema, Pope John's call for a pastoral Council, and Pope Paul's reiteration of this theme, had never been uttered.)

These and similar facts revealed the unyielding temper of the "remnant of Israel," as the thirty or so members of this curial group came to be called. Their conviction that, in the end, they would win caused great concern on the progressive side. Behind the scenes curial agents pursued their witch-hunt tactics in France, Germany, Spain, and even the United States, where several bishops were encouraged by the Apostolic Delegate to aid him in ferreting out "dangerous" theologians and journalists. Pressures were also put on official representatives of the Catholic press in America to improve the public image and whitewash the reputation of Cardinal Ottaviani, who now began to grant interviews. Commenting on the widely circulated story that he had tried to silence Karl Rahner, the celebrated Austrian theologian who served as a Council *peritus* during the first session of the Council, Cardinal Ottaviani said:

This is completely false. This whole matter was completely unknown to me until I heard others speak of it. Neither I nor anyone else in the Holy Office, either directly or indirectly, suggested that Father Rahner should leave Rome. Quite the contrary. Twice I invited Father Rahner to address the members of the Preparatory Commission on Theology.

However, Father Rahner in an interview in the *Catholic Reporter*, of Kansas City, had this to say:

It is generally known that I had difficulties with the Holy Office, whose chairman is Alfredo Cardinal Ottaviani, in Rome before and at the beginning of the Council. These difficulties were based for the most part on efforts to subject my future published works to a special Roman censorship.

In the weeks preceding the opening of the Second Session, the relationship of the Curia with the American Catholic universities was the subject of a meeting in Washington. After the Federation had elected Fr. Theodore Hesburgh, C.S.C., the president of Notre Dame University, as its new president to succeed Msgr. William McDonald, rector of the Catholic University of America, Father Hesburgh was asked by an official of the curial Congregation of Seminaries and Universities to relinquish his new office in favor of Msgr. McDonald. This example of Roman determination to maintain control, in the very face of the expressed wishes of the universities themselves, could not have been more crudely demonstrated. To his great credit, Father Hesburgh refused to resign on the score that he had to honor his obligation to the Federation, having already accepted its highest elective office. A resolution on the relationship between the International Federation of Catholic Universities and the Congregation of Seminaries and Universities within the Roman Curia was introduced and discussed with some heat on the floor. One debater cited the Curia's attempt to curtail academic freedom by means of a *monitum,* or warning, that they were not to grant honorary degrees without the approbation of the Holy See, an obvious censure indirectly aimed at St. Louis University and Boston College, who earlier in the year so honored Father Hans Küng, the theologian whose appearances at Catholic universities and elsewhere have been warmly received by the American laity. The implications of this kind of remote control are delicate, and could cause the most serious difficulties in accreditation for American Catholic universities as a whole. Meeting in Minneapolis, the National Catholic College Federation, a different group, voted an "absolute and unequivocal condemnation" of Catholic University of America's famous ban of Father Küng and three distinguished American theologians. The resolution stated that Catholic University helped "propagate the image of Catholics as religious automatons."

As a preamble to the Second Session, the Pope's reception of the Roman Curia was scheduled for 10 A.M. on September 21, 1963. To the surprise of some, who had forgotten the Pope's reputation for punctuality, he entered the doorway of the Hall of Benedictions—an enormous room over the porch of St. Peter's Basilica—on the dot of ten, and, a slim figure in white, walked the length of the room, which was already crowded with dozens of cardinals, scores of prelates, and hundreds of clerical and lay officials of the Curia and workers at the Vatican. As he stood near his throne on the dais, a few latecomers of high rank, who had obviously set out for their destination at the usual Roman pace for such occasions, had to trudge to their places toward the front of the hall while the Holy Father waited patiently to begin. Still standing, he told his audience that because the formal talk he had prepared for them might prove to be long, he was declaring the rest of the day a holiday. The crowd broke into pleased applause. He added that in view of the increased cost of living in Rome (rents, for example, had gone up thirty per cent that summer) he was also giving each of them a raise. Louder applause and happy murmurs. The Pope then sat down and began a historic discourse.* Though it was somewhat overshadowed by his address at the opening of the Council, eight days later, its importance was evi-

* Full text is printed in the Appendix, p. 338.

dent. That he intended it to be heard by the world, and not
only by the Roman Curia, was clear from the fact that he
could have arranged an off-the-record reception and not permitted the release of his text. It was obvious that he wanted
everyone, especially the twenty-three hundred Council
Fathers (many of whom were converging on Rome from
various continents at that moment), to hear and understand
his words. He used phrases of great tact, courtesy, and praise,
yet at the same time he clearly expressed every theme of
reform that had been raised at the First Session of the Council by spokesmen for the progressive viewpoint, Speaking as
one who knew his audience well, he reminded them that
he himself had served for thirty years in the ranks of the
Curia. He had called this meeting at the beginning of his
reign, he told them, in order to greet those present and to
express to them his veneration, gratitude, and encouragement. Another reason for the reception, he said, was "the
very beautiful and serious moment being lived by the whole
Church"—namely, Vatican Council II. He thought that the
Curia should take careful stock of this great event—not that
it had failed to understand the enormous importance of the
Council during the first session. "On the contrary," said the
Holy Father, "the Council's extraordinary and complex
dimensions were discerned more fully by the Curia than by
any other sector of the Church or public opinion, even to the
point of at times allowing a certain stupor and apprehension
to show." When he spoke of the necessity for accord between
the Pope and the Curia, he seemed to be putting some of its
members politely on notice: "We are certain that no hesitation regarding the principal wishes of the Pope will ever
come from the Curia, and that the Curia will never be suspected of any differences of judgment or feeling with regard
to the judgments and feelings of the Pope." To make his
message perfectly clear, he referred to himself at this point

as "the Pope who today has made the legacy of John XXIII his own, and has also made it a program for the entire Church." He then spoke of the Curia's critics, and said it was understandable that a body whose present form goes back to 1588, and whose most recent reorganization was in 1908, "should have grown ponderous with venerable old age, shown by the disparity between its practices and the needs and usages of modern times." He added that the Curia needs "to be simplified and decentralized, and to adapt itself to new functions," and, after referring to Pope John's word *"aggiornamento,"* he concluded simply, "Various reforms are therefore necessary." He then made one of the most significant statements in the address, foreshadowing a major topic of the Council debates—that of collegiality, or the sharing of the government of the Church by the Pope *and* the bishops—and indicating that the de-Italianization of the Curia is inevitable:

We will say more: If the Ecumenical Council wishes to see some representatives of the episcopacy, particularly bishops heading dioceses, associated . . . with [the Pope] in the study and responsibility of ecclesiastical government, it will not be the Roman Curia that will oppose it.

Toward the close of his talk, he uttered a fervent message: "People everywhere are watching Catholic Rome, the Roman pontificate, the Roman Curia. The duty of being authentically Christian is especially binding here. We would not remind you of this duty if we did not remind ourself of it every day. Everything in Rome teaches the letter and the spirit—the way we think, study, speak, feel, act, pray, serve, love." He ended with the prayer that "this old and ever new Roman Curia" might shine like a light in the Church of God. He had carried his audience with him completely, and after he concluded, the applause was so great and prolonged that he had to intone the words of the papal blessing to stop it. All over Rome, in the days that followed, many members of the Curia expressed their joy at the talk and their gratitude that the Pope had defended them and shown such appreciation of their work. It apparently did not cross their minds that, as Michael Novak later wrote in *Commonweal,* "the talk was a two-edged sword." *Il Tempo,* an ultraconservative paper, gave its readers what was probably the most peculiar printed report of the talk. Its headline read, "POPE ANNOUNCES RAISE FOR ALL VATICAN WORKERS," and under this was quoted the Pope's praise of the Curia. There was not a word about reform.

The Council's opening ceremony, on Sunday, September 29, 1963, was impressive, if less formal than the rites at the First Session. Instead of marching in procession through St. Peter's Square, the bishops strolled casually, with mitres in hand, to their seats in the nave of the Basilica. Though Pope Paul, preceded by the Swiss Guard and the College of Cardinals, was borne on the *sedia gestatoria* from the bronze doors of the Papal Palace to St. Peter's, he dismounted inside the Basilica. In place of the papal triple tiara, he wore a mitre, like the other bishops, and instead of giving the bishops the customary papal blessing, he contented himself with greeting his colleagues in the episcopate with waves of the hand as he walked down the central aisle to the Confession of St. Peter, where his throne was placed. After the Solemn Pontifical Mass, the Pope made his profession of faith and received the homage of the cardinals. Then the Council Fathers professed their faith, viva voce, and Pope Paul began his opening address.

While unusually long—an hour and four minutes—it was

a magnificent discourse,* reasserting the purpose of the Council as inaugurated by Pope John XXIII and indicating the concrete steps by which *aggiornamento* would proceed. Pope Paul's voice was somewhat hoarse, but his enunciation was clear and his diction precise, and the Council Fathers, the observer-delegates from non-Roman religious communions, the lay auditors, and the invited guests all knew that they were participating in one of the great moments in Church history. Pope Paul expressed the joy he felt at the regathering of the Fathers, who, by the time the Council finally concludes its business, "with one voice alone will give their message to the whole world." He explained that he had first intended to send the bishops the customary encyclical letter of a new pope; instead, he said, "let this address be a prelude not only to the Council but to our pontificate." He assured them that, as Pope, he had "no idea in mind of human domination, nor are we jealous of exclusive power," and that "our sole desire is to exercise the divine mandate, beloved brethren, that through you and by you has made us Supreme Pastor." He said that Pope John had called this Council "doubtless under divine inspiration," thereby mending "the broken thread of Vatican Council I" and banishing the fear, "wrongly deduced from that Council, that the supreme powers conferred by Christ on the Roman Pontiff were sufficient to govern and vivify the Church without the assistance of Ecumenical Councils."

He then announced four points as the Council's principal aims. First, the Church must impart to herself and to the world a new awareness of her inner nature. Despite great progress in theology since Vatican Council I, the Church still does not have a clear notion of herself that is likely to impress the modern world. This definition need not take the form of dogma, he said, but could be made as an explicit and

* Full text is printed in the Appendix, p. 347.

authoritative declaration. Second, there must be a renewal
and reform of the Church—"not by turning upside down the
present way of life or breaking with what is essential and
worthy in her tradition" but, rather, "by stripping it of what
is unworthy or defective." Then, as Pope Paul discussed the
third principal aim of the Council—the unity of all Christians—an impressive and moving incident occurred. He
turned around to face the tribune to his left, where the observer-delegates from other Christian communions were
seated. He said that their presence at the Council stirred
great hope in his heart, as well as a feeling of sadness at their
separation. "If we are to blame in any way for that separation," he said to them, "we humbly beg God's forgiveness,
and ask pardon, too, of our brethren who feel themselves to
have been injured by us." This unprecedented and historic
utterance no doubt shocked some of the Fathers who have
insisted that the Church is without stain or blemish, but to
the majority of the Pope's listeners it was a great moment.
Before taking up the final theme—the dialogue between the
Church and the world today—Pope Paul saw fit to point out
the vacant benches of those bishops who are suffering under
restraint, and in prisons, for their faith. "We must be realists," he said, "and not hide the savagery that reaches into
this Council from many areas. . . . In certain countries,
religious liberty, like other fundamental rights of man, is
being crushed by principles and methods of political, racial,
and anti-religious intolerance. The heart grieves that there
are still so many acts of injustice against goodness." He said
that "while the light of the science of nature is increasing,
darkness is spreading over the science of God" through the
destruction of intellectual and moral integrity. "Progress is
perfecting, in a wondrous way, every kind of instrument that
man uses, but his heart is declining toward emptiness, sadness, and despair," he said, and concluded, "The Church

today stands ready to aid the oppressed, the poor, and the suffering. Let the world realize that the Church looks on it with profound understanding and sincere admiration, with the frank desire not to conquer but to serve, not to despise but to appreciate, not to condemn but to comfort and save." The Pauline Council had begun.

II

The Debate on "The Church"

As THE BISHOPS GATHERED in the great conciliar hall of St. Peter's for the first business session of the second phase of Vatican Council II, on Monday morning Sept. 30th at 9 A.M., they were unusually talkative, exchanging greetings and congratulations as new arrivals, both bishops appointed during the intersession and about 75 Apostolic Prefects sitting for the first time, were attempting with difficulty to find their proper seats. The first person to be heard over the microphone was one of the council Undersecretaries, Monsignor Villot, requesting the Fathers to make the responses to the mass in unison, slowly and distinctly. As a thoughtful touch of the new Pope, the first conciliar mass was to be celebrated in the Ambrosian rite by His Excellency the Archbishop of Milan, Giovanni Colombo, the successor of Montini on the throne of St. Ambrose. The voices of Archbishop Colombo and of the Pope are so remarkably alike that it was not difficult for the Fathers to imagine that they were listening to the mass of the Holy Father himself.

According to the pre-announced agenda, the first item of business was to be the schema *De Ecclesia* on the nature of the Church. The text before the Fathers represented a completely new version of the schema originally submitted for consideration by the Theological Commission during the final days of the First Session which had come in for heavy criticism as a wholly inadequate expression of the Council's mind on this all-important crucial theme. In fact, it would be more accurate to speak of the fusion of various drafts. Chapters I and II, for which the Theological Commission was exclusively responsible, were based largely on a draft by the Louvain theologian G. Philips in which key portions of the original schema had been incorporated. Other drafts which influenced the final version were one, largely scriptural in inspiration, by Karl Rahner, S.J.; another less comprehensive in nature which also furnished some of the ideas which would be incorporated in Schema 17; and finally a French draft based largely on a study of Fathers G. Thils and J. Daniélou published in *Etudes et Documents* (Jan. 15, 1963). Chapters III and IV were worked out by mixed or joint committees with the assistance of the Commission for the Apostolate of the Laity and the Commission for Religious Orders.* Under the circumstances it is not surprising that one of the objections raised against the new version (Cardinal Gracias) was that it betrayed its patchwork origin and was lacking in uniformity. However, there were many virtues which helped to compensate for defects. The schema, in four chapters, ran to 78 printed pages, most of which were devoted to footnotes, so that the actual text was not very long:

* *Le Monde,* October 2, 1963; *Herder-Korrespondenz,* Nov. 1963, p. 91.

Ch. I   The Mystery of the Church (6½ pages of text);
Ch. II   The Hierarchic Constitution of the Church with
         special reference to the Episcopate (3 pp. of text);
Ch. III The People of God and the Laity (6¾ pp. of text);
Ch. IV   The Vocation to Sanctity in the Church (5½
         pages of text)

Before the Second Session the Coordinating Commission had
decided to recommend that the section on the People of
God be removed from Chapter III and brought forward as a
new Chapter II, thus giving the whole schema greater co-
hesion and logic. This would tend to emphasize the idea of
the basic equality of all members of the Church before distinctions were made according to office or charisma. As many
of the speakers seconded this recommendation, it is certain
that the final text will reflect the proposed change.

It was truly surprising that a text as "liberal" as the
present one could have come out of the Theological Commission in view of the known theological orientations of its
chairman and vice-chairman, Cardinals Ottaviani and
Browne. As the debate progressed, both cardinals had very
little to say except with regard to one or two key points, the
collegiality of the bishops and the revival of the diaconate,
preferring to refrain, publicly at least, from all comment on
the schema as a whole. According to unconfirmed reports
the elaboration of the present text was achieved only after a
prolonged struggle within the Theological Commission itself, with the chairmen ultimately unsuccessful in their attempt to impose a more conservative document on the
progressive-minded majority.

Before the discussions began on *De Ecclesia,* Secretary
General Archbishop Felici mounted the rostrum and made
a series of important announcements. He drew the attention
of the Fathers first of all to the changes that had been made

in the conciliar *Ordo,* pointing out what Articles had been
changed and commenting on each one briefly. The purpose
of the changes was twofold, he said: to facilitate the work of
the Council, and to protect the rights of those Fathers who
found themselves in a minority as the result of a vote. The
law of every Council must be a moral unanimity: this meant
that everything which tended to divide the Council into a
majority and a minority representing two opposing tendencies should be avoided.

The rules regarding the interventions were then read first
in Latin by Archbishop Felici and afterward by the five
Undersecretaries in their respective languages. The Fathers
were requested specifically to observe the provisions of
Article 57 of the *Ordo* which required: 1) that the complete
text of a speech, duly signed, must be submitted to the Secretariat at the conclusion of every speech; 2) that the Fathers
who have the same observations to make on a given subject
should arrange to have one or more speak on their behalf;
3) that the Fathers should avoid repeating what others have
said, if need be by withdrawing their names from the list
of speakers. Those who speak on behalf of others should
attach a list of the names of those on whose behalf they are
speaking. Signatures are not necessary. Moreover, in accordance with Art. 33, the speakers must submit to the Secretariat three days beforehand a summary, or preferably, the
full text of what they intended to say.* The summary should
be more than a mere outline, it should contain, briefly, the
principal arguments to be presented. During the speeches a
two minute warning signal would be sounded in the telephone near the microphone where the bishop is speaking,

---

* The intention was to allow the Moderators a better opportunity for
guiding the Council by eliminating needless repetitions, but the Secretariat,
in effect, eluded their control, remaining subject directly to the Secretary of
State, and this measure was rendered nugatory in practice. R. Laurentin,
Bilan de la deuxième session, Paris, 1964, p. 204.

indicating that eight minutes have elapsed and only two remain in which to conclude his remarks.

The Secretary General then announced that His Holiness had laid down the following rules with regard to the Council secrecy: the obligation of secrecy applied in full force to the contents of the schemata and to the discussions and conclusions reached in sessions of the Council Commissions. But with reference to the discussions in the council hall during the General Congregations, His Holiness recommended that a maximum moderation and prudence be observed at all times and in all places.

As Henri Fesquet remarked in *Le Monde*:* "The secrecy of the council *tombe en quénouille*—is shattered." For the essential thing was what was said in the debates on the floor and no attempt would now be made to keep this from journalists. Prudence and discretion replaced the draconian rules hitherto in effect. As a matter of fact, he went on, the rules were inapplicable and knowledge about what took place in the council aula during the First Session did reach the public anyway. The new regulations were in accord with the words of Pope Paul VI himself when he said that the Council would "open a window on the world." And more in accord also with one who is himself the son of a journalist and aware of the problems of the press. As the Pope said the following day, Tuesday, while receiving the journalists accredited to the Council, with regard to the lesson to be drawn from the first session: a loyal and objective reporting under the responsibility of the various national hierarchies is more profitable to the Church than misguided timidity and vain efforts to hide what was going to be published anyway by others with more or less regard for the truth.

The Fathers were also told on Monday that there would be no further appointments of Council Experts—Periti—

* *Le Monde*, October 2, 1963.

since the number of those appointed was more than adequate to meet the needs of the Council. As a matter of fact, several additional appointments were actually made, for various special reasons, but not on a large scale.

It was then announced that following an initial discussion of the schema *De Ecclesia* in general, a vote would be taken in accordance with Art. 31 by a simple *placet* or *non placet* to determine whether the text was acceptable as a basis for discussion in detail. Cardinal Agagianian, Moderator for the day, then announced the discussion of the schema *De Ecclesia* and began by expressing a word of greeting on behalf of the Council Presidents to all, especially the apostolic prefects who were sitting for the first time, the lay auditors, and the non-Catholic observers. He invited the Fathers to resume their deliberations under Pope Paul VI and to be inspired by the remarks he made in his opening address on Sunday.

As President of the Theological Commission which had prepared the draft, Cardinal Ottaviani opened the debate by reading the text of a speech distributed to the Fathers along with the official *"relatio"* of Card. Browne. Ottaviani said briefly that the deposit of faith must not only be guarded, it must also be presented to all (*Non solum depositum fidei servare oportet, sed omnibus proponere*), referring to a dual responsibility of the Church which it is difficult or wrong to separate. The cardinal observed, somewhat laconically perhaps though in a perfectly amiable tone, that the first session had shown that the Council must speak in a way that can be understood by all, Catholics and non-Catholics. The schema may not be perfect, but it is impossible to satisfy everybody.

The Vicepresident of the Theological Commission, the Irish Dominican Cardinal Browne, then took the floor and read his official "report" explaining briefly the plan and content of the schema. He mentioned that 372 amendments had been proposed at the first session and afterward, with which the Commission had had to deal: 1 on the title, 9 on the preamble, 165 on chapter I and 206 on chapter II.

Cardinal Frings of Cologne spoke first in the name of the sixty-five German and Scandinavian Fathers. He began with the significant words *"Valde placet,"* thus indicating that the schema was basically satisfactory to him. This was no small tribute to the work of the Commission—in view of the critical attitude of the speaker—and meant that the schema had indeed undergone fundamental changes since the last session. Cardinal Frings approved the schema's pastoral and ecumenical spirit, its avoidance of a juridical and apologetic tone which would not have been fitting for a Council, its reliance on Scripture and tradition, and its treatment of non-Christians. However he stated that the question of who is and who is not a member of the Church could not be decided in this schema. And he had a number of criticisms. He questioned whether the scriptural quotations were always the best or the most concrete. There was much more on the infallibility of the Pope than on the teaching office of the bishops. He wished that the Church's relationship to the Blessed Virgin and the saints had been set out more clearly. Finally he expressed his thanks to Paul VI who in his opening address, "courageously, not as a tactic but because it is the truth," had acknowledged the faults of the Catholic Church in the separation of the Churches and had humbly asked pardon for its share of the responsibility.

The Cardinal Archbishop of Genoa spoke much more briefly. The schema offered a good basis for discussion, he said, but it must be amended because some statements were not precise enough and certain things were missing. Theological progress was not achieved by saying things loosely and less clearly than before. Silence concerning certain points might give rise to false deductions. The expression "universal priesthood" of the faithful, for example, was open to various interpretations.

The Armenian Patriarch Batanian said that the schema was good, but did not bring out clearly enough a number of points: the universal priesthood of the faithful, the authority of the hierarchy in directing the apostolate, the necessity of interior spirituality. With regard to the first point he wanted a clearer distinction between the priesthood of the faithful and that of the hierarchy.

The Archbishop of Saragossa in Spain thought that the schema was good but that it would not be very meaningful to non-Christians. There was nothing in the chapter on the hierarchy about patriarchs—a notable omission. The statements about equality in the Church needed clarification. Priests and deacons should be considered separately from the section on bishops. There was a needless juridical tone at times and too much emphasis on the papal primacy. All these points were raised as well by other speakers.

The Italian prelate of the Order of Malta, Bishop Ferrero di Cavallerleone asked that the schema on the Blessed Virgin be attached to *De Ecclesia*. It was not possible to speak of the Church without speaking of Mary, he said.

Archbishop Florit of Florence praised the text for its clear, positive, biblical and ecumenical approach, especially for what it said about the laity and the college of bishops. But there were some defects. The title might better be *"De Ecclesia Christi."* Treating the Church as a Mystery created a psychological problem for the faithful who were inclined to think of the mysterious as something unknowable. The theology of the college of bishops should also be better explained, as well as the nature of an ecumenical council. He wished also that the schema *De Revelatione* could be discussed concurrently with the present schema so that the problem of revelation might be considered in another context. The text sometimes gave the impression of being more of a theological treatise than a conciliar constitution.

Archbishop Ngo-Ding-Thuc of Hué in Vietnam, brother of the murdered president, began by launching into a number of details instead of speaking on the schema in general and was interrupted by the Moderator, Cardinal Agagianian. Resuming his discourse, the archbishop talked about a different theme, his desire that non-Christian observers should attend the Council. He was undoubtedly thinking of his own country where Buddhists greatly outnumber the Christians and very often have a wrong impression of the Church from what they see of it in colonial or former colonial lands. The Council could help to dispel these illusions.

Bishop Gargitter of Bressanone in Italy speaking last on Monday, also praised the schema, but said that the notion of the "people of God" ought to be treated before that of the hierarchy and could be developed without detriment to the place of the hierarchy. The Church was born from the side of Christ on the cross and the schema ought to express more clearly therefore that the Church and its members were sharers in Christ's passion.

The debate continued Tuesday on the schema as a whole, the first speaker being the Cardinal Archbishop of Santiago de Chile, who delivered his address in the name of 44 Latin American bishops. The schema was good, he thought, but the suggestion of the Coordinating Commission that the chapter on the "People of God" should come before that on the Hierarchy ought to be followed and the same categories ought to be used in both, i.e. the text should speak of the Sacerdotal, Regal and Prophetic People of God. The notion of *"communio,"* or the unity of all the faithful in Christ, ought also to be developed. There was not enough insistence on the eschatological aspect of the Church: the Church continues to develop or unfold. He agreed with the suggestion of Cardinal Frings that the connection of the Church with the saints in heaven should be spelled out. Then, turning to the subject of the schema on Mary, he acknowledged: "In Latin American countries devotion to Our Lady is sometimes too far removed from the proper devotional life of the Church," a statement reminiscent of John XXIII's warning to the Roman clergy against a tendency "to cultivate certain excessive devotional practices, even with respect to devotion to the Madonna." If proposed in a separate treatise, the theology of Mary would be difficult to relate to the whole doctrine of Christian salvation. Therefore he recommended that the schema on Mary should be incorporated in the present schema on the Church.

Speaking in the name of numerous bishops from Africa and Madagascar, Cardinal Rugambwa said that he found the schema generally acceptable, however it did not bring out clearly enough the connection between the Mission of the Church and the Mission of Christ, namely with respect to the evangelization of the world, or, in other words, to the dynamic missionary role of the Church everywhere. The Church, he said, everywhere and always, is sent to all non-Christians, not merely to those "in foreign missions." This universal mission should be brought out. "Mission is needed everywhere, therefore the Church is everywhere missionary." The relation between this idea of mission and the People of God should be expressed clearly.

The Exarch for the Ukrainians in Canada, Archbishop Hermaniuk, observed: "The schema pleases me because of its scriptural emphasis, its use of Oriental theology, its insistence on collegiality, and its ecumenical spirit. But the collegiality of the bishops is not explained clearly enough. It seems to be mentioned as something accidental, whereas the government of the Church ought at all times to be collegial." Echoing a thought contained in the Pope's opening address which would be taken up by quite a few speakers later, he was the first to suggest on the floor the need for some kind of an episcopal senate to advise the Pope. "This government could take the form of a large college, a kind of episcopal council beside the Pope, which would include the patriarchs, the cardinals who are residential bishops or archbishops, and delegates from episcopal conferences or missionary areas." There was no true collegiality apart from the Pope of course. The way the terms "college and its head" or "body with its head" were used gave the impression that the Pope was separate from the episcopal college, which is not true. Instead of such frequent references to "Roman Pontiff," more ecumenical-sounding expressions such as "Pastor of the universal Church" should be used. He proposed the use of the term "Supreme Pontiff" rather than "Roman Pontiff" to show that the Pope's role as the successor of Peter was more important than that of the Bishop of Rome.*

Speaking in the name of the French bishops, Archbishop Garrone of Toulouse said that the schema was acceptable as a whole, however a number of points needed clarification: 1) the schema on Mary should be incorporated in *De Ecclesia* in order to preserve a better theological balance—an idea supported by numerous subsequent speakers; 2) the expression Kingdom of God should be added to the list of biblical images by which the Church was defined; this would help explain its eschatological, dynamic and missionary dimensions; 3) the notion of an episcopal college should be spelled out more fully with reference to Scripture which has much to say about the unity of the episcopal body; 4) a grave defect was the absence of any treatment of Tradition. Unless this concept was spelled out in connection with and in relation to the Church, there would be difficulty in carry-

* *L'Italia,* Oct. 2, 1963.

ing on the dialogue with the separated brethren. Bishop Vuccino, on Friday, also urged the claims of Tradition to be considered in *De Ecclesia*, "because of the intimate relation between the Word of God and baptism. The Word must be proclaimed before baptism is received," he said. Revelation, Scripture and Tradition ought to be treated in one schema.

Bishop Elchinger, Coadjutor of Strasbourg, offered a number of observations which in the main were similar to those of Archbishop Garrone. He too felt that the schema on the Church should include a chapter on Mary. The prerogatives of Mary, that is, her singular place in the People of God, exist only with respect to Christ and the Church.

The Bishop of Cuernavaca in Mexico agreed with Cardinals Silva Henriquez and Frings with regard to the latter point. It was desirable to demarcate the boundaries of Marian devotion to correct certain tendencies in popular devotion, and in order to explain the matter better to non-Catholics who sometimes have wrong notions about the Church because of these excesses. "Devotion to Mary and the saints, especially in our countries, at times obscures devotion to Christ."

By contrast, the Cardinal Archbishop of Tarragona, speaking on Thursday, was to sound the only dissenting note on this theme among the council's early speakers. In the name of 56 Spanish bishops, he put in a strong plea for keeping Mary separate from *De Ecclesia*, "because the mystery of Mary is greater than the mystery of the Church. There is danger that she would be seen in a merely passive role as representing the Church, as the Church's eldest daughter, and not as the mother of the Church by her vivifying influence." However, if the Marian schema was to be added, he asked that it be made Chapter II and should in content be as profound and extensive as the subject deserved.

The debate on the schema as a whole was brought to a

close on Tuesday with several warning notes by Italian bishops whose remarks about "difficult terminology" revealed that they were not abreast of recent theological thinking, while the Belgian Bishop Guffens was interrupted by the Moderator for wandering from the subject and sat down in confusion without delivering the rest of his talk.

The Council was then asked to vote on the following proposal:

"Does this schema please you in general as a basis for pursuing the discussion chapter by chapter?"

The Secretary General shortly afterward announced the results:

2301 votes in all
2231 favorable votes (*placet*)
  43 unfavorable votes (*non placet*)
   3 votes proposing amendments (*iuxta modum*)
  24 invalid votes.

The votes proposing amendments were counted as invalid because there were only two choices allowed: *placet* or *non placet*.

While the voting was taking place the Secretary General announced that the Coordinating Commission had decided on the following order of discussion for the schemata at this session, "time permitting":

De Ecclesia;
De beata Virgine Maria, Matre Ecclesiae;
De Episcopis et regimine dioecesium;
De Apostolatu laicorum;
De Oecumenismo.

In the remaining time on Tuesday, discussion was begun on Chapter 1, the Church as a Mystery, by Cardinal Ruffini,

Archbishop of Palermo.* In general the cardinal praised the
text but said that it was too repetitious and its language too
inexact in places. He offered a large number of amendments,
criticizing especially the inappropriateness of certain biblical
quotations and remarking apropos of the statement that "the
Church is a sacrament": "For a long time the term sacrament has been reserved to the seven sacraments; because its
use with reference to the Church is obscure today and needs
long explanations, it is contrary to the pastoral orientation
of the Council. This term was often used heretically by
George Tyrrell, apostate priest and leader of the Modern-
ists." His principal point however was that a distinction
should be made between the foundation of the Church on
Peter, and its foundation on the Apostles. The statement
that "Christ founded the Church on both Peter and the
Apostles together" had no biblical testimony, he said, and
could lead to error. "Only to Peter did Christ say: *Tu es
Petrus.* In Ephesians 2:20 Paul only wishes to say that the
Apostles were the first to adhere to Christ, the Cornerstone
of the Church, after the manner of a foundation wall upon
which the faithful are *superaedificati.*" There should be a
distinction between charisms in the Church and the functions of the hierarchical government of the Church. He
criticized also what the schema had to say about the Church
as both a divine and a human society, as the Mystical Body
and as a visible society, for Pius XII had said in *Mystici
Corporis* that the Mystical Body and the Church were one
and the same reality and there was danger of introducing a

* The numbered paragraphs of the Introduction and Chapter I of the
schema *De Ecclesia* were as follows: 1. Introduction; 2. The eternal design of
the Father; 3. The mission of the Son; 4. The Spirit sanctifying the Church;
5. The Church as the Mystical Body of Christ; 6. Other images of the
Church; 7. The Church as a Pilgrim on earth; 8. The Catholic faithful;
9. The bonds of the Church with non-Catholic Christians; 10. On bringing
non-Christians to the Church.

dualist conception, whereas the two notions should be kept strictly together.

The last speaker of the day was Archbishop Aramburu of Tucumán in Argentina, who said that the schema must not only expound the nature of the Church but serve as a basis for all the other conciliar acts. He proposed mention of the idea of the eucharist as a source of the Church's unity.

At noon on Tuesday the Holy Father received some 400 journalists in Rome to cover the Council in the Hall of the Consistory, along with the members of the Council Press Committee. After congratulating newspaper editors, radio broadcasters and other who had assigned to Rome "so many reporters" to cover the Council, he said (in French):

"We have already had occasion to tell you of the esteem we hold for journalists, and how aware we are of the important place they occupy in the world of today. . . The honor of your profession demands on your part objective reporting and constant concern for the truth. . . This is a difficult task, as we well understand, for this imposing assembly has some similarity with large human gatherings, when in reality it is quite different. In fact, there could be the temptation to search out certain well-known "friends" such as nationalism, conflicting tendencies, parties, historical and geographical differences, as for example between East and West. If attention is limited to these externals, or if there is emphasis upon them, then the reality of things is altered, even falsified. For all the bishops are endeavoring to avoid giving any substance to these divisions, in order on the contrary to be guided by the objective divine truth which they profess and by the fraternal charity which animates them. Certainly discussion in the council hall is free and of various kinds. But if it undoubtedly bears the stamp of the various backgrounds of the bishops, it is nonetheless not determined by closed minds or prejudice. . .

It is largely your task to see to it that the entire world, alert and waiting, gets the information it needs in order to understand the progress of this great assembly. . .

Rest assured in any case that the ones responsible for the organization of the Council will do their best to satisfy your desires. . . .

Although the Pope admitted that the Fathers' opinions might be colored by their origins and backgrounds, he still insisted that the discussions in the Council were not characterized by *parti-pris*. This was true, but observers noted that some of the Fathers still seem confused about the real significance of the *"balzo in avanti"*—Pope John's phrase for the leap forward into modernity that the Council has inspired —though they seemed to accept it all with a spirit of humility and a sense of humor. One French prelate was overheard to say in Bar Jonah: "To be a good Council Father, you need the patience of Job and the wisdom of Solomon, and it also helps if you have a cast-iron bottom, *alors!*" The bishops were obliged to sit each morning through two and a half hours of Latin oratory, delivered in such dissimilar accents as lilting Italian, nasal French, gutteral German, broguish Celtic, and rasping American. Most of the Council Fathers sat there silently deploring the lack of a simultaneous-translation system and straining to make something of the speech whenever an interesting speaker took the microphone. There was no difficulty for anyone with an ear for Latin when Archbishop Pericle Felici, the Secretary General of the Council, had the floor; his clear, loud, and agreeable voice lingered consciously on the vowels, and he commanded a flow of Latin that enabled him, by an emphasis or a turn of phrase, to indulge in much appreciated pleasantries. The Council's Lay Auditors were assigned an interpreter, Monsignor Achille Glorieux, but the one American auditor—James J. Norris, assistant to the executive director of the Catholic Relief Services, which are run by the American bishops—had no need for his translations. He is a personal friend of Pope Paul, who was heard to say to him on his arrival, "Well, Jim, we

have made you a Council Father." As far back as 1946, Norris
worked with the then Monsignor Montini, who was in the
Vatican Secretariat of State, setting up the International
Catholic Migration Committee. Though the Council Auditors could not speak in the debates in St. Peter's, they were
given copies of all the Council documents and were asked
for technical advice by the commission in charge of drawing
up the schema on the apostolate of the laity.

On the sidelines of the Council, one of the greatest single
differences between the first session and the second was the
change in press relations. On Monday, September 30th, Secretary General Felici announced to the Council, in a complicated Latin sentence before which Cicero would have
paused, that for all practical purposes the secrecy of the debates was no more—though he advised supreme prudence
and caution in quoting speeches.

The daily press bulletins were prepared each morning by
the Press Office under the direction of Msgr. Fausto Vallainc,
as follows: seven priests experienced in journalism compiled
the bulletin each day. Two of them sitting at a table in the
right transept of the basilica had the task of writing the bulletin. Five others took notes on the different interventions,
then summarized what they had taken down quoting key
phrases whenever this seemed necessary. Their drafts were
then handed to the table which prepared the bulletins by
weaving together the various versions handed in. In order
to be sure that the words of the speaker had been heard and
recorded correctly, the text of the bulletin was always based
upon the notes of the priest who spoke the same language as
the speaker, this because of the wide differences in pronounc-
ing Latin depending upon the original language of the speaker
—Italian Latin did not sound at all like American or German
Latin, etc.—and because it was simply necessary to admit the
fact that what they were dealing with was in most cases not

Latin at all, but English, German, French, Italian or Spanish *translated* into Latin.*

The various language press conferences began to shape up during the first few days under the general auspices of the Press Committee presided over by Archbishop Martin O'Connor. Archbishop Andrea Pangrazio was the member of this Committee responsible for the Italian Press; Archbishop René Stourm for the French press; Bishop Hermann Wittler for the German press; Bishop J. Cirarda for the Spanish press; Bishop Albert Zuroweste for the English-language press.** Each day, as in the last session, a briefing in the rooms of the Press Office immediately after the daily session on the content of the speeches. Father Edward Heston, of the Holy Cross order, briefed the American and English journalists; Father F. B. Haubtmann of *La Croix* briefed the French journalists; Msgr. G. Fittkau the German journalists; Fr. F. Farusi, SJ, the Italian journalists; and Fr. C. Calderón the Spanish journalists.† The American bishops, and the Americans only, also decided to have a discussion or panel meeting each afternoon to provide a fuller briefing, with members of the hierarchy and other persons being invited to address the journalists on special topics. This was under the chairmanship of the Paulist Father John Sheerin, editor of the *Catholic World*. The panel consisted of Father Francis J. Connell, CSSR, Fr. Gustave Weigel, SJ, Fr. Frederick McManus, Msgr. George Higgins, Fr. Bernard Häring, CSSR, Fr. Robert Trisco, and

---

* Cf. interview of Père François Bernard, A.A., editor of *La Croix* and responsible for the French section of the Press Office, published in *La Semaine religieuse d'Angers,* Oct. 27, 1963.

** Nine other episcopal members were also responsible for areas, as follows: J. Rezende Costa, for the Portuguese press: H. Thiandoum, for Africa; O. McCann, for the missionary press; E. D'Souza, for the Far East; J. Khoury, for the Oriental Churches; G. De Vet, for the Dutch press; H. Bednorz, for the Slavic press; M. McGrath, for the Latin-American press; and H. Routhier, for the Canadian press.

† Other Press Office members briefing the press were: Fr. P. Almeida, SJ, the Portuguese press; Fr. S. Wesoly, the Polish Press.

Fr. F. McCool, SJ, as the more or less permanent members.
Those on the panel, of course, had all attended the morning's
session and could speak from their personal knowledge of
what had taken place. After a few days, the principle news-
papers reporting the daily sessions in depth, *Il Quotidiano,
La Croix, L'Avvenire d'Italia, Le Monde, Le Figaro,* in particular, began to identify the speakers consistently, and the
official press bulletins also began the practice of devoting a
paragraph to a speech, thus making it easier to identify what
each Father had said, though the bulletins refrained from
affixing names to the paragraphs in order to escape responsibility for the digests. The English bulletin was not merely
a translation of the Italian, the first out, but an independent
summary based on the notes of Father Heston and other
experts. The French, Spanish and German bulletins were
more like the Italian, with differences here and there.

The Moderator presiding on Wednesday was Cardinal
Doepfner.

Before the business of the day was taken up, Msgr. Villot,
a council Undersecretary, read in French a message from the
Lay Auditors to the Council:

"Conscious of the historical event which has taken place as
a result of the decision of the Holy Father to invite qualified
Lay Auditors to take part as observers in the Council sessions,
these Auditors consider it a duty to express to the Council their
emotion, joy and profound gratitude of the laity whom they
have the honor to represent and to fulfill this responsibility by
attentively following the work of the Council and its decisions,
and redoubling their prayers for its success."

As Henri Fesquet* noted, this message gave rise to various
comments of a somewhat cynical nature. Some said, for
example: "This colorless ecclesiastical language hardly befits

* *Le Monde,* Oct. 4, 1963.

laymen. It employs the very type of sentimentalized terminology which the laity complain about in pastoral letters. Are the laity to attend the Council as the mere mouthpieces of the clergy?" Whatever truth there is in remarks of this kind, he goes on to say, the Fathers applauded this statement with marked reserve (*une extrême discrétion*) and they can hardly be blamed for this.

The discussion continued on Wednesday on the Introduction and Chapter I.

Speaking in the name of 153 Brazilian bishops (but mentioning the names of those who offered specific amendments) Cardinal de Barros Câmara said that it should be explicitly stated in the Introduction that dogmatic definitions are to be found only where the words of the text indicate that the Council intends to define truths of faith. The reason was in order to avoid abuses of the Council's text and distortion of its meaning. In contrast to this prudent reserve, caution appeared to be thrown to the winds on Friday by the Spanish Archbishop García Martínez who claimed that enough light had been thrown on the question of whether infallibility extended to virtually revealed truths, necessarily connected doctrine, and dogmatic facts, "for a solemn definition to be made on this point" and thus "complete the work of Vatican Council I." A majority of theologians would probably not agree.

The Cardinal Archbishop of Bombay, Cardinal Gracias, spoke next and said that the Introduction should be shorter and should give a brief history of salvation, indicating that Christ's redemption was for all men. "Why say that the language of the Council should be adapted to modern times? Let us use this language instead of saying that we should use it."* Greater clarity and order were desirable in Chapter I.

* *La Croix*, October 4, 1963.

The religious and spiritual side of the Church should be brought out more clearly; it should not be considered as a "state within a state," as some Catholics maintain who "want to be more Catholic than the Pope." The Church should be presented as ministering to and serving the world, as Pope Paul VI pointed out in his opening address. The Church grows in the world only to save and enrich it morally and spiritually. This idea should be developed especially with reference to the missionary action of the Church. The cardinal quoted Cardinal Newman to the effect that since Catholics were a minority they should attempt to prevail not by numbers but by their example and zeal. He observed apropos of the unity of Christians, that this was less important than union with God and quoted the English aphorism, in English, "Too many cooks spoil the soup," changing the last word so that it would be better understood.*

The intervention of Cardinal Alfrink of Holland on Wednesday made a deep impression, particularly on the non-Catholic Observer Delegates. He criticized the expression in the schema "Peter and the Apostles" for implying that Peter was not an Apostle. It would be better to substitute some other phrase such as "Peter and the *other* Apostles." "No one," he added, "wishes to deny or lessen the primacy of Peter, but it is necessary to restore the Pope to his place in the apostolic college. The Church has twelve foundations. Peter is the rock." Peter's place in the college and his primacy should be dealt with simultaneously for they are inseparable. Christ's words "Whatever you shall bind on earth . . ." (Mt. 18:18) were said to *all* the Apostles. And the Apocalyptic vision of the New Jerusalem "The wall of the city having as a foundation the Twelve, and in them the names of the Twelve Apostles" (Apoc. 21:14) was not merely eschatological. In Scripture, apocalyptic imagery was taken

* *The New York Times,* October 3, 1963.

from what was already realized in time. A further indication of this truth was the liturgical practice of having twelve crosses representing the Apostles in consecrated churches. "That all the Apostles together constitute the foundation does not detract from Peter's singular place among them," he said, thus throwing down the exegetical gauntlet to Cardinal Ruffini.

The Bishop of Haarlem van Dodewaard, speaking in the name of the Dutch Bishops' Conference, observed that the relationship between the visible and invisible elements of the Church "is not well elaborated." "Neither the unity nor the distinction between 'the community of love and grace' and the 'complex of the means of salvation' is made clear." Under one aspect the Church referred to all those for whom redemption was actually effective, for example, all those who profess the faith of Abraham; under other aspects, the Church was seen as the universal means for applying redemption. Thus, on the analogy of the Incarnate Word, we spoke of the Church as a living instrument, a sign, a means of salvation operating through the Spirit of Christ for the building up of the Mystical Body; the Church as a servant of Christ was a sign raised among the nations.

The first American speaker was the Bishop of Manchester, New Hampshire. Introduced by the Moderator as an English bishop, he brought laughter when he began by saying that the Bishop of Manchester, England, happened to be one of the "separated brethren." Bishop Primeau felt that certain statements in the schema were ambiguous regarding membership or incorporation in the Church. It was necessary to bear in mind certain distinctions, he said, "incorporation in the Church, incorporation in God, incorporation on earth, in purgatory, in heaven," and so forth. The Council should define the relationship between the Catholic Church and other Christian communities. This question—so important for ecumenism—came down to asking what the ecclesial reality was of those communities that were non-Catholic. "The Council would make a giant step forward if it acknowledged the Protestant claim to be 'Churches'." Admittedly this was a question that was still under serious study. He also touched on the theme of the relations between Church and state.— In a press interview later the same day, Bishop Primeau enlarged on the latter idea, observing that there was nothing in the present draft on the subject.

"I myself think that the Council should say something on the matter. I do not think the Council should go into particulars, nor into the particular relationships that exist between the Church and state. But some general principles should be laid down."

He said that such matters as the freedom to carry out the Church's mission would be an example of what might be covered by the Council. He acknowledged that such a statement might be more useful for America than for some other countries.

"In our country the Protestant intelligentsia are always asking for a definite statement on Church and state. In our pluralistic societies we have some kind of basic principles."
"We have not come here just to rubberstamp the status-quo," he said; "there are knots to be cut."

The same theme was enlarged upon by the Abbot of Downside, Dom Christopher Butler. It was not sufficient for the schema to confine itself to the relationship between the Church and non-Catholic Christians *individually*, the question must be faced of whether there was any relationship between the Church and those communities as such. "These communities, in so far as they follow the counsels of Christ, have supernatural qualities, although as supernatural societies they are incomplete."—Since there was a distinction between the Kingdom of Christ and the Kingdom of God, the Church must be identified as the Kingdom of Christ. The Kingdom of God had apocalyptic as well as eschatological significance. "This distinction will also help ecumenical relations," he commented.*

The concern of a rather large number of speakers with what may be called the ecumenical implications of the schema on the Church indicated that there was a kind of general consensus on this point, which may be summed up by saying that what most desired was a thoroughly biblical definition of the Church based on such scriptural images as the People of God or Kingdom of God, one that would be meaningful to Protestants, Orthodox and even non-Christians, and as free as possible, therefore, from the traditional post-biblical terminology—largely of a juridical inspiration—which has characterized Catholic speculation on the nature of the Church in recent centuries. As Cardinal Bea pointed out, it was futile to think that any impression could be made on non-Catholics by employing the sterile terminology of past centuries already compromised by divisions and misunderstandings. What was needed was a return to the Bible or apostolic age, some common ground on which Christians could be expected to agree particularly in the light of recent biblical research. In the opinion of many speakers, while the present schema was on the right road, it had not yet fully attained this goal.

One of the most important speeches on this theme, delivered by Cardinal Lercaro on Thursday, set the tone of the debate, and was confidently believed by many observers to reflect the views of Pope Paul himself.** For this reason all

* *La Croix*, Oct. 4, 1963.
** *L'Avvenire d'Italia*, Oct. 4 and 6, 1963; cf. *La Civiltà Cattolica*, Nov. 2, 1963, p. 300-303.

of the speeches of Cardinal Lercaro merited and received ample attention during both sessions. They were also reproduced almost verbatim in the Bolognese newspaper *L'Avvenire d'Italia,* an organ faithfully reflecting the critical left-of-center policies, ecclesiastical and political, of the cardinal himself, thus assuring these views wide publicity.

Cardinal Lercaro's speech was divided into three parts. In the first part, after a few preliminary remarks praising the work of the Theological Commission, he listed three corrections which ought to be made to eliminate any possible misunderstanding over words constantly recurring such as "Church," "society," "Mystical Body," which seemed to be used in different senses. The text said that the Church as a visible society and the Church as the Mystical Body were identical (text: *non duae res sunt, sed una tantum*). Cardinal Ruffini had said on Tuesday that the visible Church and Mystical Body could not be distinguished (*nullatenus distinguuntur*) and were "coextensive." Cardinal Lercaro held that this was true in one sense, but not in another. "Church and Mystical Body are two distinct aspects which coincide perfectly in the essential order and according to the constitutive norm of the Divine Founder, but not in the same fully verifiable identical way in the existential or historical order. In the latter order the two aspects are not coextensive but reflect certain tensions and will reflect them till the end of time, when the true identity between Church and Mystical Body will be revealed." He therefore seconded the proposed amendment suggested by Cardinal Alfrink clarifying these distinctions, "lest unfounded conclusions be drawn, as happened after "Mystici Corporis"—a reference to the controversy in the Church after the publication of Pius XII's famous encyclical on the Church as the Mystical Body in 1943.

His second correction related to membership in the Church. The cardinal emphasized that belonging to the Church

through baptism was not an ecumenical "novelity" invented
in order to please the separated brethren, but a traditional
theological truth. Baptism made a person a member of the
Church. Neither schism, heresy, nor apostasy could completely
break this bond. "All the baptized belong to the Church
(the Oriental Code expressly says so) regardless of the schisms
or apostasies that may occur afterward." Like Card. Bea on
numerous occasions, including his intervention later the
same morning, Lercaro insisted that the proper way to speak
of membership or incorporation in the Church was of complete or incomplete membership. Therefore in section 8 of
Chap. I where a definition was given of *"fideles Catholici"*
or full members—as those who recognized the Church's perfect structure and all the means of sanctification, that is, those
who were united to Christ by belonging to the visible society
which is governed by the Pope and the bishops, by the bonds
of faith, the sacraments, discipline and ecclesiastical communion—the introductory adverbs *"reapse et simpliciter
loquendo,"* which many Fathers considered too restrictive,
should be changed to *"plene et complete"*—fully and completely. "This is suggested not only or principally for ecumenical reasons as a kind of condescension toward the separated brethren; but primarily because the doctrine according
to which baptism validly received incorporates once and for
all in the Church as a visible society has always been Catholic
doctrine" (*"è la dottrina cattolica di sempre"*). His third correction was that the relation between the Church and the
eucharist be brought out more clearly, the latter being not
merely a sign of unity but a dynamic entity. "In the eucharist
the faithful are gathered together and constituted as the
Elect People of the New Testament, existing as an anticipation of the Kingdom of Heaven, reconciled and united to
the Father. In the eucharist, by consuming the unique Bread
which is the real Body of Christ, the Church exercises the

final and most perfect act of which it is capable on earth; it is truly the *Ecclesia;* by its eucharistic action the Chuch is formally and essentially constituted as a *coetus culticus*—a worshiping community."

His second important point was to the effect that the dynamic nature of the definition of the Church should be brought out more clearly. Scripture was fond of calling the Church a new people, a new creation (*novum genus, nova creatio*). These ideas should be stressed, "since recapitulation in Christ is not just a psychological or ethical assimilation or merely a religious consecration." The Church was a new presence in the world; its witness, service, preaching were not just a history of the Church but *are* the Church. A new creation meant a new birth and the pains of childbirth. "The Church is the womb in which this cosmic rebirth takes place. Hence its dynamic nature, its essential existence not only or principally as a structure but as a *dynamis,* a dynamic force, whose significance and nature should be spelled out in *De Ecclesia.*" He did not think, in this connection, that the proposals by Cardinals Rugambwa or de Barros Câmara, Bishop Ancel or others "could be suspected of being an attempt to introduce into a dogmatic constitution a kind of phenomenology of the situation and concrete activity of the Church in our times"— referring to objections by conservative theologians to what those prelates had urged. Their proposals were not concerned merely with external attributes but with the very "essence of the Church." The mystery of the Church could not be explained adequately by reference merely to principles governing its activity, mention must be made also of principles governing its existence or nature. "According to the Gospel, the Church's present mode of existence is that of a *martyrion*—a witness of the truth of the Gospel to all nations, and a *diakonia*—a service, which should cause it always to be humble and the servant of all." The Church was sent primarily to the lowly, the humble and the poor, and did not expect anything in return. It was sent also to all nations, all races, all civilizations, and ought never to consider itself permanently tied to any one.

His third observation related to the revision of the text. So many fine things had been said in the Council that a complete revision was obviously necessary. "The Theological Commission is probably not equal to this task. It would be a good idea to ask those Fathers who have spoken well on this subject to assist it in its labors. This would merely be an application of Art. 65 which allows the Fathers to be heard in the Commissions. It would be a good idea to invite Cardinals Silva Henriquez, Gracias, Rugambwa, Bishop Guano and Bishop Ancel to confer with each other and get in touch with the Theological Commission so that the new definition of the Church will correspond more fully to the aspirations of the men of our time."* It is doubtful whether the cardinal expected that this indirect public rebuke to Card. Ottaviani who had refused on the whole to solicit the cooperation of other Commissions or encourage participation by experts in the work of his Theological Commission, would have much effect but he seemed to feel obliged to make the statement anyway for the record.

Following Cardinal Lercaro's lead, the idea of poverty was stressed particularly on Friday, the Feast of St. Francis of Assisi, by Cardinal Gerlier, Archbishop of Lyons, who quoted from the moving appeal of Cardinal Lercaro toward the end of last year's session as well as words of Pope John XXIII and Pope Paul VI, to the effect that the poor and those who suffered were particularly close to the Church. He endorsed the proposal of 13 East African Bishops that the Introduction should say something about this place of the poor in the Church. The schema did not develop suf-

* *La Croix,* Oct. 4, 1963.

ficiently what he called the theology of the poor, namely
that they made present in the Church the mystery of Christ
by living his poverty and his passion among us. Christ identified himself with them and what was done for them was
done for him. Later the same day Bishop Himmer of Tournai,
Belgium, stressed the idea of service to the poor, if the
Church wished to reveal its true face to the poor. "We shall
be judged with regard to the charity we have shown to the
poor, because of the presence of Christ in them."

A number of speakers followed Lercaro in dealing with
membership in the Church, finding the expressions in the
schema inadequate or misleading. Archbishop Van den Burgt
of Pontianak, Indonesia, said that while Catholics may be
the only "complete or perfect" members of the Church, theologically speaking, a real membership in the Church could
not be denied to Protestants. For Bishop Van Kelsen of
Kroonstad, South Africa, the schema was not sufficiently
positive in its approach to the separated brethren: when dealing with Protestants it failed to mention the Bible and baptism which they had in common with Catholics, and when
dealing with the Orthodox it failed to mention their valid
orders and eucharist. The words *"reapse et simpliciter"* had
obviously been added for the sake of clarity, but he found
that theologians were uncertain what they meant exactly—
he himself disclaimed any pretension to technical theological
knowledge. According to Archbishop Baudoux of Saint-
Boniface, Canada, the treatment of the bonds between the
Church and non-Catholic Christians in Paragraph 9 was
defective. He agreed with Dom Butler that non-Catholics
could not be dealt with merely as individuals but only as
communities with some or all of the sacraments. "We do not
know the exact relationship between such communities and
the Church, but we must recognize that God saves souls
through them," he said. A more positive approach was needed.

It should be noted that schisms and heresies had often befallen the Church because of the faults of her members and
therefore such faults should be freely acknowledged. Bishop
Marling of Jefferson City, Missouri, thought that the schema
did not bring out well enough the doctrinal basis of ecumenism. He agreed with Archbishop Baudoux that the Church,
as Mother of all, recognized that those who were not in complete union with her "nevertheless are in many ways united
through the Holy Spirit, faith in Christ, and baptism." This
union was close in the case of Orientals who shared many
things in common with Catholics. The last sentence of Paragraph 9 should contain a strong exhortation to prayer and
cooperation that there might be "one flock of Christ." All
these thoughts would be stressed again in the debate on Ecumenism. Archbishop Heenan of Westminster, speaking in
the name of the English and Welsh hierarchies, said that the
"duty of the Church and of Christians towards the separated
brethren" not only consisted in praying and reforming one-
self, as the schema stated, but involved a truly evangelical
attitude. "Every Catholic must be an Apostle. His apostolate
is performed by prayer, example and preaching." Expound-
ing the true doctrine to those separated from Catholic unity
was also an obligation.

A rather remarkable intervention along this line was that
of Archbishop Baldassari of Ravenna, Italy, on Friday. He
recalled the words of Paul VI in his opening address and insisted that it was necessary to acknowledge faults. "It is
necessary to say these things so that the ecumenical dialogue
may be started in an atmosphere of mutual pardon."* Emphasis should be placed on baptism as the door of the Church.
It was regrettable that the schema did not come out clearly
enough on this score. Instead, speaking of the "separated
brethren," almost fearfully (*timorose*), it referred to them as

* *Le Monde,* Oct. 6-7, 1963.

"those who are adorned with the name of Christian (*qui christiano nomine decorantur*)." They are much more than "adorned," they actually shared baptism in common with us. Ravenna felt particularly close to the East because of its history and traditions. Therefore its archbishop hoped that the schema might put more stress on "the common faith in the Trinity, the sacred deposit of Scripture, and the venerable traditions of the Fathers of the Church" which we shared. "Why not say these consoling things in the text?"*

The missionary dimensions of the definition of the Church were also treated by Archbishop D'Souza of Nagpur, India, following Cardinal Rugambwa, in the name of 25 bishops of northern India. The schema on Missions was unfortunately not yet ready, he acknowledged, but it was hoped that the one on the Church would at least lay down the theological foundations of the missionary concept. It must not be thought that missionary responsibilities were satisfied looking after internal missionary problems. "Much energy is devoted, even in missionary territories, to preserving the faith rather than spreading it. Unfortunately at times, in lands where the Church is established, missionary work with non-Christians is considered a work of supererogation. Today only 3 to 5 per cent of the Church's apostolic effort is directed toward the 2 billion souls who have yet to be evangelized." Bishops and religious superiors should consider a reorganization that would permit the release of surplus personnel for truly missionary work. He mentioned in this connection the French book *"France, pays de mission,"* which dealt with a renewal of pastoral methods and had had an enormous success.

Speaking on a kindred theme, Archbishop Grauls of Kitega, Urundi, in the name of 55 bishops of Burundi, Rwandi and the Congo, expressed the wish that the idea of the Church's catholicity could be brought out more clearly, that is, its

* *L'Avvenire d'Italia,* Oct. 5, 1963.

ability and obligation to assume the human values found in all cultures. Africa, for example, had a culture which was neither eastern nor western. Just as Christ when he became incarnate took on the characteristic features of the Jewish people, so the Church, which in a certain way could be said to become incarnate in peoples, should take on the values of a people or continent. "Let us never oppose unity and diversity. The Church should appropriate to itself all values, adopt all cultures. All Catholic churches have the same rights and the same dignity. Catholicism means the ability to appropriate everything."*

There were a number of criticisms also of the final Paragraph 10 "On bringing non-Christians to the Church" (*De non-Christianis ad Ecclesiam adducendis*). The Apostolic Vicar of Montagnosa in the Philippines, Bishop Brasseur, felt that a passage seemed to indicate that the difference between Christians and non-Christians could be expressed in terms of *magis et minus*—more or less. This should be corrected since it was obviously false. "The question of the salvation of the non-baptized is not yet mature enough to be defined." Archbishop Seper of Zagreb, Yugoslavia, said that this paragraph should mention the Jews who stood in a special relationship to the Church because of the Old Testament.**

Finally, Bishop Pildáin, of the Canary Islands, raised the delicate question of fallen-away Catholics. While the schema had much to say about non-Catholics and non-Christians, it failed to broach this important subject. "Both Pope Pius XII and Pope John XXIII" had expressed grave concern over this problem of masses of baptized Catholics who have virtually withdrawn from the Church. "It is a new phenomenon of our day and has been called the scandal of the century."

* *Le Monde,* Oct. 6-7, 1963.
** Cf. *New York Times,* Oct. 4, 1963.

He proposed the addition of a new paragraph treating of it. Since most of the fallen-away Catholics were found among the poor and the laboring classes, he gave strong approval to the amendment of 13 bishops of East-Central Africa that a paragraph be added to the Introduction expressing this concern.

Many speakers concentrated their remarks on Paragraphs 5 and 6 of the schema, "On the Church as the Mystical Body of Christ" and "Concerning other Images of the Church." Some found the images mentioned adequate, others wanted new ideas introduced. Bishop Romero of Jaén, Spain, wanted the notion of the Church as the Kingdom of God—occurring often in the Gospels—mentioned and used as a basis for explaining the eschatological, missionary, and social aspects of the Church. According to Auxiliary Bishop Ancel of Lyons "a new paragraph dealing with the Church as the Kingdom of God should be composed and inserted into the schema immediately after the fourth paragraph. This image reveals the Church as a society both visible and spiritual, and it explains the essence of renewal through charity, the growth of the Church and its universal mission to the whole world, as well as its eschatological goal." Other speakers suggested images such as the "Spouse of Christ" or "Family of God." The Bishop of Calahorra, Spain, noted that the image of the Mystical Body conveyed little meaning with regard to the Church as a visible society. He also criticized the ambiguous use of the word ecclesia. Sometimes it meant the "congregation of those who have been saved," and sometimes more strictly the society which Christ had founded. In view of the "militancy" of the Church in the present world, according to Bishop Franič of Split, Yugoslavia, such images as Kingdom of God and City set on a Mountain had much to recommend them, not in a provocative sense of course, but in the sense exemplified by Christ who submitted even to the cross. "We

must struggle with spiritual, not worldly arms."* The Church
as the "Family of God" commended itself particularly to the
Brazilian Archbishop de Proença Sigaud and the Bishop of
Dalat, Vietnam, Nguyen-van Hien. The former maintained
that the Church was the "family of God" not in a meta-
phorical sense, but properly speaking: "God is Father, Christ
is the first-born brother, Mary is mother, and all members
are brothers through baptism." The latter was of the opinion
that this easily graspable idea emphasizing the unity of the
Church could be appreciated especially in Asia where the
family has remained a sacred thing. "Here in the council,"
he said, "we are accustomed to refer to ourselves not as members of the Mystical Body but as brothers in Christ—*carissimi fratres* not *carissima membra*." This brought smiles to
the faces of his hearers. The following speaker, Bishop Volk
of Mainz, Germany, also brought smiles when he turned to
the Observer Delegates and addressed them as *carissimi
observatores* while stressing the point that the schema should
contain a clearer distinction between the Church as an
efficacious sign of redemption and the Kingdom of God as
the consummation of redemption.**

Several speakers, including Bishop Jelmini of Lugano,
Archbishop Martin of Rouen, and the Bishop of Majorca,
regretted the fact that almost nothing was said in the text
about the eucharist and its relationship to the Church. The
former proposed an emendation to Paragraph 5 stressing the
presence of Christ in the eucharist, the external organization
of the Church, and the People of God. The schema on the
Church and that on the Liturgy should be brought into line,
according to Archbishop Martin. "The eucharist is the summit or culmination where the Son accomplishes his mission
and where the Holy Spirit dispenses his gifts (*simul culmen*

* *La Croix,* Oct. 4, 1963.
** *Le Monde,* Oct. 5, 1963.

et fons ecclesiae)." This manner of speaking was in accordance with both Eastern and Western theology.

A more fundamental objection was raised by Bishop Jenny, Auxiliary of Cambrai, with regard to the lack of a proper Christological orientation. The text should be reorganized to bring out the following three points: 1) It should emphasize the majestic place of the person of Christ more clearly. "Pope Paul VI did just this in his opening talk on Sunday in a magnificent hymn to Christ that moved all our hearts and those of the observer-delegates." 2) It should concentrate on the Paschal Mystery. How was Christ present in the Church and how did he found the People of God? By the mystery of the cross and his resurrection. 3) It should show that the Church was the People of God, not in image only, but in reality. But the People of God and all humanity are renewed and recreated precisely through the Paschal Mystery. The Church must in this way be made to appear not as something extrinsic to humanity, but as in humanity, as humanity itself renewed.

Two important interventions on Thursday emphasized the importance of an even greater biblical approach and of the theology of the Word, relatively new ideas in recent Catholic theology. The first by Cardinal Ritter, Archbishop of St. Louis—the second American to speak in the session—said that the Introduction rightly described the Church as a sacrament of union between all men and between men and God. But by concentrating on the static aspect of the Church, the schema was silent about those things which constitute the Church's causality in relation to this union. In Paragraph 7 there should be a treatment of the salvific ministry of the Church, which should include consideration of the efficacy of the Word, together with a treatment of the sacraments. "Preaching and teaching are almost synonymous with the Church, but there is little about this in the schema." "The theology of the Word has been left in the shadows, although the Word is always living, illuminating and operating in the Church," he said. There must be a renewed emphasis on preaching. Let no one say: "This is a pastoral subject." It was primarily theological. The Word and the sacraments were elements of the Church.

The first speech of the president of the Secretariat for Promoting Christian Unity, Cardinal Bea, at this session, also was significant. Pope John, he said, had declared that the Council should express the meaning of Christian life by drawing on the primary sources of the faith. Thus a proper use should be made of Scripture and tradition in the text of the schema. The latter was not lacking in scriptural quotations, but, as Cardinal Ruffini pointed out, these were not always well chosen. Among examples, he cited 1 Tim. 3:15 *columna et firmamentum veritatis*—column and foundation of truth—which referred, he said, not to Peter and the Apostles as the text had it, but to the teachings of the Church. Ephesians 2:20-22 would have been better here.* The schema was defective also in its use of tradition and the documents of the magisterium. There was too much quotation from later sources. Whenever possible sources prior to the Reformation and before the schism in the eleventh century should be used, because there was more chance that these would be understood by the separated brethren. Even references to Vatican Council I and the Council of Trent should be cited with due regard for the present situation. For example, in discussing the prerogatives of the Pope in convoking and confirming an ecumenical council, only canon 227 of the Code is cited in the text, but this was not accepted as binding by the separated Oriental Churches. Unless there was careful atten-

---

* "You are built upon the foundation of the Apostles and prophets, Jesus Christ himself being the chief corner stone. In him the whole structure is closely fitted together and grows into a temple holy in the Lord."

tion to this ecumenical aspect in all quotations from the Bible
and tradition, the schema would fall short of its goal which
was to promote the restoration of unity.

Cardinal Richaud of Bordeaux also felt that many more
quotations from Ephesians should be included in the Introduction, "because this represented the earliest theology of the
Church."

Apart from the speakers already mentioned, the Italian
contribution to the debate of the first week was not notable.
Bishop Carli of Segni, the spokesman for the conservative
wing of the Italian hierarchy, contented himself with second-
ing Cardinal Ruffini as to the dangers that might arise from
a misunderstanding of the phrase "Peter and the Apostles"
which was used so often in the text. He made a strong appeal
for the foundation of the Church on Peter alone, and quoted
a number of scriptural references and Vatican Council I
purporting to show that Peter was "the one foundation of
unity both for the Apostles and for all believers." He concluded with the customary warning: "We must avoid the
danger of seeing the primacy of the Pope only according to
his position as the head of the episcopal college." The same
thought seemed to be echoed by Bishop Campagnone of
Anagni, while Archbishop D'Avack of Camerino felt that the
treatment of the place of the faithful in the Church was a
step back from the doctrine expounded in *Mystici Corporis!*
Finally, Bishop Pocci, speaking on behalf of Cardinal Micara,
Vicar of Rome, who was ill, voiced concern over "certain
widespread errors about the Mystical Body and the Church's
relationship to non-Catholics." Failure to condemn these
errors might scandalize the faithful. The conservative Vicar
of Rome was obviously not in sympathy with the thinking
which had produced *De Ecclesia*. He also felt there was need
for condemning those who denied the existence of hell.

Winding up the debate on Chapter I, Cardinal Browne

said that all the suggested amendments would be taken into account by his Commission. Speaking as a Father, he proposed that the word *"sacramentum"* in the Introduction with reference to the Church, should be understood in the sense of *"sacramentum amoris Christi erga totum genus humanum"* —sacrament of the love of Christ for the whole human race, thus replying to Cardinal Ruffini who had questioned the suitability of the term in its present context.

On Thursday, at the close of the morning's discussions, the Secretary General, Archbishop Felici, had announced that no pamphlets or booklets were to be distributed to the Fathers without the permission of the Council Presidents. On Friday at the beginning of the deliberations, he qualified this statement to mean that such permission was necessary only within the confines of the council hall. The remarks had been misinterpreted or magnified in certain organs of the press as an official ban on certain books about the Council which the Vicariat of Rome had attempted to have withdrawn from sale in Rome.* It referred actually to mimeographed sheets and booklets with which the Fathers were constantly being bombarded in order to influence their voting. Last year there was a flurry of such, notably certain notorious pamphlets by Msgr. Spadafora and Msgr. Romeo on the biblical question accusing the Biblical Institute of heresy. Later, during the present session, Father Balič would attempt to invade the council precincts in this way—in spite of the official ban— with his pamphlet on the Marian schema.

Discussion of Chapter II of the schema on the Church, entitled "The Hierarchial Constitution and especially the Episcopate" began on Friday of the first week and continued for one and a half weeks. The principal topics around which the debate revolved were the controversial proposal in Para-

* Works by X. Rynne, R. B. Kaiser, Teilhard de Chardin, H. de Lubac.

graph 15 to revive the diaconate, and the relationship of the Bishops to the Pope as head of the episcopal college, or the idea of episcopal collegiality as such, whether the bishops constituted a "college" or "corporate body" in any sense other than a merely metaphorical one. The numbered paragraphs of Chapter II were as follows:

11. Preface;
12. The Institution of the Twelve Apostles;
13. The Bishops as Successors of the Apostles;
14. The Episcopate as a Sacrament;
15. Priests and Deacons;
16. The Episcopal College and its Head;
17. The Relations of the Bishops in the College;
18. The Ministries of the Bishops;
19. The Teaching Office of Bishops;
20. The Sanctifying Office of Bishops;
21. The Governing Office of Bishops.

The debate on this Chapter was the longest, and in some respects the most repetitious and boring, during the entire Second Session, lasting eight and a half mornings or a full week and a half. But it was likewise, unquestionably, one of the most important, owing to the key issue of collegiality, rightly considered as the touchstone of a structural renewal of the Church, just as the liturgical innovations and schema were to be the guarantee of a liturgical or spiritual renewal. The debate on collegiality was in fact the primary *raison d'être* for the second session and the core of the new vision of herself which the Church must acquire, according to Pope Paul in his opening address. It was partly in order to prepare the ground for definitive action that such protracted debate was allowed—there must be no accusation that enough time had not been allowed for a thorough discussion—and partly also, no doubt, because of indecision on the part of the council presidency, perhaps of the Pope himself.

The debate tended to revolve around a number of key themes most of which were enunciated on the very first day: the idea of collegiality as such and whether the episcopate constituted a college or corporate body; the relationship of such a college, if it existed, to the papal primacy; the question of whether there should be an episcopal "senate" to advise the Pope, a topic that would be aired more fully later on when the schema on Bishops would be taken up; the sacramentality of the episcopal office; the position of priests with respect to bishops; the functions of a hierarchy, the oriental patriarchs, and a number of subsidiary questions. Most speakers of course spoke on a variety of themes, but in general a summarization of their views pro or con with respect to these main topics will give the reader an adequate idea of the tenor of the debate on this chapter.

Perhaps the least disputable part of the chapter was the issue of the sacramental character of the episcopate. Paragraph 14 takes a positive attitude and declares the episcopate the "highest degree of the sacrament of order." If adopted, this would put an end to a question that has been debated since the Middle Ages, namely whether episcopal consecration involved the conferring of a sacramental grace, or merely conferring on one who already had the fullness of the sacrament of order, greater jurisdiction or authority. The majority of theologians have long taught the former opinion, which was confirmed by Pius XII in his constitution *Sacramentum ordinis*. Left open in the present text was the question of whether episcopal consecration also admitted to the episcopal college, or how and when a bishop became a member of the college. The answer to both questions was apparently settled by the test questions of October 30. There was almost unanimous agreement then that the episcopate was sacramental, with only 107 bishops voting against the view that membership is acquired through consecration. Archbishop Guerry

explained the importance of the whole question on the first
day of debate (Oct. 4). The schema did not bring out clearly
enough its importance. Two important consequences flowed
from this truth: 1. a radical change was bound to come about
in the relations between bishops and priests. So far the priesthood has been regarded as an end in itself and the episcopate
looked upon as adding to it merely a greater power, authority
or jurisdiction, not a sacramental grace. It would be better to
bring out the filial relationship between priests and bishop,
and of the latter as constituting the unity of the presbyterate
gathered around him (*presbyterium*). 2. If the episcopate
was a sacrament, the bonds between episcopal consecration
and the Apostolic college appeared in a clearer light. Through
episcopal consecration, all the bishops admitted to their college
a new bishop-member. The college was seen as having a sacramental structure. Moreover, by his consecration, the bishop
became responsible for spreading the Gospel to the whole
world before he assumed responsibility for his own diocese.
These ideas were developed more fully in an interview which
the bishop gave to *La Croix* the same day.*

The very opposite point of view was asserted by the next
speaker, Archbishop García y García de Castro of Granada,
Spain. Many still held the opinion, he said, that the episcopate was not a sacrament and was differentiated from the
priesthood merely in the jurisdictional sphere. Priests after
all could be the extraordinary ministers of the sacrament of
order. This would be difficult to explain if the episcopate
were regarded as the fullness of the sacrament. Accordingly
much of the language in Paragraph 14 must be changed.

Archbishop Florit was favorable to the idea of sacramentality, but felt that the language of the schema needed improvement. Bishop Doumith of Lebanon wanted it made clear
that not only the grace but also the power of the episcopate

* *La Croix*, Oct. 6-7, 1963.

came from episcopal consecration (Oct. 9). In the opinion of Archbishop Urtasun of Avignon, the question was quite mature for definition, being evident from liturgical as well as theological tradition. A practical reason would be that it would show that the bishop was united to his clergy not only juridically but sacramentally. A clear statement that episcopal consecration was the source of the threefold power of bishops mentioned in Paragraphs 19, 20, and 21 was desired by Bishop Cirarda, Auxiliary of Seville, Spain, while Bishop Henriquez of Venezuela explained that bishops could exercise jurisdiction as soon as they were nominated, and before consecration, because they were then acting vicariously, on the authority of the Pope, whereas after consecration they acted in their own right, though of course subject to the Pope, with his "explicit or tacit canonical mission." He criticized existing canon law which made it seem that the bishops were merely the delegates or vicars of the Roman Pontiff, and questioned the practice of having certain national episcopal conferences presided over by representatives of the Holy See or their decisions submitted to Rome for approval.

The vast majority of speakers preferred to concentrate on the much more tangible and explosive issue of episcopal collegiality. A negative note was struck at the outset by Cardinal Ruffini, who nevertheless found Chapter II satisfactory as a whole. The expressions "People of God" and "Mystical Body" should not be used separately as if they were two different things, as the text seemed to imply. The cardinal defended his interpretation of Eph. 2:20,* which Cardinal Alfrink had seemed to criticize. "Apostles" in this passage did not refer strictly to the Twelve, but rather to men gifted with the charism of the apostolate, just as the prophets were gifted with the charism of prophecy. Therefore *"fundamentum"* in the passage should be taken in a wide sense as

* See p. 73 for text.

"preachers of the Gospel." Others besides the Apostles had
the charism of the apostolate. He said: "I still have not
been convinced that Christ constituted the Apostles as a
College," or that the episcopal college succeeded the Apostolic
college, for, with the exception of the Council of Jerusalem,
the Apostles did not act in a collegial manner. On a purely
practical plane, of course, it was possible for the bishops to
act as a college, with the Pope's permission. In speaking of
the relations between priests and bishops, the concept of
obedience must not be left out. The Greek word "*diakonia*"
was too vague to describe the office of a bishop. Finally, in
speaking of the infallibility of the bishops united to the
Pope, mention should be made of the fact that the Pope
could speak infallibly without recourse to the bishops.

Very few speeches disputed the *fact* of collegiality, that is,
that the bishops formed a body or order in the Church's
hierarchy and that they could and did act, occasionally, in a
corporate manner. But the question was whether this "cor-
porateness" or "collegiality" was of divine origin, part of the
fundamental organization of the Church, or merely of human
or ecclesiastical origin. Cardinal Siri seems to have taken a
view somewhat middle-way between the skepticism or nega-
tion of Cardinal Ruffini and the divine-right view. "There
can be no doubt," he said, "that all bishops, acting with the
Roman Pontiff, constitute a true college. The practice of
ecumenical councils clearly proves this." He approved of
what the schema said about collegiality and regarded it as
"an effective contribution to the feeling of solidarity, mutual
union, charity and reciprocal assistance, particularly among
bishops themselves." But he was concerned that the notion
of collegiality must not be considered apart from the primacy
of the Pope. "There can be no genuine collegiality among
the bishops except in union with the Roman Pontiff. In other
words, without Peter there can be no college of bishops.

Peter does not bring the college into existence, but the college draws its completion and perfection from Peter." The door seemed to be left open, though perhaps not enthusiastically, to divine origin. The same uneasy positiveness is found in a later speech (Oct. 15). "It is easy to prove that the Apostles made up one body and received a collective mission. But it is quite another thing to prove that the bishops of the Church constitute a college. One of the most convincing proofs is the practice of Councils in the history of the Church. . . . Wherever there is a Council there is a college . . ." But this doctrine must be harmonized with the papal primacy. He objected to the expression "undivided subject of full and supreme authority" as ambiguous.* "Wrongly understood it could imply that the bishops might sometimes force the hand of the Pope, but this would contradict the teaching of Vatican Council I."

The interventions of Cardinals Koenig of Vienna and Meyer of Chicago (Oct. 7) were strongly positive. The former maintained that what the schema had to say about collegiality in Chapter II was "not new teaching" but was found in tradition, oriental theology, the theological manuals, and the practice of ecumenical councils. It was held moreover even by those Fathers at Vatican Council I who upheld papal infallibility, and while there was some fear at that time that the doctrine constituted a threat to the papal primacy, this was no longer the case today. The teaching "was approved unanimously by the Theological Commission" and was a response to the hope expressed by Pope Paul in his opening

---

* Paragraph 16 states: ". . . The Roman Pontiff in his own right has full and universal authority over the Church; however the college of bishops, which succeeds the college of Apostles in pastoral teaching and government, or rather in which the Apostolic body continues to endure, constitutes with its head the Roman Pontiff, and never without this head, the undivided subject of full and supreme authority over the universal Church (*indivisum subiectum plenae et supremae potestatis in universam Ecclesiam*) . . ." French translation in *La Croix*, Oct. 17, 1963.

address that the episcopate and its functions should be "examined more deeply." For the Cardinal of Chicago there was no question that Christ entrusted his Church to the College of the Twelve Apostles, for this was the clear testimony of the New Testament. He then cited a number of passages proving the permanence and continuity of the collegial authority handed on to the Apostles, and the early Church's interpretation of Christ's actions in this sense (Mt. 28, Jn. 14:16, Acts 2:14 & 37, Acts 6:2 & 6, etc.). The idea of collegiality was of course juridical, but the New Testament was not a code of law and therefore did not offer a juridical explanation of the facts recounted in its pages.* In his speech on Oct. 11, Archbishop Gouyon, Coadjutor of Rennes, also stressed the evidence from early church history supporting the collegial nature of the episcopal office, the practice of writing letters to other churches, the holding of local synods, the collegial nature of the consecration of bishops, and so on. The custom of having three co-consecrators was not purely formal. It was the expression of the fact that the new bishop was entering the college of bishops. "There has never been any exception to this rule in any liturgies, not even by the Roman Pontiff."

In contrast to these positive assertions of collegiality there were not lacking dissenting voices which questioned the validity of the concept and were critical of the language of the schema. The Archbishop of Palmas in Brazil, Msgr. de Proença Sigaud (Oct. 9), speaking in the name of "many"

* He thus seemed to spike in advance the opinion of Archbishop Dino Staffa, Secretary of the Congregation of Seminaries and Universities, who in a mimeographed paper spread among the council members in St. Peter's—and therefore against the explicit prohibition of the Secretary General—claimed that the term "college" meant "a group of equals with one given primacy of position," and suggested that if the concept were applied to the bishops it would destroy the primacy of the Pope. This was a purely juridical consideration, and quite foreign to conciliar thought. But the tactic was typical of certain curial officials.

bishops, went so far as to characterize the teaching that the Apostles constituted a college *iure divino* a "new doctrine." This would mean that the government of the Church was not monarchical but collegiate. The traditional teaching of the Church was otherwise, according to the archbishop. Bishops were not responsible for the whole Church but only for a portion of it which they had in their charge, except on the rare occasions when they were called together by the Roman Pontiff. "Care should be taken to avoid setting up anything resembling a World Parliament of bishops governing the Church conjointly with the Roman Pontiff." For Bishop Mansilla of Burgos, Spain, the term "collegiality" was ambiguous. "Tradition does not provide us with apodeictic arguments for the collegiality of the bishops in the strict juridical sense." (Oct. 10) The intricate historical questions involved in the transmission of power from the Apostolic College to the episcopal college seemed to impress Archbishop Van den Hurk of Indonesia, who felt that this was something which could not be settled by a Council, though he was otherwise favorable to the sacramentality of episcopal consecration and the restoration of the diaconate. Cardinal Quiroga y Palacios of Santiago de Compostela, Spain, likewise had his doubts about the exact meaning of such a term as "college of bishops." It was not clear, he thought, whether Christ had constituted the bishops as a juridical moral person or whether the idea of collegiality merely designated the totality of the bishops. That collegiality was of divine law "does not yet seem to have been conclusively proved."

A negative approach was manifested also by Archbishop Slipyi of the Ukrainian Church who, under normal circumstances, might have been expected to be enthusiastically for the notion of collegiality. He was quite categorical: "Strictly speaking, the bishops do not constitute a college." His explanation was that colleges belonged to the juridical order, whereas the links that bound the bishops together were of a sacramental character. The bishops were no more of a college than the human family. While he balked at the word, there were traces in his speech that he partly accepted the idea by recognizing that bishops, through consecration, acquired a "direction toward the whole Church." In this his first speech on the council floor since his dramatic liberation from Soviet captivity earlier in the year, he somewhat startled his supporters by asserting roundly toward the end: "Our own faithful of the East and the Orthodox would be greatly strengthened if our principal Metropolitan See of Kiev were raised to patriarchal rank." This wish seems to have been gratified, in part at least, by his recent elevation to the rank of "Great Archbishop," a title not hitherto conferred by the Holy See but found in the East, the virtual equivalent of primate or patriarch.

Archbishop Nicodemo of Bari agreed with Cardinal Quiroga y Palacios that "stronger arguments must be adduced to prove the divine institution of the doctrine of collegiality." Bishop Flores Martín of Barbastro, Spain, concurred and suggested that since it was difficult to prove the divine origin of collegiality, perhaps the Fathers would consider whether there were sufficient reasons for defining it as a matter of ecclesiastical law (Oct. 11). If collegiality were of divine law, he surmised, "the Pope would be obliged to set up a permanent council of bishops, which is certainly not true." Speaking later, Archbishop Lefebvre, Superior General of the Order of the Holy Spirit, while accepting the idea of a college of bishops as broadly demonstrable both from Scripture and tradition, warned against any diminution of the supreme jurisdiction of the Pope which he felt would be involved in the suggestion of a "senate" of bishops. The only convincing proof for episcopal collegiality, according to Bishop Enciso Viana of Majorca, Spain, "came from the fact of ecumenical

councils in the Church." Bishops have certainly acted col-
legiately, but the idea of collegiality was not a necessary one
in the Church. In fact it would weaken the Pope's authority.

This last argument was the principal weapon of the objec-
tors. Most speakers, however, dealing with the problem of
the relationship of a collegial episcopate to the papacy, came
to a positive conclusion and maintained that there was no
danger to either from a frank acknowledgment of the claims
of both and stressed the intimate, inseparable connection between them. On Monday Oct. 7, Patriarch Maximos IV Saigh,
Melkite Patriarch of Antioch, delivered what might be called
the keynote speech on this particular issue, laying the cards
squarely on the table as was his custom, and speaking in
French as was also his habit. It was reported that he had
encountered difficulties in getting his name on the roster of
speakers until it had been arranged by the Secretariat that a
mentor should "translate" his speech into Latin in strict com-
pliance with the rules. This was in the early days of the
Session. Later on such punctiliousness was not considered
necessary. He first observed that the definition of the papal
primacy by Vatican Council I had been exaggerated through
abusive interpretations and that it had thus become an
obstacle to reunion. The primacy itself, clear enough according to the Bible and tradition, was not at issue, but the misinterpretation and abuses of it in practice. Since the Council
proposed to prepare the way for union, it should not be
satisfied merely to repeat Vatican Council I but should
clarify and complete the doctrine on the primacy by acknowledging the unquestioned rights of the episcopate. "We should
endeavor to express the proper balance," he said, "by keeping
the following points in mind. 1. It should be stressed in the
schema that the real 'Head' of the Church is Christ and
Christ alone, not the Pope. 2. The Pope as 'Head' of the
Church should be spoken of with due regard to his position

as a successor of Peter, since a successor cannot have more power than the one whom he succeeds. Peter was one of the Twelve, but also the head of the Apostolic college; the Pope is one of the bishops, but the head also of the Church. 3. The power of the Pope does not destroy the power of the bishops. The head gives order to the body but is not separate from the body. 4. The universal authority of the Roman Pontiff should be understood as a means of service or ministry. *Thou art Peter* must not be understood apart from *Confirm thy brethren*. 5. Finally, the appointment of bishops is not restricted by divine right to the Roman bishop. The restrictive practice of the Latin Church should not be made a law for the whole Church."*

A similar explanation of the oriental position on collegiality and the papal primacy was offered by the Melkite patriarchal vicar for Egypt, Archbishop Zoghby (Oct. 16), who criticized the language of the schema for its emphasis on Western theology and developments. The doctrine of the primacy, he said, which the Oriental Church did not deny, had gone through so many changes and suffered so much elaboration since the separation that it could not be recognized by the Orthodox. Unless this Western emphasis were modified, dialogue with the Orthodox would be made difficult. There was too much emphasis on the dependence of the bishops on the Pope. Whenever mention was made of the authority of the bishops, attention was always called to their subordination to the Pope, which suggested that papal authority was nothing except some kind of limitation on the power of the bishops. The purpose of the primacy—a wonderful gift to the Church—was not to destroy or limit the bishops, but to safeguard and protect their authority. "The greatest gift conferred on Peter was his membership in the Apostolic college." Patriarch Meouchi of the Maronite

* *La Documentation Catholique*, Nov. 3, 1963, col. 1458-60.

Church in Lebanon (Oct. 15) said substantially the same thing the day before, coming out foursquare on behalf of the divine institution of the Apostolic and episcopal colleges, of the role of the Roman Pontiff as head of the college, exercising his authority *with* the bishops, and approving of the language of the schema with respect to an "undivided subject of supreme authority."

There was a lack of agreement among modern exegetes, according to Bishop Charue of Namur, Belgium, as to the meaning of Ephesians 2:20, though the early Fathers were almost unanimous in understanding it as referring to the Apostles of the New Testament: "You are built upon the foundation of the apostles and prophets with Christ Jesus himself as the chief cornerstone." Nevertheless that Epistle presented the Church as founded on the gospel preached by the Apostles, he maintained, and so from the whole context of the Epistle the Apostles were to be considered as the foundation of the Church (Oct. 8). The scriptural arguments on behalf of collegiality were further marshalled by Cardinal Liénart of Lille in his intervention on Oct. 9. Various passages were cited to prove that "Christ made a special choice of the Twelve . . . Christ conferred the primacy on Peter within the college . . . Peter was not outside the college nor against the college . . . We cannot deny the divine institution of the Apostolic college, nor did the powers of this college die with its members . . ." However the solution to the present problem was not in seeking out particular texts but rather in reading the Gospel in its continuity and "seeing what Christ did in the foundation of his Church." He concluded by observing that the twin authorities in the Church, that of Pope and bishops, were intended to collaborate not collide with each other in the common service. The "supreme service" exercised by the Pope preserved unity; while the service of the bishops dispersed throughout the world yet inseparably united to the Pope, manifested the catholicity of the Church. Concurring with the Belgian and French speakers, Archbishop Weber of Strasbourg (Oct. 9) noted that the term *"dodeka"*—"twelve"—was already used in a technical sense in 1 Cor. 15, where it is found in a passage taken from the early oral tradition of the Church.

Cardinal de Barros Câmara of Brazil (Oct. 10) was in favor of speaking out "fearlessly" on the issue of collegiality and saw no conflict with the primacy because of the intimate union between bishops and Pope. The subject of papal infallibility also claimed attention. Two Fathers, Archbishop Descuffi of Smyrna, Turkey, and Archbishop Shehan of Baltimore, Maryland, both speaking on the same day (Oct. 10), dealt with the theme at length in unusually frank terms. Both viewed the dogma, or rather its misinterpretation, as an obstacle to the dialogue and suggested concrete ways in which to get around the difficulty. The former suggested a new paragraph entitled *"De Magisterio Ecclesiae"* (the teaching authority of the Church), explaining the infallibility of Church and Pope and clarifying the language of the definition reached at Vatican Council I, particularly the phrases *"ex sese"* and *"non ex consensu Ecclesiae."* After the former he wished to add: *"scilicet, ex speciali assistentia divina"*; and to replace *"consensu"* by *"assensu."* The text as it now stood could imply—though the interpretation would be false—that the Pope was infallible by himself, or even in opposition to the Church, or conversely that the Church, infallible when taken as a whole, could be in opposition to the Pope's infallibility. "The two infallibilities should not be opposed, but composed." Archbishop Shehan asked for the inclusion in Paragraph 19 of a statement such as: "Such definition is never to be understood as against the consent of the Church. For since we believe the Pope to be infallible through divine assistance, by that very fact we believe that

the assent of the Church will never be lacking to his definition, because it cannot happen that the body of the bishops
will be separated from its head, and because the universal
Church cannot fail."

Speaking on Monday of the third week (Oct. 14), Cardinal
Frings of Cologne elaborated on an expression by Cardinal
Meyer the previous week and said that while collegiality did
not appear in ancient tradition as a strictly determined juridical concept, it was nevertheless just as clear as the doctrine
about the primacy. There was ample evidence in antiquity
of the practice of collegiality and this practice at times assumed
juridical forms, for example, the sending of so-called *"litterae
communicatoriae"* (letters of communion). Not all truths of
the faith were equally clear from the beginning, and he cited
as examples the assumption of Mary, the papal primacy, and
papal infallibility. Since collegiality belonged to the essential
structure of the Church, it was up to the Council, he maintained, to put this in the proper light.

The opposition, as we have said, concentrated on the dangers of the idea of collegiality, dangers to the papacy, to the
unity of the Church, the risk of disobedience, of subjection
of the Church to the civil authorities, and was voiced for
the most part by Spanish prelates or by Italians close to the
Curia. According to the Latin Patriarch of Jerusalem, Alberto Gori (Oct. 8), the remedy against these evils was "to
retain the traditional practice of all activity being centered
in and guided by the Roman Pontiff." If too great a process
of decentralization were fostered, difficulties would be encountered in reforming abuses in local Churches. "If bishops
throw off the yoke of the tempering authority of the Pope,
then priests and laity in the diocese will be encouraged to
do likewise." There should be insistence on the authority
of the Pope and of his legates. With regard to the latter
point, he thought that papal legates should be present at

all episcopal conferences. The same fears were expressed in
a speech on the floor by the energetic Secretary of the
Roman Congregation for Seminaries, Archbishop Dino
Staffa, who did not content himself with this formal statement of his views but like certain other council members,
saw to it that his ideas were amply aired in the press and
distributed abroad.* He objected to the phrase "undivided
subject," preferring what he chose to call "the doctrine set
forth by many theologians at the time of the First Vatican
Council," namely "the doctrine that full and supreme power
is vested solely in the Pope, independently of consultation
with others." The archbishop was misinformed or a bad
historian. That Council decreed no such thing, as was made
clear by Bishop Gasser, secretary of the Theological Deputa-
tion which had drawn up the infallibility decree, in a report
to the council on July 11, 1870, and by Bishop Fessler, council secretary, in a famous exposition of the decree approved
by Pius IX.** On the archbishop's behalf it can be said that
he was merely expressing a widely held—though erroneous
—opinion that adoption of the doctrine of collegiality would
mean "replacing the monarchical structure of the Church
with an aristocracy." The irony is that the Church never has
been a monarchy in the strict sense of the term—merely has
seemed to be such owing to historical circumstances—and it
was only justice, many thought, as well as high time, that its
government be returned to something more nearly approaching its original divinely appointed constitution.

Bishop Temiño Saiz of Spain flatly denied that collegiality was "divinely instituted" (Oct. 11). For the Assessor of
the Holy Office, Archbishop Parente (Oct. 14), it was true
that "bishops are true teachers and judges for the universal
Church, but always dependently on the Pope." The pre-

* See footnote, p. 82.
** F. Dvornik, *The Ecumenical Councils,* New York, 1961, p. 103 and p. 104.

eminent position of Peter must be safeguarded at all costs.
Bishops never surpass, much less equal Peter, the foundation. Peter was made by Christ the unique foundation of the
Church; the other Apostles were associated with Peter as
subordinates, "as deeper parts of its walls, but not as its
foundation." The archbishop appeared to leave the door
open on the question of whether collegiality was an apostolic *datum* but indicated that he was not favorable to the
idea of any meaningful episcopal co-responsibility with the
Pope in the government of the universal Church—the real
crux of the matter. Bishops received both the power of order
and power of jurisdiction—distinctions introduced later by
canon lawyers he said—at their consecration as a sharing in
the "single, undivided power" conferred by Christ on his
Church. "The Pope does not create the jurisdiction of the
bishop; rather he makes it possible for a bishop to exercise
it." But it was "inconceivable" that any bishop should exercise it "independently."

Some speakers felt that the language of the schema was
not sufficiently strong on collegiality. Bishop Sauvage of
Annecy, for example, criticized the last words of Paragraph
13 for implying that the successors of Peter and the successors
of the Apostles had no relationship to each other. Others
that it was too strong because the question of collegiality by
divine law was not sufficiently mature for definition (Archbishop García de Sierra y Mendez, Oct. 14).

Although the rules provided that no speaker should be
applauded, there were occasions when the Fathers took the
law into their own hands. One such was after the ringing
speech by the new young auxiliary of Bologna, Bishop Giuseppe Bettazzi, winding up a rather repetitious and long
session on Friday, Oct. 11. It was his "maiden speech." Mixing audacity with humor in masterly proportions, he declared: "Although I am young and Italian, I intend to speak

about collegiality. There is no doubt that by his consecration a bishop becomes a member of the episcopal college which succeeds to the Apostolic college, and that this college has a universal jurisdiction over the whole Church. This view is neither Gallican nor anti-Roman. Since the time of the Council of Florence the Popes have said as much, and even a number of theologians regarded as being among the most intransigent, such as the great inquisitor Torquemada, are in agreement on this point. Moreover this universal jurisdiction is of divine right, while a bishop's power over his own diocese is only of positive law. For if a bishop's power over his own diocese were of divine right, how could bishops pass from one diocese to another without giving the impression of committing adultery?"—he observed, referring to the ancient doctrine that bishops are "wedded" to their sees. "The power of universal jurisdiction is both in Peter and in the college of bishops. It is impossible to separate these two aspects of the same universal jurisdiction. This brings us to the heart of the debate. Vatican Council I was not against this way of expressing things, it simply refused to solve the problem and said so. Scripture, tradition and the liturgy all take this for granted. Those who doubt that the bishops have a part with the Pope in governing the whole Church are the innovators." In conclusion he cited the collect for the feast of St. Mathias: "O God, who hast associated blessed Matthias with the college of Your Apostles" (*qui beatum Matthiam Apostolorum tuorum collegio sociasti . . .*)." *Quid Melius?*—was any further proof needed?

The issue could not have been put more succinctly. Cardinal Lercaro, Moderator for the day whose auxiliary Bettazzi was, allowed a smile to creep across his face, as the majority of the Fathers, roused from their slumbers, clapped loudly. Some interpreted the speech as a sign that Cardinal Siri's influence over the Italian episcopate (as president of the

Italian Episcopal Conference) was waning. If so, the conservative bloc among the Italian bishops lost no time in disavowing Bettazzi's "betrayal" of the cause. On Monday, Bishop Carli of Segni, generally regarded as the spokesman on the floor for this bloc, delivered a point by point refutation of what the young bishop had said, denying that the word *collegium* was appropriate either for the Apostles or the bishops and preferring the use of some such vague expression as "episcopal body" or "episcopal communion," contesting the pertinence of his references to Torquemada or Bellarmine, and maintaining that what Vatican Council I had decided on this point was clearer than the present text. It had always been something of a mystery as to just how the Secretary General Archbishop Felici drew up the lists of daily speakers. Theoretically all names had to be handed in well in advance but when there was need for the conservative bloc to reply on the floor to some intervention which they considered particularly dangerous or outrageous, it was noted that they had little difficulty in sandwiching in their speakers at the last minute.

A subsidiary problem, crucial to the debate, was that of apostolic succession. Nobody denied the fact that the bishops succeeded the Apostles, but the question was how, in what way, with what powers, corporately or individually, with all or only some of their authority. Paragraph 13 skirts these questions, while asserting the fact. Cardinal Ruffini, as we have seen, doubted that the succession was corporate or collegial. For Archbishop Veuillot, Coadjutor of Paris, the language of the schema did not express with sufficient clarity that the notion of apostolic succession was a scriptural *datum*. When the Lord told the Apostles: "Go and teach . . . ," he conferred on them a mission and gave them powers which were to be handed on to their successors. The New Testament showed, moreover, that the Apostles did, in fact, hand on their powers, and that they handed them on in a collegial manner. The bishops which Paul placed at the head of the communities founded by him became his collaborators in the same ministry and the same responsibility. Therefore it was apparent that collegiality was an essential mark of the episcopate from the beginning despite the allegations of certain speakers.

Archbishop Jaeger of Paderborn (Oct. 10) pointed out that not all the powers of the Apostles were transmitted to their successors, namely their extraordinary personal prerogatives. It was essential to express this doctrine more clearly because of its ecumenical repercussions. The text hinted at the distinction—a commonplace in Catholic theology—but did not spell out the details. Protestant theology, in general, recognized a sharper distinction than Catholic theology between the apostolic period or period of the founding of the Church and the subsequent "period of the Church," different norms being applicable to each. It was important therefore to state what the Catholic position was.

Several speakers, following the lead of Archbishop Hermaniuk* and acting on the advice of the Pope himself in his talk to the Curia on Sept. 21, broached the subject of concrete ways in which collegiality could be made effective and greater collaboration between the bishops and the Pope assured. According to Bishop de Smedt of Bruges, collegiality had always existed in the Church but there was need today, more than ever, for it to be emphasized that the role of Peter in confirming the brethren and serving as a center of unity was much greater and could only be carried out with the help of others. "We who are farther away, desire the same ease of access to Peter as the Italian bishops." This could be realized by some form of internationalization of the

* See p. 48.

Curia.* The following speaker, Bishop Zazinovic of Yugo-slavia, while cool to the principle of collegiality said that "it would be advisable to set up a permanent episcopal com-mission with representatives of all nations, with regular meetings, and with authority to decree changes even in the prevailing practices of the Roman Curia." He cited Pope Leo the Great's relations with the Council of Chalcedon (451 A.D.) as an example of the way in which relations should be governed between the episcopal college and the Pope.

A similar stand was taken by the Master General of the Dominican Order, Father Fernandez. The subordinate role of the college of bishops with respect to the Pope was stressed. If it were deemed advisable to set up some kind of an episcopal advisory commission, it would have only the power given it by the Pope. The symbolical as well as practical value of such a body was stressed by the Coadjutor Bishop of Portsmouth, Bishop Holland, speaking in the name of the English and Welsh bishops. He suggested some organ chosen from members nominated by the various episcopal conferences, as a "sort of continuation of the spirit which inspires this council." Christ founded the Church on Peter and the Apostles. Such a body was needed to give concrete expression to the Church being ruled by the Pope with the episcopal college. "As the saying goes in legal circles, it is not sufficient that justice be done but it is necessary to show that justice has been done."

The main emphasis of the chapter was on the episcopate—as the title indicated—the other ranks in the hierarchy being dealt with only cursorily and *en passant* as it were. In the intention of the framers the role of the priesthood, pri-marily a pastoral question, would be dealt with in the sepa-rate schema, "On the care of souls" (*De Cura animarum*),

* *La Croix*, Oct. 9, 1963.

which was to be debated later. However this was not a sufficient justification, in the opinion of some speakers, for the
relative downgrading of the priesthood which the present
text seemed to imply. Bishop Beck, of Salford, England, for
example, remarked on the lack of a clear definition of the
Christian priesthood as such. The text should offer a summary of the doctrine of the New Testament on the priesthood and its place in the Church. This presentation should
stress the oneness of the Catholic priesthood with that of
Christ and point out that no other priesthood and no other
sacrifice beyond those of Christ are required. There would
be difficulty later on in dealing with the question of the
"priesthood of the laity" unless the whole concept were
clarified in its constitutive elements. The same thoughts
were offered by Bishop Añoveros of Cadiz, Spain, who criticized Paragraph 15 (Priests and Deacons) for not treating
the traditional teaching which regarded priests not only as
collaborators of the bishops, but as participating in their
teaching, sanctifying and ruling office. He objected to the
phrase "second-rank priests" (*sacerdotes secundae dignitatis*)
used to describe them because it implied that they were mere
delegates of the bishop and did not share directly in a
divinely appointed order.

Archbishop Conway, of Armagh, Ireland, was of the opinion that the subject merited a separate chapter. The text
devoted 9 pages to the episcopate and 7 pages to the laity,
but priests had only one-half a page and then were considered
primarily in relation to the episcopate. With the world
shortage of vocations, the Council should exalt rather than
minimize the glory of the priesthood. "The First Vatican
Council," he said, "is said to have left the bishops in the
shade because of its desire to exalt the papacy. It might be
said of the Second Vatican Council because of its emphasis
on the episcopate that it has left the priesthood in the shade."

Archbishop Hurley of Durban, South Africa, favored dividing the chapter into three parts, devoted to the episcopate,
priesthood, and diaconate. The priesthood was treated too
casually. As a matter of fact, he said, the bishop often has no
contacts with his people except through the priest. The priest
was the hands and feet, the ears, eyes, and very voice of the
bishop. More emphasis was needed on the idea of the local
Church, not only as an administrative center, but in its
theological significance, according to Bishop Schick, Auxiliary of Fulda. This would lead to consideration of the parish
and a better delineation of the role of the priest. "The
universal Church and the local Church are two essential
poles of the one Church," he observed, reflecting an idea
dear to the Orthodox (Oct. 10). Bishop Renard of Versailles
drew attention to the ancient teaching that priests constituted, together with and under the bishop, a *presbyterium:*
they were not only the bishop's ministers, but also his senate,
his counsel. The priesthood was a ministry of the Word as
well as of the mass. The bishop should appear as the father
of his priests. A short introduction to Chapter II was needed,
according to Bishop Boillon, of Verdun, France, on Christ
the Priest, explaining the office of bishop in the light of a
participation in His roles as Prophet, Ruler and Mediator.

A number of other criticisms deserve attention. Bishop
Martínez Gonzáles of Zamora (Oct. 9) and Bishop Galea of
Malta (Oct. 10) both felt that the schema played down the
"juridical" side of the hierarchy in favor of a more spiritual
mission and that this would encourage the return of errors
already condemned long ago. "Hierarchical order demands,"
said the former, "that authority come directly from on
high. . . The hierarchy cannot be considered as representatives of the people. They are the ministers of God and the
dispensers of the mysteries of Christ." The latter wanted
greater recognition of the distinction between the hierarchy

of order and the hierarchy of jurisdiction. Bishop Browne, of Galway and Kilmacdaugh, Ireland (Oct. 9), wanted the relationship of the bishop to his diocese brought out for theological reasons similar to those alleged by Bishop Schick. He regretted that the text said practically nothing about the diocese. Its failure also to deal with the institution of the patriarchate was regretted by the Coptic Bishop Ghattas of Thebes, Egypt, who commented that the schema viewed the relationship of the episcopate to the Church almost exclusively through Latin eyes and understood the Universal Church as virtually synonymous with the "Latin" Church. He too was in favor of some kind of episcopal "senate" for the Pope. Finally, Bishop Pont y Gol of Spain found the schema to be excessive in its use of such terms as "authority," "power," and the like. This was at variance with the mind of Christ. Something too should be said about the degree to which Orthodox bishops (whom the Catholic Church admits are validly consecrated) participated in the mission of Christ because of the doctrine of the apostolic succession of the bishops (Oct. 11).

One or two speakers also commented on the idea of the "Church of the Poor," a subject brought up earlier by Cardinal Lercaro. Cardinal de Arriba y Castro of Spain maintained that it needed clarification. Insistence on the concern of the Church for the poor should not be interpreted to mean that the Church intended to do nothing to improve the lot of the poor. There was a serious obligation on the part of the Church to help improve the over-all economic situation. The task of improving the lot of the poor should not be left to the Marxists. Fulfilment of this duty could be greatly helped by the establishment in Rome of a central office, or Roman Congregation, to coordinate study of social problems and assist in promoting social justice everywhere in the world (Oct. 8).

Although not crucial from the theological point of view, the suggestion for a "restored diaconate" contained in Paragraph 15 (Priests and Deacons) consumed a considerable amount of time and was of course seized upon by the press as a godsend rescuing the debate from boredom.*

The first to speak on this controversial theme was the Cardinal of New York, Francis Spellman, in his "maiden speech" on the floor at this Session (Oct. 4). He praised Chapter II as "very well composed" except for Paragraph 15. The proposal to resurrect the diaconate as a permannet degree of the hierarchy was a disciplinary matter, he felt, which should not be included in a dogmatic constitution. The question then arose whether it should be treated anywhere else and his sentiment was that it should not for the following reasons. 1. Although it was true that the diaconate had formerly been a permanent office in the Church, it was now merely a transitional stage toward the priesthood. The cardinal failed to bring out, however, that this was true only of the Latin Church, not of the various Oriental Churches. It was clear that the chief difficulty for him was along practical lines. Permanent deacons would have to be prepared for their functions, but "it is hardly or not at all possible to establish seminaries for candidates for the priesthood. How then can other houses be provided for

---

* The pertinent passage in Paragraph 15 reads as follows: ". . . Bishops and priests are assisted by deacons, in a lower rank of the hierarchical order. They help with the celebration of the sacrifice (mass), they are the extraordinary ministers of solemn baptism and holy communion, and they may perform various tasks connected with public charity, preaching and administration, as shall be assigned to them by competent authority. Although in the Church today the diaconate is regarded for the most part as a step toward the priesthood, this discipline has not always been in force and is not everywhere in force today. The diaconate can in the future be exercised as a proper and permanent rank in the hierarchy, when the Church considers this advisable for the good of souls, either in certain areas or in all. In which case it belongs to the ecclesiastical authorities to decide whether such deacons shall be bound by the law of celibacy or not." Translation in *The Pilot* (Boston), Oct. 12, 1963 (slightly modified).

deacons?" 2. The main reason why permanent deacons became obsolete, it seems, was the need of the ministry for
more priests, an organizational reason. "But this condition
still prevails in almost the entire world." 3. Many lay religious and members of lay institutes today carry out the
functions formerly performed by deacons, and the number
of laymen in the service of the Church is continually growing and being fostered. There would appear to be no need
for permanent deacons on this score. 4. The proposal to revive permanent deacons stems mostly from liturgists who
wish to restore ancient ways without taking into account
present conditions. Le Monde quotes the cardinal as having
said here: "Let us not indulge in archeology."* Pius XII in
"Mediator Dei" warned against considering something as
good simply because it was old. 5. Seminarians obviously
want to become priests. This is a sign of their divine vocation and nothing should be done to interfere with this.
"God exercises his Providence over the Church according
to present conditions" the cardinal concluded. "It must be
decided whether it is better to by-pass the divine will and
have fewer priests along with permanent deacons, or more
priests without them."—It was obvious that practical considerations dominated the cardinal's thought throughout
and that he, or his advisers, had little sympathy for the pas-
toral-theological side of the question developed by modern
theologians such as Karl Rahner. Other speakers would point
out that the alternatives were not quite as stark as the Cardinal of New York had suggested.—In a press interview later
the same day at the Grand Hotel, Cardinal Spellman repeated the substance of what he had said on the floor. "The
reason I am against it," he said, "is that it is unnecessary."
When it was pointed out that many bishops in Latin Amer-

* Le Monde, Oct. 6-7, 1963.

ica and other areas felt differently, he commented tersely:
"Let them say so."*

Cardinal Bacci of the Curia likewise criticized Paragraph
15 (Oct. 4) and thought that the proposal for a married
diaconate, to which it would open the door, was dangerous.
Times have changed and old ideas were not always the best,
he said. New seminaries would be needed because married
deacons and celibate priests could not be educated in the
same institutions. The number of priestly vocations would
be sure to decline even further, for youth was always prone
to choose the easier way. The *"finestrella* (little window)
opened would soon become a *"finestra"* (full-scale window).

The inclusion of the proposal was defended by Cardinals
Doepfner and Suenens, both council Moderators, in two important speeches on Oct. 7 and Oct. 8. The former insisted
that the measure was in accordance with the Council of
Trent which decreed that the functions of the diaconate
should not be exercised except by those invested with the
order, whereas in present-day practice these functions were
very often performed by priests. The present text merely
laid the dogmatic foundations for a possible change in the
Church's discipline, he was careful to point out, it did not
impose any change. It made it possible for its restoration in
those areas where it was felt that there was a particular need
for this step, owing to the shortage of priests. Nothing could
be done, in any case, without the approval of the Holy See,
as the wording of the decree indicated. New seminaries
would not be required, he felt, because it was a question of
"sacramentalizing" functions already existing, not of introducing new ones. Those already trained for certain activities
should receive the corresponding sacramental grace to help
them carry out these functions more perfectly. Institution

* *The New York Times,* Oct. 5, 1963.

of a married diaconate could possibly entail danger for a
celibate priesthood if the choice of such deacons were made
indiscriminately, but properly handled this question need
not be an insuperable obstacle. Cardinal Suenens stated the
crux of the matter as follows: "The purpose of this restoration would be to attribute greater prominence to the diaconate in the hierarchy of the Church, while at the same
time making it possible for vast segments of the faithful to
enjoy in greater abundance the gifts which flow from the
supernatural riches of the Church." It was not merely a
question of ordaining laymen for tasks which laymen could
do quite as well as laymen. "The work entrusted to such
deacons would proceed from the order they received." The
new arrangement was intended, of course, for places where a
stable diaconate was necessary for the growth of the Church.
As examples, he cited small communities segregated from
others, or large communities where it was difficult to experience the Church as a family. In concluding, he asked that
this question be put to a vote at the end of the discussion on
Chapter II.

It was mainly bishops in predominantly missionary areas
who were eager for the change, but even here there were
differences of opinion. Not all of the African or Asian
bishops were enthusiastic. Cardinal Landázuri-Ricketts,
speaking in the name of the Peruvian Episcopal Conference
and of 58 other South American bishops on Tuesday, Oct. 8,
voiced the largely favorable reaction of that area to the
proposal. He stressed the practical advantages, especially for
the wide tracts typical of South America where there were
so few priests in proportion to the numbers of the faithful
and there was no prospect, in the immediate future, of improving the situation. While admitting the strength of arguments in favor of retaining celibacy, he thought that the
contrary arguments were more "weighty" and a married

diaconate could be justified. Cardinal Richard of Bordeaux (Oct. 9) also did not think that a restored diaconate would endanger the priesthood. It would help to put the priesthood "in a better light." "Many youths are afraid to enter the priesthood because they see priests engaged in mean tasks with little time for study or prayer." In fact, a better calibre of priest would result if vocations could be channeled, some into the diaconate, some into the priesthood. The problem of training deacons would have to be worked out in much the same way as the training of late vocations.

The two Yugoslav bishops, Seper and Franič, took opposite points of view. The latter, speaking for the 16 Latin bishops of the country, declared that a married diaconate would be harmful to a celibate priesthood. He maintained that the Orthodox, while allowing a married clergy below the rank of bishop, esteemed celibacy and had difficulties with those in a married state which were not to be overlooked. Italian speakers were divided over the question, some were in favor, others against, but they appeared united on the possibility of the dangers to celibacy if the proposal went through. Cardinal Cento (Oct. 10) wished no relaxation in the law of celibacy if the diaconate were restored. Bishop D'Agostino of Vallo di Lucania was flatly opposed. Bishop Costantini of Sessa Aurunca would have a permanent diaconate restricted to lay brothers and members of secular institutes, thus avoiding difficulties over celibacy and finances. Bishop Carraro of Verona agreed with Cardinal Cento. Speaking in the name of 38 bishops from Portugal, Bishop Alvim Pereira of Mozambique, was not in favor of the restoration, but if it were allowed, the law of celibacy should be imposed. Many of the speakers in their opposition gave the impression that they were dealing with a subject that was somehow "tabu," as one Oriental bishop put it, and their strictures on a married clergy, he said, cast doubt on whether such a clergy was capable of leading an exemplary life.*

Discussion of the possibility of a married diaconate offered the European press of course a golden opportunity for speculating on one of its favorite topics, the celibacy of the clergy, particularly as regards a possible relaxation of the norms for priests. Some of the comments were restrained and factual, but in the more sensational press free rein was given to the imagination. The reports continued throughout the Second Session. The French bishops, in particular, were said to be contemplating the recommendation of a change in the existing legislation. To put an end to these rumors they were finally impelled to issue a communiqué from Rome denying that there was any basis for such *informations fantaisistes,* and pointing out that in spite of hardships in individual cases, "the Latin Church had no intention of giving up a law which, even though of ecclesiastical origin, was based on the Gospel and inspired by the complete gift of the priest to Christ and the Church." They noted also that no Father had suggested any such change in the existing legislation on the floor of the Council.** Nevertheless behind the scenes, and outside the confines of the council hall strictly speaking, it appears that the subject was being given a certain amount of serious attention among the experts. A document drawn up by a prominent religious in Rome commenting favorably on the possibility of a relaxation of the existing rule was circulated.† A certain amount of pontifical pique over the fact that these persistent rumors of change seemed to be aired under French auspices may have occasioned the Pope's velvet-gloved warning to the French episcopate when receiving them in audience on November 18, 1963: ". . . Con-

---

* *Herder-Korrespondenz,* December 1963, p. 1944.
** *Le Figaro,* Nov. 15, 1963.
† *Le Monde,* Nov. 27, 1963.

tinue to watch with the greatest care over these doctrines and these currents of thought . . . thus any deviation will be prevented, and any intervention by higher authority intended to clarify the matters will be rendered unnecessary." Others interpreted the papal remarks as a veiled warning on the subject of collegiality. Reports circulated in Rome that the Pope had been critical of the French Church at his meeting with the French bishops. To put an end to speculation, the French Catholic newspaper *La Croix* published the text of his remarks on December 31, 1963. While full of praise for France and especially for French efforts in the intellectual and pastoral fields, the speech nevertheless contained these rather mysterious words capable of a variety of interpretations.*

Chapter III of the schema on the Church, which the Council took up on Wednesday, October 16, and debated for one and a half weeks, as long as the debate on Chapter II, was divided into six paragraphs, as follows:

22. Introduction;
23. The Equality and Inequality of the Members of the Church of Christ;
24. The Universal Priesthood, as well as the *sensus fidei* and the Charismata of the Faithful;
25. The Apostolate of the Laity with respect to Salvation;
26. The Relation of the Faithful to the Hierarchy;
27. Exhortation.

It was entitled "Concerning the People of God and particularly concerning the Laity." Earlier, the Coordinating Commission had recommended removing the paragraph or section on the "People of God" and bringing it forward as a separate, new Chapter II, immediately after Chapter I on

* Robert Rouquette, S.J., in *Etudes*, February 1964, p. 241.

the Mystery of the Church. The suggestion, attributed to Cardinal Suenens, was printed and proposed to the Fathers in a separate booklet containing the written *"Emendationes"* to the text of the revised schema submitted by the bishops. If the suggestion is adopted by the Council, the new arrangement of the chapters of the whole schema would be (unless further changes occur):

Chap. I —The Mystery of the Church.
Chap. II —The People of God in general.
Chap. III—The Hierarchic Constitution of the Church.
Chap. IV—The Laity in particular.
Chap. V —The Vocation to Sanctity in the Church.

Cardinal Ruffini began the debate with a frontal attack on the new theology of the laity on which the chapter is based. The clergy today were more than ever in need of the assistance of the laity, but this did not authorize us to speak of a "mission of the laity." The text said that the laity have a mission directly from Christ, whereas, as a matter of fact, their mission came to them only through the hierarchy. "They do not share in the mission conferred by Christ on the Apostles," he said bluntly. Laity and clergy seemed to be on the same level according to the schema with respect to the task of spreading the gospel, but this was simply not true. Unless the vague and ambiguous terminology in the text was cleared up, bishops and pastors might encounter difficulties when disagreements arose between clergy and laity. It was dangerous to speak of the "rights" of the laity without defining their limits. It was wrong to refer to the episcopal office as a "service" (*servitium*): this tended to reduce respect for authority. And he objected finally to the implication that charisms, or special gifts, were common in the Church, whereas, today, as a matter of fact, they were very rare.

As President of the Conciliar Commission for the Apostolate of the Laity which had helped prepare the text, Cardinal Cento who spoke next praised it and thanked those directly responsible for their work. It would serve as a good statement of principle. Like many of the following speakers, he approved of the proposed division of the material suggested by the Coordinating Commission.

A point frequently attacked by conservative-minded prelates were the statements in the schema about the "universal priesthood" or "priesthood of the faithful," which, in their mind, seemed to imply a whittling away of the traditional distinction between a hierarchical priesthood and the rest of the faithful. Bishop Rastouil of France praised what the schema had to say about the distinction between the universal priesthood of all Christians and the ministerial or hierarchical priesthood. It had always been Catholic teaching, of course, that there was only one priesthood, that of Christ, and all, in different ways, shared in it. "Christ," he said, "communicates his unique priesthood to the Church through baptism, confirmation, and orders, in order to continue His work of redemption." Thus it was true to say that the basic nature of the Church was priestly. He went on to say that while priests were aware of their dignity, the laity were ignorant of the power conferred on them through the characters of baptism and confirmation. At this point he was interrupted by the Moderator for wandering from the subject.

To Cardinal Bacci, on the other hand, what the schema had to say on this point was ambiguous and objectionable. To speak of the laity as sharing in a "universal priesthood" without further qualification might seem to imply that they shared in the hierarchical or sacramental priesthood of the ordained priest. The layman offered only "spiritual sacrifices," not the body of Christ, the priesthood of the laity was of a generic kind, with the word being understood in a meta-phorical, not a literal sense.

It was all very well, said Bishop Elchinger of Strasbourg, to emphasize the communal importance of such ideas as the Mystical Body, the People of God, the family of believers, the universal communion of the sons of God through baptism and the sacraments, but experience proved that such ideas were usually understood juridically and abstractly by the faithful. The problem was to get rid of the prevailing deep-rooted sense of individualism and make the feeling for a Catholic community a reality and daily experience. Too many Christians approached the sacraments in a purely personal sense, for their own satisfaction, without any awareness of the corporate nature of their membership in the Mystical Body. The Council must do something about reviving a communal sense in place of rampant individualism.

The historical as well as the theological importance of the chapter were stressed by Bishop Wright of Pittsburg. He felt that, while there was room for improvement, the text expressed very well the basic ideas on the apostolate of the laity. "The faithful have been waiting for four hundred years for a positive conciliar statement on the place, dignity and vocation of the layman." He said that the laity knew that their priesthood differed from the ministerial priesthood of the clergy, but that they wanted the hierarchy, in a formal conciliar statement, to put an end to the false notion that the Church was only "clerical." The traditional negative attitude toward the layman—he was *not* a cleric, *not* a religious—must be replaced by a more positive approach.

Almost all the speakers dealt with this question of the proper definition of the layman, from one angle or another. Paragraph 26, dealing with the relations between the laity and the hierarchy, was a frequent target of comment.

The charge that the granting of more freedom to the laity

would endanger the hierarchy's freedom of action or authority was answered by Bishop Hengsbach of Essen, Germany, who said that there was more danger in not recognizing their responsibility, for without their help the hierarchy could not fulfill its obligations today and if it ignored them it would be frustrating the Holy Spirit who was given to all for the growth of the Church. "We should not forget that at the first Pentecost, the Holy Spirit descended on the Apostles and the laity alike."

The theological presuppositions of the apostolate of the laity were also brought out by Cardinal Gracias in a long speech which the Moderator stopped on account of time (Oct. 18). The apostolate must be presented in a practical and realistic way as grounded on a firm basis. Some of the members of the hierarchy either did not want or would not seek the collaboration of the laity, and when the latter offered their services they gave the impression that they were accepting them as a privilege granted to the laity. But the truth was that the laity were not only invited but had a right to take part in the mission of the Church. Conflicts were inevitable between the laity and clergy over this matter of collaboration, at least until the respective responsibilities of both were better defined. It would be wrong to imply that the "day of the priest is over."

The African Cardinal Rugambwa concurred with much of what the Indian cardinal had said. He asked for a better definition of the layman, not in juridical terms, but showing his participation in the mysteries of the life of Christ. This participation reached its peak when he shared in offering the sacrifice of Christ. The basic doctrine on the apostolate of the laity should be more clearly expressed in Paragraph 25 and then incorporated in the theological manuals and canon law. Speaking in the name of some of the Fathers, he asked for an increase in the number of Lay Auditors at the

Council so that they would be better representative of different areas and professions.

Bishop Picachy of India found the treatment of the dignity of the laity acceptable, but not the part dealing with the relations between laity and hierarchy. The text put undue emphasis on the sole obligation of obedience and did not stress the fact that the clergy *wanted* their collaboration. He recalled the words of St. Augustine to the effect that while bishops and pastors were shepherds in charge of sheep, in the sight of the Divine Good Shepherd, they too were sheep along with their people.

The very opposite was urged by the Italian Bishop Melendro, who said that the text should emphasize more clearly the need for obedience and the fact that all authority acts in the name of God. The Council had a *munus*—a duty, to point out certain unspecified "errors" which were said to be rampant in the Church today. He appealed to what Cardinal Micara had said earlier and to Pope Paul in support of this thesis.

To forestall misconceptions, the text should speak of "the hierarchy and the rest of the people of God," according to Bishop Schröffer of Germany, who praised the emphasis on the concept of the People of God but said that the treatment did not take into sufficient account recent thought.

The passage in the Exhortation at the end of the chapter which urged the laity not to be "ashamed of the Gospel" (*Ne erubescant Evangelium*) was hardly appropriate for them, opined Archbishop Golland-Trinidade of Brazil. The words were applicable primarily to the clergy and religious. If applied to the laity, there was danger that those who were much closer to the voices of the poor and of workers might say that the clergy who preached but did not live a life of poverty, humility and charity were the real embarrassment. This disparity between precept and example was the greatest obstacle to the expansion of the Church and the increase in priestly vocations.

Bishop McGrath of Panama City also criticized the unrealistic and negative approach to the layman. The laity were not "little acolytes," at the base of a clerical pyramid, subject to everyone. Echoing Bishop Wright, he said that it was out-of-date to present the apostolate of the laity today as something under the thumb of the hierarchy or as "clerical." The Church today appeared too often to be dominated by an "escapist philosophy" and wholly preoccupied by the supernatural. The task of every Christian was to take part in the great work of bringing to perfection the work of creation by getting rid of inequities and eliminating poverty.

A more positive approach was also called for by Bishop Ménager of France, who said that the Lay Auditors had found the text disappointingly "negative, clerical and juridical." They had opened the eyes of the Conciliar Commission on the Apostolate of the Laity when shown the text. The respective roles of the liberty of the laity and the authority of the hierarchy must be spelled out much more clearly, stated Bishop Primeau of Manchester, New Hampshire, or "there was danger that laymen would lose interest in the mission of the Church" and eventually fall away. He was afraid that Paragraph 26 on the relations between the laity and the hierarchy would do more harm than good for it stressed obedience, when what was needed was an emphasis on lay initiative, freedom and responsibility. The impression would be gained that the whole function of the layman was to *"credere, orare, oboedire, solvere"* (believe, pray, obey, pay). It was important, particularly, for the clergy to encourage lay "intellectuals" whose work was so necessary to the Church and acknowledge their right to freedom of investigation. He concluded with "We should put these principles into action by giving our Lay Auditors an opportunity to be heard in the Council."

The distinction in the text between clergy and laity was still too sharp in the opinion of Archbishop Seper of Yugoslavia. When ordained to the hierarchy the clergy did not lose their place as part of the people of God. Thus it was not correct to say that Christian activity in the world was *primarily* the responsibility of the laity, as though the clergy had only a supplementary responsibility in this field. The apostolate of the laity did not involve merely a carrying out of plans conceived by the hierarchy, the layman's part also extended to planning.

To promote a greater "dialogue" between the hierarchy and the laity, finally, Bishop Ruotolo of Italy suggested the creation of a new Congregation for the Laity in Rome to be staffed by laymen as well as clergy.

The great ecumenical importance of this chapter of the schema was pointed out by Archbishop Jaeger of Paderborn, Germany, particularly the idea that the entire Christian people was called upon to carry on the work of Christ and was bound by the obligation to preach the gospel. The oneness of the new People of God should be stressed, because St. Paul said that, with Christ, they were nailed to the cross. More attention should be paid to the eucharist as the principle of unity within the people of God. He mentioned the early Church and its literal interpretation of the meaning of *"communio."* The distinction between the ministerial and universal priesthoods as being one of "essence" and not "degree," which some speakers had drawn, was not adequate or in accordance with the real facts. Theology taught that they both had certain similar and dissimilar elements: they were similar in both being a "consecration in the Holy Spirit"; dissimilar in that "consecration as a minister" was a setting aside for special tasks of one who was already "consecrated in the Holy Spirit." The hierarchical priesthood was a setting aside or further consecration within the ranks of "universal priests."

The sharing of the laity in the eucharistic sacrifice as the "peak" of his priestly activity was also mentioned by Bishop de Smedt of Bruges, a member of the Secretariat for Promoting Christian Unity. He said that the text should bring out more clearly the relationship between the apostolate of the laity and the threefold functions of Christ as Priest, Prophet and King, by exercising a priestly office: their lives should be religious and offered to God, with the eucharist as the apex; a prophetic office: a truly Christian life bore witness to Christ and His Church; a kingly office: concrete human life, both individual and social, was to be ordered according to God's will and informed by charity.

Cardinal Lefebvre of France was happy, he said, to agree with Bishop de Smedt that the dignity of the laity consisted chiefly in their priestly character and approved of what he had said about their priestly, prophetic and kingly roles. References to the "kingly" nature of Christian life were also made by Bishop Tomasek of Czechoslovakia, and Bishop Darmancier, Vicar Apostolic of the Willis Islands in the South Pacific. According to the latter, it would provide the dogmatic basis for a consideration of the temporal activity of the faithful. Man's dominion over the created world manifested his kingly character and thus was in close relationship with his priestly role in the Church.

Rising to speak on Monday, Oct. 21, 1963 for the first time since his brief remarks opening the discussion on the schema, Cardinal Ottaviani exercised the unwritten prerogative of his order to speak on whatever topic he chose, regardless of conciliar rules, and reverted to the discussion of Chapter II which the Council had left behind some days before.—It is worth noting that none of the Moderators

thought fit to call him to account for this flagrant flouting
of the rules, nor of course did the Secretary General Archbishop Felici pose any objection when his speech was submitted in advance, if indeed it was.—The Cardinal of the
Holy Office seemed to speak without benefit of manuscript,
though he may have merely been unable to read because of
failing eyesight—in any case his command of Latin is so
prodigious that he could speak extemporaneously in that
language, to great effect, if he so wished. He began by an
attack on three of the *periti* or council experts (unnamed
but assumed to be Rahner, Ratzinger and Martelet) whom
he accused of soliciting various groups of bishops in favor
of a married diaconate. He said that the *periti* should stick
to their lasts: it was the business of the bishops to do the
conciliar thinking and that the experts ought not to be
lobbying or offering suggestions unasked. Despite his charge,
the cardinal's manner was pleasant. When a later speaker
(Bishop Kozlowiecki) rose and pointedly addressed the cardinals, bishops, observers and "Beloved *Periti*," the cardinal
acknowledged this rebuke with a large gracious smile. His
proposal for resurrecting the office of acolyte—a minor order
in the early Church and now only one of the stepping-stones
to the higher orders of deacon, priest and bishop (present-
day altar-boys are not real acolytes)—was untimely and unrealistic, being motivated, in part at least, by the age-long
concern felt at the Holy Office that any breach in the wall
of celibacy would start an avalanche of requests for dispensa-
tions close to home which could not be controlled. His remarks about the *periti* were also unseasonable, for he had
scarcely delivered them, when one of his spokesmen, Father
Carlo Balič, a Yugoslav Franciscan, specialist in Mariology
and consultor of the Holy Office, began distributing a pamphlet to the Fathers in the Council hall—in contravention
of what Archbishop Felici had repeatedly warned against

from the pulpit—which had been printed by the same Vatican Press which printed the official schemata and booklets distributed to the Council members. As an ironical note, it was pointed out by *Le Monde** that the above-mentioned memorandum of the *periti* favoring a restoration of the diaconate did not mention a "married" diaconate at all. Either Ottaviani had forgotten or—because of his bad eyesight—was unable to read what his advisers had presumably written.

While praising the general lines of the chapter, Cardinal Meyer of Chicago found that the text was not realistic enough about certain facts of life: men continued to be sinners and even after their entrance into the Church they were weak and liable to lapses into sin. Hence the appropriate petition in the "Our Father": "Forgive us our sins . . ." Christian life had a double aspect: the heavenly and the terrestial. This idea was conveyed in liturgical texts and in countless other ways, in particular by the prayer *Adsumus* which the Fathers recited every day before beginning their labors. Consequently there should be a paragraph proclaiming that the Church was the home for the weak and struggling, "before we describe the Church as being without stain or wrinkle." Jesus said: "I have not come to summon the just, but sinners."

The prophetic role of the laity was stressed by Bishop Larraín of Chile. He felt also, with Cardinal Meyer, that a clear distinction was not always made between the stainlessness of the Church and the failings of its members. Historically speaking, the People of God had not always fulfilled their ministry. Renewal in the Church was always necessary.

Speaking for the more than 40 Spanish and 30 other

* *Le Monde,* November 1, 1963.

bishops, as well as some Auditors, Bishop Moralejo of Spain criticized the chapter for not dealing sufficiently with the problem of the presentation of Catholic thought on the subject of the apostolate of the laity in terms that would be intelligible to modern man or in accordance with present-day thinking, as John XXIII and Paul VI had asked. It was unnecessarily technical and theological in language; the order in which the material was presented was not logical, proceeding from the less known to the better known; and certain important subjects relating to the Church such as the continuation of Christ's work, its entirely spiritual mission, its call to self-denial and charity, and the weakness of its human members, were not touched upon at all. He proposed that these defects be rectified and that a catechism adapted to the modern world be issued by the Council.

Instead of the expressions "universal priesthood of the laity" and "ministerial priesthood of the hierarchy," Archbishop Cooray of Ceylon felt that it would be better to speak of the "spiritual priesthood of the laity" and the "sacramental priesthood of the Church's official ministers." The point being that, whereas the hierarchical priesthood worked for the sanctification of the Church primarily through sacramental means, the laity worked through such spiritual means as prayer, apostolic activity, and the radiation of sanctity in personal and social life.

In an important speech on Tuesday, October 22, one of the Moderators, Cardinal Suenens, replied to Cardinal Ruffini's criticism that the schema made too much of the subject of charisms (*charismata*), or special gifts of the Holy Spirit to the Church, by saying that in his opinion it touched rather lightly on the subject. Charisms *do* exist in the Church today and recognition of the fact was needed if a balanced view of the Church were to be arrived at. Such gifts were not mere peripheral phenomena or accidental appendages to the

Church, but belonged to its very nature. "The Holy Spirit is given to the whole Church, not just to its pastors." The Church was a "pneumatic reality," founded not only on the Apostles but on "prophets" as well. It was wrong to think of the charisms of the early Church as entirely extraordinary: Paul mentions such things as teaching, the discerning of spirits, etc. The Church would be undisciplined without the shepherds, but without the charisms it would be sterile. Paul's admonition should be heeded: the shepherds should not "stifle the Spirit" of the faithful. He had a number of concrete suggestions. The schema should develop the charismatic as well as the ministerial structure of the Church; it should extol the importance of charisms, underline the role of prophets (who aroused others to practice the Gospel), show the relationship between charisms and the shepherds in a more constructive way, and expound St. Paul's doctrine of the freedom of the children of God. On a more practical level, he urged that the number of Lay Auditors should be increased and that women should be invited to join their ranks, for "Unless I am mistaken," he said, "women make up one half of the world's population."

The cardinal's reference to the attendance of women at the Council, of course, immediately evoked a number of ironical comments in the press. The cynical right-wing *Il Borghese,* in an article entitled *"Il Feminismo di Sua Eminenza"* conjured up all sorts of supposed horrors that would result from taking the proposal seriously, from a resurrection of the scabrous days of "Popess Joan" and "furtive Boccaccio-esque encounters" to the dire prospect of an "Aristophanian Parliament of Women." It cited the editor of *The Tablet* (London) to the effect that "I had hoped in the near future to be included among the Lay Auditors at the Council, but it appears now that my wife will beat me to it," as a result of the intervention of "the paladin of ecclesiastical neo-feminism."*

An attempt was made on the same and the following day to offset the favorable reception accorded the speech of Cardinal Suenens. The text of the schema was correct in reflecting Pauline usage of the term "charism," according to Archbishop Florit of Florence, Italy, but care must be taken lest the term be misunderstood. This was true particularly today, he said, in view of prevalent "anti-conceptualist theories" which preferred an infused knowledge of theology or mystical theology to theology as an objective science and discipline. The word *dona* was safer than *charismata*.

The third intervention at this Session by Cardinal Siri of Genoa proved to be in a more conservative vein than his two previous efforts. The question of the subjection of the laity to the hierarchy must be treated more explicitly, otherwise there would be misunderstandings. He saw no valid reason— unlike the vast majority of speakers—for moving the section on the People of God to an early position in the schema. The term "added nothing to the general notion of the Church" and had nothing to do with any important aspect of the constitution of the Church. He also took exception to what he called "the sweeping conclusions" expressed on the floor about the implications of the universal priesthood of the faithful. The treatment in the chapter should be more restrained, because while it was necessary to stimulate the piety and zeal of the faithful, this must be done with a proper sense of proportion. As regards charisms, he said that while nobody denied that they could occur as manifestations of the Holy Spirit, the important thing was that they were to be subject to the teaching authority of the Church. There was "no room for a Church within the Church," or a Church full of "illusions."

* *Il Borghese,* October 31, 1963.

The role of the Holy Spirit in influencing the mission of the Church through charisms was stressed by the Maronite Archbishop Ziadé, who observed that this was better expressed in eastern than western theology. He agreed with Cardinal Suenens that it should be emphasized for theological, ecumenical and pastoral reasons.

But the contribution of the Orient was not entirely positive. A word of warning about easy assumptions concerning the universal priesthood of the laity was voiced by the Chaldean Patriarch of Babylon, Paul II Cheikho. Oriental theology, he claimed, was much less specific on the point than western theologians seemed to be. There was only one priesthood, that of the hierarchy and care must be taken not to leave the door open so that the laity would be inclined to interfere in things which properly belonged to the hierarchy. The laity had the mission to preach the Gospel, as witnesses, but not to share in the priesthood. As a practical step he said that it might be advisable to let the Observer Delegates who assisted devoutly at mass each morning and listened carefully to what was said, be heard themselves once a week either in the council hall or elsewhere.

The doctrine of the universal priesthood of the faithful was particularly important for those areas where the Church was unable to operate fully, particularly by promoting Catholic action, noted Bishop Arnerič of Yugoslavia, who also emphasized that the role of the Christian family needed more treatment in the schema. He warned, however, against a real danger to the Church from laymen who appeared as good Catholics but in reality were not and refused to obey the hierarchy, a cautious reference to painful current situations in satellite countries.

Dissatisfaction with the organization of the chapter was stated in blunt terms by Bishop Muldoon who observed: "It is becoming increasingly clear that the contents of this

chapter are not worthy of an ecumenical council. As it stands
the chapter is a shapeless mass of ideas." He singled out as its
"original sin" the lack of a basic theological principle which
could serve to unify and organize the whole. He proposed as
a new title "Concerning the Dignity and Vocation of Christ's
Faithful" and said that the chapter should clearly determine
the dogmatic foundation of the supernatural dignity of the
faithful, namely their incorporation in the Mystical Body
of Christ and their "co-incorporation" among themselves.
With this as a basis, the rest would follow.

Bishop Hakim of Israel commented unfavorably on the
failure of the schema to take into account the relations of
the Church with the non-Christian world. The chapter's "tri-
umphalism" was still annoying to those who had hoped that
after the first session this sort of approach would have been
abandoned. The text seemed to have been conceived as a
confirmation of ecclesiastical power, whereas the plain fact
of the matter was that the Church was not alone in the world.
Its strength was in the Word of God, not in self-glorification.
The Church covered only a small part of the world, numer-
ically. It would be more accurate to describe it as *"valde
pusillus grex"*—a very small flock. Apart from the question
of non-Christians, many speakers indicated that they clearly
had no concept whatsoever of what other Christian Churches
taught on a number of points and their remarks were plainly,
though unconsciously, insulting to them. For example, on
the subject of a married clergy. He endorsed the proposal
of Cardinal Suenens that the place of women in the apostolate
of the laity should be exalted—notice being taken, for example, of the great work they were doing in Catholic Action. A
conciliar definition of their dignity was needed because
in many countries their position was still insufficiently
respected.

The subject of discrimination was brought up in another

connection by Bishop Tracy of Baton Rouge, Louisiana, who criticized Paragraph 23 on the equality and inequality of the members of the Church of Christ. A statement ruling out any discrimination on account of race was sorely needed, he said, for it was impossible to reconcile racial discrimination with belief that God created all men equal in rights and dignity, as Christianity teaches. Such a statement would also make clearer what St. Paul meant when he said that there could be no distinction between Jew and Greek among Christians. It would help bishops to instruct their faithful with regard to the question of racial prejudice, and reassure those who had been humiliated by racial discrimination. It would also provide a good basis for future treatment by the Council of the subject of racial equality in greater detail.

Opinions differed among the Fathers as to whether there should or should not be included in the present chapter some treatment of the relationship which ought to obtain between Church and State. In Paragraph 25 on the Apostolate of the Laity, after quoting Mt. 22:21: "Render unto Caesar the things that are Caesar's, and unto God the things that are God's" the text goes on to say that while on the one hand the faithful should avoid any undue interference of the Church in purely civilian matters, on the other hand they should also oppose any "unfortunate separation" (*infaustae separationi*) between them or opposition on the part of the earthly City to God and His Church, because no human activity can be removed from the jurisdiction of God (*Dei imperio*). The use of the word "unfortunate" to describe the separation of Church and state rankled with the American and quite a few other bishops, who saw nothing "unfortunate" about a pluralist solution which has increasingly come to be recognized as decidedly preferable and more logical under present-day circumstances, quite apart from the fact that many hold it to be better grounded theologically than the old "Constantinian" view of Church-State relations which has dominated thought especially in the Latin-tradition countries of southern Europe. Bishop Klepacz, speaking for the Polish bishops, stated that the delicate matter could not be dismissed in a few words, especially ill-chosen ones, because too much was at stake, as the experience of the Church with totalitarian states, in Poland, for example, showed. "Separation, rightly understood," he observed, "could benefit both Church and state; it gives the Church an independence that is invaluable." Corcordats were not always the blessing that the Vatican represented them to be: they often rendered the Church subject to the state especially in financial matters. The word *infaustae* must go, and the whole topic should be treated either at greater length here or in Schema 17.

Archbishop Shehan of Baltimore, speaking in the name of the American hierarchy, and voicing the latter's concern, expressed in their annual conference just held in Rome, concurred in the judgment of Bishop Klepacz. The treatment of the problem of Church-State in the schema was entirely inadequate. It pertained primarily not to the laity but to the whole Church. He voiced the view of the American bishops that the section should be completely redone or the subject dropped altogether. Speaking then on his own behalf, he took exception to what the chapter had to say about "the world." It was necessary, following the example of Christ, to distinguish between the world in a disparaging sense and the men who lived in it. This would help to clarify the mission and scope of Catholic action. It would also clarify preaching about "the world" and provide a better understanding of the Christian vocation to holiness, serving to foster a proper love for the world and the Church's mission to bring Christ to the world. His final remarks were interrupted by the Moderator, who asked him to wait while a question about the voting was clarified, but the archbishop did not resume his talk.

The term "separation" was not univocal but analogous, noted Bishop Boillon of France, because it admitted of various interpretations under different circumstances. The Council should wait before taking up the whole question of Church-state relations until the declaration on religious liberty to be presented by the Secretariat for Christian Unity had reached the floor and been considered. This would provide a basis for a fraternal discussion on the council floor. The same sentiments were voiced by the Mexican Bishop of Cuernavaca, Mendez Arceo. The separation of Church and state could not longer be considered as a tolerated "hypothesis" because in some countries with constitutional regimes it was positively approved according to the supreme juridical norm in question, the common good of a particular church or nation.

Many of the Fathers were concerned about the schema's apparent lack of relevance to "the world" or to practical questions facing laymen who lived in the world, as well as its inadequate treatment of a widespread feeling on their part that they had no responsibility for, or share in, an apostolate at all. Bishop Scandar of Egypt opined that this was perhaps due to a lack of schools and catechists, but this explanation, if true, was only part of the picture. Other bishops believed that the roots of the problem lay much deeper and suggested ways in which to overcome the laity's negativistic attitude.

The promotion of lay organizations and associations of all kinds seemed to Bishop Hannan, Auxiliary of Washington, D.C., a good way to cause the laity to have a greater awareness of their role in the Church. They must be urged to realize that in activities of this kind, whether business, social and civic, they were being true witnesses to the faith and fulfilling the obligations of their apostolate. The clergy, especially bishops, must provide for closer contacts with the laity in this regard. Canon 1520 of the Code referred to lay advice, but only in temporal matters. The initiative must be taken by bishops to establish organs for consultation with the laity.

Bishop Bednorz of Poland wanted the schema to mention more specifically that one of the most basic practical forms of the lay apostolate was the work done by parents in educating their children and instilling in them the principles of their faith, a thought echoed by Bishop Philbin of Ireland. The schema might give the wrong impression that the Church was concerned only or principally with the after-life. Greater attention should be paid in this chapter to a concern for justice in this world, for greater social justice, and mention should be made of the natural virtues, industry, temperance, self-discipline, etc. which all understood, according to Bishop Philbin. The dignity of the Christian family should be exalted and the example of Mary and Joseph cited.

The Archbishop of Durban, South Africa, Denis Hurley, agreed with Bishop Philbin that the relationship between the earthly and the heavenly City was not brought out clearly enough in the text. The latter did not make plain what belonged to Caesar and what belonged to God. The problem treated here should be not so much that of Church-State, as of "the Church and human society." The faithful were warned about mixing the religious with the profane, but then were told that they must avoid separating the two. "We seem to be telling them to make an omelette without breaking the eggs." The implication should be removed from the text that the "world" was the sum-total of everything that was an enemy of God, said Bishop Geise. Christian teaching with regard to the world was positive and this should be brought out in relation to the layman. In his daily life the layman consecrated the "world" to God. Ideas to be incorporated in Schema 17 should not be completely passed over here.

The Master General of the Dominicans, Father Fernandez, concurred in what Bishop Hannan had said earlier about lay associations. Catholic charitable organizations certainly merited praise, but Catholic organizational activity was still far short of what it should be in many areas, for example communications. The lay apostolate could help advance the Kingdom of God through organizations aimed at a juster distribution of wealth, at developing new ways of exercising charity, or other works such as missionary schools. It might be helpful to set up an International Central Commission to coordinate efforts along these lines.

Finally, the role of the layman with respect to the missions called for more attention, according to Archbishop Gopu of India. Experience showed that the laity in missionary areas were less zealous for the spread of the faith than the laity in Europe or America. The missionary character of the Church needed particular emphasis in this chapter.

On Sunday, October 13, 1963, Pope Paul seized the occasion of the first beatification of his pontificate to show his appreciation for Americans and his respect for the American way. Assisting at the afternoon ceremonies in St. Peter's honoring the new *beatus*—the Pope does not take part in the solemn mass in the morning during which the proclamation of beatification is made public, the degree declaring it having been signed several days before or even weeks earlier —the Holy Father praised the virtues of American Catholicism as demonstrated by the new blessed John Nepomucene Neumann, an immigrant from Bohemia, who arrived in New York penniless in 1838, worked as a missionary in northern New York before joining the Redemptorist Order, became a naturalized citizen, succeeded the bluff and beloved Irishman Francis Patrick Kenrick as Bishop of Philadelphia 1852, and died, in true pioneer fashion, on Vine Street in the center of the city with his shoes on at the age of 49 in January 1860. Referring to a book entitled "Sanctity in America," written by Cardinal Cicognani when Apostolic Delegate in Washington, D.C., Pope Paul seemed to go out of his way to exorcise once and for all the ghost of pseudo-heresy known as "Americanism" in theology text-books, which was concocted, before the turn of the century, by a French theologian, the Abbé Félix Klein, who thought that the American way stressed the active instead of the passive virtues. Pope Leo XIII in a letter to the American hierarchy in 1908, known as *Oceano longinquo,* warned against such activism hinting that it stemmed from a theological misapprehension, and historians of the Church in the United States have been divided ever since on whether such a tendency really existed, the *sanior pars* holding that there was not sufficient theological depth in the United States at the time to generate a heresy. The following week at a similar ceremony honoring the Passionist missionary, Father Dominic Barbieri, who had received John Henry Newman, the future cardinal, into the Catholic Church in 1846, Pope Paul took occasion to praise the contribution of the English to the well-being of Christianity down through the centuries. In a third beatification on Sunday, November 3, 1963, he stressed the apostolate for youth, particularly youth of the working classes, that had brought Don Leonardo Murialdo, another late nineteenth-century priest, to the honors of the altar as a *beatus*. A fourth and a fifth beatification, of Vincenzo Romano and Nunzio Sulprizio, followed on November 17 and December 1, respectively. With the exception of the first candidate, this spate of Italian beatifications could not but strike some observers as a rather strange commentary on the subject which the Fathers took up during the remaining week of October, namely Chapter IV on the Vocation to Sanctity in the Church, implying as it did—whether deliberately or not is beside the point—that heroic sanctity was predominately an Italian monopoly. Students of the scene were also reminded that it was not infrequently the habit of the Curia to reply to attacks on the Church occasioned by a particular scandal by making some move in the beatification-canonization process of a priest or religious relative to the area where the attack had occurred, and wondered what could have occasioned such a concentration of effort, apart from the fact that the illness and death of John XXIII had no doubt held up some cases.

Chapter IV was divided into nine paragraphs, as follows:

28. Introduction;
29. The Universal Vocation to Sanctity;
30. The Different Ways in which Sanctity can be pursued;
31. The means to Sanctity and the Evangelical Counsels;
32. The Observance of the Counsels in a Way of Life approved by the Church;
33. The Profession of States of Perfection in the Church;
34. Under the Authority of the Church;
35. Consecration to the Evangelical Counsels to be Honored;
36. Conclusion.

Two thirds of the text related to Religious Orders, although the subject was clearly one that concerned the whole Church. As in the case of Chapter III, there was a widespread feeling that much that was said here duplicated, and in some respects, perhaps even conflicted with special schemata devoted to the subject which were to be taken up later. There was also the impression that the text had been rather hastily drawn up and that ideas had been lumped together which did not seem to belong either to the chapter on the Mystery of the Church or the chapter on the People of God. Although only three days were devoted to the final chapter of *De Ecclesia,* the extreme repetitiousness of the rather long roster of speakers coming at the end of an already long drawn-out exhausting debate, coupled with the feeling that the topic of sanctity hardly merited conciliar discussion, helped swell the rising tide of dissatisfaction with the course of the Session which began to manifest itself during the last two weeks of October. As one American bishop expressed it, after listening to speakers dwell on the importance of sanctity in the life of the Church for the hundred and first time, he was frankly bored by the whole subject.

A number of speakers pointed out the vagueness of the text with regard to a definition of holiness and its failure to present the idea within a scriptural context. The idea of sanctity was viewed too much from an ethical point of view and not enough as a grace, a gift of God, or from a Christocentric point of view. Holiness, after all, was essentially a sharing in the holiness of Christ. Sanctity was never perfect on earth, Bishop Schoemaker of Indonesia pointed out, but consisted in a continuing effort to respond to the divine invitation. This was important *pastorally,* because Christians who were conscious of their faults would not consider that they had achieved any state of consummated perfection, as the schema says. It was important *ecumenically,* because Christians of the Reformation found it difficult to understand sanctity apart from the general objective sanctity of the People of God. Instead of speaking of "acquiring a state of perfection," it would be better to speak of a "state of imitating Christ according to the evangelical counsels." This would eliminate the implication that the religious life represented a perfection achieved, whereas it only denoted a greater effort at striving toward perfection.

Cardinal Léger welcomed the stress of the text on the holiness of the laity but said that it could be improved. For too long, he maintained, monastic sanctity had been regarded as the only real sanctity in the Church, the ideal being unattainable for the secular clergy and the laity. However, it was necessary to go even further and bring out the sanctity involved in leading a married life, in family activity, and in other activities of the layman. The cardinal expressed it as his opinion that no true lay spirituality would be developed until laymen entered the intellectual life of the Church in greater numbers. Laymen should be allowed to obtain theological degrees and to teach in seminaries. He, too, pointed out that too much stress on such terms as "those in a state of perfection" tended to blur the central theme of the chapter, which was the vocation of all to sanctity.

Both Cardinals Urbani and Cento regretted the failure of the text to bring out more clearly the idea of the communion of saints and the connection between sanctity on earth and the saints in heaven. According to the former: "We cannot live out our own vocation to holiness without reference to those in heaven who offer their merits and continual intercession for our sanctification." The veneration of the saints, he maintained, was not an obstacle to Christocentric worship, because the saints were not persons separated from Christ but intimately united to him. As president of the conciliar Commission for the Apostolate of the Laity, Cardinal Cento formally requested that more attention be paid to encouraging the canonization processes of laymen. He cited the French writer Daniel-Rops to the effect that the health of the Church could be measured by the number of her saints. The following day Bishop Emannuel of Germany seconded the cardinal's remarks about the canonization of laymen.

Cardinal Ruffini was critical, as usual, about a number of details. Since the schema was dogmatic, it should treat of sanctity from a dogmatic point of view: holiness was not only a vocation, it was also present as one of the main marks or notes of the Church, through the latter's union with Christ, her means of sanctification, and the holiness of her members.

The traditional distinction between the degrees of sanctity should also be brought out more clearly: ordinary or common sanctity, and heroic or extraordinary sanctity. He objected particularly to the sentence in the Introduction: "In the mystery of the Church . . . all are called to holiness" as inflated, and said that it made the Church sound like the Archangel Gabriel announcing something new. The term *"mysterium,"* used five times in this chapter, was too obscure and tended to imply that we knew nothing about the nature of the Church, but this was not true. Though as an object of faith the Church was a mystery, we knew considerable about its nature since it had visible elements in the social and juridical orders. Such expressions as the "Church of charity" which Pope Paul VI had used in his opening address—were dangerous, according to Cardinal Ruffini, as implying a separation between a visible and an invisible Church, or a distinction between a Church of charity and the juridical Church.

The severest criticism of the chapter was that by Cardinal Bea. The text did not distinguish sufficiently between the holiness of a Church on earth, in a state of pilgrimage, and that of the Church in heaven or at the end of time. The former was dynamically holy but never perfectly so, the latter perfectly holy. It was not realistic to speak only of a Church of saints, the Church also consisted of sinners while here on earth. If the Church were simply holy, there would have been no cause for the Protestant Reformation. In support of his second major criticism, he cited a number of texts showing how inadequately the chapter treated its subject-matter from the viewpoint of Scripture, and declared that this treatment was "unworthy of the Council." The passage containing Paul's programmatic declaration of Christian holiness, for example: "This is the will of God, your sanctification," was omitted altogether. But this and other texts gave a whole

New Testament teaching on sanctity. Since some of these texts also spoke of man's capacity to do good in a moral sense, their inclusion would be a response to those who thought that man himself was so corrupted that he was incapable of good and had to rely on a purely "extrinsic" justification. Since they were also frequently quoted by the Fathers of the Church, mention of them could serve as a bridge for a dialogue with non-Catholics on this particular point.

Apart from these negative criticisms of general import, quite a few of the speakers commented favorably on the insistence of the chapter that *all* Christians were summoned to holiness, not merely certain classes or groups. There was *one* divine commandment applicable to all, but there were different means or ways of achieving the goal. Also welcomed was the emphasis on the ecclesiological and eschatological aspects of a life pursued according to the evangelical counsels, rather than solely upon the ascetical aspects. As Cardinal Doepfner pointed out, it was the ancient tradition of the Church that the religious life was to be led for the entire people of God. The religious were not to lead a life for themselves, but were called along with other groups to form a united Christian people.

A number of speakers like Bishop Franič of Yugoslavia found the treatment inadequate with respect to the position of the bishop and sanctity. The bishop should be presented as the model or pattern of sanctity for his people, particularly the clergy. But if this claim or ideal were to be taken seriously, bishops would have to show more care in ordering their lives according to the counsel of evangelical poverty, "especially since rich living is a scandal to so many today." He praised the example of "our brother Orthodox bishops," who ever since the seventh century had taken a vow of poverty, chastity and obedience prior to their consecration as bishops. He also recommended a private vow of poverty for diocesan priests, to complete their vows of chastity and obedience.

The German Benedictine Abbot Reetz repeated the suggestion that the expression "state of perfection," in use since the time of St. Thomas Aquinas in the 13th cenutry, should be dropped because of its ambiguity. The vocation to sanctity applied to all, though not all were summoned to use the same means or follow in the same path. Misconceptions on this point had prompted Nietzsche to write that no one was as proud as a monk. The better term was "religious," since this had been used in a technical sense ever since the 6th century. Finally, some speakers were of the opinion that the general treatment of sanctity should be transferred to the chapter on the People of God, and the present chapter reserved exclusively to the religious state.

On Thursday, October 31, 1963, Pope Paul took part in ceremonies celebrating the opening of the academic year at Lateran University. Present were a distinguished gathering of some thirty cardinals, the rectors of Roman universities, and a quorum of interested prelates. In the absence of Cardinal Micara, Grand Chancellor of the university, who was ill, the Pope was perfervidly welcomed by the Rector Magnificus, who made resounding references to the Holy Father's earlier association with the Lateran, both as a student 1922-23 and a professor 1930-37. In actual fact, during those years the then Monsignor Giovanni Battista Montini had lectured on the history of Vatican diplomacy primarily for the students of the College of Ecclesiastical Nobles which prepares for careers in the Vatican's diplomatic service and had delivered conferences on moral and doctrinal topics to members of the Federation of Italian Catholic University Students (FUCI), as the Pope made plain when he recalled "the brief years in which we first as student, then as teacher, attended the *Apollinare* from which this university was born" and said, with a gracious smile, that he "was not tempted to vanity—since we lack the genius and time to give a glorious account of our twofold attendance." The principal speaker for the occasion was the Stigmatine professor Father Cornelio Fabro, considered one of the ablest Italian clerical philosophers. His hour-long speech was a grandiose defense of thomistic philosophy replete with learned assertions about its competency to handle the existentialist problems of the hour and plentiful references to German philosophers from Hegel and Kant to Feuerbach, Jaspers and Heidegger.

Throughout the Pope's talk his tone was calm and affable, his manner of delivery positive. Though warmly praising the speaker, he made no mention of St. Thomas Aquinas or thomism, despite Roman sensibilities on this score. More ominous were the hopes he expressed for the future of the Lateran. "We are convinced of the beneficent role of this Pontifical University of the Lateran . . . and of the stimulus which its presence affords to all those who have at heart Catholic culture and the training of students, both clerical and lay, who show an aptitude for scientific research, for teaching, and for those tasks which require a specific higher ecclesiastical and academic indoctrination." Then lowering his voice but retaining his affable tone, he said: "Our hopes are all the more justified in that, on the one hand, they expect that a smoothly functioning organization, a seriousness of purpose, and a persistent effort toward improvement will spur on all, both teachers and students alike, to impart to this university the virtues and merits commensurate with the excellence of its name; and, on the other hand, that its contribution in the concert of great and celebrated Roman institutes of higher ecclesiastical learning will be that of sincere recognition, fraternal collaboration, loyal emulation, mutual reverence and amicable concord, *non mai d'una gelosa concorrenza, o d'una fastidiosa polemica, non mai!—*

never jealous or irksome polemics, never!" These words were greeted by a tremendous outburst of applause among the students which immediately communicated itself to the rest of the assembly. The Rector Magnificus, Monsignor Piolanti, sat stunned, then quickly recuperating joined in the demonstration. These incisive words at the very end of his talk and especially the repetition of "never" put an end to whatever plans certain clerical minds had been nurturing to absorb all the ecclesiastical institutes of higher learning in Rome, including the Jesuit-run Biblical Institute, information about which came to light soon after Pope John's announcement regarding the summoning of Vatican Council II.* He then concluded by saying that Lateran University would in that case have its positive mission to fulfill and "it will then always be favored by our affection and supported by our apostolic blessing."

SUMMARY

Sunday, September 29, 1963—SOLEMN OPENING OF SECOND SESSION. MASS: celebrated by Dean of Sacred College, Cardinal Tisserant. GOSPEL: enthroned by Archbishop Pericle Felici, Secretary General.
—Address by His Holiness, Pope Paul VI.

* See *Letters from Vatican City: Vatican Council II (First Session)*, New York, 1963, p. 51.

September 30, 1963, Monday—37TH GENERAL CONGREGATION.

MASS: Archbishop Giovanni Colombo of Milan, in Ambrosian rite.

GOSPEL: Archbishop Pericle Felici.

MODERATOR: Cardinal Agagianian.

PRESENT: 2,258 Fathers.

—Announcement by Secretary General of changes in Rules of Procedure, and of change in rule of conciliar secrecy.

SUBJECT: debate on the schema *De Ecclesia,* in general.

SPEAKERS: introductory remarks by Cardinal Agagianian as Moderator, Cardinal Ottaviani as president of Theological Commission, and Cardinal Browne as vice-president of the same commission.

1. Cardinal Josef Frings (Archbishop of Cologne) (approves it as a whole, criticizes details).
2. Cardinal Giuseppe Siri (Archbishop of Genoa) (approves).
3. Patriarch Ignace Pierre XVI Batanian (Armenian Patriarch of Cilicia, Lebanon) (priesthood of faithful and hierarchy, authority of latter).
4. Archbishop Casimiro Morcillo González (Zaragoza, Spain) (certain omissions, too much on primacy).
5. Bishop Carlo A. Ferrero di Cavallerleone (Tit., Italian) (schema on Mary should be included in *De Ecclesia*).
6. Archbishop Ermenegildo Florit (Florence, Italy) (criticizes form).
7. Archbishop Pierre-Martin Ngo-Dinh-Thuc (Hué, South Vietnam) (Church and non-Christians).
8. Bishop Giuseppe Gargitter (Bressanone, Italy) (People of God before hierarchy).

October 1, 1963, Tuesday—38TH GENERAL CONGREGATION.

MASS: Archbishop John Charles McQuaid of Dublin.

MODERATOR: Cardinal Lercaro.

PRESENT: 2,229 Fathers.

SUBJECT: Schema *De Ecclesia,* in general.

SPEAKERS:

1. Cardinal Raul Silva Henriquez (Archbishop of Santiago de Chile) (eschatological aspect of Church, inclusion of Mary in present schema).

2. Cardinal Laurean Rugambwa (Bishop of Bukoba, Tanganyika) (missionary nature of Church).
3. Archbishop Maxim Hermaniuk (Ukrainian Exarch, Canada) (episcopal "senate" in Rome).
4. Archbishop Gabriel Garrone (Toulouse, France) (inclusion of Mary and section on Tradition).
5. Bishop Primo Gasbarri (Auxiliary, Velletri, Italy) (Church and state).
6. Bishop Arthur Elchinger (Coadjutor, Strasbourg, France) (sections on Word of God, Tradition, inclusion of Mary).
7. Archbishop Armando Fares (Catanzaro, Italy) (clearer statement of teaching of Church prefixed to each paragraph).
8. Archbishop Adrian Djajasepoetra (Djakarta, Indonesia) (insufficient Christological basis).
9. Bishop Joseph Guffens (Tit., Belgian) (favorable).
10. Bishop Giocondo Grotto (Prelate Nullius of Acre and Purús, Brazil) (unclear terminology).
11. Bishop Sergio Méndez Arceo (Cuernavaca, Mexico) (collegiality, inclusion of Mary.)
12. Bishop José Pont y Gol (Segorbe-Castellón, Spain) (written).
—Vote on schema as basis for discussion. Total: 2,301. Placet: 2,231. Non placet: 43. Invalid: 27.

SUBJECT: Chapter I of schema, on Mystery of Church (*De mysterio Ecclesiae*).

SPEAKERS:

13. Cardinal Ernesto Ruffini (Archbishop of Palermo, Sicily) (criticizes biblical quotations, treatment of papal primacy and Mystical Body).
14. Archbishop Juan Carlos Aramburu (Tucumán, Argentina) (eucharist as source of unity).
—Papal audience to council journalists.

October 2, 1963, Wednesday—39TH GENERAL CONGREGATION.
MASS: Archbishop Thomas Cooray of Colombo, Ceylon.
MODERATOR: Cardinal Doepfner.
PRESENT: 2,288 Fathers.
—Archbishop Villot, Undersecretary, reads Message of Lay Auditors to council.
SUBJECT: Chapter I, on Mystery of Church.

SPEAKERS:

1. Cardinal Jaime de Barros Câmara (Archbishop of Rio de Janeiro) (doctrinal authority of schema, Church as Kingdom of God).
2. Cardinal Valerian Gracias (Archbishop of Bombay) (Introduction should be shorter).
3. Cardinal Bernhard Alfrink (Archbishop of Utrecht) (Peter and the Apostles).
4. Cardinal Achille Liénart (Bishop of Lille) (written).
5. Bishop John Ambrore Abasolo y Lecue (Vijayapuram, India) (criticism of phrase "Lumen gentium").
6. Bishop Jan van Dodewaard (Haarlem, Holland) (membership in Church).
7. Archbishop Charles de Provenchères (Aix-en-Provence, France) (holiness in the Church).
8. Bishop Anastasio Granados García (Auxiliary of Toledo, Spain) (twofold mission of Holy Spirit).
9. Bishop Enrico Romolo Compagnone (Anagni, Italy) (clarification of Christological basis; Peter and the Pope).
10. Bishop Franjo Franič (Split, Yugoslavia) (Church Militant, Secretariat for Study of Atheism).
11. Bishop Felix Romero Menjibar (Jaén, Spain) (Church as Kingdom of God).
12. Bishop Luigi Carli (Segni, Italy) (Church founded on Peter alone).
13. Bishop Guillaume Brasseur (Vicar Apost. of Montagnosa, Philippines) (questions schema on salvation of non-Christians).
14. Bishop Alfred Ancel (Auxiliary of Lyons, France) (social implications of concept Kingdom of God).
15. Bishop Emilio Guano (Livorno, Italy) (analogy between Church and Incarnation).
16. Bishop Jesús Enciso Viana (Mallorca, Spain) (Church as Bride of Christ).
17. Bishop Ernest J. Primeau (Manchester, New Hampshire) (Church and state, incorporation in Church).
18. Dom Christopher Butler (Abbot of Downside, England) (membership in Church, non-Catholics).
19. Bishop Arturo Tabera Araoz (Albacete, Spain) (written).

—Press panel conference of Fr. Karl Rahner, S.J., on concept of Church.

October 3, 1963, Thursday—40TH GENERAL CONGREGATION.
MASS: Archbishop Jean Baptiste Zoa of Yaoundé, Cameroon.
MODERATOR: Cardinal Suenens.
PRESENT: 2,262 Fathers.
SUBJECT: Chapter I, on Mystery of Church.
SPEAKERS:
1. Cardinal Giacomo Lercaro (Archbishop of Bologna and Moderator) (identity and differences between Church and Mystical Body, suggests certain Fathers be heard in Theological Commission).
2. Cardinal Benjamin de Arriba y Castro (Archbishop of Tarragona, Spain) (keep Mary as a separate schema).
3. Cardinal Carlo Confalonieri (Curia) (Holy Spirit and Church).
4. Cardinal Paul Richaud (Archbishop of Bordeaux, France) (revision of Introduction in light of Ephesians).
5. Cardinal Joseph Elmer Ritter (Archbishop of St. Louis, Missouri) (more emphasis on theology of the Word).
6. Cardinal Augustin Bea (Curia) (criticism of biblical quotations and use of scripture and tradition).
7. Archbishop Franjo Seper (Zagreb, Yugoslavia) (better use of scriptural images, mention of Jews).
8. Archbishop Geraldo de Proença Sigaud (Diamantina, Brazil) (Church as Family of God).
9. Archbishop Emile A. Blanchet (Tit., Rector of Catholic Institute, Paris) (written).
10. Bishop Abilio del Campo y de la Bárcena (Calahorra-Logroño, Spain) (meanings of *ecclesia*).
11. Bishop Simon Hoa Nguyen-van Hien (Dalat, Vietnam) (Church as Family of God).
12. Bishop Jacinto Argaya Goicoechea (Mondoñedo-Ferrol, Spain) (written).
13. Bishop Hermann Volk (Mainz, Germany) (more emphasis on Word of God and eucharist).
14. Bishop Antonio Pildáin y Zapiáin (Canary Islands, Spain) (fallen-away Catholics).

15. Bishop Angelo Jelmini (Apost. Administrator of Lugano, Switzerland) (ecumenical suggestions, eucharist).
16. Archbishop John Heenan (Westminster, England) (ecumenical responsibilities).
17. Archbishop Félix Scalais (Léopoldville, Congo) (three biblical images of Church).
18. Archbishop Eugene D'Souza (Nagpur, India) (theology of Church's missionary task).
19. Bishop Gerard van Velsen (Kroonstad, South Africa) (criticizes attitude toward Protestants, Orientals).
20. Archbishop Herculanus van der Burgt (Pontianak, Indonesia) (complete and incomplete membership, Protestants).
21. Archbishop Joseph Martin (Rouen, France) (discrepancy between this schema and that on Liturgy in treatment of Church).
22. Bishop Vincenzo Enrique y Tarancón (Solsona, Spain) (written)

—Announcement of Secretary General about distribution of printed material to Fathers without permission of Council Presidents.

October 4, 1963, Friday—41ST GENERAL CONGREGATION.
MASS: Bishop Francesco Filippini, Vicar Apostolic of Mogadiscio in Somalia.
MODERATOR: Cardinal Agagianian.
PRESENT: 2,256 Fathers.
SUBJECT: Chapter I, on Mystery of Church.
SPEAKERS:

1. Cardinal Pierre Gerlier (Archbishop of Lyons, France) (Church and poverty).
2. Cardinal Raul Silva Henriquez (Archbishop of Santiago de Chile) (written).
3. Archbishop Antoine Grauls (Kitega, Burundi) (Catholicity of Church needs emphasis).
4. Archbishop Maurice Baudoux (Saint-Boniface, Canada) (treatment of non-Catholics inadequate).
5. Archbishop Salvatore Baldassari (Ravenna, Italy) (bolder ecumenical approach).
6. Bishop Joseph M. Marling (Jefferson City, Missouri) (doctrinal basis of ecumenism needs clarification).

7. Bishop Henri Jenny (Auxiliary of Cambrai, France) (more emphasis on place of Christ in Church).
8. Archbishop Giuseppe D'Avack (Camerino, Italy) (schema less clear than *Mystici Corporis*).
9. Bishop Charles Himmer (Tournai, Belgium) (Church and poverty).
—Cardinal Browne concludes debate on Chapter I on behalf of Theological Commission.

SUBJECT: Chapter II, on Hierarchy and Episcopate (*De ordine hierarchico et in specie: de episcopatu*).

SPEAKERS:

10. Cardinal Francis Spellman (Archbishop of New York) (praises chapter, but criticizes paragraph 15 on deacons).
11. Cardinal Ernesto Ruffini (Archbishop of Palermo, Sicily) (no biblical basis for collegiality).
12. Cardinal Antonio Bacci (Curia) (criticizes diaconate).
13. Archbishop Emile Guerry (Cambrai, France) (sacramentality of episcopate).
14. Archbishop Rafael García y García de Castro (Granada, Spain) (episcopate not a sacrament).
15. Archbishop Pierre Veuillot (Coadjutor of Paris) (apostolic succession is scriptural).
16. Archbishop Antonio Gregorio Vuccino (Tit., resident in France) (schema on Revelation should be included).
17. Bishop Carlos Eduardo Saboia Bandeira de Mello (Palmas, Brazil) (papal primacy and episcopate).
18. Archbishop Fidel García Martínez (Tit., Spanish) (time to define infallibility of Church and councils).
19. Bishop Filippo Pocci (Auxiliary of Rome) (on behalf of Cardinal Vicar Micara, condemns certain errors.)
20. Cardinal José Quintero (Archbishop of Caracas, Venezuela) (written).
21. Archbishop Paul Dalmais (Fort-Lamy, Equatorial Africa) (written).
22. Archbishop Gilbert Ramantoanina (Fianarantsoa, Madagascar) (written).
23. Archbishop Jean Wolff (Diego-Suarez, Madagascar) (written).
24. Bishop Pablo Barrachina Estevan (Orihuela-Alicante, Spain) (written).

25. Bishop Juan Hervás y Benet (Prelate Nullius of Ciudad Real, Spain) (written).
26. Father Aliprando Catani, Prior General of Camaldolese Hermits (written).
27. Bishop Ernesto Gonçalves da Costa (Inhambane, Mozambique) (written).
28. Bishop François Nestor Adam (Sitten, Switzerland) (written).
—Conference of Father Yves Congar, O.P., on collegiality.

October 6, 1963, Sunday
—Archbishop Martin J. O'Connor says mass for journalists in Sant'Ivo.
—Press conference of Archbishop Heenan of Westminster on ecumenism and charity.

October 7, 1963, Monday—42ND GENERAL CONGREGATION.
MASS: Bishop Pierre Marc Théas of Tarbes and Lourdes, France.
MODERATOR: Cardinal Lercaro.
PRESENT: 2,275 Fathers.
SUBJECT: Chapter II, on Hierachy and Episcopate.
SPEAKERS:
1. Cardinal Giuseppe Siri (Archbishop of Genoa) (reservations about collegiality).
2. Cardinal Paul-Emile Léger (Archbishop of Montreal, Canada) (collegiality, sacramentality of episcopate, ministry).
3. Cardinal Franziskus König (Archbishop of Vienna) (Pope and bishops as "foundation").
4. Cardinal Julius Döpfner (Archbishop of Munich) (diaconate).
5. Cardinal Albert Gregory Meyer (Archbishop of Chicago) (collegiality).
6. Cardinal Bernhard Alfrink (Archbishop of Utrecht, Holland) ("Peter and the Apostles").
7. Cardinal Joseph Lefebvre (Archbishop of Bourges, France) (collegiality and primacy).
8. Cardinal Laurean Rugambwa (Bishop of Bukoba, Tanganyika) (universal mission of bishops).
9. Patriarch Maximos IV Saigh (Melkite Patriarch of Antioch, Lebanon) (collegiality and primacy).
10. Bishop Pietro Massa (Nanyang, China) (opposes diaconate).

11. Bishop Juan Ambrose Abasolo y Lecue (Vijayapuram, India) (episcopate a sacrament).
12. Archbishop Ermenegildo Florit (Florence, Italy) (sacramentality of episcopate and priesthood).
13. Bishop Emile Joseph de Smedt (Bruges, Belgium) (collegiality, internationalization of Curia).
14. Bishop Carmel Zazinovic (Auxiliary of Krk, Yugoslavia) (permanent episcopal commission).
15. Bishop George Andrew Beck (Salford, England) (priesthood).
16. Bishop Jan van Dodewaard (Haarlem, Holland) (Pope and college).

October 8, 1963, Tuesday—43RD GENERAL CONGREGATION.
MASS: Cardinal Tappouni, in Syrian rite.
MODERATOR: Cardinal Döpfner.
PRESENT: 2,298 Fathers.
SUBJECT: Chapter II, on Hierarchy and Episcopate.
SPEAKERS:
1. Cardinal Benjamin de Arriba y Castro (Archbishop of Tarragona, Spain) ("Church of the Poor").
2. Cardinal Valerian Gracias (Archbishop of Bombay, India) (scriptural quotations, missionary aspects).
3. Cardinal Juan Landázuri Ricketts (Archbishop of Lima, Peru) (diaconate).
4. Cardinal Leo Jozef Suenens (Archbishop of Malines-Bruxelles, Belgium) (diaconate).
5. Patriarch Alberto Gori (Latin Patriarch of Jersualem) (reservations about collegiality, papal legates).
6. Archbishop Dino Staffa (Curia) (reservations about collegiality).
7. Bishop Jean Rupp (Monaco) (collegiality).
8. Bishop Joseph Reuschen (Auxiliary of Liège, Belgium) (collegiality and Fathers).
9. Bishop André Charue (Namur, Belgium) ("Peter and the Apostles").

October 9, 1963, Wednesday—44TH GENERAL CONGREGATION.
MASS: Archbishop Rohrbacher of Salzburg, Austria.
MODERATOR: Cardinal Suenens.
PRESENT: 2,278 Fathers.

SUBJECT: Chapter II, on Hierarchy and Episcopate.

SPEAKERS:

1. Cardinal Achille Liénart (Bishop of Lille, France) (no antinomy between college and primacy, church authority not *potestas* but *servitium*).
2. Cardinal Paul Richaud (Archbishop of Bordeaux, France) (diaconate).
3. Bishop Antonio Añoveros Ataún (Coadjutor of Cadiz, Spain) (priesthood).
4. Bishop Emile Blanchet (Rector of Catholic Institute, Paris) (theological import of schemata).
5. Archbishop William Conway (Armagh, Ireland) (new chapter on priesthood).
6. Bishop Eduardo Martínez Gonzáles (Zamore, Spain) (juridical and pneumatic aspects of hierarchy).
7. Archbishop Franjo Seper (Zagreb, Yugoslavia) (diaconate without celibacy).
8. Archbishop Jean Weber (Strasbourg, France) (scriptural basis for collegiality).
9. Archbishop Denis Hurley (Durban, South Africa) (priesthood).
10. Archbishop Geraldo de Proença Sigaud (Diamantina, Brazil) (dangers of collegiality, of "parliament of bishops").
11. Bishop Biagio D'Agostino (Vallo di Lucania, Italy) (opposes diaconate).
12. Bishop Michael Browne (Galway and Kilmacdaugh, Ireland) (dioceses).
13. Bishop Michel Doumith (Maronite, Sarba, Lebanon) (episcopate in oriental theology, sacramentality).
14. Bishop Franjo Franič (Split, Yugoslavia) (dangers to primacy, opposes diaconate).

October 10, 1963, Thursday—45TH GENERAL CONGREGATION.

MASS: Archbishop P. Kinam Ro of Seoul, Korea.

MODERATOR: Cardinal Agagianian.

PRESENT: 2,265 Fathers.

SUBJECT: Chapter II, on Hierarchy and Episcopate.

SPEAKERS:

1. Cardinal Jaime de Barros Câmara (Archbishop of Rio de Janeiro, Brazil) (collegiality).

2. Cardinal Fernando Cento (Curia) (diaconate, with celibacy).
3. Bishop Emanuele Galea (Malta) (distinction between hierarchy of order and hierarchy of jurisdiction).
4. Bishop Eduard Schick (Auxiliary of Fulda, Germany) (more emphasis on local church).
5. Archbishop Lorenz Jaeger (Paderborn, Germany) (difference between powers of Apostles and bishops).
6. Archbishop Joseph Descuffi (Smyrna, Turkey) (new chapter on magisterium)
7. Archbishop Bernard Yago (Abidjan, West Africa) (diaconate).
8. Bishop Demetro Mansilla (Vicar Capitular of Burgos, Spain) (ambiguity of "collegiality").
9. Archbishop José Maurer (Sucre, Bolivia) (diaconate).
10. Archbishop Lawrence Shehan (Baltimore, Maryland) (infallibility).
11. Bishop Isaac Ghattas (Coptic, Thebes, Egypt) (patriarchates).
12. Bishop Alexandre Renard (Versailles, France) (priesthood).
13. Archbishop Casimiro Morcillo González (Zaragoza, Spain) (doubts about collegiality).
14. Father Aniceto Fernandez, Master General of Dominicans (doubts about collegiality, commission of bishops, opposes diaconate).
15. Archbishop Joseph Urtasun (Avignon, France) (sacramentality of episcopate).
16. Archbishop Paul Yü Pin (Nanking, China) (diaconate).
17. Archbishop Antoine Henri van den Hurk (Medan, Indonesia) (episcopate sacramental, Apostles and bishops).

October 11, 1963, Friday—46TH GENERAL CONGREGATION.
MASS: Archbishop Fernández Feo-Tinoco of San Cristobol, Venezuela.
MODERATOR: Cardinal Lercaro.
PRESENT: 2,249 Fathers.
SUBJECT: Chapter II, on Hierarchy and Episcopate.
SPEAKERS:
1. Cardinal Fernando Quiroga y Palacios (Archbishop of Santiago de Compostela, Spain) (reservations about collegiality).
2. Archbishop Josyf Slipyi (Ukrainian Metropolitan of Lviv,

Soviet Russia) (reservations about collegiality, Ukrainian patriarchate).

3. Bishop Vittorio Costantini (Sessa Aurunca, Italy) (reservations about diaconate, collegiality, episcopal commission).
4. Bishop Manuel Talamás Camandari (Ciudad Juárez, Mexico) (diaconate).
5. Bishop Hermann Wittler (Osnabruck, Germany) (clarification of powers of episcopate).
6. Bishop José Cirarda (Auxiliary of Seville, Spain) (sacramentality of episcopate).
7. Archbishop Enrico Nicodemo (Bari, Italy) (basis of collegiality unclear, commission of bishops).
8. Archbishop Paul Gouyon (Coadjutor of Rennes, France) (collegiality in early Church).
9. Bishop Jaime Flores Martin (Barbastro, Spain) (difference between unity and collegiality).
10. Bishop Albert C. de Vito (Lucknow, India) (reservations about diaconate).
11. Archbishop Marcel Lefebvre, Superior General of Holy Ghost Fathers (doubts about collegiality, senate of bishops).
12. Bishop Angel Temiño Saiz (Orense, Spain) (collegiality not of divine origin).
13. Bishop Pierre Boillon (Verdun, France) (priesthood).
14. Bishop Paul Rusch (Apostolic Administrator, Innsbruck, Austria) (collegiality).
15. Bishop José Pont y Gol (Segorbe-Castellón, Spain) (treatment too "authoritarian").
16. Bishop Giuseppe Bettazzi (Auxiliary of Bologna, Italy) (collegiality).

October 14, 1963, Monday—47TH GENERAL CONGREGATION.
MASS: Archbishop Mihayo of Tabora, Tanganyika.
MODERATOR: Cardinal Doepfner.
PRESENT: 2,242 Fathers.
SUBJECT: Chapter II, on Hierarchy and Episcopate.
SPEAKERS:
1. Cardinal Joseph Frings (Archbishop of Cologne, Germany) (collegiality and primacy in early Church).
2. Cardinal Joseph Ritter (Archbishop of St. Louis, Missouri)

(clarification of dogmatic and practical aspects of collegiality, diaconate).

3. Archbishop Pietro Parente (Curia) (Peter as foundation, college subordinate to Pope).
4. Archbishop Custodio Alvim Pereira (Lourenço Marques, Mozambique) (reservations about diaconate).
5. Bishop Vincenzo Jacono (Tit., Italy) (infallibility).
6. Bishop Fortunato Da Veiga Coutinho (Coadjutor of Belgaum, Indonesia) (clarification of relations between college and head).
7. Bishop Henri Vion (Poitiers, France) (bishop as pastor).
8. Archbishop Joseph Schneider (Bamberg, Germany) (scriptural proof of collegiality).
9. Bishop Patrick Cleary (Nancheng, China) (clarification of authority of magisterium).
10. Bishop Jean Sauvage (Annecy, France) (revision of section on apostolic succession).
11. Archbishop Segundo García de Sierra y Mendez (Coadjutor of Oviedo, Spain) (doubts about collegiality, opposes diaconate).
12. Bishop Petar Čule (Mostar, Yugoslavia) (reservations about diaconate).
13. Bishop Marijan Oblak (Auxiliary of Zara, Yugoslavia) (priesthood).
14. Bishop Joseph Höffner (Münster, Germany) (distinction between *potestas* and *munus*).
15. Bishop Giuseppe Carraro (Verona, Italy) (diaconate, with celibacy).
16. Archbishop Armando Fares (Catanzaro, Italy) (vote on diaconate, collegiality not clear enough to define).
17. Bishop Jorge Kémérer (Posadas, Argentina) (diaconate).
18. Archbishop Paul Zoungrana (Ouagadougou, Upper Volta) (diaconate, with celibacy).
19. Bishop Luigi Carli (Segni, Italy) (collegiality doubtful).

October 15, 1963, Tuesday—48TH GENERAL CONGREGATION.
MASS: Bishop Granados García, Auxiliary of Toledo, in Mozarabic rite.
MODERATOR: Cardinal Suenens.
PRESENT: 2,239 Fathers.

SUBJECT: Chapter II, on Hierarchy and Episcopate.

SPEAKERS:

1. Cardinal Giuseppe Siri (Archbishop of Genoa, Italy) (reservations about collegiality).
2. Cardinal Stefan Wyszynski (Archbishop of Gniezno and Warsaw) (opposes application of political terms to Church, Mystical Body, "Church Militant").
3. Patriarch Paul Pierre Meouchi (Maronite Patriarch of Antioch, Lebanon) (collegiality and primacy).
4. Bishop Narciso Jubany Arnau (Auxiliary of Barcelona, Spain) (diaconate).
5. Archbishop Thomas Couray (Colombo, Ceylon) (infallibility).
6. Bishop Jesús Enciso Viana (Majorca, Spain) (doubts about collegiality).
7. Bishop Jean Gay (Basse Terre, Guadeloupe) (reservations about diaconate).
8. Bishop Dino Luigi Romoli (Pescia, Italy) (diaconate, with celibacy).
9. Bishop Jan Mazur (Auxiliary of Lublin, Poland) (missionary aspect, priesthood).

October 16, 1963, Wednesday—49TH GENERAL CONGREGATION.

MASS: Bishop Scandar of Assiut, Egypt, in Coptic rite.

MODERATOR: Cardinal Agagianian.

PRESENT: 2,259 Fathers.

SUBJECT: Chapter II, on Hierarchy and Episcopate.

SPEAKERS:

1. Bishop Joachim Ammann (Tit., Switzerland) (nuncios).
2. Bishop Pietro Carretto (Vicar Apostolic of Rayaburi, Thailand) (diaconate).
3. Bishop Luis Eduardo Henriquez Jimenez (Auxiliary of Caracas, Venezuela) (sacramentality of episcopate, collegiality, no need for papal delegates to preside over episcopal conferences).
4. Archbishop Elias Zoghby (Tit., Melkite Patriarchal Vicar for Egypt) (oriental tradition on episcopate).
5. Bishop Gaston Jacquier (Auxiliary of Algiers) (collegiality).
6. Bishop Thomas Holland (Coadjutor of Portsmouth, England) (organ for whole episcopate).

7. Bishop Bernardino Echeverría Ruiz (Ambato, Ecuador) (collegiality).
8. Archbishop Cesar Antonio Mosquera Corral (Guayaquil, Ecuador) (diaconate, with celibacy).
9. Bishop Jozef Drzazga (Auxiliary of Gziezno, Poland) (reservations about diaconate).

SUBJECT: Chapter III on Laity.

SPEAKERS:

10. Cardinal Ernesto Ruffini (Archbishop of Palermo, Italy) (apostolate of laity from hierarchy, not Christ directly, passive infallibility, charismata) (spoke 22 minutes).
11. Cardinal Fernando Cento (Curia) (thanks Theological Commission for inclusion of chapter, clarification of priesthood of laity).
12. Cardinal José Maria Bueno y Monreal (Archbishop of Seville, Spain) (reservations about People of God, prefers Mystical Body).
13. Cardinal Antonio Bacci (Curia) (reservations about priesthood of faithful).

October 17, 1963, Thursday—50TH GENERAL CONGREGATION.
MASS: Bishop Aramburu of Tucumán, Argentina.
MODERATOR: Cardinal Lercaro.
PRESENT: 2,259 Fathers.
SUBJECT: Chapter III, on the Laity.
SPEAKERS:

1. Bishop Louis Rastouil (Limoges, France) (fuller treatment of priesthood).
2. Bishop Stanislaus Lokuang (Tainan, China) (universal priesthood).
3. Bishop Franz Hengsbach (Essen, Germany) (reorganization of matter).
4. Bishop John Wright (Pittsburg, Pennsylvania) (positive side of chapter, rejection of "clerical" Church).
5. Bishop Pietro Fiordelli (Prato, Italy) (Christian family).
6. Archbishop Marcel Dubois (Besançon, France) (meanings of People of God).
7. Bishop Candido Padin (Auxiliary of Rio de Janeiro, Brazil) (relation of bishop to faithful as good shepherd).

8. Bishop Joseph Gopu (Hyderabad, India) (laity in missionary countries).
9. Bishop Léon Elchinger (Auxiliary of Strasbourg, France) (more emphasis on communal experience, avoidance of individualism).
10. Bishop Philip Hannan (Auxiliary of Washington, D.C.) (witness of laity).
11. Bishop Luigi Civardi (Tit., Curia) (theological clarification of apostolate of laity).
12. Archbishop Ismaele Mario Castellano (Siena, Italy) (practical aspects of apostolate, clarification of Latin terms).
13. Archbishop Louis Mathias (Madras, India) (new pontifical institute for catechists).
14. Bishop Herbert Bednorz (Auxiliary of Katowice, Poland) (Catholic parents engaged in apostolate).
15. Bishop Enrico Compagnone (Anagni, Italy) (treatment first of hierarchy, then of People of God).
16. Bishop Federico Melendro (Anking, China) (more emphasis on obedience and authority, errors are rampant)
17. Bishop William Philbin (Down and Connor, Ireland) (care of Church for world and poor).

October 18, 1963, Friday—51ST GENERAL CONGREGATION.
MASS: Archbishop Djajasepoetra of Djakarta, Indonesia.
MODERATOR: Cardinal Doepfner.
PRESENT: 2,217 Fathers.
SUBJECT: Chapter III, on Laity.
SPEAKERS:

1. Cardinal Jaime de Barros Câmara (Archbishop of Rio de Janeiro, Brazil) (laity share in priesthood of Christ).
2. Cardinal Valerian Gracias (Archbishop of Bombay, India) (rights and duties of laymen).
3. Cardinal Laurean Rugambwa (Bishop of Bukoba, Tanganyika) (theology of laity).
4. Bishop Paolo Sani (Den Pasar, Indonesia) (clarification of definition of layman).
5. Bishop Lawrence Picachy (Jamshedpur, India) (clarification of relations between hierarchy and laity).
6. Dom Godefrido Dayez, President of Benedictine Congrega-

tion of Belgium (distinction between religious, members of secular institutes, and laity).

7. Bishop Joseph Schröffer (Eichstätt, Germany) (definition of laity).

8. Bishop Arturo Tabera (Albacete, Spain) (sanctity should be treated here, not in Ch. IV).

9. Bishop Paternus N. J. C. Geise (Bogor, Indonesia) (special section on laity's functions).

10. Bishop Giuseppe Vairo (Gravina, Italy) (ambiguous terms should be avoided).

11. Bishop Pablo Barrachina Estevan (Orihuela-Alicante, Spain) (clarification of People of God and priesthood of faithful).

12. Archbishop Lorenz Jaeger (Paderborn, Germany) (Church as People of God).

13. Archbishop Léon-Etienne Duval (Algiers) (missionary tasks of laity).

14. Bishop Michal Klepacz (Lódz, Poland) (Church and state, weaknesses of concordats).

15. Bishop Emile de Smedt (Bruges, Belgium) (priesthood of faithful needs emphasis).

16. Bishop Gilles Henri Alexis Barthe (Fréjus-Toulon, France) (Christian hope).

October 21, 1963, Monday—52ND GENERAL CONGREGATION.
MASS: Bishop Cristea, Apostolic Visitor for Rumanians.
MODERATOR: Cardinal Suenens.
PRESENT: 2,294 Fathers.
SUBJECT: Chapter III, on Laity.
SPEAKERS:

1. Cardinal Albert Gregory Meyer (Archbishop of Chicago, Illinois) (Church and sinners).

2. Cardinal Alfredo Ottaviani (Curia) (acolytes as deacons, *periti* criticized).

3. Archbishop Raymond-Marie Tchidimbo (Conakry, Guinea) (dangers of spiritual colonization).

4. Archbishop Thomas B. Cooray (Colombo, Ceylon) (clarification of universal priesthood).

5. Bishop Karol Wojtyla (Vicar Capitular of Kraków, Poland) (People of God).

6. Archbishop Denis Hurley (Durban, South Africa) (Church and world).
7. Archbishop Adam Kozlowiecki (Lusaka, Northern Rhodesia) (Church on pilgrimage and Church Triumphant).
8. Bishop Juan Hervás y Benet (Tit., Prelate Nullius of Ciudad Real, Spain) (relate text to *Humani Generis* and *Mystici Corporis*).

October 22, 1963, Tuesday—53RD GENERAL CONGREGATION.
MASS: Archbishop Sanchez Beguiristain of Concepción, Chile.
MODERATOR: Cardinal Agagianian.
PRESENT: 2,238 Fathers.
SUBJECT: Chapter III, on Laity.
SPEAKERS:

1. Cardinal Antonio Caggiano (Archbishop of Buenos Aires, Argentina) (title should be "Laity in Church of Christ").
2. Cardinal Leo Suenens (Archbishop of Malines-Bruxelles, Belgium) (theology of charismata).
3. Archbishop Henrique Heitor Golland Trinidade (Botucatú, Brazil) (collaboration of laity with hierarchy).
4. Bishop Giuseppe Ruotolo (Ugento, Italy) (Roman Congregation for Apostolate of Laity).
5. Archbishop Casimiro Morcillo González (Zaragoza, Spain) (theological rather than juridical definition of laity needed).
6. Bishop Jules Victor Daem (Antwerp, Belgium) (stress newness of concept People of God).
7. Bishop Sebastião Soares de Resende (Beira, Mozambique) (universal priesthood).
8. Bishop Vicente Enrique y Tarancón (Solsona, Spain) (section on public opinion in Church).
9. Father Johann Schütte, Superior General of Society of Divine Word (treatment of sanctity in this chapter).
10. Bishop Marius Maziers (Auxiliary of Lyons, France) (better definition of role of laity).
11. Archbishop Franjo Seper (Zagreb, Yugoslavia) (laity and clergy).
12. Bishop Mark Gregory McGrath (Auxiliary of Panama) (Church not a hierarchic pyramid, treatment of laity too negative).

13. Bishop Jacques Eugène Louis Ménager (Meaux, France) (text too negative, clerical, juridical).
14. Archbishop Ignace Ziadé (Maronite, Beirut, Lebanon) (role of Holy Spirit and charismata).
15. Bishop Alfonso Uribe Jaramillo (Auxiliary of Cartagena, Columbia) (priesthood of faithful).

October 23, 1963, Wednesday—54TH GENERAL CONGREGATION.
MASS: Archbishop Shehan of Baltimore, Maryland.
MODERATOR: Cardinal Lercaro.
PRESENT: 2,234 Fathers.
SUBJECT: Chapter III, on Laity.
SPEAKERS:

1. Cardinal Joseph Lefebvre (Archbishop of Bourges, France) (priesthood of clergy and laity cannot be separated).
2. Patriarch Paul II Cheikho (Chaldean Patriarch of Babylon) (universal priesthood not ripe for definition).
3. Bishop Manuel Larraín Errázuriz (Talca, Chile) (prophetic role of faithful).
4. Bishop John Farmer Healy (Gibraltar) (include treatment of human suffering).
5. Bishop Jão Przyklenk (Januária, Brazil) (definition of layman, dogmatic and non-dogmatic elements).
6. Bishop Biagio D'Agostino (Vallo di Lucania, Italy) (twofold mandate of laity from baptism and hierarchy).
7. Bishop Rafael González Moralejo (Auxiliary of Valencia, Spain) (text not in keeping with present needs).
8. Bishop Guillaume Marie van Zuylen (Liège, Belgium) (terminology too abstract).
9. Archbishop Lawrence Shehan (Baltimore, Maryland) (criticizes term "unfortunate" with regard to Church-state separation).
10. Bishop José Pedro da Silva (Auxiliary of Lisbon, Portugal) (better definition of apostolate of laity).
11. Bishop Josip Arnerič (Sibenik, Yugoslavia) (family, obedience to hierarchy).
12. Bishop Manuel Fernández-Conde (Córdoba, Spain) (concept of layman too negative).
13. Archbishop Ermenegildo Florit (Florence, Italy) (criticizes use of charisma).

14. Bishop Ernest J. Primeau (Manchester, New Hampshire) (statement on lay initiative, freedom, responsibility).
15. Bishop Alexandros Scandar (Assiut, Egypt) (education of laity).

October 24, 1963, Thursday—55TH GENERAL CONGREGATION.
MASS: Archbishop Bertoli, Nuncio in Paris.
MODERATOR: Cardinal Doepfner.
PRESENT: 2,236 Fathers.
SUBJECT: Chapter III, on Laity.
SPEAKERS:

1. Cardinal Giuseppe Siri (Archbishop of Genoa, Italy) (opposes chapter on People of God, subjection of laity to hierarchy, ambiguity of term priesthood of laity, reservations about charismata).
2. Father Aniceto Fernández, Master General of Dominicans (International Central Commission for organized charity).
3. Bishop Pedro Cantero Cuadrado (Huelva, Spain) (meaning of *sensus fidei, sensus Ecclesiae*).
4. Bishop Thomas William Muldoon (Auxiliary of Sydney, Australia) (text mixes theological and practical).
5. Bishop Robert E. Tracy (Baton Rouge, Louisiana) (section condemning racial discrimination needed).
6. Bishop Alfred Ancel (Auxiliary of Lyons, France) (clearer definition of apostolate, scriptural basis).
7. Bishop Georges Hakim (Melkite, Akka, Israel) (triumphalist tone, place of women).

October 25, 1963, Friday—56TH GENERAL CONGREGATION.
MASS: Bishop Gomes Junqueira of Nova Lisboa, Angola.
MODERATOR: Cardinal Suenens.
PRESENT: 2,192 Fathers.
SUBJECT: Chapter III, on Laity.

1. Bishop Pierre Boillon (Verdun, France) ("Church of the Poor").
2. Bishop Sergio Méndez Arceo (Cuernavaca, Mexico) (elimination of section on Church-state).
3. Archbishop Antoni Baraniak (Poznan, Poland) (rights of laity).

4. Bishop Frantisek Tomasek (Auxiliary of Olomuc, Czechoslovakia) (parents as teachers).
5. Bishop Michel Darmancier (Vicar Apostolic of Wallis Islands, Oceania) (kingly office of faithful).
6. Archbishop Raffaele Calabria (Benevento, Italy) (meaning of *sensus fidei*).
7. Bishop Fortunato da Veiga Coutinho (Coadjutor of Belgaum, Indonesia) (greater role for laity in apostolate).
8. Bishop Joseph Bartholomew Evangelisti (Meerut, India) (meaning of term People of God in East).

SUBJECT: Chapter IV, on Vocation to Sanctity.

SPEAKERS:

9. Cardinal Paul Richaud (Archbishop of Bordeaux, France) (penance and mortification need emphasis).
10. Cardinal Raul Silva Henriquez (Archbishop of Santiago de Chile) (eschatological significance of sanctity).
11. Bishop Guillaume Schoemaker (Purwokerto, Indonesia) (sanctity as gift of God).
12. Bishop Marcello González Martin (Astorga, Spain) (bishop as example of holiness).
13. Bishop Luigi Morstabilini (Veroli-Frosinone, Italy) (heroic sanctity).
14. Bishop André M. Charue (Namur, Belgium) (distinction between religious and those in world).
15. Archbishop Joseph Urtasun (Avignon, France) (treatment of sanctity after People of God).
16. Bishop Stjepan Bäurlein (Srijem, Yugoslavia) (secular priests are in state of perfection).

October 28, 1963, Monday
—Address of Cardinal Suenens commemorating fifth anniversary of election of Pope John XXIII, following low mass celebrated by Pope Paul VI, in St. Peter's basilica.

October 29, 1963, Tuesday—57TH GENERAL CONGREGATION.
MASS: Archbishop Slipyi of Lviv, in Ukrainian rite.
MODERATOR: Cardinal Agagianian.
PRESENT: 2,204 Fathers.
SUBJECT: Chapter IV, on Vocation to Sanctity.

SPEAKERS:

1. Cardinal Manuel Conçalves Cerejeira (Patriarch of Lisbon, Portugal) (virtues of laity).
2. Cardinal Jaime de Barros Câmara (Archbishop of Rio de Janeiro, Brazil) (mixture of theological and juridical).
3. Cardinal Thomas Norman Gilroy (Archbishop of Sydney, Australia) (holiness of bishops).
4. Cardinal Ernesto Ruffini (Archbishop of Palermo, Italy) (danger of terms: Mystery of Church, Church of Charity).
5. Cardinal Quiroga y Palacios (Archbishop of Santiago de Compostela, Spain) (too ethical, insufficient scriptural presentation).
6. Cardinal Julius Döpfner (Archbishop of Munich) (evangelical counsels, holiness as a gift).
7. Archbishop Antonio G. Vuccino (Tit., France) (insufficient scriptural presentation).

October 30, 1963, Wednesday—58TH GENERAL CONGREGATION.

MASS: Archbishop de Miranda Vilas-Bôas of Paraíba, Brazil.
MODERATOR: Cardinal Lercaro.
PRESENT: 2,157 Fathers.
SUBJECT: Chapter IV, on Vocation to Sanctity.
SPEAKERS:

1. Cardinal Paul-Emile Léger (Archbishop of Montreal, Canada) (holiness for all, secular clergy, laity).
2. Cardinal Giovanni Urbani (Patriarch of Venice, Italy) (treatment of communion of saints).
3. Cardinal Fernando Cento (Curia) (sanctity as note of Church).
4. Cardinal Augustin Bea (Curia) (text insufficiently biblical or realistic, careful use of word "perfection").
5. Bishop Gérard Huyghe (Arras, France) (evangelical counsels and religious vows).
6. Bishop René Fourrey (Belley, France) (no treatment of specific lay spirituality).
7. Archbishop William Conway (Armagh, Ireland) (no treatment of prayer).
8. Bishop John J. Russell (Richmond, Virginia) (participation in holiness of Christ).

9. Archbishop Angel Fernandes (Coadjutor of Delhi, India) (too much on holiness of religious).
10. Bishop Franjo Franič (Split, Yugoslavia) (evangelical poverty).
11. Bishop Sebastião Soares de Resende (Beira, Mozambique) (criticizes linking of "perfection" and religious life).
12. Bishop Dominique Hoang-van-Doan (Quinhon, Vietnam) (degrees of sanctity).
13. Abbot Benedikt Reetz, President of Beuron Benedictine Congregation (abandon term "states of perfection").

October 31, 1963, Thursday—59TH GENERAL CONGREGATION.
MASS: Archbishop van Lierde, Sacristan of His Holiness.
MODERATOR: Cardinal Doepfner.
PRESENT: 1,941 Fathers.
SUBJECT: Chapter IV, on Vocation to Sanctity.
SPEAKERS:

1. Cardinal Benjamin de Arriba y Castro (Archbishop of Tarragona, Spain) (modern world unsympathetic).
2. Bishop Isidor Markus Emanuel (Speyer, Germany) (canonize more laymen).
3. Bishop Juan Gonzalez Arbeláez (Tit., Columbia) (holiness of parish clergy).
4. Archbishop Joseph Martin (Rouen, France) (ecumenical aspects of religious life).
5. Archbishop Petrus Canisius van Lierde (Curia) (promotion of sanctity).
6. Bishop Karl Leiprecht (Rottenburg, Germany) (difference between religious and non-religious not one of dignity).
7. Bishop Michal Klepacz (Lódz, Poland) (lack of proportion).
8. Bishop Ildefonso M. Sansierra (Auxiliary of San Juan de Cuyo, Argentina) (scriptural quotations inadequate, section on poor and working classes).
9. Archbishop Joseph Parecattil (Ernakulam, India) (treatment of poverty and chastity inaccurate).
10. Bishop Andrea Sapelak (Apostolic Visitator for Ukrainians, Argentina) (no treatment of martyrdom).
11. Bishop Joaquim Lopes de Moura (Portalegre, Portugal) (more about love of God and of neighbor).

12. Bishop Simon Hoa Nguyen-van Hien (Dalat, Vietnam) (duties of parents).

13. Father Leo Volker, Superior General of White Fathers (no treatment of holiness of missionaries).

14. Archbishop Pacifico M. Luigi Perantoni (Lanciano, Italy) (inadequate treatment of religious state).

15. Abbot Jean Prou, President of French Benedictines (inadequate treatment of prayer, contemplative life).

16. Bishop Giocondó Grotti (Prelate Nullius of Acre and Purús, Brazil) (responsibility of bishops for apostate priests).

17. Archbishop Joseph Mark Gopu (Hyderabad, India) (eliminate expression "secular clergy").

18. Bishop Eduard Schick (Auxiliary of Fulda, Germany) (no real definition of sanctity in text).

19. Father Augustin Sepinski, Minister General of Friars Minor (reorganization of whole chapter).

20. Abbot Christopher Butler, President of English Benedictines (no treatment of theology of grace).

III

Crisis in the Council; the Debate on "Bishops"

✠

IT BECAME CLEAR at the midpoint of the second session that Vatican Council II was in crisis. Five weeks after convening and five weeks before adjourning, a kind of malaise had spread among the Council Fathers as the debates in St. Peter's droned on. "If things continue to go on like this," one American bishop was heard to say, "we might as well all pack up and go home." Cardinal Cushing returned to Boston not long after the session began and did not come back.* The single schema, *De Ecclesia* on the nature of the Church, had taken twenty-three days to debate—half the total debating days allotted for the Session—yet under the Council's proced-

---

* There were repeated notices in the press about the installation of a simultaneous translation service, which the cardinal had offered to pay for, but by the end of the session nothing was operational.

ure, a final document was nowhere in sight. The work of revision was far from done: the schema faced amendment in the Theological Commission, whose president was Cardinal Ottaviani; the amendments decided on by the Commission must be brought back to the Council and voted on, and there was plainly not time enough at the Session; then new suggestions resulting from the voting would have to be studied and, if acceptable, subsequently incorporated in the schema; finally the individual chapters of the schema would have to be brought back to the Council for final acceptance. As the debate on the liturgy schema last fall clearly indicated, the process of revision would take at least another year. At this pace, with sixteen schemata still on the Council's agenda, many prelates were saying that by the time the last document was approved, the Church would be ready for Vatican Council III and a new *aggiornamento*. Why, after the Council opened with such optimism and energy and goodwill, were things moving so slowly? The suspicion grew that the conservative minority was only waiting for the day when more and more bishops, restive and frustrated by the slow and tedious pace, would ask for permission to go home to their own dioceses, where so much important administrative and pastoral work awaited them. As the number of Council Fathers dropped, the authority of the Council as a whole would diminish and that of the Roman minority increase. According to Douglas Woodruff,* the responsibility for the slow pace must rest on what could be called the Salisbury school of thought at the Council:

It has been dawning on many Fathers, as October has passed, that there is a very strong body of trought, with Curial Cardinals at its head, which has been quietly satisfied at the very slow progress that is being made.

Of the Lord Salisbury, who was Queen Victoria's last Prime

* *The Tablet (London)*, Nov. 2, 1963.

Minister, it is related that some of his colleagues proposed to raise a new issue of public interest and concern, to which others objected, saying it would lead to a great deal of speech-making, public controversy and argument, and that at the end nothing would happen. "And is not that," said Lord Salisbury, "precisely what we want?"

This school of thought was not only content with the slow progress, but unfortunately it was—and is—in an excellent position to see that it remained slow.

An incident occurred about this time which, while not strictly concerned with the course of the Council, nevertheless serves to illustrate the way in which the minority was prepared to override papal wishes when it suited its purposes. It also lifts the veil, slightly, on the long-known alliance between this minority and the Italian political and economic right-wing. The incident concerns the pastoral letter which the Italian bishops issued, "from the Council," on the subject of the dangers of communism, dated November 1, 1963. Speculation had been rife in the Italian press for some time as to the nature of the expected document. Some commentators, in anticipation, hailed it as a blow against Pope John's alleged policy of "softness" toward communism which had resulted, so they claimed, in the surprising large number of votes polled by the Italian Communists in the last election in the spring. Others were fearful that it might upset the delicate balance between politics and religion in Italy established by Pope John and possibly also endanger the prospects for coming to some kind of an understanding with the communist regimes of Eastern Europe in the interests of ameliorating the condition of the Church there. Such a policy had already borne fruit in the release of Archbishop Slipyi from Soviet imprisonment earlier in the year, and the release of Archbishop Beran of Prague during the first few days of the Second Session, and there was continual speculaton that

something would soon be done about the fate of Cardinal
Mindszenty. When finally published, the pastoral letter turned
out to be much less sensational than the predictions and bore
obvious signs of having been "watered down." To offset this
disappointing impression, right-wing elements circulated the
story that the document had really been fathered by the Pope
himself, while Archbishop of Milan. Worried by communist
gains in the April elections, he had discussed with Cardinal
Siri, President of the Italian Episcopal Conference, the possibility of issuing some kind of condemnation, but publication was held up by the death of Pope John. Reflecting on
the matter after his own election as Pope, and influenced by
numerous visitors of course, Pope Paul was said to have
decided on a re-orientation of Vatican policy toward a closer
"surveillance" of Italian political life, away from the aloof-
ness of his predecessor, and to have commissioned Cardinal
Siri to consult with the Italian bishops about the preparation
of a suitable text announcing the new policy. According to
some versions, a draft was on the Pope's desk by October 17,
which he kept for a week and then handed back to Siri, with
suggestions for toning down the language, in particular sub-
stituting the term "atheistic communism" for the more general "atheistic Marxism," thus avoiding any undue ruffling
of feathers in the Socialist camp. The occasion for the publication was said to have been determined by the alarming
news—duly conveyed to the Pope—that fifty members of the
Christian Democratic party were prepared not only to kick
over the traces of the party position on an alliance with the
Socialists, but to go so far as to ally the Christian Democrats
with the Communists in a popular front. Rumors in connection with the imminent resignation of the Italian government tended to confirm speculation of this sort and made
it seem plausible.*

* *L'Europeo,* November 17, 1963, article by Renzo Trionfera.

That there was some kind of a disagreement between the Pope and those who had been behind the document emerged when Vatican Radio and the official Vatican newspaper *L'Osservatore Romano* came out with conflicting interpretations of the significance of the pastoral letter. The line of the former was that it amounted to a *dura condannazione* of communism without distinctions. The following day the newspaper appeared with a much more nuanced article, full of all kinds of mitigating phrases and tying it in with other papal pronouncements on social questions.* It appears that the Pope had intended to have both follow the same line but he had been beaten to the punch by the conservatives who appeared at the radio station first with their own interpretation.** That something went wrong appeared from the unusual vehemence of editorial comment in *L'Avvenire d'Italia,* a Bolognese paper, generally reflecting the personal views of Cardinal Lercaro, which castigated the conservative Rome daily *Il Tempo*—often the mouthpiece for the Holy Office line—for "specializing in the distortion of ecclesiastical documents and Vatican news" and alternating alarmist interpretations of conciliar decisions with sensational revelations about the imminent statement of the Italian bishops. Specifically with regard to the latter point, it was charged with having "raised a cry of victory in announcing the publication of the bishops' pastoral letter, claiming that it supported their own narrow and politically-motivated views." The *Il Tempo* technique was described by the Bolognese paper as "a clericalism of the laity ignoring the reality of the Church and its mission, putting on the same plane for use in the controversies of the hour, a speech by Lombardi [a communist leader of Nenni's Socialist Party], an intervention by a bishop

* *L'Osservatore Romano,* November 3, 1963.
** *Corriere della Sera,* November 3, 1963.

from Vietnam, Cardinal Mindszenty, a dip in the stock market, a pastoral letter of bishops and a party document."

The prospects for any rapid revision of *De Ecclesia* seemed dim. It was known that the Theological Commission in charge of the work might convene only when summoned by its president, Cardinal Ottaviani, and that he had seen fit to convene it only once a week. It also became known that the bishops' speeches on the Council floor, from which the Commission theoretically ought to be obtaining the amendments to the schema, were not being circulated to the Commission for twelve days at a time. Finally, as their sense of frustration and anxiety grew, many of the Fathers realized that Cardinal Ottaviani apparently did not regard the daily debates in St. Peter's as having any legislative force whatever. If the Council Fathers had merely an advisory, rather than a legislative, function and the Theological Commission was free to follow or disregard the Fathers' wishes as it saw fit, what guarantee was there that the true will of the Council was being expressed? As the crisis mounted, and the Fathers sought for a solution to the deadlock, they found that they faced a real dilemma. The Council had four bodies of authority, excluding the Pope, to which they could appeal—the four Moderators, the twelve-man Presidency, the ten-man Coordinating Commission and the six-man Secretariat. Which body took precedence? The rules of the Council did not make this clear.

Though no one outside the Council, and very few inside, were aware of it, the first stage of the crisis broke on October 15th. The man who brought it to a head was Cardinal Suenens, Primate of Belgium, who was the Moderator that day. He announced that it had been decided to seek a test vote to enable the Council to express its mind on four important points.* He did not spell them out, stating that

* See p. 102 for an earlier suggestion along this line.

papers outlining them would be distributed for study the
next day, but it was generally accepted that these points
would relate to collegiality—the relationship of the College
of Bishops with the Pope in the government of the Church
—and to the proposed restoration of the diaconate, or order
of deacons, to the ministry. There had already been many
keen exchanges on these topics among the Fathers in the
debate on *De Ecclesia.* Oddly enough, the official communiqué
for that day made no mention of this unusual announcement.
It was, however, noted at the press briefing that afternoon,
and it struck most observers as an eminently sensible way to
speed up the work of the Council and help the Theological
Commission in its work of rewriting the schema. Yet at the
Council meeting on the next day, the papers promised by
Cardinal Suenens were not distributed. Cardinal Agagianian,
who was the Moderator, explained that the four points would
not be handed out because the chapter of *De Ecclesia,* closed
for discussion the day before, had been reopened at the request of a group of Council Fathers. This delay gave rise
to the expression, "mystery points," in news stories, but
everyone assumed that the mystery would be cleared up in a
matter of days. The rest of that week was quiet. The Council
Fathers received complimentary sets of the first Vatican
stamps issued in Pope Paul's pontificate; the texts of the amendments to chapter four of the liturgy schema were distributed
on October 18th; four days later the amendments for chapter
five of this schema, and a monograph on the various forms
of the lay apostolate throughout the world, were handed out.
It was now seven days since Cardinal Suenens' announcement,
and the four points were as much of a mystery as ever. Many
of the Council Fathers began to suspect that the delay concealed a real crisis behind the scenes, and they were right.

On the evening of Wednesday, October 23rd, a summit
meeting of the Council authorities—Moderators, Presidents,

Coordinators and Secretariat—was held in the Vatican. The
Moderators had announced the proposed test-vote on the
four points on their own authority alone, and Cardinal
Suenens had made his announcement in St. Peter's without
consulting the other bodies. This move had been protested
by the Presidents as being *ultra vires,* beyond the powers of
the Moderators. And Secretary General Archbishop Felici
had threatened to resign if his authority was undermined,
as he thought it was by the Moderators' action. This was the
essence of the crisis. What took place at the summit meeting?
It later developed that there had been two votes, one after
the other. On the first vote, the results were 11 to 9 against
the right of the Moderators to propose a test-vote. Had this
result been allowed to stand, the Council might have broken
up in confusion. At the second vote, the results were again
11 to 9, but in favor of the Moderators. What happened was
that the wording of the propositions had been changed, eliminating the suggestion that a *married* diaconate be allowed,
which, it was claimed, would have scandalized such areas as
Italy, Spain and the United States, and dividing the third
proposition in two, making the *divine* origin of collegiality a
separate question. These two "sacrifices," it is said, were sufficient to bring about the shifting of two votes, in the Moderators' favor. Did the Pope have any part in this change? He
certainly arbitrated the matter, perhaps suggesting the changes
in question.* It was also decided at the summit meeting to
hold a vote on whether the separate schema on Mary should
be incorporated in *De Ecclesia* or not.

If the Council Fathers expected to find evidence of a crisis
at their meeting on Thursday, October 24th, they were disap-

---

* According to Abbé René Laurentin, in *Le Figaro*, November 11, 1963.
The *Time* account, Nov. 8, 1963, disclosed only half of the story, the Abbé
maintained, representing Cardinal Suenens as having suffered a defeat on
only one vote.

pointed. Instead, Cardinal Doepfner, the day's Moderator, announced that two cardinals would discuss the pros and cons of presenting the doctrine on the Blessed Virgin Mary as a separate schema, or as part of the schema on the Church. He then told the Fathers that a vote would be taken on this question the following week. The two viewpoints were then argued by Cardinal Santos of Manila and Cardinal Koenig of Vienna, and the texts of their speeches distributed to the Fathers the following day, Friday. Thursday night Romans were speculating wildly, as only Romans can, about the outcome of the summit meeting. Had there finally been a showdown? What had Pope Paul done, since he alone could now settle the matter? On Friday *L'Osservatore Romano* carried an item indicating that the Moderators had seen the Pope. It was also known that a number of bishops, and several delegations of bishops from particular countries, in their anxiety over developments, had gone to see the Pope to ask him to intervene. At this low point it was announced that on Monday, instead of a regular Council meeting, Pope Paul had arranged to say a special mass in memory of John XXIII, commemorating his election as Pope on October 28, 1958. Cardinal Suenens, it was stated, would give the address. On Sunday night, October 27th, in the papal palace, the Pope and Cardinal Suenens dined alone.

Meanwhile this weekend was the occasion for an extraordinary and intensive propaganda barrage on behalf of a separate schema on the Blessed Virgin Mary. This seemed to have no direct connection with the procedural deadlock in the Council, or the outcome of the summit meeting, but the desire for a separate schema on Our Lady was deeply identified with the Theological Commission and the Curial party, even though the issue at stake here was the manner of presentation, rather than the doctrine alone. Propaganda for the separate schema was so intensive as to startle many of the bishops. Leaflets were handed to them on the steps of St. Peter's, pamphlets arrived in their mail, and the Italian press joined in the campaign by printing absurd stories of "foreign" bishops wishing to tarnish the glories of Our Lady. Early in the session Secretary General Felici had uttered strong warnings against distributing pamphlets in the council hall. Yet Father Carlo Balič, a Yugoslav Franciscan, a consultor in the Holy Office, under Cardinal Ottaviani, did not hesitate to use the Vatican Press, which printed the official schemata of the Council, to run off a pamphlet soliciting the bishops' votes in favor of a separate schema on Our Lady. This pamphlet looked like an official conciliar document, with the same format and typography, though slightly smaller in dimension, and not only bore the Vatican Press imprint, but Father Balič went so far as to classify it "SUB SECRETO," like an official schema, before it was distributed in St. Peter's. This abuse of a position in the Curia by someone not a Council Father scandalized many of the bishops; they knew the action must have had the sanction of someone higher up. Father Balič's pamphlet was not only an impassioned plea for a separate schema on the Blessed Virgin, but it tried to make the bishops believe that the forthcoming vote was a matter of taking sides "for" Our Lady, or "against" her, rather than voting for a separate schema or for incorporation of the doctrine in another schema. Altogether, this Roman weekend of "secret" propaganda, campaigning, and Council uncertainty and crisis, was a strange and uneasy one.

On Monday morning, October 28th, St. Peter's was completely filled by 8:30 A.M. and the excitement in the basilica was very great. As Pope Paul walked in, small and slight and almost lost behind the halberds of his guards, the bishops stood up and applauded loudly. As the Pope said the introductory prayers before mass, he lost his place and looked embarrassed, and this very human occurrence invoked his audience's sympathy. As the journalist priest, Father Raymond Bosler, wrote in the *Catholic Reporter* of Kansas City:

He endeared himself to everyone present when he muffed the prayers at the foot of the altar. It was the sort of thing you would have expected from John, but not from Paul, the perfect diplomat always in complete control of himself. *He* was human, too. And every bishop and priest offering the mass with him was glad he had stumbled over the prayers, for it made the Holy Father seem closer.

After mass, Cardinal Suenens mounted the ambo, or pulpit, erected at the side of St. Peter's. He appeared calm, dignified, and very serious as he put on his glasses and took out his manuscript. He looked at Pope Paul on his throne on the papal altar, and then started his speech. He spoke in French, a significant departure from the expected Latin, and he made certain that all could follow him by having arranged for the distribution of advance texts in other languages. His address represented a supreme effort to revive the spirit of Pope John XXIII at the flagging Council. It was a moving talk in itself, but it was also full of overtones of the crisis now facing the Council Fathers, though this was never directly mentioned. Cardinal Suenens reminded his hearers that many of them had regarded Pope John, on his election, as a transitional pope. He had been transitional in only one sense, the Belgian cardinal said; he had opened a new era for the Church and laid the foundation for a transition from this century into the next. Though Pope John had died, he was still present in their midst in the person of Pope Paul, who was continuing John's work, said the cardinal, and who had been given to the Church "to endow the prophetic intuitions of his predecessor with form and substance." For those inclined to fear the spirit of freedom and renewal, he quoted Pope John's words: "We have no reason to be afraid. Fear comes only from a lack of faith." He recalled the Johannine spirit in

Paul VI's opening address to the second session: "On each line and between the lines, the same breath of the Pentecost was perceptible. We heard the same invitation to openness and dialogue, to doctrinal and pastoral charity, the same insistence on constructive, positive work, the same solicitude to translate the Gospel's eternal message into language modern men can understand." At the conclusion, there was a great round of applause. The Roman ear is attuned to nuance, and it got the message—the Cardinal was saying that Pope Paul's Council had begun, and in case anyone had any doubts, the Council was going to continue along the pastoral and ecumenical lines laid down by Pope John. As Cardinal Suenens left the pulpit, Pope Paul stood up. He was smiling broadly. Cardinal Suenens strode with long steps to the papal altar, kissed the Pope's ring, and then stood up to be embraced warmly by the slim figure in white. The scene was full of deep feeling and elicited another round of applause that echoed through the basilica. Pope Paul had made his position clear.

At the Council meeting the next morning (Tuesday, October 29th), the nature of the victory was revealed. Secretary General Felici announced that, "by order of their Eminences, the Cardinal Moderators," a paper containing five (rather than four) points would be distributed for study so that the Fathers could vote on them the following day. Archbishop Felici stressed the fact that the vote would serve to indicate the general mind of the Council on these points, to "assist" the Commission in its revision of the text. Despite the possibly qualifying implication of the Secretary General's last phrase, it was clear that the Moderators were no longer *ultra vires*. An extremely important test in the Council had been won. At this point ballots were distributed in order to settle another question, one that had inspired so much propaganda by the Curial party: should the doctrine on the Blessed Virgin Mary be treated in *De Ecclesia* or in a separate schema? A close vote was expected, but no one thought it would be as close as it turned out. Of the 2,193 votes to be cast, a 51% majority would decide the question, since it was a procedural matter. (There were 5 void votes, incidentally, because a few bishops forgot to mark their ballots with the special magnetic pen that made it possible to tabulate the votes quickly in the electronic computer.) When the Secretary General announced the results, there was a profound silence. The Fathers had voted 1,074 for a separate schema, and 1,114 for incorporating the doctrine in *De Ecclesia*. Only forty votes separated the two groups. It would be difficult to describe it as a victory for the progressives, since the issue was not a clear-cut one. But one thing was clear: even though they had made such a fuss, and used such extreme measures as faked Council documents, the Curial party had lost by a slim margin.

The following morning (October 30th) the Council voted on these fateful points (called *propositiones*):

1. Does it please the Fathers to have the schema declare that episcopal consecration is the highest degree of the sacrament of order?

2. Does it please the Fathers to have the schema declare that every bishop, legitimately consecrated in communion with the bishops and the Roman pontiff, who is their head and principle of unity, is a member of the episcopal body (*membrum esse corporis episcoporum*)?

3. Does it please the Fathers to have the schema declare that the body or college of bishops (*corpus seu collegium episcoporum*) succeeds the College of Apostles (*collegio Apostolorum*) in the task of preaching the gospel, sanctifying and shepherding the flock; and that it, together with its head the Roman pontiff and never without this head (whose right of primacy—*ius primatiale*—over all shepherds and faithful remains safe and entire) enjoys a plenary and supreme authority over the universal Church

(plena et suprema potestate in universam ecclesiam pollere)?

4. Does it please the Fathers to have the schema declare that the said authority belongs to the college of bishops *(collegio episcoporum)* united with its head by divine right *(iure divino)*?

5. Does it please the Fathers to have the schema declare that the opportuneness should be considered of restoring the diaconate as a distinct and permanent grade of the sacred ministry, according to the needs of the Church in the various areas?

Bishop John J. Wright of Pittsburg called the occasion a "turning-point" in the history of Vatican Council II, and indeed it was. The vote on the first four points was overwhelmingly in favor; that on the fifth point, favorable, with a somewhat reduced majority:

1.	Favorable—2,123	Unfavorable—34	Invalid—0
2.	Favorable—2,049	Unfavorable—104	Invalid—1
3.	Favorable—1,808	Unfavorable—336	Invalid—4
4.	Favorable—1,717	Unfavorable—408	Invalid—13
5.	Favorable—1,588	Unfavorable—525	Invalid—7

Was the crisis now over? By ordinary standards, there would have been no question about it. But Cardinal Ottaviani was no ordinary man. Losing a battle is not the same as losing a war, and there are some warriors who never admit that they are beaten. In warfare, this came be a most admirable quality, but the ecumenical Council was summoned to increase unity, not to do battle. Nevertheless the votes on the five points in no way guaranteed by themselves that the Council's wishes would necessarily be carried out by the Cardinal President of the Theological Commission. The "turning point" vote of October 30th was followed by a four-day holiday of the Council, beginning with the feast of All Saints on November 1st and ending with Italy's Armed Forces Day on November 4th. During this period Pope Paul

VI sent a letter to Archbishop Parente, directing that the Theological Commission resume more regular and frequent meetings. At the first such meeting, Cardinal Ottaviani was reported as having stated flatly that the Council's votes on the five points were merely "directive," and would not be considered binding on his Commission. It was now apparent that the Council was again headed for an impasse. This impression was strengthened by a report that the president of the Liturgical Commission, Cardinal Larraona of the Curia, at a meeting of his body had exclaimed, "Before God, I have not been putting obstacles in the way of this group's work!" To the Roman mind, this could be interpreted only as meaning that he had been chided by the Pope for having done just that.

In this unhappy atmosphere, the debate was begun on the second schema to be taken up at the Second Session, on Tuesday, November 5, 1963. The document was entitled "On Bishops and the Government of Dioceses," and it was bound to set off fireworks because its first chapter dealt with the explosive subject of relations between the bishops and the Roman Curia. The schema was not long, consisting of 25 pages of text with notes, and two Appendices, the whole not totalling over 38 pages. There were thirty-seven numbered paragraphs.*

---

* The schema was divided into the following chapters and paragraphs:
      1. Introduction.
CHAPTER   I—The relations between the bishops and the sacred congregations of the Roman Curia.
      2. Prooemium.
     I—Bishops' Faculties.
      3. Fundamental principle.
     II—The praxis of the sacred congregations with respect to the bishops.
      4. Fundamental principle.
      5. The coopting of bishops to advise the sacred congregations.
CHAPTER II—Coadjutor and Auxiliary Bishops.
      6. Prooemium.
      7. Definition of Coadjutor and Auxiliary.

In his introductory remarks, Cardinal Marella, president of the Commission which presented the schema, was immediately on the defensive, stating that due to excellent modern communications and the outstanding competence of members of the Curia, "it is a fact that the Roman Curia has accurate and precise knowledge of each diocese. The customs, usages, mentality and genius of each place is well appreciated here," he said. This claim was greeted with all but audible derision on the part of the great majority of the Council Fathers, whose dissatisfaction with the Curia was mainly due to its parochial and Italianized outlooked. To make matters worse, in his *relatio* on the way the schema had been prepared and description of its contents, Bishop Luigi Carli of Segni all but admitted, by disclosing dates and other information unwittingly, that the final text had been the work of but a few Curial officials in Rome who had not bothered to consult the other members of the commission. The details were disclosed by speakers in the course of the debate. Bishop Gargitter of Bressanone, Italy, charged: "The text as we now have it is certainly not the one drawn up by the Preparatory Commission. It expounds its doctrine under the one-sided light of insistence on the rights and the central organs of the Roman Curia. On the contrary, it should proceed under the light of basic theological principles dealing with the nature of the episcopal office, and should follow through with a practical explanation of the bishops' powers and duties."

Bishop Jean Rupp of Monaco supported this contention. After making an ironical reference to "this shining model of Roman brevity," he continued: "The original text drawn up by the Preparatory Commission was much more complete and better balanced, thanks to the work of Father Felix Cappello, S.J., now deceased. In the meantime the text has undergone several surgical operations. . . . The present text contains few new elements and even when it offers new solutions for problems it almost immediately indicates a loophole through which it will be possible to escape applying the principle indicated." Bishop Correa León of Colombia charged that fully one half of the members of the Preparatory Commission were not given an opportunity to express their minds on the text of the schema now submitted to the Council." And he said further "that the report read in the name of the Commission this morning was not drawn up in conformity with the procedural rules of the Council" and challenged the right of Bishop Carli to act as secretary and *relator* of the Commission. On Nov. 13 Bishop Carli answered this accusation, claiming that he had been voted in by a two-thirds majority on a secret ballot, causing one American bishop to remark that the vote was probably three to two with but five members out of x number present. Archbishop Leo Binz of St. Paul, a member of this Commission, later referred to the schema as an "unhappy proposal" with "no real introduction, no connecting link, and no conclusion." He explained that five chapters of the original schema had been deleted after it had been returned by the Coordinating Commission. He likewise spelled out Bishop Carli's cryptic remarks in his *relatio* by revealing "that a final version of the schema was completed in March 1963, but that only the bishops near Rome and the experts in Rome had been invited to review it." Archbishop Binz indicated that the main difficulty was that the schema avoided the subject of the collegiality of the bishops, stating that their relations with the Curia should be in effect strengthened, and that the internationalization of the Curia could be effected by naming bishops from various parts of the world as members and consultants of various curial congregations. It did grant however that the regional or national conferences of bishops were useful bodies for coordinating the apostolic work of the Church.

Cardinals Liénart of Lille, McIntyre of Los Angeles, Gracias of Bombay and Richaud of Bordeaux led off the debate on the acceptability of the schema as a whole as a basis for discussion. The first referred to Pope Paul's remarks

to the Roman Curia calling for representatives of the episcopate to assist the supreme head of the Church in his care
and responsibility for the government of the Church, and
said that now was the time to respond to the Pope's wishes.
This could be accomplished by inserting a new chapter in the
schema under discussion on "The relations between the Pope
and the College of Bishops." Cardinal McIntyre foresaw
trouble if episcopal conferences were provided with a firm
juridical basis, as the schema proposed. This could conflict
with the recent debate on the collegiality of bishops and by
interposing a new organ between the Pope and the bishops,
could "lead to a radical change in the structure of church
government so as to endanger her very unity." While finding
the text weak from certain points of view, the Cardinal of
Bombay thought that it could serve as a useful basis for
discussion. In particular he wanted a better definition of the
diocese and noted that papal representatives—nuncios and
delegates—would be better prepared to deal with the problems of the areas where they were sent, if they acquired a
better knowledge of the languages of the Orient and of the
customs and special traditions obtaining there. Cardinal
Richaud criticized the characterization of the faculties of
bishops as "concessions" of the Holy See and thought that the
schema would be given greater coherence and unity if it
were based on a clearer expression of episcopal collegiality
and the sacramentality of episcopal consecration. In any reorganization of the Curia along international lines, it was
important to include the heads of dioceses so that its work
would be better coordinated and directed more realistically
toward actual conditions. The schema needed complete rewriting. What was wanted, according to Bishop Gargitter,
was a spelling out in practice of dogmatic principles enunciated in the schema on the Church. There must be an
efficacious decentralization and internationalization of the

Curia. The privileged position of certain western nations should be done away with. Bishops could cooperate in assisting the Pope rule the Church in various ways: through commissions of bishops, or through a council of bishops called to Rome for the purpose by the Pope.

The extreme juridical tone of the schema was criticized by Bishop de Bazelaire of France, who said that there was no trace of the doctrinal lines on the episcopate laid down in the schema on the Church. In accordance with the principle of subsidiarity, there was no reason why bishops today could not freely exercise certain powers which the Holy See formerly reserved to itself. It was not correct to call these powers "concessions" of the Holy See. The schema appeared to fluctuate between two views. In the Introduction it spoke of bishops as true pastors with all the powers necessary for their office; but in paragraph 3 it spoke of granting faculties as a "concession."

Archbishops Garrone and Marty of France and Archbishop Baudoux of Canada were all three highly critical of the schema's omission of the basic notion of collegiality. According to the latter, "The approach used in the present text amounts to a downgrading of bishops because it speaks of a *granting* of faculties to them." He also suggested, as other speakers would later, that the traditional terminology which distinguished between titular and residential bishops was no longer applicable today and a new terminology should be found. Since episcopal consecration incorporated a bishop into the episcopal body or college and therefore conferred on him a share in the government of the Church, the traditional distinction was not logical. All bishops were true pastors and responsible for the whole Church.

The debate on Wednesday, still on the acceptability of the schema as a whole, was led off by Cardinal Ruffini who made a number of points. While critical of the text in detail, he thought that it could serve as a basis for discussion. Answering those who had regretted the lack of any reference to the idea of episcopal collegiality, he maintained that this idea had not been sufficiently developed by the debate on the Church. Cardinal Lercaro, he said, had given his assurance that the vote of the bishops on the five points would not prejudice any final conciliar decision. The vote had been merely indicational or directional, and was not definitive. Consequently it would be wrong to base any firm conclusions on it. The treatment of episcopal conferences in the schema was obscure, as Cardinal McIntyre pointed out. It was noted that the Cardinal of Palermo's remarks about collegiality and the vote on October 30th were a public statement of what Cardinal Ottaviani had been saying privately, within the confines of the Theological Commission. As such, they were accepted as a challenge by the majority, and the subject became a bone of contention between conservative minority and progressive majority throughout the remainder of the Session.

Cardinal Koenig of Vienna concurred in the judgment that before speaking of relations between the bishops and the Curia, the text should deal with "Bishops with and under the Roman Pontiff collaborating in the government of the universal Church" and that there should be an international college of bishops in Rome assisting the Pope. With regard to episcopal conferences, he mentioned the fruitful experiences of the American and German bishops with their respective conferences as an example of how such bodies could function effectively with merely moral, and not juridical, authority. The Cardinal of Utrecht brought out that a body of bishops functioning in Rome as advisers to the Pope would not be a representative parliament, but a *sign* of episcopal collegiality and an instrument by which the collegial will of the bishops could be made effective. It would serve the same purpose as the episcopal conference on a lower level. If such a body were authorized, he went on, the Curia would then become an executive instrument or branch of the legislative power of the bishops collaborating with the Pope.

The principle of subsidiarity was further stressed by Cardinal Bea. It was valid for the Church as well as for other societies. What could be done well enough on a lower level should not be preempted as a privilege or prerogative by a higher level. Special circumstances in the history of the Church had given rise to such intermediate bodies as the patriarchates and the Roman Curia. Nevertheless the rule still held that what bishops could do for themselves, they should be permitted to do without undue interference from on high, unless liberty of action needed to be curtailed for the common good. The establishment of some kind of episcopal body in Rome to help the Pope, according to norms laid down by him, would have an ecumenical importance in that it would lay to rest traditional accusations of a lust for power, ecclesiastical imperialism, curialism and over-centralization on the part of Rome. Such charges could only be answered by deeds, not words.

The next speaker, Cardinal Browne, Vice President of the Theological Commission, supported Cardinal Ruffini in rejecting the contention that it was a defect of the present schema that it did not take into account the notion of collegiality. "From yesterday's talks," he said, "I suspect that some Fathers think that the word *college* can be taken in a strictly juridical sense, but it seems to me that such a meaning can in no way be admitted." The whole idea needed to be "studied, weighed, and judged" by the Theological Commission, but he gave no indication when this arduous task would be completed. His words "We must await the report of the Theological Commission for a clarification of this basic point before we can take any concrete action" seemed to suggest that the Commission had no intention of moving unless it were prodded by higher authority.

Following this casting of doubt on the very basis of the present discussion as expressed in the debate on the Church, Archbishop Veuillot drew the logical conclusion that it would be useless to go on to discuss the details of the present schema and that this should be put off until *De Ecclesia* had been confirmed by the Council. The same thought was echoed by other speakers. Bishop Hodges, in the name of the bishops of the United States, accepted the schema as a basis for discussion, but maintained that it must be correlated with the teaching on the episcopate recently formulated as a result of the debate on the Church. In order to protect popular reverence for the authority of the Pope, Bishop Cooray of Ceylon suggested that further debate should be confined to written proposals given to a special commission which would be assigned the task of working out an agreed text that could be voted on in the usual way.

After a number of other speakers had been heard, the Moderator for the day, Cardinal Suenens proposed a standing vote on whether the schema was acceptable as a basis for further discussion. The result was 1,610 votes in favor of acceptance, 477 for rejection, with 13 invalid votes. The outcome somewhat surprised observers who had gained the impression from the critical tenor of the remarks that an outright rejection of the schema was possible. But this would have eliminated all debate on a number of important issues connected with the relations between the Pope, Curia and bishops, which the majority wanted to air more fully.

The doughty, eighty-five-year-old Maximos IV Saigh, the Melkite Patriarch of Antioch, then took the microphone as the morning's last speaker. Speaking in French, as usual, he said that whoever put this schema together seemed to think that the Church of God consisted of the Pope and the

Roman Curia. "This corresponds neither to the nature of the Church," he said, "nor to the needs of the times." He went on to say that the Pope is not only the Bishop of Rome and Patriarch of the West, but Supreme Pastor of the Universal Church, "and it is this final title that absorbs all his other functions." Hence the Pope cannot rule the Church merely with an administrative body, the Roman Curia, nor even with a College of Cardinals. The latter group, he said, are the succsesors of the parish priests of Rome and, merely in their office as cardinals, have nothing to do with the Universal Church as such. Instead, said the aged speaker, the Pope now needs a College of Bishops, in which the patriarchs, those cardinals who are bishops of large diocese around the world, and an elected group of bishops from all regions could serve. This College of Bishops, he concluded, "would assist the Pope, only at his request, in governing the Church and providing for its needs." As the Council Fathers poured out of St. Peter's, they told one another that the speech of Patriarch Maximos could not fail to have verbal repercussions.

Though the Council meeting on the following day, November 7th, was marked by the important intervention of Cardinal Ritter of St. Louis, speaking for a large number of American bishops, proposing that the chapter be redone in the spirit suggested by the majority of the Fathers, with the title changed to "The relations between the bishops and the Apostolic See," instead of the Roman Curia, and though the Armenian Patriarch, Ignace Pierre XVI Batanian, made a vigorous defense of the Curia in an obvious attempt to offset the impression made by the Melkite Patriarch, and though Archbishop Florit of Florence, in the name of fifty bishops, called for the establishment of a super-Congregation of Bishops in Rome that would outrank all existing congregations as a concrete expression of collegiality, while at the same time asserting that "Yesterday . . . some went too far"

in praise of the idea, the real fireworks did not occur until
the meeting on Friday, November 8th. It began with a mild
suggestion by Cardinal Câmara of Rio de Janiero that, in
accord with the needs of the Church and the expressed desires
of Pope Paul, some action be taken to set up a body, or
senate, of bishops in Rome. A speaker then rose who turned
this meeting of the Council into a historic one. He was the
cultured and drily witty Cardinal Frings of Cologne, a scriptural scholar and a graduate of the Pontifical Biblical Institute. Formerly a mountain-climber but now ailing at 76, the
Cardinal touched on the heart of the Council's problems.
"The vote of October 30," he said, "is perfectly clear, even
though indicative. I am astonished that Cardinal Browne,
vice president of the Theological Commission, has put this
vote in doubt. The Commission has no other function but to
execute the wishes of, and obey the directives of, the Council. Furthermore," he added, "we must not confuse administrative roles with legislative ones. This also goes for the
Holy Office, whose methods and behavior do not conform
at all to the modern era, and are a cause of scandal to the
world. No one should be judged and condemned without
having been heard, without knowing what he is accused of,
and without having the opportunity to amend what he can
reasonably be reproached with."

At this point many bishops, though applause is forbidden
during the Council debates, clapped loudly and long. He
then went on to say that too many prelates were employed in
Curial offices, and stated candidly that the episcopacy should
not be conferred on anyone as a reward for services. "It is
not necessary to be a bishop in order to serve in the Roman
Curia, nor even to be a priest," he went on. "Certain tasks
of these bureaus can be perfectly carried out by laymen. We
have talked a great deal about the laity at this Council; they
should be given the places for which they qualify. This re-

form of the Curia is necessary," he concluded. "Let us put it into effect." There was a sort of stupefied silence when he ended, then the Council Fathers again broke out into sustained applause. The two speakers who followed, Cardinal Lercaro of Bologna, a Council Moderator, and Cardinal Rugambwa of Tanganyika, both made an important proposal: that the Council send the Pope a petition that he could make into a separate constitution, creating the new body of bishops to be associated with him in serving the Church. The Cardinal Archbishop of Bologna spoke from the Moderators' table. He noted that the discussion of paragraph 4 and 5 as to the feasibility of establishing some kind of an episcopal body to advise the Pope had so far been too dogmatic in tone, whereas what was needed were arguments or suggestions regarding the opportunities or practical means for establishing organisms capable of fulfilling this role. Certain principles must remain inviolate: "a) the Roman Pontiff enjoys by divine right a supreme jurisdiction over the whole Church; b) also by divine right the supreme pontiff may exercise such jurisdiction without any juridical dependence on the bishops; c) to help him in the government of the Church, the Pope may make use of the instruments which he considers the most opportune; d) the episcopal body also has power, together with and under the Pope, to teach and govern; e) nothing prevents the Pope from using the episcopal body or any organ consisting of his representatives to study the most important problems faced by the Church, however the final judgment always remains that of the Pope. In fact the Holy Father is free to follow one method or another of judging the opportuneness of creating new organs to advise him and help him coordinate and decide with regard to the most important matters affecting the Church. This is the role which consistories performed in the Church until the sixteenth century." The Cardinal then concluded with these measured words: "However this participation in the government of the Church cannot be effected either by delegating certain bishops representing episcopal conferences, nor by creating a new congregation that will interpose itself between the Pope and the existing dicasteries. The problem transcends not only the schema under discussion, but the Council itself, the moment that it touches on the rights of the Pope. The expression of a desire is one thing, a decree is something else; therefore the whole question should be stricken from the schema and elaborated later in the form of a *votum* (petition) to be presented to the Pope for the renewal of the Curia or for the participation of the bishops in the government of the Church."

Cardinal Rugambwa delivered an equally measured, impressive appeal. But all eyes were on Cardinal Ottaviani, who was to be the next speaker. When he rose, a tremendous hush settled on the gathering.

In a voice shaking with rage and emotion, he said, "I most profoundly protest against the accusations made against the Congregation of the Holy Office. Without any doubt, it is due to lack of knowledge (*nescientia*). I use this word advisedly, so as not to use another which would not be charitable. One commits a great mistake in not realizing that the Holy Office is always assured of the help of the most eminent and the most solid men." He pronounced the next words slowly and emphatically. "In attacking the Holy Office, one attacks the Pope himself, because he is its Prefect." As this point, applause was heard from the Italian and Curial group, so carried away that they forgot it was forbidden. "There is much talk," Cardinal Ottaviani went on, "of the divine right of collegiality, as if it had been defined. However, nothing of the sort has been done, and it is the Theological Commission alone that can define it. I respect the Moderators, but why did they not ask the Theological Commission to prepare the points put to vote on October 30th? It is the Commission, and it alone, that is competent here, and not the Moderators." He then stated that the best theologians had told him no basis could be found in holy scripture for collegiality. "I am astonished that the Fathers can speak of collegiality in the juridical sense of the term. When Christ said to Peter: 'Feed my sheep,' He included the other Apostles in this group."

Ottaviani was followed by Cardinal Browne. The Dominican cardinal pointed out that the higher officials and consultors of the Roman Congregations are not appointed by the Holy See but are chosen freely and personally by the Pope himself. If collegiality were to confer on the bishops the right to participate in the government of the Church, the Pope would be obliged to recognize and respect this right and as a consequence would no longer enjoy a true primacy over the whole Church. These propositions seemed to imply a "co-government" of the Church. As formulated, they seemed to be in conflict with the constitution *Pastor aeternus* of Vatican I on the papal primacy and infallibility. If adopted they would mean that it would no longer be Peter who was guiding and feeding the sheep, but the sheep Peter—*sed oves Petrum*. If the collegiality of the bishops should be given a purely juridical interpretation, the authority of the Pope would no longer be plenary and supreme. "*Venerabiles Patres, caveamus*—Venerable Fathers, let us be on guard."

These words, too, brought forth applause, emphasizing the division of the council over this matter. The majority interpreted them, rightly, as a virtual throwing down of the gauntlet to the idea of *aggiornamento* and to the Pope probably viewing the scene on his closed TV circuit.

Later in the morning, while on the subject of Chapter II of the schema, Cardinal Ruffini took the occasion to attack what Patriarch Maximos IV Saigh had said earlier in the

week about an episcopal "Senate" and in criticism of the
Roman Curia. Speaking with hardly concealed anger, he
said, "I have heard in this gathering a severe and offensive
speech against the Roman Curia. I say it is unacceptable!
Reparation has happily been made by the Patriarch Batanian,
my dear friend and colleague. I publicly thank him in the
name of Cardinal Siri, president of the episcopal conference
of Italian bishops." This last remark seemed to imply that
the Roman Curia really was an exclusively Italian affair. In
this tense and overwrought atmosphere, the brilliant intervention of Archbishop Eugene D'Souza, of India, brought a
much needed return to calmness and to issues rather than
personalities.

"I hear," he said, "that the thinking of the Council on
collegiality is not clear, and that our vote of October 30th
can be considered as invalid and illegitimate. It is mockery
to speak thus, when 80% of the Fathers have replied in a
perfectly clear manner to a series of questions that were no
less clear. Further, their answer is in total conformity with
the address of Pope Paul VI to the Roman Curia itself. I beg
you not to reduce this question of collegiality to nothing but
its juridical aspect, for the pastoral care of souls, our *raison
d'être*, depends on this collegiality." He then went on to say
that the schema they were debating was not pastoral enough,
and did not correspond to the intentions of this Pope or his
predecessor. "It proposes that the bishops be given a few
more memberships in the Curial congregations. Is this why
2,200 Council Fathers have been summoned here?" he asked.
"The bishops have already resisted the many pressures that
have been put upon them. How much more pressure will
there be, when they have been scattered to their dioceses?"
He then made an important distinction between the Curia
and the Council. "The Roman Curia," he said, "does its job
in a context quite different from an ecumenical Council. Yet,

in every field, today's context is totally different from yesterday's. The administrative problems of today cannot be resolved by the Curia in the same way as in the past." After recalling the scriptural verse, "the letter killeth," Archbishop D'Souza concluded: "Suspicion has been cast on certain authors without saying why, without specifying what part of their writing is to be praised, and what part requires correction. The more we love the Pope, the more we believe in his primacy. Why, then, this outcry, as if the Church were in peril?"

That afternoon it was reported that Pope Paul VI phoned Cardinal Frings, to express his approval of what he had said on the Council floor. (Among other things, the Cardinal had said that "the Holy Office is a cause for scandal in the world.") On the same afternoon, the Pope also agreed to see Cardinals Ottaviani, Antoniutti and Siri.* If the Secretary of the Holy Office came to seek the Pope's support, he did not receive it. Cardinal Ottaviani was said to have been so upset by this rebuff that he considered whether he ought not to resign. (This reminded Romans of his similar encounter with Pope John XXIII during the First Session on November 18, 1962, during the debate on the schema, "On the Sources of Revelation," prepared by his Theological Commission. These debates revealed that Cardinal Ottaviani and his followers, on this subject too, were out of step with the thinking of most of the Council Fathers. That day Ottaviani called on Pope John and complained about the dissension. "Dissension?" Pope John is said to have replied. "Don't you recall that at Trent the dissension became so heated that an Italian bishop tore the beard of a Greek bishop? Nevertheless, the Council of Trent is remembered today as one of the great events in the history of the Church." Ottaviani then said, "If this dissension goes on much longer, the dignity of the Holy

* *Le Monde*, November 14, 1963.

Office will be in danger, and I may resign." Pope John calmly replied, "You will stay. There will be no resignations.") One year later, in more heated circumstances, Cardinal Ottaviani was again talking of resigning.* It is reported that Pope Paul was particularly displeased because Cardinal Ottaviani did not confine himself to a defense of the Holy Office, but attacked the person of Cardinal Frings in a regrettable manner by implying ignorance and bad faith. It was also reported that the Patriarch Maximos IV Saigh had received apologies from Cardinal Ruffini, for the latter's attack on his person in his speech on the Council floor on this memorable day of November 8th.**

The day was not quite over, however, for a preview showing of Otto Preminger's new film, *The Cardinal*, was scheduled in the evening. The showing had been arranged under the auspices of the Holy Office itself, in that congregation's palace to the left of St. Peter's basilica. Cardinal Ottaviani naturally presided as host on his own grounds. Word of the fireworks in St. Peter's only a few hours earlier had already spread all over Rome, and photographers and journalists were everywhere. When the Cardinal arrived in person, there was a great flurry of flashbulbs. The film version of Henry Morton Robinson's novel, and the strange occasion of this screening, received a truly Gallic review by Henri Fesquet, who reported on them in *Le Monde*, "From a puerile but readable enough novel, the U.S.A. has made a film that is not only stupid but in dubious taste. Nothing is lacking, not even an

---

* *Il Tempo* (November 15, 1963), published a denial by Cardinal Ottaviani's office that he had been received in audience, had ever thought of resigning, or that his language had been offensive to Cardinal Frings.
** *La Croix* (November 16, 1963) explained that confusion over the audiences was compounded by an error of *L'Osservatore Romano*, which reported Cardinal Frings as having been received on Friday whereas he had been received on Thursday along with the German and Austrian bishops. But not all audiences are announced! Cardinal Siri was seen leaving the Pope's office on Saturday morning, but his name was not on the official list.

amourette between the ecclesiastical hero and a young girl with tender eyes. The Council Fathers gave this film the reception it deserved, but many were astonished that their leisure time had been put to such bad use. At the first session of the Council in the fall of 1962, things had been arranged better by a showing of Bresson's film, *The Trial of Jeanne d'Arc*. It is true that this year, under the circumstances, the showing of such a film at the Holy Office would have had the appearance of a provocation. But between the authentic history of the most famous victim of the Inquisition, and the insipid story of a film that is religious in name only, it should have been possible to find some less questionable distraction for the Council Fathers."

The tension caused by the Frings-Ottaviani exchange on Friday continued to the end of the Session. The question uppermost in men's minds was whether the Holy Father would take cognizance of what was apparently a challenge thrown down by the Cardinal of the Holy Office. It was known that the Council Moderators had two long audiences with the Pope on Saturday and Sunday, November 9th and 10th. Important decisions, including what to do about the present impasse were discussed, but only part of the veil was lifted when later it became evident what steps the Theological Commission was to take Monday and Tuesday. Meanwhile, considerable uncertainty prevailed and questions were raised as to why the Pope did not act. The Holy Father however did begin to take off his gloves, in a characteristically velvet-gloved fashion so that most missed the point. In a moving ceremony on Sunday, November 10, 1963, Pope Paul took formal possession of the Lateran basilica, Rome's cathedral, having delayed his ceremonial entrance for five months, in order to emphasize the continuity with the Church of earlier centuries when a new pontiff performed the rite surrounded by as many bishops as could be gathered to-

gether. Hence in the course of his discourse Paul stated:
"Today this basilica, as never before . . . holds almost the
entire episcopate of the world present here to receive
splendidly and solemnly the latest of her pontiffs, the lowliest
and most humble in the line of Popes. He has no right to
enter as lord and master, other than the irrefutable right of
having been canonically elected Bishop of Rome." *Il Tempo,*
the conservative Rome daily, in one of its habitually slanted
interpretations, ignored the first part of the Pope's remarks
and quoted him as having referred to himself as the "Supreme
Pontiff and Master and Lord of the Universal Church"—
words which he had not uttered at all. In fact, the Pope's
speech was the very opposite in tone from a lordly assertion
of extreme papalism. It certainly was not an overt defense
of Cardinal Ottaviani on Friday, as the paper claimed. There
was nothing in it either suggesting that Paul was now emulat-
ing "Pope Martin V" in the fifteenth century as another
"dominator" of Councils. On the contrary, the Pope's speech
contained a veiled but definite warning to the Roman people
to mend their ways and receive the reforming work of the
Council—a theme which *Il Tempo* preferred to pass over in
silence.*

Shortly before this, on Thursday Nov. 7th, the Vatican
newspaper announced that the Pope had received in special
audience the Archbishop of Freiburg in Germany, the editor of the German Catholic publishing house of Herder
Verlag, and one of the latter's principal authors, the famous
German theologian Father Karl Rahner, S.J., who had been
accused by Cardinal Ottaviani some weeks before in a speech
on the floor of having solicited bishops on behalf of a married diaconate.** In the course of the audience Pope Paul
expressed his deep "appreciation" to Father Rahner for his

* *Il Tempo,* November 11, 1963.
** See p. 114.

profound theological knowledge and works, which, along
with those of the French Dominican Father Yves Congar, had
had such an influence on shaping the course of the Council.
Congar was later to be awarded a "Masterate of Theology"
with the full approval of the Pope. The "rehabilitation" of
both men—who had suffered for years at the hands of the
Holy Office because of their supposedly "dangerous" ideas—
was Paul's way of replying to the campaign of fear and suspicion which the Holy Office was still waging on all fronts.
(An eloquent article by Abbé René Laurentin in *Le Figaro* on
December 9, 1963, entitled simply "The Price of Vatican
Council II," listed the vexations, bannings and even banish-
ments of which Père Congar had been the victim over the
years, from 1935 until the present time. He is now fortunately back teaching and carrying on his studies at Le
Saulchoir.)

The "lull after the storm" wrote Henri Fesquet of the
resumption of the debate on "Bishops," on Monday November 11th. This was only partly true. On the side-lines, all
during the week, there was considerable anxious speculation
about the problem of religions liberty, for it was known that
a statement drawn up by Cardinal Bea's Secretariat for Unity
had been submitted to the Theological Commission last
June. It was to form Chapter V of the schema on Ecumenism,
the next topic to be taken up by the Council, but so far no
action had been taken. The Theological Commission had
prevented it thus far from being printed, and rumor had it
that Cardinal Ottaviani had even refused to discuss the draft.
When pressure began to build up in favor of getting it
printed, Ottaviani was reported to have failed in a bid to the
Pope to get the measure tabled.* Instead he was told to have
his commission meet, discuss the statement, and bring it to

* *The New York Times,* November 12, 1963.

a vote. Credit for this decision can be given to Cardinal Spellman who is known to have presented a petition to the Holy Father, signed by the majority of American bishops, urgently requesting that the document on religious liberty be taken up at the second session. The distribution to the Fathers on Friday November 8th of the text of Chapter IV of the schema on Ecumenism, on the Jews, naturally increased the pressure for a prompt consideration of Chapter V. The atmosphere was tense with expectancy.

Monday and Tuesday, November 11th and 12th, were some kind of a landmark in the history of the Council, for it was then that Cardinal Ottaviani suffered defeat on his own territory. At a meeting of the Theological Commission on Monday, called by the cardinal to consider whether Chapter V on Religious Liberty should be "reported out," Bishop Charue asked Father John Courtney Murray, S.J., an expert on church-state relations, Council *peritus* and consultor of the Commission—fortunately present at this session, through the efforts of Cardinal Spellman, after having been "disinvited" to the first session—to speak on the subject. As the Jesuit weekly *America* (November 30, 1963) described the scene: "The President of the Commission, Cardinal Ottaviani, is almost blind. He did not recognize or distinguish the tall figure of Father Murray when he spoke . . . before the Commission's members and consultants. Cardinal Ottaviani, one hears, leaned over to his neighbor, Cardinal Léger, to ask who was speaking. The Canadian cardinal, perhaps to spare Father Murray any unwelcome publicity at that point, replied simply: *'peritus quidam'* (One of the experts)." On Tuesday the Commission proceeded to a vote. Previously a subcommittee of the Commission headed by Cardinal Léger, to which the chapter had been turned over for examination, had, by a vote of 3 to 2, approved the text in principle but recommended its release to the floor unani-

mously.* Cardinal Ottaviani tried to delay the fateful vote
on Tuesday by making a great many long-winded explanations and offering a number of wild suggestions, all of which
were voted down by the impatient commission members.
Finally the members shouted: "Bring the measure to a vote!"
When the vote was counted it turned out to be 18 to 5 in
favor of reporting the text to the floor, with 1 invalid vote.**
The five opposing votes were apparently those of Cardinal
Ottaviani, Cardinal Browne, Cardinal Santos, Archbishop
Parente and Archbishop Florit, who constituted the small
ultra-conservative coterie which had repeatedly held up or
frustrated the work of a more progressive majority. The
document went at once to the printer and was in the hands
of the Fathers when they began discussion of the schema on
Ecumenism the following week.

Pursuing the debate on Monday, Cardinal Spellman came
out with a rather ambiguous statement on collegiality and
the Curia. He declared that there was much misinformation in
the press on both these topics. "The theology we all learned
in the seminary teaches us that the Pope alone has full power
over the entire Church. He does not need the help of others.
As far as the Roman Curia is concerned it is only an executive organ of the Holy Father. Consequently it is not up to
us to try to reform or correct it. We can only offer suggestions and recommendations." He concluded with this warning: "Let us be careful about proposing anything that may
be at variance with the decrees of previous councils or papal
pronouncements."

Cardinal Confalonieri, Secretary of the Congregation of
the Consistory, tried to calm the ruffled waters by posing as
a conciliator and observing that the Curia was not all bad.
In ten years as bishop of Aquila he had had ample experi-

* *Il Quotidiano*, November 13, 1963.
** *Le Monde*, November 14, 1963.

ence of the difficulties bishops encountered in their dealings with the Curia but criticism must be tempered with praise. Reform of the Curia was necessary but the initiative must come from the Pope, acting courageously—*"viriliter."* "Let us address our humble requests to him."

This is precisely what the Fathers did. For some days it had been rumored that Cardinal Silva Henriquez of Santiago de Chile would speak on the need for an episcopal senate to advise the Pope and would make concrete proposals in response to the wish expressed by the Pope himself in his opening talk to the Council on Sept. 29. But the cardinal never spoke. Instead, it is reliably reported that he submitted to the Moderators on Wednesday Nov. 13 a document signed by over 500 hundred Latin American, Canadian, African and Indian and other bishops, respectfully requesting the Pope to indicate his pleasure about the matter of episcopal advisers. "The Fathers of the Council request that the Supreme Pontiff determine the principles and methods of the aid which the Roman Pontiff himself indicated might be added to himself in the way of greater cooperation of the bishops of the entire world. . . . Just as the Supreme Pastor should according to the command of the Lord confirm his brethren, so by the same token his brethren should know that it behooves them to give to the Supreme Pontiff serious and efficacious support . . ." The document cited the Pope's own words about the reform of the Curia on Sept. 21, particularly the need for a greater decentralization, and expressed the willingness of the bishops to aid in this task in whatever way seemed appropriate. Once in the hands of the Moderators however—the fact was never officially announced—this was the last the Council would hear of the petition. The perplexity of not a few of the bishops was only slightly relieved by the Pope's vague reference, in his closing talk, to the problem of greater episcopal cooperation in the government of the unversal Church.*

Following Cardinal Confalonieri on Monday, Cardinal Doepfner, one of the Council Moderators speaking on the theme under discussion, the subject of auxiliary and coad-jutor bishops, kept alive the tension by replying to Cardinal Ottaviani's contention on Friday that the famous vote of October 30 on the five points of the Moderators had been merely indicative and was not binding. Said he, obviously speaking for the other Moderators: "Certain interventions in the last few days have implied that an enemy—*inimicus homo*—has sown cockle in the field while the father of the family was sleeping. But this vote was decided on by the Moderators, who are in charge of directing the course of the Council according to the rules. After reflecting on the matter for fifteen days, they proposed certain questions based on the language and significance of the schema itself. One cannot therefore say that the Moderators have acted furtively —*furtim*—in introducing the word "college" into the questions. This word is found in several places in the text of the schema approved by the Theological Commission and presented by it to the Council. This vote was taken to help clarify the matter for the Fathers. It is purely indicative, to be sure, but what has been indicated is also perfectly clear and cannot lightly be ignored."

Regarding one of the more practical matters under debate, namely whether bishops should retire at a certain age, Archbishop Mingo of Monreale, Sicily, now sixty-two himself, said that it was a *"Dura lex sed necessaria"*—a harsh but necessary law—that bishops should retire at the age of sixty-five, as the schema recommended. On the other hand, Bishop De Vito of Lucknow, India, felt that this requirement was

* *The New York Times,* Nov. 16, 1963; *Il Tempo,* Nov. 17, 1963.

completely unacceptable: "It would be just as outrageous as attempting to change the course of the moon."

Bishop Caillot, the coadjutor bishop of Evreux, France, insisted that the practice of naming auxiliary bishops as titular bishops ought to cease. "This custom causes amazement. No one, except the Benedictines, knows where these titular sees are. They are usually nothing but ruins." Coadjutors and auxiliaries should have the title of the see where they are assigned. All auxiliaries should share the episcopal ministry together. Bishops who resigned should become *emeriti* of the see they formerly occupied.

Three American cardinals spoke on Tuesday Nov. 12 on the touchy subject of episcopal conferences. The issue under discussion was whether such bodies in future should be able to make decisions juridically binding on the members or merely moral or hortatory decisions. Debate on this theme revealed a rather sharp division between the Fathers. Father Gustave Weigel, S.J., summed up the basic difference when he said at a press conference: The Continental mind holds that you do not have any kind of an agreement unless it is written down and spelled out in law. The Anglo-Saxon mind on the other hand believes that the less law there is the better. As much as possible should be left to the moral sphere.

The three American cardinals curiously represented three tendencies among the Fathers. Cardinal McIntyre of Los Angeles—who opinions were seconded the following day by Cardinal Spellman—was definitely not in favor of juridically binding decisions and not enthusiastic about episcopal conferences at all. He said: "Episcopal conferences can be accepted if they are on a voluntary basis but are to be deplored if they assume a strictly juridical character. The authority given to such a body always tends to take on greater expansion. . . . Wanting to give a national conference juridical character could be interpreted as an attack on the Roman Curia and

thus as an indirect attack on the infallibility of the Pope."
This view was extreme. Few thought that such conferences
harbored any threat to papal infallibility. When asked later
why the cardinal had seen a danger to infallibility in episcopal conferences, Father Weigel delivered himself of one of
his famous bon mots: "We must remember that Cardinal
McIntyre probably sees much farther than most of us do, if
he can be said to see at all."

A more moderate position was represented by Cardinal
Meyer of Chicago, who said that rather than run the risk of
restricting the freedom of action of the individual bishop,
binding force should be accorded only to decisions taken by
episcopal conferences concerning matters referred to them
by the Holy See. He remarked also that the presidents of
such conferences should be elected by secret ballot. This
view probably represented that of the majority in the
Council.

A third position was voiced by Cardinal Ritter of St. Louis,
who came out in favor of juridically binding decisions as
proposed in the draft text. The Bishop of Lódz, Poland,
Msgr. Klepacz, made an interesting suggestion that the president of episcopal conferences should be in charge of relations
between church and state in given countries, and not papal
nuncios or apostolic delegates. Of more significance was the
important intervention by Cardinal Suenens, one of the
Moderators, on the need for legislation about enforced retirement for bishops. "To expect bishops to agree to resign
voluntarily," he said, "is like brandishing a sword in the
water." "Old age creates a hiatus between the bishops and the
modern world. One has only to look around at sees governed
by aged prelates." Sixty-five was a reasonable age for retirement from every point of view.

In spite of the strong, authoritative statement of Cardinal
Doepfner on Monday, Bishop Carli of Segni, the gadfly of

the ultra-conservatives, had the presumption to say on the
floor on Wednesday: "The votes of October 30 are of doubtful validity since they were taken without a previous official
'report' on both sides of the question and contrary to Article
30 No. 2 of the Rules in that the Fathers were not given
enough time for deliberation."

Speaking at the American bishops' press panel on Wednesday after his speech on the floor in the morning, on the subject of auxiliary bishops, the chubby-faced, youthful-looking
Auxiliary Bishop of Philadelphia, Gerald McDevitt, displayed a delightful sense of humor when explaining his plea
that auxiliaries should be regarded a full-fledged bishops and
not be hedged about, as they were at present, by all kinds of
restrictions. Said he: "When I was made a bishop I was given
a three page description of my titular see somewhere in the
south of Tunisia. After reading it I lost any desire ever to
visit it. I understand that there is nothing there but a couple
of goats and palm trees." Apropos of the subject of enforced
retirement for bishops, he remarked that he had done his
doctoral in canon law on resignation from ecclesiastical office.
Every year he noted that his thesis was still among those
listed for sale by Catholic University. When asked how he had
dared to speak out on the subject of auxiliaries, being one
himself, he replied: "I understand that my salary has already
been cut."

In a press interview on Wednesday granted to the Divine
Word news service, Cardinal Ottaviani showed that he was
conceding nothing, publicly at least, and reiterated everything he had said on the council floor the preceding week,
supporting what Bishop Carli had said in the morning of
the same day. He came out explicitly against "any episcopal
consulative body to advise the Pope" as an infringement of
the "universal and immediate supreme authority of the Pope."
All the sheep of Christ must agree to "follow the directions

of the pastor appointed by Him. There must not be any exception to this rule, not even for bishops," he said, rejecting the idea of any meaningful collegiality of the bishops. He repeated that the five propositions of the Moderators voted on by the Council on October 30 were merely an indication of the "thought of the Council Fathers" and that they "had not been formulated as a result of any discussion, but were proposed by the Moderators without being submitted to the Theological Commission which was competent in the matter, since they treated of matters touching the dogmatic sphere." His Commission, Ottaviani said, would have "rendered the language more precise, eliminating certain equivocal and ambivalent expressions, contained especially in the third proposition on the college of bishops, which governs with the Pope." He did not elaborate, but the Moderators had already pointed out that the five propositions were suggested by the language of the schema on the Church which the Theological Commission itself had presented to the assembly. Ottaviani concluded with the usual statement that "we must have confidence in the Holy Father who will put into practice all the prudent measures capable of aiding him in the government of the Church" while at the same time openly opposing the will of the Pope as expressed by the Moderators who were directing the Council according to his wishes.

The following day the Archbishop of Utrecht, Cardinal Alfrink, replied to Carli and Ottaviani, by observing that what the Council Fathers wanted was not a juridical definition of "collegiality" but only a declaration of Catholic teaching on the universal authority of all bishops together with the Pope, in accordance with the words of the official report of the Theological Commission long in the hands of bishops, that "the bishops gathered with the Pope in Council or dispersed through the world (but in communion with him)

enjoy supreme authority in the Church." The Moderators
were urged to see to it that this doctrine was made clear in
some kind of a statement.

The debate on Bishops and Dioceses came to an end on
Thursday and Friday amid undertones of contrasting opinions about the relative size of bishoprics and overtones of the
still raging controversy between Cardinal Ottaviani and the
progressive majority. Bishop Sorrentino of Bova, Italy, urged
that the numerous small Italian dioceses, the boundaries of
which had not been changed for over a thousand years, should
be consolidated in the interests of greater efficiency. The
Lateran Treaty with Italy (1929) had envisaged a redrawing
of boundaries, but nothing had been done because of local
pride and resistance to change. Bishop Massimiliani of Civiltà
Castellana, Italy, on the other hand, put in a strong plea for
the small diocese, nothing that "because there were many
bishops in Italy, Protestantism could not get a foothold." He
might have added that excessive fragmentation was partly
responsible for the present indifferentism and anticlericalism.
The Archbishop of Astorga in Spain, Monsignor González,
brought up the interesting subject of the need for a greater
distribution of ecclesiastical wealth. Some parishes were rich
while others, in the same diocese, were disgracefully poor and
the contrast was very disedifying. More attention should be
paid to "the social function of property." Before the close
of the debate on the schema, Msgr. Zoghby, Melkite Patriarchal Vicar for Egypt, stressed the importance of synodal
government in the Oriental Churches, relating this to the
proposal for more episcopal conferences in the West. He
said that it was hopeless to attempt any appeal to the separated Orthodox Churches unless respect were shown for this
basic principle of church government. The trouble was that
all real power had been taken away from the Oriental synods
by the Roman Congregation for the Oriental Churches and

that this must be restored. Moreover there was too much fear of nationalism as a bad thing. Some nationalism was good and helpful. The rise of numerous nations in recent years "has proved that national sentiments do not prevent peoples from working together in harmony and on a basis of equality."

Taking cognizance of the unrest among the Council Fathers—it was known that a number of prelates in private audiences had expressed their concern about the confusion caused by the airing of differences over the meaning of the October 30th vote on the floor as well as by the slowness of the debates—Pope Paul summoned another extraordinary meeting of the Council summit for Friday afternoon, November 15th, this time deciding to preside over it himself. The meeting was held in the Hall of Congregations on the third floor of the Vatican Palace. The Pope arrived alone at 6:15 P.M. and remained until the end some two hours later. He began the proceedings with the usual prayer *Adsumus* with which all conciliar deliberations begin. The main business at hand was a report (*Relatio*) on the work of the Council, delivered by Cardinal Lercaro, one of the Moderators. Each of the cardinals and bishops present then offered his comments. According to certain *"indiscrezioni"* which leaked out immediately afterward, there was widespread approval of what the Cardinal of Bologna had said. Also discussed, these sources said, were the preparations for a solemn public session at the end of the present Session, the organization of the intersession period, and the prospects for the Third Session. The majority of the Fathers present were in favor of holding the latter in the autumn of 1964, but the Pope himself was said to be undecided and unwilling to come to a final decision until he had sounded out more of the Council members.*

The text of Cardinal Lercaro's "Report" was distributed

* *La Croix*, November 17-18, 1963.

RELATIO

QUAM, IN CONVENTU EM.RUM CARDINALIUM CONSILII PRAESIDENTIAE COMMISSIONIS DE NEGOTIIS CONCILII COORDINANDIS ET MODERATORUM CORAM SS. D. N. PAULO PP. VI IN AEDIBUS VATICANI HABITO DIE 15 NOVEMBRIS 1963, LEGIT E.MUS CARD. IACOBUS LERCARO MODERATOR; QUAEQUE ADPROBATA, EX VOTO PATRUM, PATRIBUS OMNIBUS COMMUNICATUR

Beatissime Pater,

Ea quae praecipua manifeste patent in labore quem secunda sessione Concilii iam perfecimus omnibus nota sunt. Satis igitur est breve summarium delineare:

1. Quinque schematum quae secundae sessioni proposita sunt duo tantum omni ex parte pertractata sunt: id est schema *de Ecclesia* et schema *de Episcopis et de regimine dioeceseon.*

2. Schema *de Beata Virgine Maria* maiori paucis sententiis parti Patrum visum est ad Commissionem remittere ut in schema *de Ecclesia* extremum caput includeretur, secundum congruentem cohaerentemque de Ecclesia rationem. Id nondum in promptu est quod disputetur, etiam propter magnam molem laboris quae uni Commissioni de Doctrina committitur.

3. Reliquorum schematum *De Oecumenismo* et *De Apostolatu Laicorum,* quae ne delibata quidem sunt, alterum evidentiorem nexum habet cum praecipuis schematis *De Ecclesia* partibus et ad principia ipsa pertinet quae magis propria sunt Concilii Oecumenici propter quaestionum subtilitatem et propter earum perennem vim; alterum, quamquam nodos in agendo difficiles et graves spectat, aspectus habet et partes quae magis sunt descriptivae, ad principia minus pertinent et magis sunt temporibus temporumque mutationibus conexae. Id est cur in oeconomia et aequabilitate laboris, quem ad hoc tempus perfecimus, schema *De Oecumenismo* praecedere voluimus.

Opening page of *"Relatio"* by Cardinal Lercaro, delivered on November 15, 1963 to the Fathers on December 2, 1963—in a Latin translation although he delivered it in Italian. Large extracts were printed by the Bolognese paper *L'Avvenire d'Italia.** However, coming at the time when it did, this important disclosure was virtually ignored by the world press, yet it contains—and was intended to make public—a whole program of action for the intersession period and beyond. In typical Pauline fashion, the program was revealed, indirectly, in the form of a critique. After a brief review of the Second Session in the form of an appraisal of *De Ecclesia* and *De Episcopis,* a few words about the decision to attach the schema on the Virgin Mary to the former instead of having it as a separate document, and a word about the coming schemata to be debated, *De Oecumenismo* and *De Apostolatu laicorum*— Cardinal Lercaro made an important observation: he said that the procedure adopted in voting the amendments to the Liturgy schema had revealed the value of what the Liturgy Commission had done as a norm for the future. This had shown in fact "how confusion and serious delays can occur if a commission—even though there may be valid reasons for so doing—offers a single text on doubtful and controversial matters without any alternative, thus passing judgment itself on important amendments proposed by the Fathers. Therefore the commissions from now on should not presume to resolve *on their own authority* the requests and demands of certain episcopal conferences, but should 'order and evaluate the amendments,' as the Regulations declare, so that the general congregation of the Council may be able to compare, read and decide for itself among the amendments proposed."

He then took up a number of practical points concerned with the debates on the floor, which in the general opinion had seemed to drag excessively. Many petitions had been received by the Moderators to do something about this situa-

* *L'Avvenire d'Italia,* December 2, 1963.

tion. In general what they had done was to apply the existing rules more rigorously without introducing any essential change and by using their authority more directly. "It was not considered appropriate to alter the Rules at this stage." Most of the bishops approved of the way the Moderators had handled the situation. He then put his finger on one of the crucial points. "An acceleration of the work of the Council depends more on quickening the rhythm at which the Commissions work, some of which have too many competences and tasks. Acceleration depends also on the Commissions paying more heed to and giving a readier response to the mind of the general congregation, in accordance with their subordinate nature. . . ." Driving home the validity of the five propositions, he said that further acceleration would be achieved if we follow the procedure adopted . . . namely, by having "the Moderators pick out certain important questions in each discussion summarizing the gist of the debate and intended to serve as a guide for the commissions, and propose these questions to the assembly for a vote."

Cardinal Lercaro concluded with a number of general observations. The course of the debates had shown that the Fathers were manifesting an increasing sense of catholicity of thought; the whole episcopate was clearly behind the Pope, and there was no trace today of any of the separatist movements typical of the past. The present assembly "strongly and sincerely" (*fortiter et sincere*) adhered to what Vatican Council I had decided about the papal primacy and infallibility. The mind of the Church was turned away from narrow factional rivalries toward the great missionary horizon before it, the cardinal concluded. One could say about these remarks what was said about Cardinal Bea and Pope John during the first session: though the voice and words were those of Cardinal Lercaro, the thoughts were clearly those of Pope Paul VI.

SUMMARY

November 5, 1963, Tuesday—60TH GENERAL CONGREGATION.
MASS: Patriarch Paul II Cheikho, Chaldean Patriarch of Babylon, in Chaldean rite.
MODERATOR: Cardinal Suenens.
PRESENT: 2,107 Fathers.
SUBJECT: Schema on Bishops and Dioceses, in general.
SPEAKERS:

1. Cardinal Achille Liénart (Bishop of Lille, France) (new chapter on bishops and Pope).
2. Cardinal James Francis A. McIntyre (Archbishop of Los Angeles, California) (critical of episcopal conferences).
3. Cardinal Valerian Gracias (Archbishop of Bombay, India) (nuncios and apostolic delegates).
4. Cardinal Paul Richaud (Archbishop of Bordeaux, France) (conflicts with principles of collegiality).
5. Bishop Giuseppe Gargitter (Bressanone, Italy) (not text of Preparatory Commission, internationalization of Curia).
6. Bishop Jean Rupp (Monaco) (text inadequate, inconsistent with collegiality).
7. Bishop Narciso Jubany Arnau (Auxiliary of Barcelona, Spain) (inadequate treatment of role of bishops).
8. Archbishop Louis de Bazelaire de la Ruppierre (Chambéry, France) (too juridical).
9. Bishop Pablo Correa León (Cúcuta, Columbia) (irregularities in preparation of text).
10. Archbishop Gabriel Garrone (Toulouse, France) (illogical order, wrong tone).
11. Archbishop François Marty (Rheims, France) (collegiality ignored, drastic revision needed).
12. Archbishop Maurice Baudoux (St.-Boniface, Canada) (thorough revision in light of *De Ecclesia*).

November 6, 1963, Wednesday—61ST GENERAL CONGREGATION.
MASS: Archbishop Natale Mosconi of Ferrara, Italy.
MODERATOR: Cardinal Suenens.
PRESENT: 2,136 Fathers.
SUBJECT: Schema on Bishops and Dioceses, in general.

SPEAKERS:
1. Cardinal Ernesto Ruffini (Archbishop of Palermo, Italy) (collegiality not settled, its dangers).
2. Cardinal Franz. Koenig (Archbishop of Vienna, Austria) (international college of bishops in Rome, national conferences).
3. Cardinal B. Alfrink (Archbishop of Utrecht, Holland) (central episcopal organ in Rome, Roman Curia as executive).
4. Cardinal Augustin Bea (Curia) (theological presuppositions of schema should be made clearer, organ of bishops in Rome).
5. Cardinal Michael Browne (Curia) (idea of collegiality unclear).
6. Archbishop Pierre Veuillot (Coadjutor of Paris) (discussion dependent on *De Ecclesia*).
7. Archbishop Fernando Gomes dos Santos (Goiania, Brazil) (*"Non placet"* in name of Brazilian bishops).
8. Bishop Pierre Dib (Coptic, Cairo, Egypt) (discrimination against Orientals).
9. Bishop Carlos Eduardo Saboia Bandeira de Mella (Palmas, Brazil) (complete revision, faculties of bishops not "granted").
10. Archbishop Hermann Schäufele (Freiburg, Germany) (central organ in Rome, auxiliaries and coadjutors).
11. Bishop Alejandro Olalia (Lipa, Philippines) (more stress on collegiality).
12. Bishop Francis Simons (Indore, India) (power of Roman Pontiff supreme, not absolute; Curia inadequate).
13. Bishop Giuseppe Ruotolo (Ugento, Italy) (too rigid and dry).
14. Bishop Joseph Hodges (Wheeling, West Virginia) (should be correlated with collegiality).
15. Bishop Rafael González Moralejo (Valencia, Spain) (Pope's election belongs to episcopal college).
16. Father Aniceto Fernandez, Master General of Dominican Order (collaboration between secular and religious clergy).
17. Archbishop Thomas Cooray (Colombo, Ceylon) (criticism of Roman Curia should be in writing).
18. Archbishop Maxim Hermaniuk (Ukrainian, Winnipeg, Canada) (should be correlated with collegiality).

SUBJECT: Schema on Bishops, Introduction and Chap. I, on Bishops and the Curia (*De Rationibus inter episcopos et sacras Romanae Curiae congregationes*).

SPEAKER:

19. Patriarch Maximos IV Saigh (Melkite Patriarch of Antioch, Lebanon (criticizes timid reform of Curia proposed, calls for new "Sacred College" of bishops in Rome).

November 7, 1963, Thursday—62ND GENERAL CONGREGATION.

MASS: Bishop Pieter Anton Nierman of Groningen, Holland.

MODERATOR: Cardinal Agagianian.

PRESENT: 2,155 Fathers.

SUBJECT: Chapter IV of *De Ecclesia*.

SPEAKER: Cardinal Doepfner summarized the remarks of those who still had a right to be heard on Chap. IV but had renounced the right to speak, viz. Cardinal Rugambwa, Bishop Lucey, Bishop Helmsing, Archbishop Tawil, Archbishop Kozlowiecki, Bishop Reuss, Father Deschatelets, Father Van Hees, Father Hage, Archbishop Zoa, Father Jannsens, Bishop Compagnone, Bishop Corboy, Bishop Patroni, Abbot Kleiner, Father de Hornad, Bishop Guilly.

SUBJECT: Schema on Bishops, Introduction and Chap. I, on Bishops and the Curia.

SPEAKERS:

1. Cardinal Joseph Elmer Ritter (Archbishop of St. Louis, Missouri) (divine-law powers of residential bishops).
2. Patriarch Pierre XVI Batanian (Armenian Patriarch of Cilicia, Lebanon) (criticism of Curia must not be exaggerated).
3. Archbishop Ermenegildo Florit (Florence, Italy) (new Central Congregation of Bishops in Rome, collegiality not yet defined).
4. Bishop José Souto Vizoso (Palencia, Spain) (gratitude to Pope for "granting" faculties).
5. Archbishop Paul Gouyon (Coadjutor of Rennes, France) (apostolic college of bishops in Rome).
6. Bishop Piotr Kalwa (Lublin, Poland) (jurisdiction of bishop over diocese).
7. Bishop Fidel García Martínez (Tit., Spain) (faculties of bishops).

8. Archbishop Owen McCann (Capetown, South Africa) (consultative episcopal body).
9. Bishop Michael Browne (Galway, Ireland) (collegiality overestimated, revision of Curia, episcopal senate).
10. Bishop Antonio Ferreira Gomes (Oporto, Portugal) (essentiality of collegiality, need for cardinalate questioned).
11. Bishop Sergio Méndez Arceo (Cuernavaca, Mexico) (better integration of parts).
12. Archbishop Herculanus van den Burgt (Pontianak, Indonesia) (college of bishops).
13. Archbishop Ignace Ziadé (Maronite, Beirut, Lebanon) (episcopal faculties, *"pusillus pastor"*).
14. Bishop Aurelio del Pino Gómez (Lerida, Spain) (Curia should be praised, idea of episcopal senate erroneous).
15. Bishop Francis Mazzieri (Ndola, Rhodesia) (missionary bishops and Pauline Privilege).
16. Archbishop Joseph Attipetty (Verapoly, India) (nominations of bishops).
17. Bishop Pablo Barrachina Estevan (Orihuela-Alicante, Spain) (better treatment of local church).
18. Bishop Eduardo Mason (Vicar Apostolic, El Obeid, Sudan) (Curia, Church need *"aggiornamento"*).

November 8, 1963, Friday—63RD GENERAL CONGREGATION.
MASS: Bishop Hadrianus Ddungu of Masaka, Uganda.
MODERATOR: Cardinal Agagianian; Cardinal Lercaro.
PRESENT: 2,148 Fathers.
SUBJECT: Schema on Bishops, Introduction and Chap. I, on Bishops and the Curia.
SPEAKERS:
1. Cardinal Jaime de Barros Câmara (Archbishop of Rio de Janeiro, Brazil) (competence of Curia should be reformed, episcopal group in Rome).
2. Cardinal Joseph Frings (Archbishop of Cologne, Germany) (importance of vote on collegiality, criticism of Holy Office, too many "honorary" bishops).
3. Cardinal Giacomo Lercaro (Archbishop of Bologna, Italy) (clarification of idea of episcopal college, suggests study and message to Pope).

4. Cardinal Laurean Rugambwa (Bishop of Bukoba, Tanganyika) (immediate creation of central body of bishops, petition to Pope).
5. Cardinal Alfredo Ottaviani (Curia) (rejects Frings' contention about Holy Office, minimizes vote on collegiality).
6. Cardinal Michael Browne (Curia) (collegiality is contrary to Vatican Council I).
7. Archbishop Antoine Khoreiche (Maronite, Sidon, Lebanon) (revision of canon law).
8. Bishop Anastasio Granados García (Auxiliary of Toledo, Spain) (importance of local church).
9. Bishop António de Castro Mayer (Campos, Brazil) (collegiality not sufficiently demonstrated).
10. Bishop Vittorio Costantini (Sessa Aurunca, Italy) (avoid criticism of Curia and leave to Pope).
11. Archbishop Eugene D'Souza (Bhopal, India) (critics of collegiality mock bishops, inadequacy of Curia, need for episcopal senate).
12. Bishop Joseph Schoiswohl (Seckau, Austria) (principle of subsidiarity applied to bishops, episcopal faculties).
13. Bishop Eduardo Martínez González (Zamora, Spain) (greater theological precision).
14. Archbishop Marcel Lefebvre, Superior General of Holy Ghost Fathers (cardinals are Pope's senate, juridic collegiality cannot be proved).
15. Archbishop Carlos Rodríguez-Quíros (San José, Costa Rica) (remove obstacles to episcopal jurisdiction).
16. Bishop António Pildaín y Zapiáin (Canary Islands, Spain) (written).
17. Bishop Cyril John Zohrabian (Armenian Tit.) (written).
18. Bishop Ireneo Chelucci (Montalcino, Italy) (written).

SUBJECT: Schema on Bishops, Chap. II, on Coadjutors and Auxiliaries.

SPEAKERS:

1. Cardinal Ernesto Ruffini (Archbishop of Palermo, Italy) (thanks Patriarch Batanian for defending Curia).
2. Cardinal José Garibi y Rivera (Archbishop of Guadalajara, Mexico) (resignation of bishops).

November 11, 1963, Monday—64TH GENERAL CONGREGATION.

MASS: Bishop Joseph Khiamsum Nittayo, Coadjutor of Bangkok.

MODERATOR: Cardinal Lercaro.

PRESENT: 2,141 Fathers.

SUBJECT: Schema on Bishops, Chap. II, on Coadjutors and Auxiliaries.

SPEAKERS:

1. Cardinal Francis Spellman (Archbishop of New York) (criticism of Curia not business of Council).
2. Cardinal Carlo Confalonieri (Curia) (reform of Curia up to Pope).
3. Cardinal Fernando Cento (Curia) (pension fund for retired bishops).
4. Cardinal Julius Doepfner (Archbishop of Munich) ("test-vote" indicative for Theological Commission).
5. Archbishop Corrado Mingo (Monreale, Italy) (retirement at 75).
6. Archbishop Michele Gonzi (Malta) (no compulsory retirement).
7. Bishop Manuel Alfonso de Carvalho (Angra, Portugal) (auxiliaries and coadjutors).
8. Bishop Conrad de Vito (Lucknow, India) (resignation).
9. Bishop António Añoveros Ataún (Coadjutor of Cadix, Spain) (need for coadjutors).
10. Bishop Edmund Nowicki (Coadjutor of Gdansk, Poland) (coadjutors).
11. Bishop Johann Pohlschneider (Aachen, Germany) (faculties of auxiliaries).
12. Bishop Jacinto Argaya Goicoechea (Mondoñedo-Ferrol, Spain) (*sede vacante*).
13. Abbot Benedikt Reetz, President of the Beuron Benedictine Congregation (bishops and abbots appointed for life).
14. Bishop Antoine Caillot (Coadjutor of Evreux, France) (abolition of titular bishops).
15. Bishop Peregrin de la Fuente (Tit., Prelate Nullius of Batanes and Babuyán Islands, Philippines) (exiled bishops).
16. Bishop Carlos Saboia Bandeira de Mello (Palmas, Brazil) (episcopal conferences, interrupted).

17. Abbot Egidio Gavazzi, Abbot-Coadjutor of Subiaco (abbeys as models for diocese).

18. Bishop Roman Arrieta Villalobos (Tilarán, Costa Rica) (choice of auxiliaries).

19. Bishop Richard Lester Guilly (Georgetown, British Guiana) (written).

November 12, 1963, Tuesday—65TH GENERAL CONGREGATION.

MASS: Abbot-Primate Benno Gut of Benedictine Confederation.

MODERATOR: Cardinal Lercaro; Cardinal Doepfner.

PRESENT: 2,166 Fathers.

SUBJECT: Schema on Bishops, Chap. II, on Coadjutors and Auxiliaries.

SPEAKERS:

1. Cardinal Leo Suenens (Archbishop of Malines-Bruxelles) (retirement).

2. Bishop Vicente Zaspe (Rafaela, Argentina) (theology of episcopal office).

3. Bishop Juan Hervás y Benet (Prelate Nullius of Ciudad Real, Spain) (abolition of coadjutors).

4. Bishop Franz Zak (St. Pölten, Austria) (authority of auxiliaries).

5. Bishop Hermann Volk (Mainz, Germany) (fewer auxiliaries).

6. Archbishop Raymond Tchidimbo (Conakry, Guinea) (fewer auxiliaries).

7. Bishop Jacques Le Cordier (Auxiliary of Paris) (residential auxiliaries).

8. Bishop Thomas Cahill (Cairns, Australia) (privileges of retired bishops).

9. Archbishop Josyf Slipyi (Ukrainian, Lviv, Soviet Russia) (controversies over primacy and Curia).

10. Bishop Joseph Reuss (Auxiliary of Mainz, Germany) (auxiliaries belong to episcopal college).

SUBJECT: Schema on Bishops, Chap. III, on Episcopal Conferences.

SPEAKERS:

11. Cardinal Francis McIntyre (Archbishop of Los Angeles) (decisions should not be juridically binding).

12. Cardinal Valerian Gracias (Archbishop of Bombay, India) (decisions morally binding).

13. Cardinal Albert Gregory Meyer (Archbishop of Chicago) (decisions morally binding).
14. Cardinal Joseph Elmer Ritter (Archbishop of St. Louis) (decisions juridically binding, decentralization and subsidiarity).
15. Cardinal Landázuri-Ricketts (Archbishop of Lima, Peru) (decisions not juridically binding, monarchical government of diocese).
16. Bishop Michal Klepacz (Lódz, Poland) (functions defined).

November 13, 1963, Wednesday—66TH GENERAL CONGREGATION.
MASS: Bishop Andrei Katkoff, Apostolic Visitor for Russians in exile, Rome.
MODERATOR: Cardinal Doepfner.
PRESENT: 2,164 Fathers.
SUBJECT: Schema on Bishops, Chap. II.
SPEAKERS:
1. Archbishop Angel Fernandes (Coadjutor of Delhi, India) (retirement).
2. Bishop Joseph Busimba (Goma, Congo) (auxiliaries in Africa).
3. Bishop Giuseppe Melas (Nuoro, Italy) (retirement at 80).
SUBJECT: Schema on Bishops, Chap. III, Episcopal Conferences.
SPEAKERS:
4. Cardinal Francis Spellman (Archbishop of New York) (decisions not juridical).
5. Cardinal Joseph Frings (Archbishop of Cologne, Germany) (decisions not juridical, papal approval not required).
6. Bishop Marcelino Olaechea Loizaga (Valencia, Spain) (danger of national churches).
7. Bishop Gerald McDevitt (Auxiliary of Philadelphia, Penna.) (auxiliaries and episcopal conferences).
8. Bishop Luigi Carli (Segni, Italy) (conferences not based on divine right collegiality).
9. Bishop Alfred Ancel (Auxiliary of Lyons, France) ("collegial sense" of bishops must be developed).
10. Bishop Antonio Pildáin y Zapiáin (Canary Islands, Spain) (must not restrict episcopal freedom).
11. Archbishop Emile Guerry (Cambrai, France) (conferences and idea of *koinonia*).

12. Bishop José Dammert Bellido (Cajamarca, Peru) (theological basis).
13. Bishop Garabed Amadouni (Armenian Apostolic Visitor, France) (excessive western, Latin orientation).
14. Bishop Luis Alonso Muñoyerro (Military Ordinary, Spain) (dangers, papal confirmation necessary).
15. Bishop Guy Riobé (Orléans, France) (practical suggestions).
16. Bishop Lawrence Bianchi (Hongkong) (conferences and civil authorities).
17. Bishop René Pailloux (Fort Roseberry, Rhodesia) (written).
18. Bishop Luigi Pirelli (Savona and Petigliano, Italy) (written).

November 14, 1963, Thursday—67TH GENERAL CONGREGATION.
MASS: Archbishop Raymond Tchidimbo of Conakry, Guinea.
MODERATOR: Cardinal Doepfner; Cardinal Suenens.
PRESENT: 2,168 Fathers.
SUBJECT: Schema on Bishops, Chap. III, Episcopal Conferences.
SPEAKERS:

1. Cardinal Giuseppe Siri (Archbishop of Genoa, Italy) (should be shortened).
2. Cardinal Stefan Wyszynski (Archbishop of Gniezno and Warsaw) (Polish experience with conferences).
3. Cardinal Bernhard Alfrink (Archbishop of Utrecht) (conferences and collegiality).
4. Bishop Gérard Marie Coderre (Saint-Jean de Québec, Canada) (neglects Eastern Church).
5. Bishop Edmund Peiris (Chilaw, Ceylon) (elimination of word "national").
6. Archbishop John Garner (Pretoria, South Africa) (juridically binding decisions).
7. Bishop Franjo Franič (Split, Yugoslavia) (danger of "national Curias").
8. Abbot Benedikt Reetz, President of Beuron Benedictine Congregation (read by Abbot Prou of Solesme) (conferences and heads of religious orders).
9. Archbishop Antonio Santin (Trieste, Italy) (opposes juridically binding decisions).
10. Bishop Luis Cabrera Cruz (San Luis Potosí, Mexico) (majority decisions).
11. Bishop Alberto Devoto (Goya, Argentina) (written).

12. Archbishop A. Gonçalves do Amaral (Uberada, Brazil) (written).
13. Archbishop Ismaele Castellano (Siena, Italy) (written).
14. Bishop Francesco Spanedda (Bosa, Italy) (written).

SUBJECT: Schema on Bishops, Chap. IV, on Dioceses.

15. Cardinal Maurice Feltin (Archbishop of Paris) (approves of personal dioceses).
16. Bishop Alexandre Renard (Versailles, France) (changes in diocesan structure needed).
17. Bishop Francisco Peralta y Ballabriga (Vitoria, Spain) (diocesan boundaries for large cities).
18. Bishop Franciszek Jop (Auxiliary of Opole, Poland) (residences of bishops).
19. Bishop Aurelio Sorrentino (Bova, Italy) (smaller dioceses).
20. Bishop Sebastião Soares de Resende (Beira, Mozambique) (size of diocese).

November 15, 1963, Friday—68TH GENERAL CONGREGATION.
MASS: Archbishop Tulio Botero Salazar of Medellin, Columbia.
MODERATOR: Cardinal Suenens.
PRESENT: 2,123 Fathers.
SUBJECT: Schema on Bishops, Chap. III, Episcopal Conferences.
SPEAKERS:

1. Cardinal Joseph Lefebvre (Archbishop of Bourges, France) (Council must decide on collegiality).
2. Monsignor Joannes Ferreira (Apostolic Prefect for Portuguese Guinea) (prelates nullius and conferences).
3. Bishop Elias Zoghby (Melkite Patriarchal Vicar for Egypt) (synod is eastern form of conference).
4. Bishop Michel Ntuyahaga (Usumbura, Burundi) (juridical decisions).

SUBJECT: Schema on Bishops, Chap. IV, Dioceses.

5. Bishop Stefan László (Eisenstadt, Austria) (criticizes individualistic spirit).
6. Bishop John B. Velasco (Amoy, China) (personal dioceses for displaced persons).
7. Bishop Bernhard Stein (Auxiliary of Trier, Germany) (division of dioceses).
8. Archbishop Joseph Urtasun (Avignon, France) (amalgamation of small dioceses).

9. Archbishop Dominic R. B. Athaide (Agra, India) (collaboration between Latin and Oriental rites in India).
10. Archbishop Antonio Vuccino (Tit., France) (lacks formal concept, interrupted).
11. Bishop Marcello Gonzalez Martin (Astorga, Spain) (equitable distribution of wealth).
12. Bishop Roberto Massimiliani (Civiltà Castellana, Italy) (advantages of small diocese).
13. Bishop Raul Zambrano Camader (Facatativá, Columbia) (replacement of cathedral chapters by episcopal council).
14. Bishop Fernando Romo Gutierrez (Torreón, Mexico) (criteria for dividing dioceses).
15. Bishop Alexandros Scandar (Coptic, Assiut, Egypt) (inconvenience of small diocese).
16. Bishop Antoine Khoreiche (Maronite, Saida, Lebanon) (several jurisdictions in same place).

IV

The Debate on "Ecumenism"; the Mystery
of Chapters 4 and 5

THE LAST TWO FULL WEEKS of the session, from November
18th to December 2nd, were devoted to a discussion of the
schema on Ecumenism, spelling out the Catholic attitude toward the worldwide movement known as "ecumenism" which
aims at the restoration of Christian unity. The document had
been prepared by Cardinal Bea's Secretariat for Promoting
Christian Unity, technically or theoretically by a Mixed Commission consisting of representatives of the Secretariat, the
Commission for the Oriental Churches, and the Theological
Commission, since they were the three bodies sponsoring
similar drafts presented, or intended for discussion, at the
first session which the Council had ordered to be combined
into one document. Actually, only the draft prepared by the
Oriental Churches had reached the floor in 1962 and been

debated. The revised schema now up for debate consisted of five chapters:

Chap. I—The Principles of Catholic Ecumenism.

Chap. II—The Practical Aspects of Ecumenism.

Chap. III—Christians separated from the Catholic Church.

Part I—The Oriental Churches.

Part II—The Communities which arose beginning with the 16th century.

Chap. IV—The Jews.

Chap. V—Religious Liberty.

The debate opened on Monday, November 18th, with Cardinal Agagianian in the chair as Moderator. First there was an official presentation of the schema as a whole by Cardinal Cicognani, in the name of the Mixed Commission, inasmuch as he had been the President of the only Commission (Oriental Churches) whose draft had already been discussed by the Fathers. His speech was followed by a more detailed exposition of the contents of the new schema by Archbishop Martin of Rouen, a member of the Secretariat, who spoke on Chapters I-III. Archbishop Martin's remarks in appreciation of the work of Cardinal Bea and his Secretariat were warmly applauded by the Council. The following day there was a change of plan. Instead of proceeding with the debate on the first part of the schema, in accordance with customary procedure, it was announced that Cardinal Bea would introduce Chapter IV and Bishop de Smedt Chapter V, at once. This news was greeted with tremendous enthusiasm and applause. In the opinion of some observers there was nothing quite like the spontaneous response on this occasion. Nothing the Council had discussed so far generated so much warmth of feeling. This was interpreted both as a tribute to the speakers, personally, Cardinal Bea in particular, for the tireless activity he had displayed during recent years in promoting the cause of unity, and as an expression of approval for the general ideas contained in the document. Bea explained:

The schema "On Jews," now up for examination, was begun about two years ago and in substance it was finished in May of last year. This year, with the approval of the Council Coordinating Committee, it was placed in the schema "On Ecumenism."

The Secretariat to which the care of promoting Christian Unity is given undertook the question treating the Jews not on its own initiative, but by reason of the express command of the Supreme Pontiff, Pope John XXIII of happy memory. This was given verbally to the President of the Secretariat.

After this schema was prepared, it was to be discussed in the conferences of the Central Commission in June, 1962. The discussion was omitted not because of the ideas or doctrine expressed in the schema, but only because of certain unhappy political conditions at that time.

The decree is very brief, but the material treated in it is not easy. Let us enter immediately into the heart of it and tell what we are talking about. Or rather, since it is so easy to understand it wrongly, before all else let us say what we are not talking about. There is no national nor political question here. Especially is there no question of acknowledging the State of Israel on the part of the Holy See. None of these questions is treated in the schema. Nor is there any treatment of such condition or consideration in any way. There is only treatment of a purely religious question.

The decree intends to recall in a solemn way those things which the Church of Christ by the hidden design of Divine Providence, receives through the hands of the chosen people of Israel. It receives especially, in the words of St. Paul in his Epistle to the Romans, "the oracles of God" (Rom. 3:2); that is, the word of God in the Old Testament. Besides, in the words of the same St. Paul, "who are Israelites who have the adoption as sons, and the glory and the covenants, and the legislation and the worship and the promises"; who have the fathers and from whom "is the Christ, according to the flesh, who is over all things, God, blessed forever" (Rom. 9:4-5).

In other words, not only was the whole preparation of the

work of the Redeemer and his Church done in the Old Testament, but also the execution of his work, the foundation of the Church and its propagation in the world, either in the chosen people of Israel or through members of this people whom God chose as instruments. The Church is in some sense the continuation of the chosen people of Israel, as is so well stated in *De Ecclesia* (On the Church), Chapter I, p. 7 sq., so that according to St. Paul, Christians can be called "Israelites" not indeed "according to the flesh" but because in them are fulfilled the promises made to Abraham, the father of the people of Israel (cf. Rom. 9:6-8). For in us Christians, members of the Church, the perfection of that Kingdom of God for which God selected and designated the people of Israel, is brought to fruition.

Really, it is a valid question to ask whether our preachers at times in their sermons, especially on the Passion of Our Lord, use these facts and associations of the Church to the chosen people of Israel and whether they give our necessary thanks to this people.

There are those who object: Did not the princes of this people, with the people in agreement, condemn and crucify the innocent Christ, the Lord? Did they not "clamor": Let His blood be upon us and upon our children" (Matt. 27:25)? Did not Christ himself speak most severely about the Jews and their punishment?

I reply simply and briefly: It is true that Christ spoke severely but only with the intention that the people might be converted and might "recognize the time of its visitation" (cf. Luke 19:42-49). But even as He is dying on the cross he prayed: "Father, forgive them, for they know not what they do" (Luke 23:34).

Wherefore, since the Lord emphasized, before the burial of Lazarus, speaking to the Father: "I know that Thou always hearest me" (John 11:42), it is wrong to say that His prayer to the Father was not heard and that God has not only not forgiven the fault of His chosen people but that He has rejected them.

God Himself through St. Paul assures us that He "in no way" has rejected His chosen and beloved people. For the Apostle writes to the Romans: "I say then: Has God cast off His people? By no means—God has not cast off His people whom He foreknew" (Rom. 11:1 s.). And a little below this he gives the reason: "For the gifts and the call of God are without repentance" (ibid.,

v. 29), that is God does not revoke a choice once made nor does He reject the people of Israel. Going still further, St. Paul affirms that at some time "all Israel" will be saved, both those who are of "Israel according to the flesh," as well as those who are of Israel according to the promise only. For the Apostle states: "For I would not, brethren, have you ignorant of this mystery, lest you should be wise in your own conceits, that a partial blindness only has befallen Israel, until the full number of the gentiles should enter and thus all Israel should be saved.—For as you (the Romans, insofar as they belonged to the non-Jewish people) also at one time did not believe in God, but now have obtained mercy by reason of their unbelief, so too they have now not believed by reason of the mercy shown you, that they too may obtain mercy" (Rom. 11:25-30).

Hence St. Paul, who indeed suffered so much from some Jews, having imitated the burning charity of God, said: "For I could wish to be anathema myself from Christ for the sake of my brethren, who are my kinsmen according to the flesh" (Rom. 9:3).

Therefore, the aim of this very brief decree is to call to the attention of Christ's faithful these truths concerning the Jews proposed by the Apostle and contained in the deposit of faith and to do this so clearly that in dealing with the children of that people the faithful will act in no other way than did Christ the Lord and his Apostles, Peter and Paul. St. Peter in preaching to the Jewish people on the crucifixion of the Lord said: "I know that you did this through ignorance as did your leaders . . ." (Acts 3:17). Thus he excuses even the leaders themselves. Likewise St. Paul (Acts 13:27).

The point therefore is not in any way to call into doubt— as is sometimes falsely asserted—the events which are narrated in the Gospels about Christ's consciousness of his dignity and divine nature, or about the manner in which the innocent Lord was unjustly condemned. Rather that, with these things kept fully in mind, it is still possible and necessary to imitate the gentle charity of Christ the Lord and his Apostles with which they excused their persecutors.

But why is it so necessary precisely today to recall these things? The reason is this. Some decades ago anti-Semitism, as it is called, was prevalent in various regions and in a particularly violent and criminal form, especially in Germany under the rule of National Socialism, which through hatred for the Jews committed frightful crimes, extirpating several millions of Jewish people—we need not at the moment seek the exact number. Moreover, accompanying and assisting this whole activity was a most powerful and effective "propaganda," as it is called, against the Jews. Now it would have been almost impossible if some of the claims of that propaganda did not have an unfortunate effect even on faithful Catholics, the more so since the arguments advanced by that propaganda often enough bore the appearance of truth, especially when they were drawn from the New Testament and from the history of the Church. Thus, since the Church in this Council is striving to renew itself by "seeking again the outlines of its most fervent youth," as John XXIII of venerable memory said (cf. Discourse of November 14, 1960, AAS 52/1960/ 960), it seems imperative to take up this question.

Not that anti-Semitism, especially that of National Socialism, drew its inspiration from Christian doctrine, something which is in no way true. Rather, it is a question of rooting out from the minds of Catholics any ideas which perhaps remain fixed there through the influence of that propaganda. If Christ the Lord and the Apostles who personally experienced the sorrows of the Crucifixion, embraced their very persecutors with an ardent charity, how much more must we be motivated by the same charity?

For the Jews of our times can hardly be accused of the crimes committed against Christ, so far removed are they from those deeds. Actually, even in the time of Christ, the majority of the chosen people did not cooperate with the leaders of the people in condemning Christ. Does not the Gospel say that an actual member of the Sanhedrin, namely, Joseph of Arimathea, did not agree "to their plan and their actions" (Luke 23:51)? Again, those among them who cried out to Pilate, "Crucify him" formed a very small part of the chosen people. Were not the leaders of the Jews unwilling to kill the Lord "on the feast day lest there be a tumult among the people" (Matt. 26:5)?

If therefore not even all the Jews in Palestine or in Jerusalem could be accused, how much less the Jews dispersed throughout the Roman Empire? And how much less again those who today after nineteen centuries live scattered in the whole world?

But let us set aside these considerations. Let the example of ardent charity given by the Lord and the Apostles be sufficient for us. To this example the Church must conform as perfectly as possible in teaching the Passion and Death of the Lord. In saying this we do not mean to state or to hint that anti-Semitism usually or principally arises from a religious source, namely from what the Gospels recount concerning the Passion and Death of the Lord. We know very well that anti-Semitism also has causes of a political-national, psychological, social and economic nature. But we affirm that the Church most certainly must imitate Christ's example of gentle charity toward the people through whom it received so many great benefits from God.

If and when, therefore, some or many Jews do this or that one of the things of which they are accused, Christians will be mindful of the example of St. Paul. He, while violently attacked by many of the Jews, indeed publicly denounced his persecutors who were interfering with either his freedom to announce the word of the Lord or the freedom of men to believe the Gospel (cf. I Thess. 2:15f). At the same time, however, he testified that he loved them so ardently that he would wish "to be anathema from Christ" for them. In such fashion therefore, the children of the Church also should make vigorous use of the peaceful weapons of truth, charity and patience, which weapons are surely most effective.

Lastly: since we are here treating a merely religious question, there is obviously no danger that the Council will get entangled in those difficult questions regarding the relations between the Arab nations and the State of Israel, or regarding so-called Zionism.

In December of last year, I set out in writing for the Supreme Pontiff, Pope John XXIII of happy memory, a discussion of this whole question "Regarding the Jews." After a few days the Holy Father indicated to me his full approval.

The Supreme Pontiff himself did indeed write in this way scarcely five months before his holy death. Certainly, I am not saying that the question which we are treating was settled by these words of his; for he wanted the Council to be free, just as his Successor also unquestionably wishes it. I think however, that these words of his are dear to all the Most Eminent and Most Excellent Fathers, and that at the same time, they throw light on how to follow the Lord Christ.

However, for our purpose, of much more importance, in fact simply decisive, is the example of burning charity of the Lord himself on the Cross praying: "Father, forgive them, for they know not what they are doing." This is the example to be imitated by the Church, the Bride of Christ. This is the road to be followed by her. This is what the schema proposed by us intends to foster and promote.

A communiqué on the text, released to the press, received widespread approval among Jewish communities throughout the world on the whole.*

Speaking on the subject of religious liberty, Bishop de Smedt made a historic statement:

Very many Conciliar Fathers have insistently demanded that this Sacred Synod clearly explain and proclaim the right of man to religious liberty. Among the reasons given, four principal ones should be listed:

1) Truth: The Church must teach and defend the right to religious liberty because there is question of the truth, the care of which was committed to her by Christ;

2) Defense: The Church cannot remain silent today when almost half of mankind is deprived of religious liberty by atheistic materialism of various kinds;

3) Peaceful Social Life: Today in all nations of the world, men, who adhere to different religions or who lack all religious belief, must live together in one and the same human society; in the light of truth, the Church should point the way toward living together peacefully;

4) Ecumenism: Many non-Catholics harbor an aversion against the Church or at least suspect her of a kind of Machiavelism because we seem to them to demand the free exercise of religion when Catholics are in a minority in any nation and at the same

* See Appendix p. 364.

time refuse and deny the same religious liberty when Catholics are in the majority. Religious liberty is such a grave problem in modern society that it can not be omitted in a pastoral decree on Ecumenism. Therefore, we submit to your deliberations this fifth chapter of our schema on Ecumenism. The Secretariat for Promoting Christian Unity, to the best of its ability, has carefully watched over the preparation of this material. Since we are treating of a most difficult question and at the same time one of great importance in modern life, the authors of the schema cherish the hope that your attention and pastoral consideration will amend what needs amendment and perfect what is still imperfect in the schema now offered to you. The term "Religious Liberty" has a definite meaning in our text. In the forthcoming discussion, great confusion might arise if any of the Fathers give to the expression a meaning that differs from the one intended by the text. When religious liberty is defended, it is not asserted that it is proper for man to consider the religious problem according to his own whim without any moral obligation and decide for himself according to his own will whether or not to embrace religion (religious indifferentism). Nor is it affirmed that the human conscience is free in the sense that it is as it were outside of the law, absolved from any obligation toward God (laicism). Nor is it said that falsehood is to be considered on an equal footing with truth, as though there were no objective norm of truth (doctrinal relativism). Nor is it admitted that man in any way has a quasi-right to maintain a peaceful complacency in the midst of uncertainty (dilettantistic pessimism). If anyone were to insist upon giving any of the aforesaid meanings to "Religious Liberty," he would attribute to our text a meaning which neither the words nor our intention possess. What therefore is meant in the text by "Religious Liberty"? Positively, religious liberty is the right of the human person to the free exercise of religion according to the dictates of his conscience. Negatively, it is immunity from all external force in his personal relations with God, which the conscience of man vindicates to itself. Religious liberty implies human autonomy, not from within certainly but from without. From within, man is not free of obligations toward the religious problem. From without, his liberty is offended when obedience to the dictates of his conscience in religious matters is impeded. At this point, two questions must be asked: 1) can each man claim for himself religious liberty as a sacred right given to him by God? 2) is there, and to what extent is there, a duty on the part of others to recognize the aforesaid religious liberty? Our decree, since it is pastoral, tries to treat the present matter especially from the practical point of view and, after the manner of John XXIII, will carefully strive to remove the whole question from that world of abstractions which was so dear to the nineteenth century. The question is put therefore regarding real man in his real dealings with other men, in contemporary human and civil societies.

The first pastoral problem which must be examined now by this Sacred Synod is this: how must Catholics because of their faith conduct themselves toward men who do not belong to the Catholic faith? We propose the following answer for your deliberations:

1) All Catholics are invited by Christ to strive by prayer, penance, witness and evangelizing in the Holy Spirit to bring our non-Catholic brothers to the blessing of the evangelical light and of the life of the Church. The sacred, absolute rights of God as well as the evangelical and natural truths must always and everywhere be honored and observed by them.

2) They must abstain from all direct and indirect coercion. Although God wills all men to be saved and to come to the knowledge of the truth, the disciples of Christ may not infringe upon the religious liberty of the individual person. On the contrary, they must respect and esteem the right and duty of non-Catholics to follow the dictate of their own conscience even when, after sincere and sufficient study, it errs in good faith.

What is the reason of faith why non-Catholics can be forced by no one to admit the Catholic doctrine against their conscience? This reason is found in the very nature of the act of faith. For this act, on God's part, is a supernatural gift which the Holy Spirit most freely gives to whom and when he wills; and, on man's part, it is and must be an assent which man freely gives to God.

3) All Catholics are bound, by the command of the Lord, to love and to help their non-Catholic brothers with a sincere and active charity.

At this point, the schema takes a step forward and asserts that each and every man, who follows his conscience in religious matters, has a natural right to true and authentic religious liberty. In this second part, it is proposed that the Sacred Synod solemnly demand religious liberty for the whole human family, for all religious groups, for each human person whether his conscience be sincere (*rectam*) and true or sincere and false concerning faith, provided only that he sincerely follow the dictate of conscience. Therefore, a general principle is laid down: no human person can be the object of coercion or intolerance.

What is the reason why observance of religious liberty is demanded of all? The human person, endowed with conscious and free activity, since he can fulfill the will of God only as the divine law is perceived through the dictate of conscience, can obtain his ultimate end only by prudently forming the judgment of conscience and by faithfully carrying out its dictate.

From the nature of things, in forming this judgment, whereby man tries freely to conform to the absolute demands of God's rights, neither any other man nor any human institution can take the place of the free judgment of man's conscience. Therefore, the man who sincerely obeys his own conscience intends to obey God himself, although at times confusedly and unknowingly, and is to be considered worthy of esteem.

When religious liberty is violated, then the very freedom of the human person is violated in its principal matter, in a fundamental demand, in man's ordination to the supreme and ultimate end. The greatest injury is to prevent a man from worshiping God and from obeying God according to the dictate of his own conscience.

The schema takes still another step forward and enters upon a most difficult question. Religious liberty would be fruitless and empty if men were not able to carry out the dictate of their conscience in external acts whether in private life, in social life, or in public life, or if human persons were prevented from forming religious groups whose members could worship the Supreme Deity by common and social acts and lead a religious life.

Here, however, there arises a most difficult problem. For, if a human person carries out the dictate of his conscience by external acts, there is danger of violating the rights and duties of another or of others. Since man is a social being and since in the human family men are subject to error and to sin, the conflict of rights and the conflict of duties cannot always be avoided.

From this it is evident that the right and duty to manifest externally the dictate of conscience is not unlimited, but can be and at times must be tempered and regulated for the common good.

This ordering of the common good must be done juridically in human society and belongs to public authority (*potestati publicae.*) "One of the fundamental duties of civil authorities," therefore, we read in *Pacem in Terris* (revised NCWC transl.), "is to coordinate social relations in such fashion that the exercise of one man's rights does not threaten others in the exercise of their own rights nor hinder them in the fulfillment of their duties. Finally, the rights of all should be effectively safeguarded and, if they have been violated, completely restored."

How is public authority to carry out this duty? In establishing order for the common good, public authority can never act contrary to the order of justice established by God. As St. Thomas says: "Human law is truly law to the extent that it is in accordance with right reason; and therefore it is evident that it is derived from the eternal law. In so far as it departs from reason, it is a so-called "wicked law," and therefore is not truly a law but a kind of violence" (i-ii, p. 93, a. 3, ad 2um).

Recent Roman Pontiffs again and again have bewailed the fact that not a few governments have gone too far in this matter, ignoring and violating religious liberty. In our own day, there are some regions in which tolerance in religious matters has been so little observed that the Supreme Pontiff, Paul VI, in his allocution to the Fathers of the Second Vatican Council on September 29, 1963, said, speaking of the violated right to religious liberty:

"Because of sufferings of this kind, with what sadness are we affected and how deeply we are grieved, when we behold that in some territories religious liberty, together with the other principal rights of man, is suppressed by the principles and arts of those who do not tolerate opinions different from theirs on politics, on races of men, or on religion of any kind. We are

sorrowed also by the many injuries which are done to those who
would like to profess their religion honestly and freely."

In order that we might clearly understand the doctrine of the
Church on the extent and limits of the civil power's duty relating
to religious liberty, we must, in a few words, develop the history
of this doctrine. Bear with me, Venerable Fathers, if I seem to
make more than just demands on your patience. But the Secretariat for Promoting Christian Unity is convinced that many
difficulties and confusions can be avoided in the study of the
schema if, before the discussion begins, I show very briefly what
the Supreme Pontiffs since the time of Pius IX have taught concerning the duties of public authority in religious matters.

On the question of religious liberty, the principal document
is the encyclical *Pacem in Terris,* in which Pope John XXIII
especially developed these two points of doctrine: 1) by the law
of nature, the human person has the right to the free exercise of
religion in society according to the dictates of a sincere conscience
(*conscientia recta*), whether the conscience be true (*conscientia
vera*), or the captive either of error or of inadequate knowledge
of truth and of sacred things. 2) To this right corresponds the
duty incumbent upon other men and the public authority to
recognize and respect that right in such a way that the human
person in society is kept immune from all coercion of any kind
(cf. AAS 55, 1963, p. 299; p. 264 and pp. 273-274).

Moreover, this doctrine must be understood as the contemporary terminus of a process of evolution both in the doctrine on
the dignity of the human person and in the Church's pastoral
solicitude for man's freedom. This doctrinal evolution took place
according to a two-fold law:

1) Law of continuity: The Church's doctrine and solicitude
are always self-consistent, always remain the same. This perennial
doctrine can be expressed in the words of Pope John: "The
dignity of the human person demands this, that in his actions
man should enjoy his own counsel and freedom" (ibid. p. 265).
This doctrine has its deepest roots in the Sacred Scriptures which
teach that man was made to the image of God. From this doctrine stems the continual pastoral solicitude of the Church for
man's true freedom.

2) Law of progress: The ecclesiastical magisterium adapts, explains, and defends genuine doctrine according to the demands of errors which are spread and according to the needs which arise from the development of man and of society. By this progress, the mind of the Church is led to search more deeply into doctrine and to understand it more clearly.

In this way, there has arisen in two areas a distinction which no one has explained more clearly than Pope John XXIII in his encyclical *Pacem In Terris:* 1) A clearer distinction between false philosophical teachings and the endeavors and institutions which these ideologies give rise to or nourish. While on the one hand the ideologies are always to be condmned, on the other hand the economic, social and civil institutions which have arisen therefrom can contain something that is good and worthy of approval. 2) A clearer distinction between errors and the person who errs in good faith. While on the one hand errors must always be rejected, on the other hand the man in error "does not cease to be endowed with human nature, nor does he ever lose his dignity as a person, due consideration of which must always be maintained (ibid. pp. 299-300).

These two laws of continuity and progress must be kept before our eyes always when the documents of the Apostolic See are read and interpreted.

In this way the door is opened to a correct understanding of many pontifical documents which in the nineteenth century treated of religious liberty in such words that this liberty appeared as something that had to be condemned. The clearest example is found in the encyclical *Quanta Cura* of Pius IX, in which we read: "From this completely false concept of social rule (naturalism), they do not hesitate to foster that erroneous opinion which is especially injurious to the Catholic Church and the salvation of souls, called by our predecessor Gregory XVI *"deliramentum,"* namely that the freedom of conscience and of cults is the proper right of each man, and this should be proclaimed and asserted in every rightly constituted society" (ASS 3, 1867, p. 162).

As is evident, this freedom of conscience is condemned because of the ideology of the rationalists who founded their conclusions upon the principle that the individual conscience is under no law, and, therefore, is subject to no divinely given norms. (Cf. Syllabus, prop. 3, ASS 3, p. 168). Freedom of worship is condemned also when it is based upon religious indifferentism (ibid. prop. 15, p. 170). Finally, there is condemned that separation of the Church from the State which is based upon the rationalistic principle of the juridical omnicompetence of the State, according to which the Church is to be incorporated into the monistic organism of the State and is to be subjected to its supreme authority (ibid., prop. 39, p. 172).

To understand these condemnations correctly, we must see in them the constant doctrine and solicitude of the Church concerning the true dignity of the human person and his true liberty (law of continuity). For the ultimate basis of human dignity lies in the fact that man is a creature of God. He is not God himself, but an image of God. From this absolute dependence of man upon God there flows every right and duty of man to claim for himself and for others true religious liberty. For man is subjectively bound to worship God according to the sincere dictate of his own conscience (*juxta rectam suae conscientiae normam*) because objectively he is absolutely dependent upon God.

In order, therefore, that his absolute dependence upon God might not be infringed in any way, man must not be impeded in any way by others or even by public authority from freely practicing his religion. Therefore, in opposing the philosophical and political tenets of laicism, the Church was fighting for the dignity and true liberty of the human person. In accordance with the law of continuity, then, the Church, in spite of changing conditions, has remained consistent both in the past and in the present.

Leo XIII had already started this doctrinal development when he distinguished clearly between the Church, the People of God, and the civil society, a terrestrial and temporal people (cf. *Immortale Dei*, ASS 18, 1885, pp. 166-167). By this means, he opened the way to a new affirmation of the due and lawful autonomy which belongs to the civil order and to its juridical dispositions. Because of this, it was possible to take a step forward (law of progress) toward a new judgment on "modern freedoms."

These freedoms can be tolerated (cf. ibid., p. 174; *Libertas Praestantissimum* ASS 20, 1887, pp. 609-610). And yet they were to be tolerated only. The reason was evident. For at that time in Europe, the regimes which proclaimed the modern freedoms, religious liberty among them, consciously drew their inspiration from the laicist ideology. There was danger, therefore—and Leo XIII sensed this—that the civil and political institutions of this kind of republic, since they were of laicist orientation, would lead to such abuses that they would necessarily do violence to the dignity and true liberty of the human person. In accordance with the law of continuity, what was dear to Leo XIII is always dear to the Church—the safeguarding of the human person.

With the rise of State-Totalitarianism in its various forms, Pope Pius XI brought the pastoral and doctrinal development to a new height. There is no longer any danger, as there was in the nineteenth century, that the false concept of liberty might do violence to human dignity. There is a new danger, that every kind of human and civil liberty, and above all religious liberty, will be destroyed. For this reason, the Church is beginning in a new way to manifest her concern, which through the centuries has never wavered, for human liberty and dignity. With the increase of her pastoral concern, the Church's doctrine continues to develop.

Faithfully observing the law of continuity, Pius XI maintained the unstinting opposition of the Church to anti-religious laicism: "Those things which Pius X condemned we also condemn; as often as there is in 'laicism' any meaning or purpose that is harmful or contrary to God or religion, we condemn laicism, and openly declare that it must be condemned, as alien to God and religion" (*Maximam gravissimamque*, AAS 16, 1924, p. 10).

But observing the rule of progress no less, Pius XI introduced a new distinction which was of great importance for a deeper understanding of Catholic doctrine. He made a distinction between the "freedom of consciences" and the "freedom of conscience." The latter he rejected as "equivocal," as often used by the laicist to signify "an absolute independence of conscience, which is an absurdity in man who was created and redeemed by God"; the former however, "freedom of consciences," he accepted, stating that he would joyfully fight the good fight for "freedom of consciences" (*Non abbiamo bisogno,* AAS 23, 1931, pp. 301-302).

Moreover, Pius XI not only fought for the religious liberty of the faithful, but he was at the same time compelled to show the pastoral concern of the Church on a wider basis. For not only Christian, but human reality was at stake, if we can rightly distinguish between two things that are in reality one.

By way of new advances, Pius XI developed a truly liberal and Christian doctrine when he taught: "man as a person possesses God-given rights which must remain immune from all denial, privation, or interference on the part of society" (*Mit brennender Sorge,* AAS 29, 1937, p. 159). And he continues in no ambiguous words: "The believer possesses the inalienable right to profess his faith and to practice it in a proper way. Laws which interfere with or render difficult this profession and practice are in contradiction to the natural law" (ibid. p. 160). No one, who understands the condition of the times and the purpose of this encyclical, can fail to understand the universal intent of this statement.

Deeply sharing the pastoral solicitude of his predecessor, Pius XII developed further and expanded his doctrine (law of progress). One thing he kept before his mind, the human person, created by God, redeemed by Christ Jesus, yet placed in stringent circumstances and surrounded on all sides by dangers.

In this context of doctrine and pastoral solicitude (law of continuity) we must read the text which in this matter is supreme. Enumerating "the fundamental rights of the person" which must be recognized and respected in every well-ordered society, he repeats the doctrine of Pius XI and vests it with new authority, affirming "the right to the private and public worship of God, including religious 'actio caritativa'" (*Nuntius radiophonicus* 24 Dec. 1942, AAS 35, 1943, p. 19).

The Roman Pontiff did not propose this doctrine as a tenuous opinion or as a theory belonging to the schools. On the contrary, he carries the doctrine to its juridical conclusions so that it becomes a principle according to which just limits are placed on public authority: "The chief duty of any public authority is to safeguard the inviolable rights that are proper to men and so to provide that each one might more easily fulfill his duties" (*Nuntius radiophonicus* 1 June, 1941, AAS 33, 1941, p. 200).

Here we must recall especially the doctrine of Pius XII on the limitation of the State, because it deals with the suppression of errors within society: "Could it be that in certain circumstances He (God) would not give men any mandate, would not impose any duty, and would not even communicate the right to impede or to repress what is erroneous and false? A look at things as they are gives an affirmative answer." Then, having cited the example of divine providence, he proceeds: "Hence the affirmation: religious and moral error must always be impeded, when it is possible, because toleration of them is in itself immoral, is not valid absolutely and unconditionally. Moreover, God has not given even to human authority such an absolute and universal command in matters of faith and morality. Such a command is unknown to the common convictions of mankind, to Christian conscience, to the sources of revelation, and to the practice of the Church" (*Ci Riesce*, AAS 45, 1953, pp. 798-799).

This declaration (law of progress) is of the greatest importance for our question, especially if we keep in mind what was in the past held concerning the role of the State.

At the end of this historical development comes the encyclical *Pacem in Terris*. This document comes forth as the ripe fruit of a slow process of growth which has taken place within the Church, under the light of the Holy Spirit, throughout the whole of the last century.

Our schema had already been prepared and had been studied by the Central Commission and by the Commission for Coordination when Pope John, on April 11 of this year, published his last encyclical *Pacem in Terris*. We believe that our text is in complete conformity with his perlucid doctrine, which was received within the Church and outside of the Church with unprecedented praise.

We now submit this text for your consideration. In the historical conspectus of this doctrine, we have shown that, in the pontifical documents, along with continuity, we must look for a progressive spelling out of doctrine. It is evident that certain quotations from the Popes, because of a difference of words, can be put in opposition to our schema. But I beseech you, Venerable Fathers, not to force the text to speak outside of its historical and doctrinal context, not, in other words, to make the fish swim out of water.

Let our document be studied as it stands. It is not a dogmatic treatise, but a pastoral decree directed to men of our time. The whole world is waiting for this decree. The voice of the Church on religious liberty is being waited for in universities, in national and international organizations, in Christian and non-Christian communities, in the papers, and in public opinion—and it is being waited for with urgent expectancy.

We hope that it will be possible to complete the discussion and the approbation of this very brief, but very important, decree before the end of this second session. How fruitful our work would appear to the world if the Conciliar Fathers, with the voice of Peter's successor, could announce this liberating doctrine on religious liberty!

Venerable Fathers, we will add our labors to yours. Our Secretariat will study your emendations most attentively and also with the utmost speed. We will work day and night. But our hope is in the Lord. May Jesus Christ assist all of us with His grace. If at the end of this session He asks of us: "Young men, do you have any fish?," seeing the faith and good will of this Council, He might say to their successors what once He said to the Apostles: "Cast the net to the right of the boat: and you will find" (Jn. 21:6).

Just as the debate on "Bishops" had been dominated by its "crisis"—the Frings-Ottaviani exchange and the controversy over the validity of the October 30th vote—so the discussion of Ecumenism came to be pervaded by the nagging uncertainty about the fate of Chapters IV and V at the present session. The primary concern was over the last chapter. A large majority, including most of the Americans whose interest in toleration was based in good part on the traditional American stand on separation of Church and state, were eager to have a test-vote on the chapter in principle. The minority, on the other hand, were fearful about the implications of debate on this issue, distrustful of the language employed in the text, and opposed to making any concessions to liberty which, they claimed, could be distorted by the communists and used to undermine the authority of the Church in certain traditionally Catholic areas.

In opening the debate on Monday, Cardinal Tappouni of Antioch sounded a warning note that would be repeated by almost all the Oriental prelates. After objecting to the treatment of the Orthodox and Protestants in the same chapter "because the relationship of the two to the Catholic Church is radically different," he said that "to treat of Judaism and religious liberty in this schema was out of place and most inopportune." Ecumenism was concerned with the unity of Christians. It was inappropriate for the Council to take up the matter of relations with non-Christians. The latter should be mentioned only "by accident" and if so, there should be no discrimination by showing more attention to one group than to another. The good intentions of the Fathers would be misunderstood in the Arab press.

Cardinal Ruffini observed that the term "ecumenism" really had quite a different meaning from the one given to it in the text. As employed here it was out of harmony with the authentic meaning of "ecumenical" used with reference to a Council. The word normally meant "universal," while with reference to the schema it had a special meaning pertaining to the apostolate for unity. The term was introduced into theology by Protestants and was used with reference to their conferences intended to promote unity. The term should be clarified so as not to lead to dangerous ambiguities. It would be better to give a simple description of the movement under discussion, referring to it as "The movement called Ecumenism."—The text should speak more specifically about the special bonds uniting us with our separated brethren in the Oriental Churches, who were closer to us than the various Reformed "sects": they have the hierarchy, the seven sacraments, a true eucharistic worship, and devotion to the Blessed Virgin. While, apart from baptism and—at least for some—Scripture, there were no other ties with the Protestants. If there was to be discussion of the Jews, who were here given what we might call honorable mention, then the text should also take up those other religions whose members are often less hostile to the Church than the Jews and more open to "conversion" than the Protestants, as many missionaries can testify. And likewise if ecumenism was to be extended to the Jews, "why should there not be mention also of those millions of baptized Christians who follow marxism and daily contribute to the spread of atheism?" Lastly the schema provided no concrete directives for establishing a true and effective dialogue with our separated brethren. "Contacts with the separated brethren should be maintained only by those Catholics who lead a holy life, devote themselves to continual prayer, have a sound knowledge of theology, and have the approval of ecclesiastical authority."

Speaking in the name of "some" American bishops, Cardinal Ritter of St. Louis declared that the schema was the answer to the need felt for an *aggiornamento* of the Church. The presentation of this text marked the end of the Counter-Reformation, and obliged us to make a thorough examination of conscience. Likewise it put us under obligation to hasten the desirable day of unity by fervent prayer, example and study. "We are happy to hear that Chapter V will deal with religious liberty," he said. Without a declaration of this kind by the Council there could be no mutual discussion and the door would remain closed to any real dialogue with those outside the Church. Such a declaration should not be based on motives of expediency. It should proceed from solid theological principles, namely, 1) the absolute freedom of the act of faith; 2) the inviolability of human conscience;

and 3) the incompetence of any civil government to interpret the Gospel of Christ, with consequent independence of the Church from civil authority in the accomplishment of its mission.—In the text greater attention should be paid to the celebration of the eucharist as a symbol of unity and to the importance of the liturgy generally. There should also be a clear affirmation of the validity of the sacraments and orders of the Oriental Churches. The text should be cleared of any expressions offensive to Protestants. There was no valid reason for denying the use of the term "Church" to the religious groups which originated after the 16th century. Like any other living movement, ecumenism was subject to dangers. Excessive intellectualism could make it sterile and it could likewise easily degenerate into indifferentism. This was why we needed a *vademecum* or practical guide which would provide necessary and safe directions.

The Cardinal Archbishop of Caracas felt that the schema wisely laid stress on the essential foundation of ecumenism, which consisted in interior renewal and holiness of life. Only then would the Church shine and seem attractive to those to whom it might appeal. The splendor of the Church was that of truth, not only of revealed truth, but also of historical truth. It was therefore necessary to recognize, frankly, the responsibility of Catholics for divisions in the Church. It would be desirable if in the spirit of Pope Paul VI's opening speech, the Council would make a declaration acknowledging the faults of Catholics with respect to unity, asking pardon of the separated brethren, and would affirm at the same time that the Catholic Church does not feel the least resentment for whatever it may have had to suffer in turn.

The two Spanish cardinals, de Arriba y Castro and Bueno y Monreal, found the schema satisfactory with reservations, *"Placet iuxta modum,"* said the latter. It was clear that both

were basically hostile to the modern movement of ecumenism, and skeptical as well as fearful of its possible effects
on their Church. Their remarks revealed also that they had
not studied the matter very deeply and still regarded as valid
the reservations which had caused the Holy See to refuse
all cooperation in the twenties and thirties. The former, for
example, said that a conciliar decree urging the laity to take
part in any dialogue was dangerous and inconsistent with
present laws of the Church which forbade the publication or
reading of books favoring heresy. He was particularly exercised by the thought that the "less educated faithful" would
not be able to make a good showing if they participated in
any such conversation. As far as he was concerned, ecumenism meant simply a free rein for "proselytism." The implication was, of course, that while it was all right for the
Church to engage in proselytism, the same right could not
be claimed by other groups. To make the point clear beyond
any doubt, he stated flatly: "It should not be forgotten that
only the Catholic Church has the right and duty to evangelize." The schema should be dropped. Cardinal Bueno y
Monreal thought that the wording of the text should be more
cautious, lest it appear to sanction a kind of "Pan-Christi-
anity" or religious syncretism with all its dangers of indifferentism. Too much praise of things which the Catholic
Church shared in common with other groups could obscure
the distinctions.

The Archbishop of Tokyo, Cardinal Tatsuo Doi, welcomed the schema, but was of the opinion that the missionary aspects of ecumenism required that more attention be
paid to those who were non-Christians. The fact should be
brought out more clearly that the Church respected truth
wherever it was found, among non-Christian religions as
well.

Stephanos I Sidarouss, the Coptic Patriarch of Alexandria,

Egypt, was particularly anxious that the schema avoid giving the impression that it favored any "false irenic approach to unity" by stressing more clearly the doctrinal differences which separated the Catholic Church from others, for example the doctrine of the papal primacy. He found the definition of "ecumenism" in Paragraph 9 completely unsatisfactory. And he was for dropping all mention of the Jews. If the Council insisted on taking up this touchy subject, "we shall have to face the music" when we, meaning the representatives of Arab Christianity, go home.

The most notable speech of the first day was that by Patriarch Maximos IV Saigh, and all eyes were on him as he rose to state his views. The schema deserved more than mere assent: it was the first to combine doctrinal profundity with a pastoral orientation and it served as an excellent basis for discussion. Among its positive features: it left aside all sterile polemics and false proselytism; it marked the beginning of a dialogue in truth and unity; it breathed the theology of the Church which was traditional in the East. Among its negative aspects, however, must be mentioned, above all, Chapter IV which was completely out of place. Ecumenism was devoted to the reunion of Christians, that is, was a family problem, and time should not be wasted in speaking of non-Christians, unless we were to run the risk of offending the separated brethren. "If we are to discuss the Jews," he said, "then we should likewise take up the question of Moslems, among whom we must live in a minority." This would give us a different viewpoint on the whole problem, because, as an Arab proverb had it, The man receiving blows has a different outlook from the man who only counts them. We should mobilize all our efforts to hasten the advent of perfect unity for the glory of the Most Blessed Trinity and the welfare of the human race. Finally, he hoped that the wish of the recent Panorthodox Conference of Rhodes (Sept.

1963) could be realized: that a permanent dialogue should be established between Catholicism and Orthodoxy.

In an important intervention on Tuesday (Nov. 19), Cardinal Léger of Canada declared: "The present hope for and movement toward unity are not passing impulses, but are inspired by the Gospel and the Holy Spirit. We are fearful when we realize what a burden of history we must overcome. But we must face the task of dialogue with positive and truly Catholic prudence, which not only safeguards but tends toward union." He recalled the words of Pope Paul VI who said recently: "One purpose of the Council is to open every possible way to the unity of Christians." The present schema reflected this kind of prudence and merited approval, in fact it was sorely needed by the bishops as an expression of principle on the local level. The Cardinal of Vienna made an important observation about the nature of ecumenism which had perplexed many. "We should avoid any impression that Catholic ecumenism is a closed and perfect system. We are only at the beginning. The dialogue, together with prayer and the Holy Spirit, may lead us to new aspects and a more profound understanding of ecumenism." This remark was offered with special reference to those critics who kept insisting that the idea of ecumenism was "vague" and therefore dangerous. According to the American Jesuit Father Weigel, the beauty about the ecumenical movement was that it remained something fuzzy and ill-defined; it was desirable to keep it that way and not allow it to become petrified if further progress was to be made.

Bishop Elchinger, Coadjutor of Strasbourg, France, described the schema as a "grace" and a "blessing" of God. Its existence was due to the work of many leaders like Cardinal Mercier and theologians like Père Lagrange, who had much to suffer in their day because of the lack of sympathy for their ideas. If progress was to be made, we must recognize frankly the faults of the Church. While the Church was holy, God had entrusted his gifts to sinful men, to vessels of clay. It was important to recognize, for example, that the Reformers did not wish to destroy the unity of the Church. They were anxious to declare certain truths which they believed had become obscured. Secondly, it was wrong to reject as totally erroneous certain assertions which contain a part of the truth. Catholic rejections of Protestantism have been too sweeping and indiscriminate. Thirdly, there was too much of a tendency to consider Revelation as something passive, whereas it was something that must always be probed and investigated. It was not sufficient to remain content with Catholic truth. "We must continue to seek the truth which we shall never possess in its entirety." This amounted to saying that the definitions of the faith were always capable of being perfected. Fourthly, we had often made the mistake of confounding unity with uniformity.

Several speakers, including Cardinal Rugambwa and Archbishop Garrone, referred to the ecumenical implications of the Commandment, "Do the truth in charity." The former observed that our attitude toward the separated brethren should be characterized by humility as we reminded ourselves that faith was a gift and that we had nothing that we did not receive. A charitable attitude required that we adopt an open mind and cooperate with non-Catholics in all possible ways, particularly in missionary areas. This principle of cooperation should be written into the text. Archbishop Garrone said that some interpreted ecumenism as meaning merely that we were to take pains not to offend the separated brethren or to be merciful to them. But true ecumenism, founded on faith and rooted in hope, was something much more positive. It did not flee from opposition or fear the light, but strove to bring about mutual understanding, in the conviction that God would arrange things in His time. "We have an obligation to practice ecumenical charity," he said. Charity could break down many walls. Charity not only made the light of faith more intent, stronger, but purified it. When we unconsciously retained as matters of faith certain non-essential elements from polemical times, or when we were not willing or able to appreciate "as truly ours truths which others have faithfully kept," our own faith suffered. Ecumenical charity could help us to appreciate the "whole treasure of faith."

While full of praise for the schema, Archbishop de Provenchères noted that there were really three steps to reunion: 1. charity; 2. dialogue; and 3. internal renewal in the Church. While the schema dealt with the first two, it neglected the last important consideration. There must be a renewal not only through the liturgical movement, but a revamping of ecclesiastical institutions, and research into theological doctrine.

For the Armenian Patriarch Pierre XVI Batanian, the schema did not emphasize sufficiently what might be called the "authoritarian" aspects of charity. Charity demanded that truth be in no way compromised. But he found that certain passages seemed to "tone down" a frank statement of Catholic truth on a number of points. For example, the phrase *"regiminis fraterna concordia"* in Paragraph 1 could be understood as referring to a union of many "equal" governments in the Church not under one head, but as arising from human consent and the love of harmony. He would prefer some such expression as *"in unitate magisterii et regiminis."* He had often heard the Orthodox say: "You fortunate Catholics. In disputes you have a supreme authority by which you can say *Roma locuta est, causa finita est."* No purpose was served by hiding or toning down the existence of a supreme authority in the Catholic Church. He agreed with his other Oriental colleagues that the Chapter on the

Jews should not appear in the schema. The Latin Patriarch of Jerusalem, Alberto Gori, also felt strongly that the Chapter on the Jews should be omitted. It was unwise to single out one non-Christian group without mentioning the others.

After this mixed bag of reactions on the first two days of debate, there was some concern in progressive circles that the schema was not going over very well. While a majority of the Council was clearly in its favor, the tenor of the remarks on the floor, amply reported in the world press, could give the impression that things were worse than they really were. Fear that the minority, who were unfortunately virtually in control of the day-to-day operations of the Council, might exploit the situation in an attempt to kill the whole schema on the basis of frequently expressed criticisms of various parts, no doubt prompted the Pope and the Moderators to agree to a separate debate on Chapters I-III with a deliberately vague promise that the last two chapters would be taken up "later." The first chapters, after all, dealt with the crux of the issue of ecumenism, and attempted to provide the "guide" which all were looking for. The issues of the Jews and religious liberty, while important in themselves, were subsidiary so far as the main argument of Chapters I-III was concerned and could, conceivably, be taken up later in another connection. But the vital question left hanging in mid-air all through these days was, Would this assurance be given? The Jewish question was frankly judged to be of less importance in the mind of most of the Fathers. But the impression was widespread that unless the Church came out strongly in favor of some kind of guarantee of religious liberty and tolerance, the absence of any statement on this subject would make a mockery of whatever the Council chose to declare with regard to ecumenism.

A minor incident at this time served to accentuate the

determination of the Curial minority not to be beaten down
or overridden. At the end of his remarks on Wednesday,
Nov. 20th to the effect that the term "ecumenism" was unacceptable as implying a confusion with "interconfessional-
ism" and that the text seemed to play down the Roman primacy in favor of a collegial form of church government,
Cardinal Bacci, chief Latinist of the Curia, stated that when
on October 30th last he had attempted to say that the expression *ius primatiale* in one of the famous Five Propositions was inaccurate and should be replaced by *ius primatus*,
he was denied permission to speak by the then Moderator. He
asked for permission on Wednesday to state this publicly. Later
in the meeting that day the Moderator Cardinal Agagianian
explained that he had been refused permission on October
30th because the Moderators considered the expression *ius
primatiale* sufficiently clear. Apparently Curia cardinals must
not be thwarted in their undeclared right to be heard, no
matter how trivial their grammatical quibbling.

The Archbishop of Chicago, Cardinal Meyer, voicing the
opinion of many American bishops put his stamp of approval on the schema as a whole. He said that he was particularly pleased that chapters IV and V formed a part of it,
although he recognized that there were differences of opinion on this score. He urged that the whole schema, including
these chapters, be accepted as a basis for discussion.

Archbishop Heenan of Westminster, speaking for the
bishops of England and Wales, accepted the schema "joyfully." He said: "Some consider Catholics in England indifferent to the ecumenical movement; indeed, some of our
separated brethren have had to go abroad to engage in dialogue. . . We do not wish to restrict freedom to attend international ecumenical gatherings. But the Council should
recommend that the dialogue be carried on normally within
the region of those taking part in it." His speech was clearly

a notification that, whatever the sins of the past, in the future the British Catholic hierarchy intended to foster dialogue and the ecumenical movement. "We declare that we are prepared to do anything outside of denying the faith, to obtain the union of Christians. We desire fuller and more frequent dialogues with all Christian denominations." It will be remembered in this connection that it was the opposition of the Catholic hierarchy in England which compelled Lord Halifax to go over to Belgium to conduct the Malines Conversations with Cardinal Mercier, in the 1920's.

The question of greater latitude in the matter of participation by Catholics in the religious services of non-Catholics, and the admission of the latter to full participation in Catholic services, was raised by Archbishop-Bishop Weber of Strasbourg. The Apostolic Prefect of Dahomey, Msgr. Chopard-Lallier, said that it was difficult for the faithful in Africa to understand why Western missionaries were so careful about avoiding worship with each other.

On Thursday (Nov. 21) two important actions took place. It was announced that the Holy Father had decided to increase the membership in the various conciliar Commissions with a view to expediting the work of the Council. Each Commission was to be increased from 25 to 30 members, except for the Commission for the Oriental Churches and the Secretariat for Unity which had 27 and 18 members, respectively. In both cases the membership would be brought up to 30. Of the 5 new members to be added to all the commissions but these, 4 would be elected by the Council, and 1 would be appointed by the Pope. In order to prepare lists of candidates, the presidents of Episcopal Conferences were requested by Archbishop Felici to convoke meetings and decide on the names they wished to vote for. The Council Fathers could vote for any names, but it would be helpful to have joint lists. The names were to be presented by Monday

NOTIFICATIO

In hunc finem ut Commissionum Conciliarium labores expeditius et alacrius procedant, SUMMUS PONTIFEX, accipiens etiam multorum Patrum postulata, dignatus est concedere ut numerus sodalium uniuscuiusque Commissionis ad triginta perducatur. Quinque igitur sodales in Commissionibus omnibus addendi sunt, exceptis Commissione de Ecclesiis Orientalibus, quae iam numerat viginti septem sodales, et Secretariatu ad christianorum unitatem fovendam, quae tantummodo duodeviginti sodales ex Patribus Conciliaribus habet: pro illa itaque tres tantum sodales eligendi sunt, pro hoc, duodecim.

Statuit Summus Pontifex ut ex quinque sodalibus eligendis in Commissionibus, unus Ipsi reservetur, quattuor a Patribus eligantur. In Commissione de Ecclesiis Orientalibus, cum duo iam electi sint a Summo Pontifice, durante intersessione, electio aliorum trium committitur Patribus. In Secretariatu ad christianorum unitatem fovendam quattuor a Summo Pontifice, octo a Patribus eligentur. Pro Commissione de Sacra Liturgia, cum haec iam expletura sit feliciter, ut speramus, suum munus, nullus alius sodalis eligendus est.

Novi sodales eligendi sunt inter Patres qui vere periti sint in materiis, quae Commissionum studio sunt subiectae, et possint Romam, durante intersessione, facile convenire.

Uti patet, eligi non possunt qui iam sint sodales in alia Commissione vel munus obeant in Coetibus directivis Concilii.

Postquam novi sodales omnes electi fuerint, Summus Pontifex concedit ut novum Vicepraesidem et novum Secretarium *additum* (hunc tamen inter Peritos), praeter iam existentes, Commissiones sibi eligant.

Ut electio expeditissime, quantum potis est, fiat a Patribus, rogantur vehementer Praesides Conferentiarum Episcopalium ut suam quisque Conferentiam congreget et Patrum nomina indicet, non plus quam tria pro qualibet Commissione (et pro Secretariatu non plus quam sex), qui proponi possint eligendi in Congregatione Generali.

Valde optandum est ut plures Conferentiae in unam coalescant, ita ut elenchum unicum exhibeant.

Manet tamen Patribus libertas alios quoque Patres eligendi.

Terminus ultimus pro exhibendis Secretariae Generali elenchis statuitur feria II proxima, dies scilicet 25 Novembris.

Omnes elenchi distribuentur Patribus feria IV sequenti, ita ut electio fiat feria V successiva.

E Civitate Vaticana, die 21 Novembris 1963.

✠ PERICLES FELICI, *Secr. Gen.*

Notification about the election of new members to the Commissions, November 21, 1963 and the voting would take place a week hence (Nov. 28). The Holy Father, it was announced, would then allow the Commissions to elect a second (or additional) Vice President and Secretary.

The first impression of this announcement was one of pessimism among council observers. It was felt that by leaving the Curial cardinals in charge of the Commissions, the Pope would undo whatever good might come out of the elections. It "fell short," in other words, of expectations. However when the results of the voting were announced in record time on Friday Nov. 29, there was at least a glimmer of hope. Some 59 episcopal conferences had accomplished the feat of agreeing on an "international list" of candidates and practically all of them were elected. Another significant detail: almost all the new members were from Europe, America and Asia, and could be described as progressives. Three Americans were elected, more than for any other country. And only 1 Italian! The Americans were Bishop Primeau of Manchester, New Hampshire, Bishop Helmsing of Kansas City–St. Joseph, Mo., and Bishop Lane of Rockford, Illinois. Bishop Ancel, Auxiliary of Lyons, France, and Abbot Butler of Downside Abbey, England, joined the Theological Commission, which then met and elected as its second Vice President, Bishop Charue of France, and its second Secretary, Msgr. Philips of Louvain, without any opposition, it was reported, on the part of Cardinal Ottaviani and Cardinal Browne, President and first Vice-President, respectively. The expectation was, as Father Häring pointed out at a press panel meeting, that the new forward-looking vice presidents, with a majority of members behind them, would be able to turn the tide against the conservative leadership. However there were many who were keeping their fingers crossed as to whether the Pope's plan to circumvent the conservatives without forcing any resignations would really work.

The same day (Nov. 21), after further discussion of the
Ecumenism schema, the Moderators suddenly announced
that the Council would proceed to an immediate vote on
acceptance of Chapters I-III as a basis for discussion. The
Secretary General added that the voting on Chapters IV and
V would take place *"proximis diebus"*—in a few days. The
voting revealed an overwhelming majority in favor of accepting the text for discussion: 1996 favorable to 86 negative,
and was considered a signal victory for the Secretariat for
Unity, on the surface at least.

In the speeches on Thursday before the latter announcement, praise for the contents continued to alternate with
discordant notes calling into question the validity of the
notion of ecumenism as such. The fact, said Bishop Flores
Martin of Spain, that Catholics shared with separated Chris-
tion brethren the indelible sacramental character and a
spiritual participation in the priesthood of Christ meant that
they must do battle with them against the snares of the devil.
The principle of cooperation, on the basis of brotherly love
and mutual aid, should be written into the schema. "The
widest possible latitude should be allowed for participation
in non-Catholic religious services in order to avoid the strug-
gles which are all too common among those who should be
living together in peace," he maintained. Archbishop Florit
of Florence disagreed with this suggestion. It was too optimistic to say that "certain elements which are common to
our separated brethren and ourselves are a manifestation of
unity," as the schema put it. "Rather they emphasize division,"
the archbishop asserted. Prayers said by ourselves and others
for unity were only externally the same; basically they were
different because of the internal personal intentions of each
one. The text had high praise for the separated brethren, but
not all were worthy of praise in the same degree. Perhaps
the better way to unity was to arouse a "holy inquietude" by

showing them what they lacked rather than to promote tranquillity of conscience by insisting on what they possessed. The questions of the Jews and religious liberty should not be considered in this schema. Religious liberty might be considered in Schema 17. The central issue remained: Could there be a natural right to diffuse a false religion in good faith? Not if this right were to be founded on the dignity of the person. To diffuse error was wrong, and one could not have a natural right to do wrong. Furthermore, error in itself was against the common good, there could therefore be no question of liberty to teach error, except in cases where it did not hurt the common good or was less harmful to the common good than a public prohibition would be.

The important thing to note about the present schema, said Bishop Hoeffner of Germany, was that it promoted union with those who cut themselves off from the Catholic Church in past centuries and now belonged to other Christian communities. The aim of ecumenism was to restore unity with these groups. "We must not act as if we were still living in the 16th century. A dialogue must be established." This was necessary because there were also countless other "separated brethren" who had abandoned all Christian confession and drifted into atheism. Ecumenism was vital as a preparation for dealing with this enormous problem.

Bishop Hervás y Benet of Spain thought that treatment of religious liberty in the schema on Ecumenism might encourage "propaganda, liberalism, and existentialism." The proper place to deal with it was in the schema on the presence of the Church in the world, Schema 17.

Both the Maronite Archbishop Ziadé and the Hungarian Bishop Hamvas welcomed the emphasis on the value of different ecclesiastical traditions and the existence of unity without uniformity. Catholics and Calvinists in Hungary were now on friendly terms, using each other's churches and cooperating in other ways, whereas not so long ago, the Calvinists were persecuted and suffered at the hands of the dominant Catholic majority.

After the announcement of a cloture, the debate continued on Chapter I of the schema concerning "The Principles of Catholic Ecumenism." The numbered paragraphs were as follows:

1. The Unity and Unicity of the Church.
2. The relation of the Separated Brethren to the Catholic Church.
3. Ecumenism.

The harshness of the integralist point of view was brought out clearly by Bishop Carli who said that the schema should state *all* the principles of ecumenism, not just a few. Among the doctrinal principles which should be uncompromisingly spelled out in Chapter I, without any attempt at equivocation, were the "uniqueness of the Roman Catholic Church" which by objective criteria was distinguished from other Churches; the axiom that "outside the Church there is no salvation"; the grave obligation on everybody to join the Catholic Church as soon as he discovered that it was the "true Church." While the separated communities possessed some of the means of sanctification—which he called the "spoils from Mother Church"—it was these gifts and not the Churches themselves which the Holy Spirit used. And the text should be corrected to remove the impression that the Spirit sanctioned separation and abandoned His unique Spouse. The first paragraph, by stating that "the Church is founded on the Apostles and prophets" implied that "the notion of the papal primacy is being obscured!" The *litigiosa vox* of "collegiality" should be omitted because it was not yet proved. It should be stated that the Apostles were the "auxiliaries" of Peter, as Vatican Council I declared. The bishop preferred to ignore not only what the Moderators themselves had repeatedly asserted, but, more to the point, what the Pope himself had just stated in his general audience the day before. Although Pope Paul did not use the word "collegiality," his words left one in no doubt as to what he meant: ". . . an organization, a hierarchy, instituted by Christ Himself, in which the first place is occupied by the Apostles, that is, the bishops, and at their head Peter, that is, the Pope."

A number of speakers on Friday (Nov. 22) contended that it was unbalanced for the schema to speak of Jews without dealing with other non-Christian bodies, but that if this was to be attempted a whole new approach would be needed. The schema as it stood was inadequate in this respect.

Bishop Huyghe of France roundly condemned what he described as an erroneous notion of ecumenism put forth by some Catholics, who equated it with "return" pure and simple to the Catholic Church in the sense of a complete "surrender" to its claims. The good lives of Catholics were the best contribution of Catholics to ecumenism, as the schema stated. There was too much of a tendency to sit back and wait for the return of others without making any changes in Catholic procedures or viewpoints. The schema was correct in speaking of reunion as involving an "approach" (*aditus*) or "access" of the others, and not of their "return." The first condition for the success of all ecumenical work was the sincere conversion of *all* Christians, Catholics as well as others. The second condition was common action, for which the schema was to be a kind of directory, suggesting concrete ways.

Archbishop Jaeger of Paderborn, Germany, congratulated the authors of the schema for using "concrete language instead of scholastic definitions." The schema presupposed what was said in the debate on the Church and at Vatican Council

I on the papal primacy, therefore it was not necessary for it to go over all this ground again. Moreover, the schema was not a dogmatic or canonical treatise, and so it would be inappropriate for it to go into these matters. He wanted the eucharist, particularly, to be mentioned as a sign of unity along with the bonds of unity listed in Paragraph 1, and for the Holy Spirit to be mentioned as the ultimate, uncreated principle of the Church's unity. Rather than say that our separated Oriental brethren had been "cut off" from the unity of the Catholic Church, Bishop Flusin of France preferred the text to say that their separation had "broken" or "weakened" the bond of unity. And he wanted a greater distinction between individuals who were personally responsible for schism or heresy and those who were born into groups thus cut off from the Church long ago.

Friday's debate was brought to a conclusion by the intervention of the Chinese Bishop Chang-Tso-huan, who directed the attention of the Fathers once again to the wider aspects of the problem. "As an example for our zeal we can take the ancient Chinese who preached ecumenism many centuries before Confucianism."

To say that a hushed silence fell over normally bustling Rome when the news broke that President Kennedy had been assassinated (about 7 P.M. Rome time) would be doing less than justice to the feeling of gloom and shock which could have been cut with a knife. Flags were immediately flown at halfmast, including the yellow and white banner of the Holy See to be seen on various buildings throughout the city. Italians of all classes were aware of their loss and showed it. In addition to the sentiments which all felt so profoundly, which Pope Paul expressed from his window on Sunday when he blessed the crowds in St. Peter's Square, his telegrams to Mrs. Jacqueline Kennedy, President Johnson, the President's parents and Cardinal Cushing were all given prominent display in the press. Rome too had its part in mourning the tragic death. Special commemorative services were held at the Episcopal Church of St. Paul on the Via Nazionale and at the Jewish Synagogue. The chief service was a solemn requiem mass celebrated on Monday by Cardinal Spellman, assisted by prelates from the American College, in the cathedral of Rome, San Giovanni in Laterano, and attended by President Segni of Italy and other high dignitaries of the government and diplomatic corps as well as most of the American colony in Rome. Among the 36 cardinals attending were Cardinals Bea, Caggiano, Suenens, Agagianian, Tappouni, Meyer, Ruffini, Landazuri-Ricketts, Pizzardo, Ciriaci, McIntyre, Ritter, Lercaro, and Wyszynski. Also present were the non-Catholic Observer-Delegates to the Council. By special permission of the Pope, the mass was celebrated at the papal altar and the proceedings were televised. Representatives of the American armed forces stood guard at the four corners of the catafalque along with four Italian carabinieri all in parade uniform, while four cuirassiers of the presidential guard stood on each side of the transept. The mass over, Cardinal Spellman approached the catafalque and gave the absolution, while all rose and the choir intoned the anthem *Libera me Domine.* The cardinal pronounced the required formula first in Latin, then in English. Afterward he delivered a few brief remarks praising the deceased President, referring to him as "that marvelous and exemplary President" and remarking on the "wave of love for our dear country" which he had evoked. "We have suffered a great loss. May God have mercy on his soul."

All day Sunday and Monday throngs of people kept filing into the American Embassy on Via Veneto to pay their respects and sign the registers, twenty-one of which had to be pressed into service, including the one normally reserved for the diplomatic corps. Next to his signature Archpriest

Vitaly Borovoy, the Russian Orthodox observer-delegate from Moscow wrote: "We have prayed for the peaceful repose of the soul of this great Christian who has sacrificed his life for a great truth: the equality of all races and the brotherhood of all peoples under God. May God receive his soul in peace and may his memory endure forever." There were also numerous spontaneous sentiments, like the following: "To the beloved, great Kennedy." "To Kennedy, missionary of brotherhood among men of peace and freedom." Beneath one expression of harsh feeling toward the assassin, a nun wrote, "Perhaps we should pray for the souls of both men."

Of the many epitaphs on President Kennedy's death published all over the world, one of the most memorable was written by Hannah Arendt in the special Kennedy number of *The New York Review of Books*. "There is a curious and infinitely sad resemblance between the death of the two greatest men we have lost during this year—the one very old, the other in the prime of life. Both the late Pope and the late President died much too soon in view of the work they initiated and left unfinished. The whole world changed and darkened when their voices fell silent. And yet the world will never be as it was before they spoke and acted in it."

On Monday November 25th, the Council was asked to vote on the revised final text of the schema on Communications Media, debated at the first session. If approved, the text was to be promulgated by the Pope as a conciliar decree on December 4th, at the closing ceremony. The rather large number of *iuxta modum* votes on this occasion—favorable but with conditions—503 to 1598 in favor (with 1 invalid vote) indicated that a rather large number of the Fathers still had reservations and were not satisfied with the final version. The belief was widespread that the adverse vote would have been even larger, except for the fact that many

U R G E N T E

Venerabiles Patres!
Relecto ante definitivam suffragationem iterum schemate
"De mediis communicationis socialis" multis Patribus textus
huius schematis ad Decretum Conciliare minime convenire videtur.
Rogantur Patres in animo considerare, an suffragium ferant
NON PLACET.

Schema enim exspectationi christianorum, praesertim in hac re
peritorum, minime respondet. Si ut Decretum promulgaretur,
Concilii auctoritas in discrimen vocaretur.

+ Hermann Schäufele, Archiepiscopus, Freiburg (Germania)
+ Angelo Fernandez, Archiepiscopus tit. Neopatrensis (India)
+ Marcus Mihayo, Archiepiscopus, Tabora (Tanganyika)
+ Carolus Jurgens, Archiepiscopus, Cuzco (Perù)
+ Michael Olcomendy, Archiepiscopus, Malacca-Singapore (Malesia)
+ Antoine van den Hurk, Archiepiscopus, Medan (Indonesia)
+ Emile de Smedt, Episcopus, Brugge (Belgia)
+ Paul Schoenmaeckers, Episcopus auxiliaris, Mechelen-Brüssel (Belgia)
+ Hermann Volk, Episcopus, Mainz (Germania)
+ Joseph Maria Reuss, Episcopus auxiliaris, Mainz (Germania)
+ Paul Joseph Schmidt, Episcopus, Metz (Gallia)
+ Maurice Pourchet, Episcopus, Saint-Flour (Gallia)
+ Hugh Boyle, Episcopus, Johannesburg (Africa meridionalis)
+ Adolf J.P. Fürstenberg, Episcopus, Abercorn (Rhodesia)
+ James Corboy, Episcopus, Monze (Rhodesia)
+ F.X. Thomas, Episcopus, Geraldton (Australia)
+ John Cullinan, Episcopus auxiliaris, Canberra Goulburn (Australia)
+ Ramon Bogarin, Episcopus, S. Juan de las Mis. (Paraquay)
+ Hanibal Maricevich Fleitas, Episc. Coadj., Villarrica (paraguay)
+ Vicente Zazpe, Episcopus, Rafaela, (Argentina)
+ Enrique Principe, Episc. auxiliaris, Santa Fe (Argentina)
+ Marcelo Mendiharat, Episcopus Coadi., Salto (Uruguay)
+ Roberto Caceres, Episcopus, Melo (Uruguay)
+ Luis Baccino, Episcobous, San José de Mayo, (Uruguay)
  P. Johannes Schütte, Superior Generalis, S.V.D.

Circular signed by 25 Council Fathers urging a *"Non Placet"* vote
on the Communications schema, November 25, 1963

bishops had not even troubled to read the text much less
give it serious consideration. The same was true of the debate
on the floor in 1962. Many thought that the subject merited
some attention but was hardly worth the time of an ecumenical Council. Some felt that it was so unworthy and com-
promising as to be voted down. To give expression to their
view, a mimeographed sheet containing signatures by 24
bishops and 1 head of a religious order, mostly Continental
prelates, was distributed to the Fathers as they entered the
basilica on Monday to cast their votes. Bishop Reuss, Auxiliary of Mainz, was behind the move. As he was entering the
basilica, the Secretary General Archbishop Felici discovered
what was being done and tried to seize the papers from the
priests who were distributing them. Bishop Reuss protested
and declared that he was entirely within his rights. Failing
to put a stop to the distribution, Archbishop Felici summoned the papal gendarmes and then rushed, in anger, into
the basilica and lodged a complaint with Cardinal Tisserant,
Dean of the Sacred College and President of the Board of
Council Presidents. In the course of the debate that morning,
Cardinal Tisserant denounced the distribution of the sheets
as a tactic "unworthy" of the Council. Later on he took the
microphone again to state that one of the bishops—whom
he did not name—claimed that he had not signed the document. This precipitate action on the part of Cardinal Tisserant caused considerable murmuring among a large number of bishops, who asked themselves why nothing similar
had been said during the voting on the schema on Mary
when Father Balič's pamphlet had been surreptitiously distributed among the Fathers, or when Archbishop Dino
Staffa's statement against the collegiality of the bishops had
been passed out in the council hall. Later a number of
bishops wrote to Cardinal Tisserant protesting his action.
Cardinal Tisserant's contention that the schema had already

been approved by a two-thirds majority in a preliminary vote as the reason why the request to vote *Non placet* was irregular, was irrelevant. To some the whole incident was but another sign that the minority were prepared to infringe the Council's freedom of action when it suited their purposes.

Criticism of the final version of the Communications Decree was summed up in a statement issued on November 16 by three American newsmen, John Cogley of *Commonweal*, Robert Kaiser of *Time*, and Michael Novak, correspondent for the Kansas City *Catholic Reporter*, the Boston *Pilot* and other papers. The statement was also countersigned under the words "This statement is worthy of consideration" by four notable theologians: Father John Courtney Murray, S.J., Father Jean Daniélou, S.J., Father Jorge Mejia, S.J., and Father Bernard Häring, C.SS.R. It claimed that the proposed decree was "not an *aggiornamento*, but a step backward," and said that where the document was "not vague and banal, it reflects a hopelessly abstract view of the relationship of the Church and modern culture. It deals with a press that exists only in textbooks and is unrecognizable to us." Singled out for censure were the "moralistic emphasis and simplistic treatment of the difficult problem of art and prudence (section 5)," its failure to mention the obligations of those who should be the sources of information (section 11), the implication that it was "endowing the Catholic press with a teaching authority and near-infallibility that is neither proper to journalism nor helpful to the formation of public opinion in the Church" (section 14), "the setting up of an intermediate ecclesiastical authority between the individual communications worker and his employer" (section 21), and giving "the state an authority over mass media which is dangerous to political liberty everywhere and which in some countries like the United States is proscribed by constitutional law" (sections 5 and 12). They asserted, finally, that "it may one

DECRETUM

DE INSTRUMENTIS COMMUNICATIONIS SOCIALIS

DE QUA AGETUR IN SESSIONE PUBLICA
DIEI 4 DECEMBRIS 1963

(Sub secreto)

TYPIS POLYGLOTTIS VATICANIS
MCMLXIII

DECRETUM

DE INSTRUMENTIS
COMMUNICATIONIS SOCIALIS

PROOEMIUM

1. Inter mirifica technicae artis inventa, quae hodiernis praesertim temporibus, Deo favente, humanum ingenium e rebus creatis deprompsit, peculiari sollicitudine Mater Ecclesia ea excipit ac prosequitur quae hominis animum potissimum respiciunt, quaeque novas aperuerunt vias cuiusvis generis nuntios, cogitata ac praecepta facillime communicandi. E quibus vero inventis ea eminent instrumenta, quae non modo singulos homines, sed ipsas multitudines totamque humanam societatem, natura sua attingere ac movere valent, sicuti prelum, cinematographeum, radiophonia, televisio et alia huiusmodi, quae proinde instrumenta communicationis socialis merito vocari possunt.

2. Novit quidem Mater Ecclesia haec instrumenta, si recte adhibeantur, humano generi valida praebere subsidia, cum multum conferant ad relaxandos et excolendos animos atque ad Dei regnum propagandum et firmandum; novit etiam homines posse ea adhibere contra divini Conditoris consilium et in suorum ipsorum iacturam convertere; immo materno angitur doloris sensu ob damna quae ex pravo eorum usu humanae consociationi nimis saepe orta sunt.

Quare Sacrosancta Synodus, Summorum Pontificum et Episcoporum, in re tanti momenti, vigilanti curae instans, suum esse censet quaestiones praecipuas tractare cum instrumentis communicationis socialis conexas. Confidit insuper suam doctrinam et disciplinam hoc modo propositam, non modo christifidelium saluti, sed etiam totius consortionis humanae progressui esse profuturam.

Title page and preface of Decree on Communications Media

day be cited as a classic example of how the Second Vatican Council failed to come to grips with the world around it."

One theory advanced for the Pope's action in allowing it to go through was that he decided it would be a good way to get rid of the measure and remove it from the Council's agenda, allowing events and experience to determine whether it should be vigorously applied or not. Since there was no question of its being regarded as infallible—this was expressly made clear on the council floor—the communications document became, as Father Gustave Weigel, S.J. described it, the "official and authentic doctrine of the Church," it did not or would not become the "irreformable and once-for-all-times doctrine of the Church." The prediction was that it would be enforced loosely, if at all.

After the voting, the debate resumed on Chapter I of Ecumenism. Cardinal Léger felt that the doctrine of unity expressed in the schema could be clarified somewhat more. Many Catholics as well as Non-Catholics thought that the Church favored an excessively monolithic unity, he said. There had been many signs in recent centuries that this was indeed the case, for example, the insistence on a uniform liturgical worship, or a uniform discipline, and a consequent neglect of legitimate freedom. Variety was still compatible with perfect obedience to the Vicar of Christ. The separated brethren had their own traditions, and the schema should bring out more clearly how these traditions could be harmonized with the essentials of unity. Particular care should be given to the question of expressing doctrinal truth in a charitable manner. It was not infrequently said that the Catholic Church possessed the whole of Christ's revealed truth. In a sense this was true, but the proper distinctions must be made. The statement glided over the undoubted fact that we were incapable of understanding perfectly the unsearchable riches of divine revelation. The transcendence of God did not contradict but rather tempered the doctrine of infallibility. "Authentic Christianity has no place for intellectual standpatism," he said, recalling words of Pope Paul to the observer delegates.

Cardinal Ritter of St. Louis also called for greater precision in dealing with the concept of unity. The pastoral, doctrinal, and ecumenical sides of unity should be brought out. Instead of the description of unity in Paragraph 1, he suggested that the text should say that unity was not desired for itself but rather because it represented Christ Himself, the achievement of His glory through a recapitulation of all things in Him. If this were done, it would then appear that the Church was a long way from its perfection in unity and holiness. From such unity, as the end and basic principle of ecumenism, flowed the need for renewal and for charity toward our separated brothers. In closing, he thanked the Fathers for their expressions of condolence on the occasion of President Kennedy's assassination.

The President of the Secretariat for Promoting Christian Unity which had prepared the schema, Cardinal Bea, rose to say that doubts about the appropriateness of the title as well as the use of the word "ecumenism" would be taken into account. There had been much talk in recent days about the "dangers" of ecumenism. He agreed that there could be such if unity was treated by men who were inspired by goodwill but were not cautious and not acting under the supervision of episcopal authority. The point of the present schema was to provide directives for those who would be authorized to deal with these questions. Directives might come from Rome, but action had to be taken on a local level. The Holy Office instruction 1949 had provided that those who took part in these matters must be well-versed and follow the Church's norms. It would be helpful if regional secretariats could be set up to promote unity in collaboration with the

Secretariat in Rome. No false irenicism would result if the movement was conducted along the proper lines. With regard to the language of the schema, he pointed out that it was addressed primarily to Catholics and it was therefore not necessary to spell out everything. Catholics could be presumed to know their own doctrine. What was necessary was to spell out only so much as was needed. Too often Catholics were ignorant of the riches to be found in the traditions of the separated brethren. Yet Popes from Leo XIII to Paul VI had praised the gifts of the Holy Spirit which they possessed. To criticize the schema for acknowledging these gifts, was to criticize the Popes. Common prayer *was* permitted by the Holy Office instruction of 1949, he maintained, but of course the faithful must be instructed in what they were doing.

The task of bishops everywhere to make their faithful aware of the lamentable facts involved in religious division was stressed by Bishop Guano of Livorno, Italy. The solution to today's problems and the effectiveness of the Gospel absolutely depended on and demanded unity. The root of all division was sin. The Church had always held and taught the principle of unity, but now it must be promoted dynamically.

The Melkite Archbishop Tawil, Patriarchal Vicar for Syria, felt that the schema had nothing to say about a "theology of division." It might be well to include a preliminary chapter on the history of unity and division. The details were complicated and there was always danger of arriving at hasty and erroneous conclusions because of a lack of knowledge in the West about Oriental theology and traditions. Because of the validity of their traditions, it would not be possible to work out anything like a uniform code of canon law for all sections of the Church.

The prospects for conversions might be reduced if the schema were acted on, according to the Master General of the Dominican Order, Father Fernandez, but the work of individual conversion and the goal of ecumenism were really two different aspects of the one apostolate of the Church. They were complementary, not incompatible. This difference should be brought out in the text.

While it was true that all elements of divine revelation were important, it was not true that all were equally important. There was a hierarchy of values among revealed mysteries and this must be taken into consideration in evaluating union and divisions. "All dogmas are to be retained, but they are not all of equal importance." Some were concerned with our final end; others with the means toward that end, e.g. the sacraments, the hierarchy, apostolic succession, etc. The schema should mention this and stress that we already have unity with the separated brethren in many truths belonging to the first category. Archbishop Pangrazio, who voiced these views, was head of the Italian section of the Council Press Office.

"Our separated brethren have a right to know what kind of a unity we are inviting them to," said Bishop Canestri, Auxiliary Vicar of Rome. He thought that the schema was vague on this point. While the text said that the separated Churches had a meaning in the mystery of salvation, it should be made clear that this was due to the fact that they retained some of the elements from their pre-Reformation days, but not precisely as separated Churches.

Toward the close of the discussion on Monday, Chapter II of the schema was taken up, which had the following paragraphs:

4. The interior renewal of the Church.
5. Conversion of heart.
6. Sanctity of life.
7. Common prayer.
8. Mutual recognition as brethren.

9. Instruction in ecumenism.
10. The manner of expressing and explaining doctrines of the faith.

The subject of the chapter was "The practical means of pursuing ecumenism" (*De Oecumenismi exercitio*).

The Spanish Cardinal Bueno y Monreal harped again on what he had said earlier about the dangers of "proselytism." Scandal and confusion were caused by preaching the Gospel differently. Proselytism must not be permitted in those areas, like Spain, where the Gospel had been preached for centuries. Nothing was worse for ecumenism, he maintained, than proselytism among already Christian communities. The schema should bring this point out.

Common prayer was one of the most important elements in helping to achieve the goals of ecumenism and its effects should not be underestimated. We should join with the separated brethren in praying for what Christ prayed and for nothing less than what he prayed, namely visible unity, according to Bishop Darmancier.

A slight dent in the minority position was perhaps registered by the speech of the Italian Archbishop Nicola Margiotta, of Brindisi, who came out in favor of removing the penalty of excommunication for those who read non-Catholic books on ecumenical matters. But he stood foursquare in favor of retaining the Index of Forbidden Books as such.

To remain insensitive or even obstinate to the ecumenical movement, said Bishop Desmazières, Auxiliary of Bordeaux, was to resist the Holy Spirit. Proximately, we were called to a humble and evangelical renewal of the Church; ultimately, to reunion. Ecumenism was not reserved to specialists, but pertained to everybody, all members alike, though in different ways. The goal should be promoted even by those bishops who did not have large numbers of non-Catholics in their diocese.

The lack of definite concrete "directives" in the schema was regretted by Bishop Martin, Vicar Apostolic of New Caledonia, with respect to ways in which the "dialogue" could be carried on. Last year Bishop de Smedt had presented norms which he hoped might have been incorporated. "Our separated brethren expect the Roman Church to enter a true dialogue in which all participants come together on an equal footing and all Churches allow discussion of their imperfections and the correction of them." He noted that the Faith and Order meeting of the World Council of Churches in 1963 at Montreal had regretted that the Catholic Church had so far refused this kind of a dialogue. Yet this was the type of discussion they were then having in the Council, in the presence of the observer delegates whose presence he welcomed. An examination of conscience was needed by all as to whether the visible Church expressed externally in her life the beatitudes of the Gospel, and whether she considered the poor as the image of Christ, who would judge the Church now and at the last day. A practical exercise of charity along this line produced faster results than endless abstract argumentation. The Church was judged by facts, not by words.

An announcement by the Secretary General on Tuesday, Nov. 26th, before the beginning of the deliberations, formalized what Cardinal Ritter had said the day before about the thanks of the American hierarchy for the expressions of condolence by the Fathers on the death of President Kennedy.

Archbishop Manek of Indonesia, in the name of 29 bishops of the area, came out forthrightly for a clear designation of Protestant Churches as *Churches,* and a correction of the cautious language of the schema which referred to them regularly as "communities." The dialogue being advocated must take place not only among individuals but among corporate bodies. They were Churches, although the Protestants were perhaps so in a less complete sense than the Orthodox. Bishop

Moralejo of Spain said that the place for the chapter on religious liberty was at the beginning of the schema. These principles must be enunciated first, for without them no ecumenical dialogue was conceivable. The text also did not make clear whether Catholics were to participate in dialogue within the framework of the primarily Protestant ecumenical movement, or whether Protestants were to be invited to discussions with Catholics under strictly Catholic auspices. The text should give clear directives on this point of cooperation.

The most notable intervention on Tuesday, from the American point of view, was that of the Auxiliary of San Antonio, Texas, Stephen Leven. As Bishop Leven explained later at the press panel meeting, he had tried unsuccessfully to speak on the floor on at least two previous occasions. His remarks related to Chapter I of Ecumenism but were equally applicable to Chapter II, when he finally succeeded in being heard. He began: "Every day it becomes more clear that we need a dialogue, not only with Protestants but also among us bishops. For there are some Fathers who have already spoken to us frequently . . . as if the only text in the Holy Bible were Matt. 16:18 'Thou art Peter and upon this rock I will build my Church.' " He went on to say that they repeatedly argued against the collegiality of the bishops. "They preach to us and chastise us as if we were against Peter and his successors or as if we desired to steal away the faith of our flocks and to promote indifferentism." Ears were naturally perked up. He continued: "They speak as if the whole doctrine of the freedom of conscience due every man, so clearly stated in *Pacem in Terris,* were offensive to pious ears." They preferred to blame non-Catholics whom they had never seen for errors rather than instruct the people in their own dioceses. Then in a series of *ad hominem* remarks, he asked: "Why are they so afraid the effects of ecumenism would not be good? . . . Why isn't there an active and functioning

Confraternity of Christian Doctrine in their parishes? . . . The prelates who seek a sincere and fruitful dialogue with non-Catholics are not the ones who show disaffection and disloyalty to the Holy Father. It is not our people who miss Mass on Sunday, refuse the sacraments and vote the communist ticket. It is not we who make little of the well known and often repeated desire of Popes Paul VI and John XXIII . . ." After getting in these barbs at an undisclosed "they," he concluded on a more harmonious note: "Venerable brethren, let us put an end to the scandal of mutual recrimination. Let us proceed in an orderly way with the examination and study of this providential movement called Ecumenism . . ."

Some of the American prelates were delighted that these things had at last been said. Others turned red in the face at the thought that they should be said at a time when the whole world was mourning the death of President Kennedy. Yet they might have asked themselves whether it were not better to speak out, or run the risk of not saying anything at all, for time was running out. The more realistic, however, were worried by a much more serious problem. As the days wore on and the debate on the first three chapters of Ecumenism seemed to be unduly protracted, the worry grew that the session might close, after all, without any definite action being taken on the remaining two chapters, Chapter V in particular, in which the American bishops were greatly interested.

Much that was said on the four last days of debate was clearly repetitious. Had the Moderators or Pope so desired, the discussion of the first three chapters could easily have been concluded on Friday, or even Thursday, and this would have allowed enough time for a vote in principle on the remaining "Mystery Chapters." The prolongation of the debate through Monday December 2 was obviously arranged to tide things over until the closing ceremonies had been reached. Earlier, it had been announced that December 3 would be devoted to another commemoration of the centenary of the Council of Trent, and December 4th, of course, had been marked for the final ceremony.

On Wednesday, November 27th, Patriarch Maximos IV declared that he was opposed to a uniform code of canon law for the whole Church. It would be "deplorable" because it would almost automatically assure Latin domination without sufficient attention being paid to the special characteristics of the Oriental Churches. It would be time wasted, from the ecumenical point of view, for the Orthodox would never consider reunion with Rome if they thought that the most that they could hope for was to be obliged to accept Latin discipline. The Latin Church had set up her hierarchy everywhere, as a result of its missionary effort. The Oriental Churches should have their share in this world-wide activity, but on a basis that respected their autonomous rights. Problems in the Near East where there were faithful of different rites could be worked out amicably. Respect for diversity, not uniformity, should be the goal.

Bishop Collin of Digne, France, called for special treatment for the Anglican Communion, because it was in a special category by itself vis-à-vis the Orthodox and Protestants. The same idea was echoed by Archbishop Gouyon and later, on Monday, by Bishop Green. Bishop Dwyer of Leeds, England, stressed the validity of what Bishop Leven had said about those who lived in the midst of non-Catholics having, in some respects, a better right to speak out on the subject of ecumenism than those bishops whose dioceses were wholly Catholic. He pointed out that "We have come a long time from the days when Catholics lived in closed communities." Polemics had waned, but union was still far off. The basic principle of ecumenism, he felt, was to take each man exactly as he was. There must be perfect sincerity on each side. There could be no preliminary accepting of conditions. The problem was how to reconcile human liberty with the authority of the Church. "Our attitude cannot be that of a mother talking to a prodigal son. We must remember that today, the one sheep is in the fold while 99 are out in the desert."

The schema gave a fine explanation of the place of the Oriental Churches in the order of things. Unfortunately, this attitude was not always reflected in practice, according to Bishop Ghattas. As one example, he cited the different Orthodox and Catholic attitudes toward marriage. Both admitted the sacramentality of marriage, but the Vatican's apostolic letter *Crebro allatae* of 1949, invalidating marriages contracted by a Catholic before an Orthodox priest, was a great blow to unity. This provision did not achieve its purpose, because the number of mixed marriages has been on the increase. In a spirit of pastoral concern, the Council should restore the former legislation in order to give proof of a genuine ecumenical spirit. Cardinal Frings, speaking on Friday, also asked for a clarification of the subject of mixed marriages. Current legislation denying the validity of such marriages if performed by someone other than a Catholic priest was an obstacle to ecumenical progress. The Church should return to the discipline in effect before the promulgation of the present code. Father Capucci, Superior General of the Basilians, also called for a revision of present marriage legislation and a mitigation of restrictions on *"communicatio in sacris"*—participation with non-Catholics in liturgical and sacramental matters. The existence of such *communicatio* in cases where it was permitted was not a scandal, but rather its absence was scandalous. Such cooperation should be encouraged on a wider scale.

At the close of the first session it will be remembered that Cardinal Lercaro had made an impassioned plea for the Church to become once again the "Church of the Poor." He stressed that the two-thirds of the world's population was still borne down by dreadful poverty and that the Council should make the task of preaching the gospel to the poor one of its principal tasks.

Many Fathers, at the end of the second session, regretted that this problem, to be dealt with in Schema 17, had still not been taken up in the concrete, although it was noted that 27 interventions referred to the theme of poverty in one connection or another. Cardinal Gerlier was one of the first to do so on Oct. 4 when he said: "The poor are the sign of the presence of Christ in the Church. We will be judged by our attitude toward them." One of the last to speak on this theme was Cardinal Gracias, who on Nov. 25th asked that the Council take up schema 17 at the beginning of the third session, and remarked that the Eucharistic Congress at Bombay in November next year would also take up this subject as one of its principal themes.

Each week during the second session a group of bishops and experts from all countries met together under the presidency of Cardinal Gerlier, Archbishop of Lyons, and Bishop Himmer of Tournai to study the doctrinal, social and pastoral aspects of the problem of underdevelopment and poverty. On Thursday Nov. 28, Cardinal Lercaro transmitted to the Pope a "petition" drawn up by the group and signed by Cardinal Gerlier, which asked that Schema 17 be taken up at the beginning of the third session and that the Congress of Bombay consider the theme too. The following day Cardinal Lercaro announced that Paul VI had agreed that schema 17 should be discussed during the third session, after the end of the discussion on De Ecclesia, which it was preferable not to interrupt. He promised that it would receive a thorough discussion after theologians and experts had worked out its terms.*

* La Croix, December 3, 1963.

On Friday, November 29th, the last day of debate but one, there was a prompt announcement of the results of the election of new Commission members the day before and joy was felt over the fact that the progressives had won this round, but the news did little to offset the gloom over the imminent prospect, now regarded as a virtual certainty, that nothing would be done to retrieve the situation so far as Chapters IV and V of Ecumenism were concerned. The grim fact had to be faced that the session would end without any vote or possibly any mention of the matter at all. Bishop Helmsing of Kansas City–St. Joseph, spoke out in the morning on behalf of calling the Protestant Churches "Churches" instead of resorting to the vague "communities" when referring to them. It was only common decency, he said, to refer to people the way they wanted to be addressed. Since the word "church" had various meanings, there was no reason why it could not be applied to those bodies which preferred to call themselves "Churches," leaving the others to be addressed as "communities" or in whatever way they pleased. A frank use of the term would go a long way toward promoting fraternal feelings. As a kind of afterthought, at the end of his talk, he interpolated the suggestion that a vote on Chapter IV and V be taken at once, that very morning. Though applause followed, he was not answered by the Moderators.

At the press panel meeting that afternoon there were many pointed questions as to why the American bishops had not done anything concrete about getting a vote on Chapter V. Why, it was suggested, when the American bishops had seen how effectively others had lobbied for what they wanted, had they not done likewise on an issue that directly concerned them? There was no satisfactory answer, except that the American bishops had not wanted to seem to bring pres-

sure to bear if there was any chance of a vote in the normal
course of events. It is doubtful, in the light of subsequent
events that even if they had lobbied, they could have changed
matters. The Pope, it seems, had already decided to postpone
a vote and this decision was irrevocable. Word to this effect
was given to the American bishops over the weekend.

On Saturday, November 30th, Oscar Cullmann, the re-
nowned Protestant theologian and an observer delegate, gave
a lecture on "The history of salvation in the New Testament." The circumstances surrounding the holding of this
talk are worth recalling. It was expected that large numbers
would attend and application was made to the Gregorian
University, the *Angelicum,* and the Biblical Institute, all
of which had halls large enough to accommodate the crowds,
but to no avail. One after the other had to turn down the
Professor's request. Finally, Archbishop Weber of Strasbourg
—the home-town of Cullmann—placed the hall of the French
church in Rome, St. Louis-des-Français, at his disposal. The
hall was packed. Monsignor Willebrands of Bea's Secretariat
introduced the speaker, extolling "what Catholic theology
owed to his work." Rumor had it that Cullmann had been
turned down by the Congregation of Seminaries, which was
in charge of these institutions, but Archbishop Staffa, secretary of the Congregation, let it be known that no request for
permission had reached his desk. It appears that the permission—or lack of it—had been handled higher up. At one
of its weekly meetings, the Holy Office had given as its reply
to a question, that the Professor should be allowed to hold
his lecture, not in a Roman university, but in a "Catholic
hall." The Holy Office no doubt thought that it was being
very liberal in the whole matter. Cullmann is on excellent
terms with Pope Paul (who invited him to have lunch with
him in the Vatican during the first session) and could have

gone to the Pope about it, but, out of modesty, he preferred not to bother him.*

Referring to "the present time in the Bible," Cullmann said that what was new about Jesus with respect to Judaism was the tension between "already" and "not yet." "We are living in the time of the Holy Spirit," he said. "This is the basis of all ecumenical dialogue. The Church is the anticipation of the Kingdom, but it is not yet the Kingdom. The dialogue between the Catholic Church and the Protestant Churches, which differ in their emphasis upon the 'already' and the 'not yet,' cannot but be fruitful." "The World Council of Churches and Vatican Council II are both signs that schism is not destined to last forever. The history of salvation advances, in spite of our imperfections and our sins." The latter was said against Bultmann who denies that there is any history of salvation at all.

Another Protestant observer delegate also had praise for the work of the Council. Dr. Skysdsgaard maintained that it was simply unbelievable, years ago, that the Roman Church would ever change. Now however, the "Roman Church is in the process of reforming itself." However he was still waiting for a "prophetic voice in St. Peter's to point out the limitations of the Church as an institution." "We all desire unity," he concluded, "but when this unity becomes a reality, no one Church will be victorious. Rather they will all be conquered, so that Christ alone may conquer." He remarked earlier in his speech that it would be a mistake for Catholics to be under the illusion that any number of Protestants looked upon the Roman Catholic Church with "nostalgia" or desired to "return" pure and simple to the bosom of a Church which they still regarded as defective. The Churches must sit down and talk over their differences as "equals" and as "equals" again be reunited. This suggestion was taken up

* *Le Monde,* December 17, 1963.

by Bishop Tomasek of Czechoslovakia on the last day of debate, Monday, Dec. 2, when he suggested that representatives of all the major orthodox confessions sit down at a "round table" with the Catholic Church at which there would be no presidency and discuss differences as equals. This in itself, he said, would constitute a great step toward reunion.

The last day was one of sharp contrasts. Little had been heard of the important opposition, but Cardinal Ruffini more than made up for this by his intervention clearly aimed at influencing the Council in its last moments. He warned against misconceptions about ecumenism "which might arise from unscholarly magazine articles"—referring no doubt to expositions by such Council experts as Father Gregory Baum, Abbé René Laurentin, Jean Daniélou, Yves Congar, Karl Rahner and others who had frequently written on this theme in recent weeks in such reputable organs as *Commonweal, Le Figaro, Le Monde, La Croix, Stimmen der Zeit*. Such misrepresentations "could mislead and confuse priests and the faithful." Instead he offered his own straight-laced, unswervingly conservative definition of "Catholic ecumenism," based on the unshakable conviction that the Roman Catholic Church had nothing to learn and nothing to be sorry for. If mistakes had occurred, they had been due to "disobedient sons," not to the Church herself, which was infallible and indefectible. His whole program was summed up in the terse words: "We strongly hope that our separated brethren will again embrace the Catholic Church of Rome." Dialogue was useful, but only to "bring back" the erring to the one true fold.

It was sobering perhaps for the Fathers to hear once again the voice of Roman *intransigenza*, lest any might have been lulled into a false sense of security by the many positive things said about ecumenism in the last few days. The next speaker,

Bishop Green of Port Elizabeth, South Africa, raised the question of Anglicanism and specifically of Anglican orders, with which the schema had not come to grips. He said that it was impossible to discuss reunion with Anglicans without coming up against the decision of Leo XIII condemning Anglican orders (1896). In justice to history and the cause of ecumenism, the whole question surrounding Anglican orders should again be examined. Scholars and theologians today were not sure that the decision of Leo XIII was the right one. It was an administrative decision, conditioned by the times, but new facts and a hopeful situation seemed to call for a review of the whole matter. The Council should also address itself to the practical question of the difficult position of married Anglican priests who sought admission to the Catholic Church.

Bishop Muldoon of Australia, in a fit of Irish pugnaciousness, took exception to the short paragraph which sought to explain the origin of the various Protestant communities. He said that as it stood, it would be sure to offend the Anglicans. It was better to say nothing about the subject at all. If it were to stand, many will criticize the Council for not having understood the heart and spirit of Protestantism. "We deceive ourselves if we think that all our separated brethren are in good faith. Many are like eagles hovering over the Church looking for what they can distort." Finally he declared that he was tired of all the breast-beating he had heard. "Some have said that all bishops should get down on their knees and confess their sins and those of their predecessors for the division of Christendom, and they cite the words of Pope Paul. But the Pope said '*If* we are in any way to blame for that separation . . .' *Salva reverentia*, we are tired of the exaggerated importuning of the Fathers. If any feel guilty, let them go to a good confessor but spare the rest of us!"

This forthright statement, intended more as a momentary expression of feeling, no doubt, than as a firm conviction, was answered later by the Abbot of Downside, Dom Butler, a trained historian as well as a theologian, who observed that the Roman Church had a share in responsibility for the separation and suggested that a paragraph be added deploring the "sins committed by Catholics or the separated brethren, which have caused or which even now continue to prolong the evil of separation." He said that "history teaches that the public confession of sins of members of the Church is the first step toward spiritual emulation." The Anglicans deserved a special mention because of their widespread following throughout the world, their patristic tradition, the active part they have always played in the ecumenical movement, and lastly because they do not consider themselves simply as Protestants but as a bridge between Protestantism and Catholicism.

The surprise of the morning was the intervention of Bishop Tomasek of Czechoslovakia, referred to above. It was useless, he said, to attempt to reach decisions without consulting the other side. A bold step would bring us a good way toward the final goal. The Moscow Patriarchate had stated, he noted, that "the way of Christian love can lead to dogmatic dialogue and thus to the desired reunion. The time is fast becoming ripe for action." The bishop could not have known about Pope Paul's projected pilgrimage to the Holy Land. His remarks may turn out to have been more prophetic than he imagined. He was certainly right in reminding his listeners that "What could not have been even attempted in the past centuries can now be carried out in a short space of time."*

The Ukrainian Archbishop Hermaniuk of Winnepeg,

---

* Bishop Tomasek later received a commendation from Patriarch Alexei of Moscow.

Canada, likewise called for "practical steps" to organize mixed theological commissions, on the diocesan level, under the general direction of the Secretariat for Unity in Rome, to further the work of ecumenical dialogue—a thought echoed by Cardinal Bea its head on a number of occasions— and urged that their full rights be restored to the patriarchs and that synod rule or government by permanent synods be restored to the Eastern Churches. Strange as these suggestions may have sounded only a year or so ago, it must be admitted, in the light of what has occurred, that it is not at all improbable that the "impossible" may come to pass. This was some gage of how far Rome had travelled on the road toward a truer appreciation of the ultimate goal of ecumenism.—As Pope Paul put it in his closing address—"To call to the one, holy Church of Christ the separated brethren."

At the conclusion of the debate Cardinal Bea summed up the impressions of the Fathers with regard to the schema on Ecumenism which they had been debating for the past two weeks. He said that the suggestions would all be carefully considered in working out a revised text to be voted on next session. Some of the proposals would be incorporated in an "Ecumenical Directory" which would be prepared for the guidance of bishops and all interested, for experience had shown that promotion of the ecumenical movement was a primary responsibility of pastors and must be cultivated on the local level, with assistance from Rome. It was regretted by many that there had not been time to discuss the controversial Chapters IV and V of the schema dealing with the Jews and Religious Liberty, but the ancient saying applied: "What is put off is not put away"—*Quod defertur non aufertur.* He repeated these words twice as if to leave no doubt in minds about the intention of the Council leaders to bring the matter up again and quiet rumors which had been circulating for some days that the conservative minority

THE SECOND SESSION

had succeeded in "burying" the dangerous document on religious liberty. The cardinal also repeated the words "There was not time"—with the same end in view. However he observed that the delay, while regrettable, could be put to good use in that it would give the Fathers time to reflect on important issues and come back with more concrete proposals the next session. Suggestions with regard to these last chapters were to be sent in to the Secretariat not later than the middle of February. Unfortunately, because the aged cardinal was slow in speaking, he was cut off before he had time to deliver the last few sentences of his discourse. The Moderators apparently thought that he had concluded when he merely paused.

It was announced in the general congregation on Monday that further consideration of a proposed message from the bishops to priests would be put off indefinitely. A text had been distributed to the Fathers on Friday last with the request that they propose amendments after considering it over the weekend. Apparently the amendments were so numerous and so serious that it became evident to the council leaders that promulgation of the text in its present form would not be possible. More than 200 suggestions had boiled down to 60 major amendments, thus making it impossible to proceed with the document as it was. The original draft was due, it was said, to Bishop Renard of Versailles.*

The meeting closed with a few remarks by Bishop Hengsbach about the schema on the Apostolate of the Laity which could not be discussed because of lack of time.

A solemn or public session of the Council on Tuesday Dec. 3rd was devoted to commemorating the closing of the Fourth Centenary of the Council of Trent, other celebrations having commemorated the event earlier in the year. The address by Cardinal Urbani was remarkable only for its

* *Le Figaro,* December 3, 1963.

"prudence." It carefully avoided saying anything that might offend the Protestant observer-delegates present in the Council hall (some of whom had absented themselves) or otherwise retard the prospects for the ecumenical movement. The contrasts between Trent and the present Council might indeed have been exploited by a more ruthless speaker to sow dissension. Trent, after all, in the minds of many represented the "triumph of the Church" over Protestantism, and had long been looked on by Protestants themselves as an apparently insuperable obstacle in the path of reunion. All these pitfalls had to be avoided. The success of Urbani in straddling a difficult fence could be measured by the lack of any interest in his talk by the Rome conservative daily *Il Tempo,* which preferred to focus its headlines on another incident of the day which occurred after the morning session. The headline "Request for a schema against Marxism at the close of the second session of the Council" made great play of a petition originating among certain Brazilian prelates that the third session of the Council take up consideration of a separate schema condemning the "errors of Marxism, socialism and communism, in their philosophical, sociological and economic aspects." The petition is said to have been signed by "more than 200 bishops." It was reported to have been handed to the Secretary of State Cardinal Cicognani on Tuesday. At the same time there was also issued a pamphlet on "The liberty of the Church in the Communist State" by a certain Dr. Correa de Oliveira, described as a university professor in Brazil. The pamphlet maintained that "it is contrary to Catholic principles to assert that the Church can exist and enjoy indispensable liberty in a communist state." A feeble, last-minute manoeuvre to draw the attention of the world away from the fundamental issues which had been before the Council at this session, and indirectly a repudiation of the policy of John XXIII laid down in *Pacem in*

Terris? The *New York Times* professed to find an anxiety among the Italian bishops, headlining its story on December 2, 1963: "Italian Bishops Resisting a Vote." The account attempted to explain, without adducing any evidence, that the "Italian bishops" had blocked discussion of Chapter V of Ecumenism on religious liberty because an avowal of its principles would be tantamount to an avowal of "atheistic communism."

SUMMARY

November 18, 1963, Monday—69TH GENERAL CONGREGATION.
MASS: Archbishop Pericle Felici, Secretary General.
MODERATOR: Cardinal Agagianian.
PRESENT: 2,090 Fathers.
SUBJECT: Schema on Bishops, Ch. IV.
SPEAKERS:
  1. Bishop Sebastian Vallopilly (Tellicherry, India).
SUBJECT: Schema on Ecumenism, in general.
SPEAKERS:
  2. Cardinal Gabriel Tappouni (Syrian Patriarch of Antioch) (separate chapter for Orthodox, exclude Jews and religious liberty).
  3. Cardinal Ernesto Ruffini (Archbishop of Palermo) (meaning of "ecumenism").
  4. Cardinal José Benjamin de Arriba y Castro (Archbishop of Tarragona, Spain) (danger of proselytism).
  5. Cardinal José Bueno y Monreal (Archbishop of Seville) (exclude Jews).

6. Cardinal Joseph Elmer Ritter (Archbishop of St. Louis, Missouri) (approves, chap. V at beginning).
7. Cardinal José Quintero (Archbishop of Caracas, Venezuela) (approves, faults of Church).
8. Cardinal Peter Tatsuo Doi (Archbishop of Tokyo, Japan) (emphasis of missionary aspects).
9. Patriarch Stephanos I Sidarouss (Coptic Patriarch of Alexandria) (exclude Jews).
10. Patriarch Maximos IV Saigh (Melkite Patriarch of Antioch) (exclude Jews).

November 19, 1963, Tuesday—70TH GENERAL CONGREGATION.
MASS: Archbishop Varghese Thangalathil of Trivandrum-Malankar, India, in Syro-Malankar rite.
MODERATOR: Cardinal Agagianian.
PRESENT: 2,182 Fathers.
SUBJECT: Schema on Ecumenism, in general.
SPEAKERS:

1. Cardinal Paul-Emile Léger (Archbishop of Montreal) (chs. IV and V should be dealt with elsewhere).
2. Cardinal Franz. König (Archbishop of Vienna) (meaning of "ecumenism," Reformation Churches should be called "ecclesial communities").
3. Cardinal Laurean Rugambwa (Bishop of Bukoba, Tanganyika) (missionary aspects).
4. Patriarch Alberto Gori (Latin Patriarch of Jerusalem) (reservations about chap. IV).
5. Patriarch Pierre XVI Batanian (Armenian Patriarch of Cilicia) (clearer formulation of certain truths, exclude ch. IV).
6. Archbishop Gabriel Garrone (Toulouse, France) (clearer theological basis).
7. Bishop Arthur Elchinger (Coadjutor of Strasbourg) (renewal of "intellectual conscience").
8. Archbishop John Charles McQuaid (Dublin, Ireland) (approves with reservations).
9. Archbishop Charles de Provenchères (Aix-en-Provence) (renewal of Church).
10. Bishop Taguchi (Osaka, Japan) (written).
11. Bishop de Castro Mayer (Campos, Brazil) (written,

November 20, 1963, Wednesday—71st GENERAL CONGREGATION.
MASS: Bishop Vendargon of Kuala Lampur, Malacca.
MODERATOR: Cardinal Agagianian.
PRESENT: 2,182 Fathers.
SUBJECT: Schema on Ecumenism, in general.
SPEAKERS:
1. Cardinal Albert Gregory Meyer (Archbishop of Chicago) (approves, including chs. IV and V).
2. Cardinal Antonio Bacci (Curia) (badly formulated, failure to emphasize primacy).
3. Bishop Angelo Jelmini (Apostolic Visitor for Lugano, Switzerland) (mention Islam along with Jews).
4. Bishop Andrea Sapelak (Apostolic Visitor for Ukrainians, Argentina) (deals with relations rather than unity itself).
5. Archbishop Casimiro Morcillo González (Zaragoza, Spain) (exclude Jews).
6. Archbishop Maurice Baudoux (St.-Boniface, Canada) (approves).
7. Archbishop John Heenan (Westminster, England) (approves, dialogue on local basis).
8. Archbishop Jean-Julien Weber (Strasbourg, France) (*communicatio in sacris* with Orthodox desirable).
9. Bishop Sergio Méndez Arceo (Cuernavaca, Mexico) ("Churches" instead of "communities").
10. Father Robert Chopard-Lallier (Apostolic Prefect of Parakou, Dahomey) (*communicatio in sacris,* danger of indifferentism).
11. Bishop André R. Jacq (Tit., Vietnam) (Church enriched by Oriental and Reformation traditions).
12. Bishop António Ferreira Gomes (Oporto, Portugal) (criticizes lack of scholastic terminology).
13. Bishop León de Uriarte Bengoa (Apostolic Vicar for San Ramón, Peru) ("ecumenism of Church" instead of "Catholic ecumenism").

November 21, 1963, Thursday—72nd GENERAL CONGREGATION.
MASS: Bishop Grutka of Gary, Indiana, Roman rite in Paleo-Slavonic language.
MODERATOR: Cardinal Lercaro.
PRESENT: 2,186 Fathers.

SUBJECT: Schema on Ecumenism, in general.

SPEAKERS:

1. Bishop Jaime Flores Martin (Barbastro, Spain) (approves).
2. Archbishop Ermenegildo Flori (Florence, Italy) reservations).
3. Archbishop Juan Aramburu (Tucumán, Argentina) (dialogue necessary).
4. Bishop Joseph Höffner (Münster, Germany) (increasing numbers of indifferent).
5. Bishop Juan Hervás y Benet (Prelate Nullius of Ciudad Real, Spain) (religious freedom in Schema 17).
6. Archbishop Ignace Ziadé (Maronite, Beirut, Lebanon) (clearer pastoral emphasis).
7. Bishop Endre Hamvas (Csanád, Hungary) (better atmosphere for dialogue today).
8. Archbishop J. da Conceiçao Cordeiro (Karachi, Pakistan) (written).
9. Bishop René Pailloux (Fort Rosebery, Rhodesia) (written).

SUBJECT: Schema on Ecumenism, Ch. I, Principles.

10. Archbishop Enrico Nicodemo (Bari, Italy), (more emphasis on dogmatic differences, heretics and schismatic "outside the Church").
11. Bishop Herman Volk (Mainz, Germany) (meaning of "ecumenism").
12. Bishop Manuel Talamás Camandari (Ciudad Juárez, Mexico) (danger of turning Catholics away from faith).
13. Bishop Luigi Carli (Segni, Italy) uniqueness of Roman Catholic Church, collegiality).
14. Bishop Antoine Abed (Maronite, Tripoli, Lebanon) (elements of truth among separated brethren).

November 22, 1963, Friday—73RD GENERAL CONGREGATION.

MASS: Archbishop Duval of Algiers, Algeria.

MODERATOR: Cardinal Lercaro.

PRESENT: 2,178 Fathers.

SUBJECT: Schema on Ecumenism, in general.

SPEAKERS:

1. Bishop Fortunato Veiga Coutinho (Coadjutor of Belgaum, India) (exclude Jews).
2. Bishop José Pont y God (Segorbe, Spain) (exclude Jews, treat religious liberty later).

3. Bishop Andreas Makarakiza (Ngozi, Burundi) (renewal of Catholicism).

SUBJECT: Schema on Ecumenism, Ch. I, Principles.

SPEAKERS:

4. Bishop Jan Mazur (Auxiliary of Lublin, Poland) (historical perspective, ecumenism not an adulteration).
5. Bishop Gérard Huyghe (Arras, France) (abandonment of "return" concept).
6. Bishop Felix Romero Menjibar (Jaén, Spain) (dangers of ecumenism).
7. Archbishop Lorenz Jaeger (Paderborn, Germany) (approves avoidance of scholastic terminology).
8. Bishop Claude Flusin (Saint-Claude, France) (separation as a "scandal").
9. Bishop Vito Chang Tso-huan (Tit., China) (ecumenism and Confucianism).

November 25, 1963, Monday—74TH GENERAL CONGREGATION.

MASS: Archbishop Antezana y Rojas of La Paz, Bolivia.

MODERATOR: Cardinal Lercaro.

PRESENT: 2,141 Fathers.

SUBJECT: Schema on Ecumenism, Ch. I, Principles.

SPEAKERS:

1. Cardinal Paul-Emile Léger (Archbishop of Montreal) (unity of Church not monolithic).
2. Cardinal Joseph Elmer Ritter (Archbishop of St. Louis) (proposes better definition of unity).
3. Cardinal Augustin Bea (Curia) (answers various objections, recognition of elements of truth in separated brethren).
4. Bishop Emilio Guano (Livorno, Italy) (sin as primary cause of separation).
5. Archbishop Joseph Tawil (Melkite Patriarch Vicar for Syria) (theology of unity and division).
6. Father Aniceto Fernandez, Master General of Dominicans (ecumenism and conversions).
7. Bishop Jean B. Gahamanyi (Astrida, Ruanda) (pastoral prudence in ecumenism).
8. Archbishop Andrea Pangrazio (Gorizia, Italy) (dynamic aspects of ecumenism).
9. Bishop Giovanni Canestri (Auxiliary of Rome) (schema too

favorable to positive elements of separated brethren, clearer definition of unity).

10. Bishop Anastasio Granados García (Auxiliary of Toledo, Spain) (distinguish between unity and unicity).

SUBJECT: Schema on Ecumenism, Ch. II, Practice.

SPEAKERS:

11. Cardinal José Bueno y Monreal (Archbishop of Seville, Spain) (dangers of proselytism).

12. Bishop Michel Darmancier (Apostolic Vicar for Wallis Islands) (common prayer for unity).

13. Archbishop Nicola Margiotta (Brindisi, Italy) (Index should be retained).

14. Bishop Stephane Desmazières (Auxiliary of Bordeaux, France) (ecumenism must not be resisted).

15. Bishop Pierre Martin (Apostolic Vicar of New Caledonia) (practical method for dialogue suggested by Bishop de Smedt should be included).

16. Bishop Kaczmarek (Auxiliary of Gdansk, Poland) (written).

17. Bishop Muldoon (Auxiliary, Sydney, Australia) (written).

November 26, 1963, Tuesday—75TH GENERAL CONGREGATION.

MASS: Archbishop Khoury of Tyre, in Maronite rite.

MODERATOR: Cardinal Doepfner.

PRESENT: 2,131 Fathers.

SUBJECT: Schema on Ecumenism, Ch. I, Principles.

SPEAKERS:

1. Archbishop Gabriel Manek (Endeh, Indonesia) (Churches of Reformation are "Churches").

2. Bishop Rafael González Moralejo (Auxiliary of Valencia, Spain) (Ch. V should be at beginning).

3. Abbot Sighard Kleiner, Abbot General of Cistercian Order (ecumenism and Mary).

4. Bishop Enrico Compagnone (Anagni, Italy) (emphasize doctrine of primacy).

5. Bishop Stephen A. Leven (Auxiliary of San Antonio, Texas) (dialogue among bishops, closed-mind attitude of some speakers).

6. Archbishop Jean Zoa (Yaoundé, Cameroon) (ecumenism and missions).

SUBJECT: Schema on Ecumenism, Ch. II, Practice.

7. Cardinal Valerian Gracias (Archbishop of Bombay, India) (petition with regard to Schema 17).
8. Cardinal Raul Silva Henriquez (Archbishop of Santiago de Chile) (ecumenism and pastoral activity).
9. Patriarch Alberto Gori (Latin Patriarch of Jerusalem) (ecumenism demands practical knowledge of both sides).
10. Archbishop William Conway (Armagh, Ireland) (thorough knowledge of faith and ecumenism).
11. Bishop Michal Klepacz (Lódz, Poland) (return to primitive testimonies of faith).
12. Bishop António Cardoso Cunha (Auxiliary of Beja, Portugal) (requires specialists).
13. Bishop Jean Gay (Basse-Terre, Guadaloupe) (eliminate unhealthy competition in missionary field.
14. Bishop Elie Farah (Maronite Bishop of Cyprus, Lebanon) (relax *communicatio in sacris,* restrictions about mixed marriages).
15. Bishop Alfonso Sánchez Tinoco (Papantle, Mexico) (practical aspects of cooperation).
16. Bishop Franz Hengsbach (Essen, Germany) (practical cooperation).
17. Bishop Charles Himmer (Tournai, Belgium) (institutional renewal).

November 27, 1963, Wednesday—76TH GENERAL CONGREGATION.
MASS: Archbishop Gray of St. Andrew's and Edinburgh, Scotland.
MODERATOR: Cardinal Doepfner.
PRESENT: 2,122 Fathers.
SUBJECT: Schema on Ecumenism, Ch. II, Practice.
SPEAKERS:
1. Bishop Jean Nuer (Coptic Auxiliary of Thebes, Eygpt) (practical cooperation between Catholics and Orthodox).
2. Bishop Vicente Enrique y Tarancón (Solsona, Spain) (methods of emplementing ecumenism).
3. Bishop Frantisek Tomasek (Auxiliary of Olomouc) (a professor for ecumenism in every seminary).
4. Archbishop Corrado Mingo (Monreale, Italy) (integral statement of Catholicism, prayer to Mary).

5. Bishop Eduard Nécsey (Apostolic Administrator of Neutra, Czechoslovakia) (remove uncharitable statements from catechisms, religious books).
6. Bishop Paul Joseph Schmitt (Metz, France) (religious liberty indispensable).
7. Archbishop Salvatore Baldassari (Ravenna, Italy) (importance of inner renewal, clear principles on cooperation).

SUBJECT: Schema on Ecumenism, Ch. III, Orthodox and Protestants.

8. Cardinal Antonio Bacci (Curia) (obscures doctrine of primacy).
9. Patriarch Maximos IV Saigh (Melkite Patriarch of Antioch) (Oriental Churches and missions, impossibility of one code).
10. Bishop Bernardin Collin (Digne, France) (*communicatio in sacris* with Orthodox, validity of mixed marriages).
11. Bishop George Dwyer (Leeds, England) (realism on both sides).
12. Bishop Henri Jenny (Auxiliary of Cambrai, France) (bond of eucharist with Orthodox).
13. Archbishop Paul Gouyon (Coadjutor of Rennes, France) (replaces *communitas* by *communio*).
14. Bishop Edoardo Mason (Apostolic Vicar of El Obeid, Sudan) (absolute need for reunion between Orthodox and Catholics).
15. Archbishop Antoni Baraniak (Poznan, Poland) (concept of "return" unacceptable).
16. Bishop Isaac Ghattas (Coptic, Thebes, Egypt), (restoration of sacramental communion).
17. Bishop Narciso Jubany Arnau (Auxiliary of Barcelona, Spain) (clarify "imperfect union").
18. Bishop Taylor (Stockholm, Sweden) (written).
19. Bishop Musty (Auxiliary of Namur, Belgium), (written).
20. Archbishop Gonçalves do Amaral (Uberaba, Brazil) (written).
21. Bishop Zak (St. Pölten, Austria) (written).
22. Bishop Bayan (Armenian, Alexandria, Egypt) (written).
23. Bishop Lorschneider (San Angelo, Brazil) (written).
24. Bishop Lokuang (Tainan) (written).

November 28, 1963, Thursday—77TH GENERAL CONGREGATION.
MASS: Very Reverend Father Sepinsky, Minister General of the Franciscans.
MODERATOR: Cardinal Suenens.
PRESENT: 2,192 Fathers.
SUBJECT: Schema on Ecumenism, Ch. II, Practice.
SPEAKERS:

1. Cardinal Joseph Frings (Archbishop of Cologne, Germany) (*ecclesia semper reformanda,* mixed marriages).
2. Archbishop Eugene D'Souza (Bhopal, India) (written).
3. Archbishop Hyacinthe Thiandoum (Dakar, Senegal) (co-operation with Jews and Moslems).
4. Bishop Vicente Reyes (Borongán, Philippines) (Church cannot lose perfection, avoid common prayers, exhort non-Catholics to better understanding of Catholicism).
5. Bishop Emile Blanchet (Tit., Rector of Catholic Institute, Paris) (intellectual understanding of position of others).
6. Abbot Benedikt Reetz, President of Benedictine Congregation of Beuron (ecumenical experiences at Beuron).
7. Abbot Hilaron Capucci, General Abbot of Melkite Basilians (change *communicatio in sacris,* marriage legislation).
8. Bishop Antonio Pildáin y Zapiáin (Canary Islands, Spain) (ecumenism and charity, 80 meetings and still no evidence of Church's interest in poor and needy).
9. Archbishop Armando Fares (Catanzaro, Italy) (danger of indifferentism, stimulate desire for unity in non-Catholics).
10. Bishop Guillaume Schoemaker (Purwokerto, Indonesia) (preparation of "Vatican Vulgate" text of Bible).
11. Bishop Garabed Amadouni (Armenian Exarch, France) (special courses in seminaries in oriental theology).
12. Archbishop Anibal Muñoz Duque (Nueva Pamplona, Columbia) (Protestant missionary proselytism in Latin America).
13. Bishop Bernardino Piñera Carvallo (Temuco, Chile) (special exhortation to poverty).
14. Bishop Lucien Lebrun (Autun, France) (fruitful experience at Taizé).
15. Archbishop Henrique Golland Trinidade (Botucatú, Brazil) (personal example alone counts in renewal).

SUBJECT: Schema on Ecumenism, Ch. III, Orthodox and Protestants.

SPEAKERS:

16. Patriarch Paul Pierre Meouchi (Maronite Patriarch of Antioch) (3 steps to unity: purgative, illuminative, unitive).
17. Archbishop Franjo Seper (Zagreb, Yugoslavia) (causes of disunity, franker recognition of validity of Oriental traditions).
18. Archbishop Casimiro Morcillo González (Zaragoza, Spain) (inadequate distinction between Orthodox and Protestants).
19. Bishop Vladimir Malanchuk (Ukrainian Exarch, France) (insert Pope Paul's words of mutual pardon in text).

November 29, 1963, Friday—78TH GENERAL CONGREGATION.

MASS: Bishop Gad, Apostolic Exarch for Byzantine-rite Catholics in Greece.

MODERATORS: Cardinal Suenens; Cardinal Doepfner.

PRESENT: 2,094 Fathers.

SUBJECT: Schema on Ecumenism, Ch. III, Orthodox and Protestants.

SPEAKERS:

1. Cardinal Fernando Quiroga y Palacios (Santiago de Compostela, Spain) (praise for Orthodox adherence to tradition).
2. Bishop Lancelot John Goody (Bunbury, Australia) (distinguish between essential and immutable, and changeable).
3. Bishop Charles H. Helmsing (Kansas City-St. Joseph, Missouri) (use term "Church" with respect to Protestants, urges vote on Chapters IV and V at once).
4. Bishop José Souto Vizoso (Palencia, Spain) (goal of unity needs definition).
5. Bishop Franjo Franič (Split, Yugoslavia) (firm principles for dialogue, separate treatment for Orthodox).
6. Archbishop Enrico Nicodemo (Bari, Italy) (legitimate diversity compatible with primacy).
7. Bishop Jean Rupp (Monaco) (more recognition of Anglican traditions, "divine transcendence" of Barth).
8. Bishop Pierre Dib (Maronite, Cairo, Egypt) (study of Oriental theology and canon law).
9. Bishop Elias Zoghby (Melkite Patriarchal Vicar for Egypt) (misunderstanding in East and West over papal primacy).

10. Abbot Atanasius Hage, Abbot General of Melkite Basilians (relaxation of legislation on *communicatio in sacris*).
11. Bishop Alexandros Scandar (Coptic, Assiut, Egypt) (proper training of clergy in Uniat Churches).

December 2, 1963, Monday—79TH GENERAL CONGREGATION.
MASS: Archbishop Thuc of Hué, Vietnam.
MODERATOR: Cardinal Agagianian.
PRESENT: 2,110 Fathers.
SUBJECT: Schema on Ecumenism, Ch. III, Orthodox and Protestants.
SPEAKERS:

1. Cardinal Ernesto Ruffini (Archbishop of Palermo) (Roman Catholic Church is infallible and indefectable, separated brethren should be invited to embrace the Church again).
2. Bishop Ernest Arthur Green (Port Elizabeth, South Africa) (question of Anglican orders should be reopened) .
3. Bishop Thomas William Muldoon (Auxiliary of Sydney, Australia) (Many separated brethren *not* in good faith, need for confession of faults doubted).
4. Archbishop Gregory Thangalathil (Trivandrum, India) (Orthodox do not always live up to their tradition).
5. Bishop Vittorio Costantini (Sessa Aurunca, Italy) (reservations).
6. Archbishop Maxim Hermaniuk (Ukrainian, Winnipeg, Canada) (mixed theological commissions under Secretariat for Unity).
7. Bishop Frantisek Tomasek (Auxiliary of Olomouc) (proposes round-table of Orthodox and Catholics).
8. Archbishop Georges Layek (Maronite, Aleppo) (regrets silence about Uniats).
9. Abbot Christopher Butler, President of English Benedictine Congregation (special mention of Anglicanism, need for confession of faults).
10. Archbishop Ignace Ziadé (Maronite, Beirut, Lebanon) (Eastern unity and pluralism).
11. Bishop Leo D'Mello (Ajmer and Jaipur, India) (prayer for unity).
12. Bishop Andreas Roborecki (Ukrainian, Saskatoon, Canada) (primacy as obstacle to reunion).

13. Bishop Jelmini (Apostolic Administrator of Lugano, Switzerland) (written).
14. Archbishop Printesis (Latin rite Archbishop of Athens, Greece) (written).
15. Bishop Terzian (Armenian Patriarchal Vicar, Lebanon) (written).
16. Archbishop Lorenz Jaeger (Paderborn, Germany) (written).
17. Archbishop Kandela (Auxiliary of Syrian Patriarchate of Antioch) (written).

—Cardinal Bea summed up the debate on Ecumenism.

—Bishop Hengsbach said a few words about the schema on the Apostolate of the Laity.

December 3, 1963, Tuesday—PUBLIC SESSION.

—Address by Cardinal Urbani commemorating close of Four Hundredth Centenary of Council of Trent.

—Addresses by Lay Auditors, Jean Guitton and Vittorino Veronese.

—Reading of Motu Proprio *"Pastorale munus"* on faculties of bishops.

December 4, 1963, Wednesday—SOLEMN CLOSING OF SECOND SESSION.

—Low mass celebrated by Cardinal Tisserant, Dean of Sacred College.

—Solemn Voting on Liturgy Constitution and Communications Decree and promulgation of same by Pope.

—Address by Pope Paul VI closing session.

V

Close of the Council; the Decrees

☒

On Wednesday December 4th the second session of Vatican Council II came to what some observers regarded as a rather inglorious end. The entrance of Pope Paul into the basilica of St. Peter's for the final solemn ceremonies was dismaying to those who witnessed the scene. Preceded as usual by the full panoply of the papal household and liveried guards, the oriental patriarchs, minus of course the doughty Melkite Patriarch of Antioch who entered the basilica in advance as a protest against Vatican protocol (which still ignored the claim to precedence implicit in the Pope's act earlier in the session),* and the college of cardinals robed in white copes and mitres, a fifth of whom seemed to be pitifully aged figures hardly able

* When he ordered the Patriarchs seated at a special table, directly opposite, and therefore by implication at least, on the same level with the cardinals. See p. xvii.

to hobble along, the Pope himself appeared carried high on the sedia gestatoria. He seemed acutely conscious of the tawdriness of all this faded splendor and perhaps even sorry that he had not decided to make a more appropriate entrance by walking the length of the nave on foot. As he passed down the central nave, the Pope scarcely looked to right or to left to acknowledge the fitful applause from the episcopal benches. Everything suddenly seemed to have a worn-out look about it, the vestments, the uniforms, the damask-draped tribunes.

By way of counteracting this impression, once he descended from the sedia, the Pope seemed to come alive, graciously turning to the non-Catholic observers and greeting them with his customarily graceful gestures, and acknowledging the applause that came from the tribunes of the diplomatic corps, the special guests and the vast throng of people crowded in the transepts and the apse. As the Pope unassumingly mounted the steps leading to his throne over the Confession of St. Peter, Cardinal Tisserant, the eighty year old Dean of the Sacred College, began the prayers at the foot of the altar in his precise but rapidly enunciated Latin which was answered by the whole congregation with equal precision and dispatch. It was noted that, in his eagerness to proceed with the mass, the cardinal had not waited for the Pope to be properly seated. A certain discontent seemed to be reflected in the rapidity with which the prelates recited in unison the words of the Gloria, Credo, Sanctus and Agnus Dei. Immediately after the mass, the Secretary General of the Council, Archbishop Felici, mounted the conciliar rostrum and instead of his usual peremptory *"Exeant omnes"*—the daily signal for unauthorized participants to leave the hall at the beginning of each daily meeting—he announced that only prelates were to occupy the seats in the bishops' tribunes, thereby dislodging a number of redfaced episcopal secretaries who had preempted the seats of bishops who were not present.

SACROSANCTUM OECUMENICUM CONCILIUM
VATICANUM SECUNDUM

CONSTITUTIO
DE SACRA LITURGIA

DE QUA AGETUR IN SESSIONE PUBLICA
DIEI 4 DECEMBRIS 1963

(Sub secreto)

TYPIS POLYGLOTTIS VATICANIS
MCMLXIII

Title page and first page of Constitution on Sacred Liturgy

Caput I

DE PRINCIPIIS GENERALIBUS AD SACRAM LITURGIAM INSTAURANDAM ATQUE FOVENDAM

I – DE SACRAE LITURGIAE NATURA EIUSQUE MOMENTO IN VITA ECCLESIAE

5. Deus, qui « omnes homines vult salvos fieri et ad agnitionem veritatis venire » (1 Tim. 2, 4), « multifariam multisque modis olim loquens patribus in prophetis » (Hebr. 1, 1), ubi venit plenitudo temporis, misit Filium suum, Verbum carnem factum, Spiritu Sancto unctum, ad evangelizandum pauperibus, ad sanandos contritos corde,[8] « medicum carnalem et spiritualem »,[9] Mediatorem Dei et hominum.[10] Ipsius namque humanitas, in unitate personae Verbi, fuit instrumentum nostrae salutis. Quare in Christo « nostrae reconciliationis processit perfecta placatio, et divini cultus nobis est indita plenitudo ».[11]

Hoc autem humanae Redemptionis et perfectae Dei glorificationis opus, cui divina magnalia in populo Veteris Testamenti praeluserant, adimplevit Christus Dominus, praecipue per suae beatae Passionis, ab inferis Resurrectionis et gloriosae Ascensionis paschale mysterium, quo « mortem nostram moriendo destruxit, et vitam resurgendo reparavit ».[12] Nam de latere Christi in cruce dormientis ortum est totius Ecclesiae mirabile sacramentum.[13]

6. Ideoque, sicut Christus missus est a Patre, ita et ipse Apostolos, repletos Spiritu Sancto, misit, non solum ut, praedicantes Evangelium omni creaturae,[14] annuntiarent Filium Dei morte sua et resurrectione nos a potestate satanae[15] et a morte liberasse et in regnum Patris transtulisse, sed etiam ut, quod annuntiabant, opus salutis per Sacrificium et Sacramenta, circa quae tota vita liturgica vertit, exercerent. Sic per Baptismum homines paschali Christi mysterio inseruntur: commortui, consepulti, conresuscitati;[16] spiritum accipiunt adoptionis filiorum, « in quo clamamus: Abba, Pater » (Rom. 8, 15), et ita fiunt veri adoratores, quos Pater quaerit.[17] Similiter quotiescumque dominicam cenam manducant, mortem Domini annuntiant donec veniat.[18] Idcirco, ipso die Pentecostes, quo Ecclesia mundo apparuit, « qui receperunt sermonem » Petri « baptizati sunt ». Et erant « perseverantes in doctrina Apostolorum et communicatione fractionis panis et orationibus ... collaudantes Deum et habentes gratiam ad omnem plebem » (Act. 2, 41-47). Numquam exinde omisit Ecclesia quin in unum conveniret ad paschale mysterium cele-

Turning to the business at hand, the Secretary in his customary felicitous Latin announced that, in accordance with Pope Paul's leave, the reading of the 37-page text of the Liturgy Constitution and the 13-page Communications Decree which was to precede the solemn voting of these measures by the Council and the Pope's solemn promulgation, would be abbreviated, much to the relief of the Council Fathers, most of whom had come prepared for a long session. He carefully reminded the Fathers to use the magnetic pencils for marking the IBM ballots in order to eliminate invalid votes, and stated that they had a choice between *Placet* and *Non placet,* thus eliminating the troublesome *Iuxta modum* or conditional vote which had caused considerable delay in the Council's proceedings. In an earlier announcement Felici had once humorously remarked that the *"modi"* proposed by the Fathers were the reason why the commissions were having trouble producing an amended text, and Bishop Rupp of Monaco had asked in the course of one of his interventions whether the modern equivalent of *Iuxta modum* might not be *à la mode?*

The actual ceremony of the promulgation began with the solemn chanting of the Creed by the assembled bishops, after which a strange voice—quickly identified as that of Cardinal Ottaviani assisting Pope Paul as the senior cardinal in the order of deacons, cried out *"Orate"*—Pray. Thereupon Pope Paul knelt at the faldstool and recited the conciliar prayer *Adsumus Domine, Sancte Spiritus*—We are here present, Lord Holy Spirit, at the end of which the same voice rang out *"Erigite"*—All stand. After the Pope had intoned the *Veni Creator Spiritus,* the Secretary General began the truncated reading of the text of the Liturgy Constitution and the ballots were collected. Some ten minutes later Archbishop Felici approached the Pope with the results and announced an overwhelming majority of 2,147 favorable to 4 recalcitrant. Thereupon the Holy Father rose together with the bishops and pronounced the solemn formula making this an official document of the Church. Contrary to the formula found in the Ordo which ascribed to the Pope alone the right to "declare, decree and approve," the Pope said: ". . . We approve (this Constitution) together with the Fathers . . ." (*Approbamus una cum patribus*), thus acknowledging the reality of the collegial government of the Church still under fire by the minority. The previous week it had been made clear that this promulgation would be disciplinary not doctrinal in character, and as a consequence would not involve the Church's infallibility. The same procedure was followed for the Communications Decree, but this time the vote reflected the uneasiness created by a campaign on the part of certain progressive circles to have this schema rejected as being unworthy of being declared a conciliar document. Apparently resentment lingered over the arbitrary action on the part of the Secretary and Council President, for the final result was 1,969 favorable to 164 against. Again Pope Paul promulgated the document. The Apostolic Protonotaries then solemnly swore, in accordance with custom, to register—*Conficiemus*—the Latin document faithfully, and the Pope launched into his address formally closing the second session.

A carefully worded, closely reasoned summation of the Council's achievements and of the tasks still ahead, Pope Paul's talk stressed the spiritual rather than the literal successes of the session. He said: "Everything in this hall and on this occasion has a symbolic significance for everything here directs the minds of those present to the contemplation of heavenly things and is a foretaste of eternal hope." Pope Paul stated that some of the goals which the Council had set itself to bring about had been reached, and he mentioned the Church's awareness and understanding of herself which he said was being brought about by a meditation in depth on the mystery involved in her inner nature. He asked, when in history the Church as a whole had ever "achieved so full a consciousness of herself, so great a love of Christ, or had ever shown so eager a determination to achieve her goal?" He insisted that the conciliar colloquy had given the bishops an unprecedented knowledge of each other and thereby enabled them to experience literally the significance of St. Paul's words which describe the Church so aptly. He then quoted Ephesians 2:19-20: "You are no longer strangers and newcomers, but rather fellow citizens of the saints and members of the household of God, built upon the foundations laid by the apostles and the prophets, where the very cornerstone is Christ Jesus." What was remarkable about the Pope's citation of this particular text was the fact that its use in the schema on Ecumenism had been challenged on the floor two weeks earlier by Cardinal Ruffini, who maintained that in employing this Pauline citation as a definition of the Church, "founded on the apostles and prophets with Christ as the cornerstone," doubt was being cast upon the Petrine foundation based on Matthew 18:16 where Christ addresses Peter: "Thou art . . . Church." Paul thus indirectly was chiding the Cardinal of Palermo—a scriptural scholar of the old school—for his dated unecumenical exegesis.

Making a Pauline contribution, the Pope revealed his thoughts with regard to the way the "revolution" in the Church was going to be carried out in the practical sphere by turning his attention to canon law, the instrument by which the Church was governed on a day to day basis. Here he noted that ecclesiastical law was not a static entity but an organic concept that developed, "extending its growth in two directions." On the one hand it should enhance the dignity of each person and office in the Church affording them greater power for development, and on the other hand it should strengthen the intrinsic demands of love, harmony and mutual respect within the community of the faithful that is guaranteed by "the unifying quality of hierarchical government." These carefully chosen and somewhat mysterious words seemed to echo the new concept of church law that Pope John had so frequently hinted at: the abandonment of the harsh menacing and condemnatory aspects which the Code of Canon Law had inherited from ancient Roman law, and a reintroduction of the liberating and encouraging aspects of Gospel law enunciated by Christ and preached as an *agape* or law of charity in the early Church. It was this direction that Pope Paul seemed intent on giving to a new codification—the recently published Oriental Code—which had been criticized at the Council as an attempt to Latinize their Churches. Later in his speech he stated explicitly that new codes were to be drawn up "both for the Latin Church and for the Oriental Churches," thus officially promising a revision of the debatable Oriental Code.

Sensitive to the criticism that the Council had appeared to be dragging its feet and lacked proper coordination, he admitted that the discussions had been "arduous and intricate" and referred to the work of the Council as "laborious," but these defects had to be borne in order to assure perfect "freedom of expression." The divergent views expressed on the council floor, far from being a source of perplexity or anxiety as the ultraconservatives keep repeating, were "proof of the depth of the subjects investigated" and a sign of this "freedom." It is reported that earlier when pressed by reform-minded bishops to intervene and end the deadlock over procedure, he had replied that he would do so only as a last resort in order not to give any side grounds for claiming that it had been muzzled by papal action.

He rejoiced that the Liturgy Constitution now made it possible "to simplify our liturgical rites" and "render them more intelligible to the people and accommodated to the language they speak." But he coupled this with an admonition: "To attain these ends it is necessary that no attempt should be made to introduce into the official prayer of the Church private changes or singular rites." The decentralization envisaged by this document must be carried out in an orderly way with the bishops in national or regional groups deciding how and how much of the change was to be introduced when the new law went into effect on the first Sunday in Lent (Feb. 16, 1964). Meanwhile, there was to be a *vacatio legis,* as Archbishop Felici announced, during which no innovations were to be permitted: This warning on jumping the gun was repeated in a boxed notice on page 1 of *L'Osservatore Romano* the following day, causing one local theologian to remark: "Since they seem to take for granted in the Vatican that the *L'Osservatore* is primarily an Italian paper, they evidently fear that the local clergy are finally feeling the revolutionary urge. They know that such a warning is useless for the Germans and many of the French who are already far advanced in the use of the vernacular, and needless for the Irish and Americans who will not move before Rome cracks the whip!"

The Pope had little to say about the controversial Communications decree, describing it as of "no small value" and expressing the hope that it would "guide and encourage numerous forms of activity" in the communications field.

Some observers discerned a veiled reference to the now famous propositions voted on October 30th and an indication of papal support for the position taken by the Moderators in the words: "As you all know the Council has addressed itself to many questions whose solutions are in part virtually formulated in authoritative decisions which will be published in time after the work on the topics to which they belong is completed." With this precise paternal admoni-

LA «VACATIO LEGIS» DELLA COSTITUZIONE «DE SACRA LITURGIA»

Avvenuta la promulgazione della Costituzione « De Sacra Liturgia » da parte del Santo Padre, S. E. Mons. Pericle Felici, Segretario Generale del Concilio Ecumenico, ha annunziato che il Sommo Pontefice stabiliva per le nuove norme, contenute nella promulgata Costituzione, una vacatio legis fino al 16 febbraio 1964, Domenica I di Quaresima.

Nel frattempo lo stesso Sommo Pontefice, con apposito documento, disporrà per la pratica attuazione della suddetta Costituzione. A nessuno è lecito applicare, di propria iniziativa, le nuove norme liturgiche sancite.

Notice announcing temporary suspension of the Liturgy Constitution, *L'Osservatore Romano*, December 6, 1963

tion, he outlined the procedure for those conciliar Commissions which had seemingly gone at their work in too slow or too unskilled a fashion:

"It is fitting . . . that the competent commissions on whose work we place so much hope, will prepare for the future conciliar meetings, in accordance with the mind of the Fathers, *as expressed especially in the general congregations* (our italics), proposals profoundly studied, accurately formulated, suitably condensed and abbreviated, so that the dis-

cussions, while remaining always free, may be rendered
easier and more brief." In effect he was saying that the commissions were intended to serve the Council, not vice versa.
Though the Pope went on to say, "We hope that the Third
Session in the autumn of next year will bring (the discussions)
to completion," he later declared (see page 335) that he had
set no time limit for the Council.

It was noted with interest that the Pope studiously avoided
any mention of the word "collegiality," but the substance of
the doctrine was clearly contained in his reference to the
Council's aim to set forth "the powers of the episcopate,
indicating how they should be used, individually and *corporately*, so as worthily to manifest the eminence of the episcopate in the Church of God, which is not an institution
independent of, or separated from, or still less, antagonistic
to, the supreme pontificate of Peter, but with Peter and under him it strives for the common good and the supreme
goal of the Church." "We are sure," he added, "that on a
subject of such importance the Council will have much to
say that will bring consolation and light."

After mentioning briefly that he was in accord with what
the Council had decided regarding the place of the schema
on the Virgin Mary, (applause)—namely to incorporate it
as a chapter in the schema on the Church, he promised that
the remaining questions proposed for consideration but not
yet discussed in the Council "would be subjected to a
thorough and deeper re-examination" so that it would not
be difficult for the next session to "obtain a judgment of the
Council on certain fundamental propositions"—once more
seeming to sanction the procedure adopted by the Moderators. Details not requiring conciliar action would be left
to post-conciliar commissions composed of bishops, experts,
members of religious orders, and cardinals. "Experience will
suggest to us how, without prejudice to the prerogatives of

the Roman pontiff defined by Vatican Council I, the earnest and cordial collaboration of the bishops can more effectively promote the good of the universal Church." These last words were a reminder that at the proper time he would announce what form a proposed episcopal "Senate" was to take.

Commentators were in agreement that this carefully worded, balanced, moderate-in-tone speech, completely lacking the enthusiasm which had marked his opening speech on September 29th, reflected the mood of the Pope and of the Council itself. He was anxious to draw up a faithful balance sheet, to say what required to be said, but not to indicate any enthusiasm for a session which, as Henri Fesquet wrote: "had more debits than credits."*

The Liturgy Constitution, the "first achievement of Vatican Council II" according to the U.S. bishops statement issued on December 4 in Rome, and a very substantial one at that—was debated on the floor of the Council and approved during the first session. This year it was necessary for the Fathers to vote on a large number of amendments to the text which the Liturgy Commission had worked out on the basis of the suggestions made in the course of the debate. These amendments were voted on in batches throughout the present session. It quickly became clear that the schema on the liturgy, as amended, was going through. To the surprise of everybody, however, a hitch developed when the voting on Chapter II (on the Mass) as a whole failed to achieve the required two-thirds majority, even though the nineteen amendments to the chapter had gone through easily. There was confusion for a moment. Later it turned out that the Fathers had failed to give the chapter their approval, not because they were against it, but because many felt that it did not go far enough. For example, the text of the schema laid down that the vernacular could be introduced into all

* *Le Monde,* Dec. 6, 1963.

the sacraments except for the essential form (e.g. the *Ego te baptizo*—I baptize thee—in the rite of baptism) which had to be kept in Latin. This was contrary to immemorial custom, some pointed out. When this restriction was removed, Chapter II (Mass) and Chapter III (Sacraments) received overwhelming support. There was henceforth no reason why even the canon, including the formula for the consecration of the eucharistic elements, could not eventually be said in English or any other modern language, if the local authorities and the Holy See approved. Father Clifford Howell, S.J., an eminent British liturgist, accurately summed up the liturgy reforms voted by the Council as follows: "The Constitution is a tremendous achievement; it proves to the whole world that all this talk about 'bringing the Church up to date' is not *mere* talk, but enlightened and purposeful discussion bearing fruit in action."* The "model" Liturgy Commission deserves all the credit possible for the commendable way in which it handled the details of steering the measure through. It was fortunate in having such vigorous progressives as Cardinal Lercaro and Archbishop Hallinan of Atlanta, among its members, and in being ably supported by a large number of equally forward-looking experts including Father Frederick McManus of Catholic University, Washington, D.C., and Godfrey Diekmann of the Benedictine Abbey at Collegeville, Minn. After one of the liturgical Commission's rather heated meetings, the French liturgist Father Mortimort gave biblical credit to the six men who had insisted on the extensive reforms called for by the majority of Council Fathers and rejected by the standpatters in the Commission, saying: "Three there are who give testimony in heaven: Bishops Hallinan, Jenny and Martin; and three there are who give testimony on earth: Fathers Wagner, McManus and Mortimort." Thus neatly distinguishing

* *Catholic Herald*, Dec. 6, 1963.

between the bishops who did the voting and the experts who prepared the texts (cf. 1 John 5:7-8).

The Liturgy Constitution accomplishes three things: a) it establishes the function of the Word of God in liturgical worship, placing the emphasis on Scripture as understood in and by modern biblical theology, and thereby furnishing a realistic bridge for a dialogue with the Protestant Churches whose worship has always been biblically rather than sacramentally oriented; b) it establishes the need and right for greater participation by the people in church worship; c) it establishes the duty of episcopal conferences to spell out the practical details of adapting the Church's worship to local conditions. The last provision is rightly seen as an important preliminary step in acknowledging the collegial character of the bishops, regarded in the light of this session's discussions as co-responsible along with the Pope for governing the Church, though the extent to which it also may mark a first stage in the loosening up of the tight control which the Roman Congregation of Rites has for many years exercised over liturgical matters remains to be seen. While certain members of the Curia can be expected to fight against any substantial relinquishment of authority to the bishops as a threat to the supremacy of papal power, it is the hope of seasoned observers, that the leaven of contact between the people and the living eucharistic mystery of the Church resulting from the application of the Constitution will work in favor of Pope John's *aggiornamento*—renewal —of the Church, despite such misgivings.

VI

The Holy Land Pilgrimage; Summary of the Second Session

THE POPE'S HISTORIC ANNOUNCEMENT that he intended to make a trip to the Holy Land was probably one of the best-kept secrets of recent years. It was a remarkable performance at a court notorious for its *indiscrezioni*. Nobody outside the immediate circle concerned had any word about what was coming until eleven o'clock, shortly before the Pope began his talk, when word was leaked to a few of the experts. But to the majority of hearers and the vast world outside, the news came as a breath-taking disclosure of incalculable significance. Nobody was prepared for it. And some time elapsed before the significance could be seen in its proper light as there was nothing except the bare fact of the announcement to go on. The Vatican could disclose no further information because nothing had as yet been settled. The details remained to be worked out. As a matter of fact, it was not until shortly before the Pope departed from Rome that the final protocol of his meetings with the Orthodox leaders was worked out, signed and sealed.

With the advantage of hindsight we can now see that the main practical purpose of the pilgrimage was to provide an occasion for a suitable encounter with Orthodox and other eastern religious leaders, specifically with Patriarch Athenagoras I of Constantinople, *primus inter pares* of the Orthodox patriarchs. But there was only the barest allusion to this in the Pope's original statement: ". . . to summon to this one holy Church our separated brethren . . ." This was all that he could say for the present in that regard, but the immediately preceding phrases of the announcement must not be left out of account, fraught as they were with meaning. Although somewhat obscurely expressed, the Pope's thought seems to have been that his pilgrimage was to be an expression of "prayer, penance and renewal" and that it was his intention "to offer to Christ His Church" in the same spirit, i.e., as a properly humble and renewed Church, to which the separated brethren would be summoned. He was careful to avoid the use of the word "return," or to imply that the Orthodox were being asked to restore unity with an "unrenewed" Church.

In spite of repeated attempts in the press and by various interested groups to make political hay out of the pilgrimage, it is clear in the light of the Pope's repeated statements, notably in his Christmas Message (December 23, 1963), in his address to the diplomatic corps (December 28th), and in numerous statements which he made while in the Holy Land, that the sole purpose of the trip was religious and spiritual. It was not intended to serve any political purpose, except indirectly by aiding the cause of world peace and mutual understanding. It was no small accomplishment to emerge from the political maelstrom of the Near East virtually unscathed ideologically-speaking.

Regardless of other factors which may have entered into the picture at the time, there can be little doubt, in the light of subsequent events, that one of the primary reasons why Pope Paul did not want a detailed debate on the floor of the Council on Chapter IV on the Jewish problem, was that he thought too heated a discussion of the matter in Rome might prejudice the success of his Holy Land pilgrimage, which had already been decided upon. The small lifting of the veil during the opening days of the debate following November 18th was enough to convince him of that. The Arab Christians were unanimously opposed to the Chapter as a part of the schema though not necessarily to the contents being treated in some other connection. And there could be no doubt that sentiment among the bishops at large was lukewarm, at best. While many were in favor of the principles involved, it was doubtful whether a majority could be mustered for approval of it as chapter IV of Ecumenism, and the unpalatable prospect therefore loomed of seeing the chapter defeated, if a test-vote were held. The initial mistake may well have been to present it as Chapter IV in the first place, but as spokesmen for the Secretariat for Promoting Christian Unity rather freely avowed this was done as much from tactical as from logical considerations. Under the circumstances, there was little that he could do except defer consideration. What specifically irked observers at the time was that he saw fit to give no assurance that it would be taken up again as part of the agenda at the Third Session. In view of the tactics of the minority, it seemed dangerous *not* to make some public statement.

The plan for a meeting with Athenagoras I seems to have matured over a period of time and therefore cannot have been a sudden last minute inspiration on the Pope's part to rescue the Council from "gloom." Two important steps in the formulation of the plan were a letter from the Pope to Athenagoras, dated September 29, 1963, replying to an earlier letter from the Patriarch congratulating him on his election as Pope, and another letter from the Patriarch to the Pope, dated November 22, 1963, replying to the Pope's letter of September 20th. In the first letter the Pope made no mention of any proposed meeting but prepared the ground for one by "confiding the past to the mercy of God" and stating that he was willing to do whatever was necessary to bring about unity. "May the Lord open our hearts to the inspiration of His Spirit and guide us toward the full realization of His will." He stated that as "successor of the coryphaeus of the Apostles" he was interested in whatever could contribute to establish "perfect concord" between Christians, and closed with the wish "May the grace of the Lord . . . the charity of the Father, and the communion of the Holy Spirit be with you." In his reply Patriarch Athenagoras suggested the establishment of friendly relations on a more intimate basis, "as became members of Christ's holy body, which is the Church," and said that there was no more precious gift that each could bring to the other than "the offering of communion in the charity which, according to the Apostle, forgives all, believes all, hopes all, bears all." And he referred to "the bond of communion in peace which formerly bound our two holy Churches together, and which is now being renewed by the grace of the Lord."

The receipt of the letter from Athenagoras during the last week of November apparently precipitated the final decision to go to Palestine and rendered impracticable any further debate on the Jewish question. In early November, the Pope's personal secretary Don Pasquale Macchi and Monsignor J. P. Martin, of the Secretariat of State, made a trip to the Near East, in the strictest secrecy, in order to prepare

the ground for a possible pilgrimage. It was revealed later
that they had visited Jordan and Israel. Diplomatic "sound-
ings" were also made through the representatives of the
Arab states and Israel accredited to the Quirinal, who visited
the Secretariat of State in a series of audiences in October
and November. It is unlikely that the subject of the pilgrimage was directly broached on these occasions, the Vatican officials probably being more interested in determining
the general background and atmosphere in which a trip
might take place, and the diplomats themselves more interested in possible reactions to the discussion of the Jewish
document.*

Once the papal intention to go on pilgrimage to Palestine
had been announced, Patriarch Athenagoras lost no time in
approving the idea and suggesting a meeting of religious
heads in Jerusalem to discuss reunion (December 6). The
intention seems to have been to clear the way for a meeting
between the Pope and Patriarch, since a broader gathering
could hardly have been arranged on such short notice.
Father Duprey, one of the high officials in Bea's Secretariat,
was dispatched to Constantinople to "explain the nature of
the Holy Father's pilgrimage" and no doubt give assurances
that a meeting with Athenagoras in Jerusalem would be
welcome. The official nature of the announcements made in
Istanbul and Rome (Dec. 10th and 12th) on this occasion,
tended to confirm the view that a meeting was being seriously considered. Further confirmation came from the Greek
Orthodox Patriarch of Antioch on December 18th, and in
the Christmas message of the Patriarch Athenagoras read on
December 25th. The latter had sounded out the other Orthodox religious leaders and won their approval to a meeting
between himself and Pope Paul. Only the Greek Church,
under the leadership of Archbishop Chrysostomos of Athens,

* *L'Avvenire d'Italia*, December 6, 1963.

remained resolutely opposed in principle, though some of the Greek hierarchy were favorable and supported the step of the Ecumenical Patriarch. The final details of the historical meeting were regulated in the most minute particulars by a formal protocol signed on the occasion of a visit to the Vatican on December 28th by the official emissary of the Patriarch and Holy Synod of Constantinople, Metropolitan Athenagoras of Thyateira, Orthodox Archbishop of Great Britain.

The Pope was accompanied to the Holy Land by Cardinal Tisserant, the Dean of the Sacred College, Cardinal Cicognani, Secretary of State, Cardinal Testa, Secretary of the Congregation for the Oriental Churches and formerly Apostolic Delegate in Jerusalem, Archbishop Dell'Acqua, Deputy Secretary of State, who had arranged the details with Metropolitan Athenagoras and Father Duprey, Archbishop Enrico Dante, Papal Master of Ceremonies, Bishop Van Lierde, the papal Sacristan, and various prelates of the papal household and Secretariat of State, including the Pope's two private secretaries and Monsignor Martin. Also included in the entourage, representing the Secretariat for Promoting Christian Unity, were Monsignor Willebrands, the Secretary, and Father Duprey, the Undersecretary of that office.

The first encounter of the Pope with an Orthodox Patriarch took place Saturday evening, the day of his arrival after the grueling experience of the Via Dolorosa and mass celebrated under unbelievably crowded conditions in the church of the Holy Sepulchre. Patriarch Benedict of Jerusalem called on the Pope at the Apostolic Delegation where he was staying, and Pope Paul then returned the visit at the villa which was the residence of Benedict. The meetings went very well. It is known that Patriarch Benedict had expressed reservations beforehand about the appropriateness of the proposed encounter, but the fact that Pope Paul agreed to receive him

first and then to return the visit and graciously took note of
the special part which Benedict had played in promoting a
better feeling between the various communities in Jerusalem
pleased him and helped to cut the ice. It was essential to
create the proper atmosphere for the meeting with Athenagoras on the morrow. The same evening after receiving
Benedict, the Pope also received the Armenian Patriarch of
Jerusalem, Derderian, who presented a special delegation of
bishops sent by the Armenian Catholicus of Cilicia, Koren I,
to greet the Pope.

Sunday was spent visiting the sites in Israel. On leaving
the Israeli authorities at the Mandelbaum Gate, before returning to the Old City of Jersualem, the Pope unexpectedly
said a few words in defense of the memory of Pius XII and
his concern for the Jews, with obvious reference to Hoch-
huth's controversial play. Back at the Apostolic Delegation, he
received Patriarch Athenagoras at 9:30 P.M. Everything took
place according to strict protocol. The Patriarch and Metro-
politans accompanying him were received at the gate by the
three cardinals accompanying the Pope, Tisserant, Cicognani and Testa, while the Pope waited to greet his guest at
the door. After putting their arms about each other and
exchanging the kiss of peace, the Pope led the Patriarch
inside for a private talk. This was supposed to last only five
minutes but actually lasted twenty. The various suites were
then presented. The Patriarch read his address in Greek:
"Most holy brother in Christ. . . The Christian world has
lived for centuries in the night of separation. Its eyes are
tired of gazing into darkness. May this meeting be the dawn
of a bright and blessed day, in which future generations,
communicating from the same chalice of the sacred body and
precious blood of the Lord, will praise and glorify, in charity,
peace and humility, the one Lord and Savior of the world."
A French translation of the speech was then handed to the

Pope and read by the Patriarch's secretary, Msgr. Simeon Amaryllios. The Pope was greatly moved by the Patriarch's words. Though protocol decreed that his own speech be reserved for the return visit tomorrow, he did remark: "I may say now that your words are the source of many fruitful thoughts."

He then handed to the Patriarch the gifts which he had brought for him from Rome, a gold chalice and a gold medal commemorating the pilgrimage. After some hesitation as to what would constitute a proper gift, the Pope had finally decided on the chalice with reference to the hoped-for restoration of fraternal communion between the two Churches. He could not have known that the Patriarch would mention the chalice in his speech! Handing the chalice to him, he said: "You have alluded to the chalice in your talk. The chalice is the living root of our fraternal love. Allow me to offer this to you as a symbol of fraternal love."

After the Pope had distributed medals to the members of the Patriarch's suite, the gathering recited the "Our Father" in unison, in Greek and Latin. Pope Paul then took the Patriarch by the arm and led him toward the door. The Patriarch said, in French: *"Oui, la main dans la main pour toujours."* He was accompanied to the gate by the three cardinals who bade him farewell. Upon leaving he remarked to one of the newsmen present: "I ardently hope that Pope Paul VI and I will one day mix water and wine in this chalice!" The Pope himself was so greatly moved by the meeting that he mentioned it the following day in his talk at Bethlehem, although this was not part of his original text.

The second encounter between Pope and Patriarch took place the next morning, Monday, January 6th, the last day of the pilgrimage, after Pope Paul returned from Bethlehem and before he was scheduled to depart for Rome. But first a word with regard to the speech at Bethlehem, carefully prepared in advance, perhaps the most important statement in the entire pilgrimage. The original text was delivered in French. It opened with a symbolic "confession of the Church of Rome" offered to Christ at the site of His nativity in the manner of Peter's confession of Christ's divinity or the offerings of the Magi:

This confession is that of the Church of Rome, the church which was Peter's and which was founded on him as a rock. For this reason, Lord, it is Your Church and lives still in virtue of its unbroken connection with Your fountainhead. Be with Your Church, defend it, purify it, give it strength and life, O Christ of the Church of Rome.

These words were promptly misunderstood by the less perceptive, both in the East and the West. Wasn't it shocking that the Pope appeared to be claiming Christ for the Church of Rome, how could this possibly be interpreted in an ecumenical sense, etc.? His intention was quite different as the context showed. The Roman Catholic Church made once again its confession of faith in the divinity of Christ and therefore belonged to Christ, who was asked to "defend, purify and strengthen" His Church—the last few words referred to the Petrine sayings quoted immediately before: "Lord, to whom shall we go . . .", "Lord, thou knowest all things, Thou knowest that we love Thee" (John 6:69 and 21:17). The implication clearly was: Are the other Churches prepared to make the same confession of faith? The words were an indirect challenge to "the others" to do likewise.

A still more significant remark followed. After addressing a few words to Catholics in full communion with the Holy See and noting that the success of the Council and its ultimate goal of imparting "new attitudes of mind, new aims, new standards of conduct" to the Church required the joyful cooperation of all, "concerted effort in which every section of the Church must play its part," he went on to address those "our Christian brothers who are not in perfect communion with us" and to state that

It is clear to everyone that the problem of unity cannot be put on one side. Today the will of Christ is pressing upon us and obliging us to do all that we can, with love and wisdom, to bring to all Christians the supreme blessing and honor of a united Church.

Then came the carefully weighed words:

Even on this very special occasion we must say that such a result is not to be obtained at the expense of the truths of faith. We cannot be false to Christ's heritage: it is not ours, but His; we are no more than stewards, teachers and interpreters. Yet we declare once again that we are ready to consider every reasonable possibility by which mutual understanding, respect and charity may be fostered so as to smooth the way to a future—and please God, not too distant—meeting with our Christian brothers still separated from us.

The door of the fold is open. We wait, all of us, with sincere hearts, our desire is strong and patient. There is room for all. Our affection goes in advance of the step to be taken; it can be taken with honor and mutual joy. We shall not call for gestures which are not the fruit of free conviction, the effect of the spirit of the Lord, who breathes when and where He wills. We shall wait for the happy hour to come.

For the present, we ask for our separated brethren only that which we set before ourselves as our objective, namely that every step toward reunion and interchange of views should be inspired by love of Christ and the Church. We shall take pains to keep alive the desire for understanding and union and we shall put our trust in prayer which, even though it is not yet united prayer, rises up nevertheless simultaneously from ourselves and from Christians separated from us like two parallel columns which meet on high to form an arch in the God of unity.

The speech closed with a "word to the world" regarding the aspirations of humanity.

These words too will undoubtedly cause rivers of ink to flow, but their message was quite simple, a message bearing the Pauline imprint but impregnated with the thought of Cardinal Bea, who probably had a hand in their composition. They disclosed a whole program. The important news was the announcement that the Roman Catholic Church stands ready to enter into a dialogue with the separated brethren on the basis of a mutual respect for truth, "inspired by a love of Christ and the Church," as the Pope put it. The Catholic Church cannot deny its own nature or what it conceives itself to be. But by the same token it declares itself prepared to recognize the sincerity of others and will not demand from them anything inconsistent with their convictions. The Pope thus appears to be ruling out both the idea of a "submission to Rome" pure and simple, as well as the reverse side of the coin, "Rome must first abandon its position as the one, true Church." His emphasis on the Church's role as the "guardian" rather than the "author" of divine revelation likewise seems intended both as a warning and an incentive. The Catholic Church cannot adopt any position inconsistent with its nature or with divine revelation on which its own authority depends; on the other hand, it is willing to join others in examining the content of that revelation ("exchange of views") with a view to reaching a common accord. Apart from these presuppositions, he seems to regard the door as wide-open, both as to the way in which such a dialogue might take place ("we are ready to consider any reasonable possibility"), and the steps that it might involve ("every step toward reunion"). Interesting is the thought that reunion is something to be achieved not all at once, but in a series of stages. However, there can be no doubt about its urgency and the necessity of taking concrete action if the wish is to become a reality. The word "fold" is almost certainly being used by the Pope in two senses: of the Catholic Church in its present form—although the Pope makes no reference to the point, he was well aware that the Orthodox Church entertains the same view with regard to itself. But it can also be understood, expectantly or by way of anticipation, of the reunited Church of the future (the "recomposed" Church, according to the expression used by the Pope in his talk at Grottaferrata on August 18, 1963). No doubt present in the Pope's mind was the thought expressed by that "Apostle of Unity," Cardinal Bea, on numerous occasions, that all baptized Christians *already* belong to the one true Catholic Church which the Roman Church conceives itself to be, by virtue of their baptism and their faith. The problem of reunion is to iron out the difficulties which prevent the realization of "perfect" ecclesiastical communion. Viewed in this light, the Pope's words are neither mysterious nor backward-looking, but a challenge to all, Catholics and non-Catholics, to get on with the business of restoring Christian unity.

The Pope arrived for his second meeting with Athenagoras at the residence of Patriarch Benedict of Jerusalem, about 9 A.M., and was greeted at the entrance according to the same protocol as was observed the day before, by Metropolitan Athenagoras and Archbishop Iakovos of the Orthodox Church of North America, in the name of the Patriarch. All then gathered in the reception room which was so very small it could barely contain those who were present. The fragile glass doors had scarcely been closed when the Pope launched into his Latin address: *"Vehementer nos commovet . . ."* He was greatly moved by the occasion, but appeared in complete control of himself, his grey-green eyes riveted on his text, unmindful of the crowded scene around him. By contrast the Patriarch appeared pale and could scarcely contain his feelings. He kept his hand on his heart and looked neither to right nor to left at those nearest him. When Paul VI recalled the figure of Pope John XXIII and the Patriarch's words with respect to him: ". . . there was a man sent by God . . ." the Patriarch smiled and from then on seemed in complete control of his emotions. After the speech had been read, the text was handed to the Patriarch. There was no translation. The Patriarch then offered the Pope his gift, which had been decided on by a special committee set up by the Holy Synod of Constantinople. The decision was in favor of a pectoral chain—called *encolpion* in the Greek Church—which is worn by bishops and is symbolic of their apostolic succession and government of the Church. The significance of the occasion was that Patriarch Athenagoras considered Pope Paul a bishop of the Eastern Church.

Pope Paul had no advance word on what the nature of the gift to him would be. His eyes lit up when he saw what it was. At once, without hesitating for a moment, he removed his Latin papal stole and put the chain on over his head, with the assistance of the Patriarch, then put the stole on over it. Other similar chains were then given to the three cardinals accompanying the Pope, and to Monsignor Willebrands and Father Duprey, officials of the Secretariat for Promoting Christian Unity, the Patriarch gave the Cross of St. Andrew, an Orthodox order awarded for special services on behalf of the Orthodox Church, in recognition of the regard in which they were held.

After the presents had been distributed, the Pope said in French: "Now we are going to read the Gospel of St. John, chapter 17, the prayer of Christ for unity." As Monsignor Willebrands held up the small New Testament volume with the Greek and Latin texts facing each other, the Pope began with a verse in Latin and was followed by the Patriarch with the next verse in Greek. The Pope was so overcome by emotion that he lost his place at least three times. The Patriarch appeared more in control of himself. The final words of verse 21: "Let them be one so that the world may believe" were enunciated by the Pope with particular emphasis. After the reading Pope and Patriarch recited the "Our Father" in unison, as on the previous day, along with the rest of the gathering. Patriarch Athenagoras at first hesitated to go beyond the words with which the Latin version customarily ends, but the Pope insisted, and they all said together the concluding phrase, which the Orthodox repeat along with Protestants: "For thine is the kingdom, the power, and the glory forever. Amen."

Pope Paul then proposed that they both bless those present. Athenagoras declined and asked the Pope to offer his blessing. "Let us bless them together," said the Pope. When the Pope began with the usual formula: *"Sit nomen Domini benedictum*—Blessed be the name of the Lord," Athenagoras said nothing, but when it came time for the actual blessing, he raised his hand high and in a majestic sweep gave his blessing along with that of the Pope. Many were moved to tears by the historical symbolism of the occasion.

A third chance encounter between Pope and Patriarch took place on the street later the same morning, as the Pope was returning from a visit in Jerusalem. The two stood for about ten minutes in private conversation. After receiving Archbishop A. C. MacInnes, Anglican Archbishop of Jerusalem and emissary of Archbishop Ramsey of Canterbury, as well as Provost Malsch, the Lutheran representative, Pope Paul left Jerusalem at 12:30 for Amman. His plane touched down at Ciampino near Rome at 6:13 P.M. The return to the Vatican along the historic Appian Way and through the heart of the city was a veritable Roman triumph, the likes of which Rome had seldom seen.

It is impossible for anyone viewing the facts dispassionately to come to any other conclusion than that this carefully planned, carefully contrived meeting—with all the attendant publicity, some of it in questionable taste, no doubt—remains a keystone in the papal view that the aims of ecumenism can only be furthered by concrete steps, by the right persons at the appropriate time, of course. It was one thing for the Fathers in the Council to discuss theoretically the advantages or disadvantages of a program for unity, in the short time allotted for this topic, it will be something else again for them to vote in the Third Session on principles of action when they have the example of what the head of the Church has now done to guide them. As some of the bishops pointed out: "Deeds count, not words." In the light of the Palestine experience, it seems safe to conclude that the Pope and his advisers, particularly Cardinals Bea and Lercaro, are determined to make a reality of what "intercommunion" already exists, through baptism, the same reverence for the Bible, the sharing of the same sacraments, etc., in the hope that by going as far as one can "in charity"—and the suggestion has already been aired, as we have seen, for a fuller sacramental communion between Orthodox and Catholics, *as of now*—and the hope voiced for a greater "openness" toward cooperation with Protestants along similiar lines, that "full ecclesiastical communion" can be established eventually on the basis of shared common experiences. In other words, for the present, there will be no ringing of church bells or chanting of *Te Deums* as at the Council of Florence in the fifteenth century, when reunion was effected temporarily between East and West, but a slow process of "reconstruction" will be inaugurated that will ultimately lead to the desired result, perhaps without any fanfare at all, at some future date.

At the close of the Second Session a gloomy atmosphere prevailed among many observers and was shared by some

of the bishops, in varying degrees. It seemed that something
of this gloom was even reflected in the Pope's final talk. The
accomplishments of the session had been distressingly small,
in spite of the tremendous effort expended. Observers also
concluded correctly that the fault lay with the relatively
small minority who were in a position to hold up the work
of the Council and were likely to continue to do so unless
they were dislodged in some dramatic move. This "doom and
gloom" attitude was reflected particularly in an article in
Time (December 6, 1963), entitled "What went wrong?"
which concluded that the Pope was "more a prisoner of the
Curia than John ever was . . ." As an intellectual he was not
a man of action and so could not be expected to cope with
the opposition of the minority effectively. The implication
was that he had given in to them and things looked exceed-
ingly bad for the Church and Council. There were many
modifications of the pessimistic line. Some darkly hinted
that the Italian and Spanish bishops had brought pressure to
bear on the Pope to drop Chapter V. "In the context of
Italian politics many purely religious and ecclesiastical matters take on political overtones. In the right-view Italian press
a criticism of the Roman Curia in the Council and the suggestion that it be placed under an international apostolic
council with the Pope are interpreted as a political gesture
in favor of the left. Why? Because it seems that in Italy the
Roman Curia has become the symbol of the anti-communist
bloc seeking to prevent a further opening to the left."* Others
have stated more bluntly that the change which alledgedly
came over the Pope sometime after the weekend of November
8th—at the time when the issue of the validity of the October
30th vote on collegiality was being so hotly debated in the
Council—was due to concern for the financial assets of the
Vatican in Italy—the fear that is, that a further drift toward

* Gregory Baum, O.S.A., writing in *Commonweal*, December 27, 1963.

the left by the Church would give added strength to the communist vote which had already reached alarming proportions in the spring election. Such an argument is scarcely plausible if one looks at the facts. And it is difficult to imagine Pope Paul being influenced by such considerations in any case. The truth of the matter is that the Holy See has much larger financial assets outside Italy than inside, the largest asset being its virtually unlimited credit with American and European financial circles through the local hierarchies. Concern for the Italian economy might cause nightmares to Cardinal Siri, but it is hardly likely that the Pope would be taken in by such parochial considerations. Father Edward Duff, S.J., in a syndicated article dated December 12, 1963, entitled "Pope upsets theories of Council pessimists," correctly assessed the situation—after he had himself helped to contribute to the gloom in several preceding articles. Nor can there be any doubt, after the events in Palestine, that Pope Paul remains determined to carry through his purposes which are still those of Pope John XXIII and the majority of the Council, but of course in his own way and in his own time. Elaborate attempts to explain a fundamental change in his thinking as the result of various conflicting interests or fears fail to hold together. His speeches, statements, actions all show a remarkable consistency. The same elements are present *after* the alleged "debâcle" of November as before. There is no need to assume a "counter-revolution."

The thesis of gloom was certainly not shared by his intimate advisers, Cardinals Suenens, Koenig, and Lercaro; nor was it shared by Frings, Ritter or Feltin who left Rome with the fullest confidence that the cause they represented would prevail whatever might be the delays or the ottavianesque difficulties still to be overcome. These were the men who were actually closest to the Holy Father in his thinking as Cardinal Montini, and with whom now, evidently, he shared an insight into the problem of implementing the reform from the lofty, timeless perspective that he had to adopt as Pope.

An indication of this manner of thinking was given by Cardinal Suenens in a lecture he delivered at the Canadian college, on Sunday December 1, attended by most of the Canadian bishops as well as the students and priests belonging to the Canadian colony in Rome. Admitting that the three schemata handled during the Second Session were not as full a work-load as they had hoped to accomplish during the ten weeks of conciliar debate, the Belgian cardinal discussed the causes for the slow pace, while insisting strongly on the unquestionable value of the achievement represented by the thorough treatment given the nature of the Church, the general, if contested, acceptation of the idea of the collegiality of the bishops, and the positive approach towards ecumenism manifested in the majority of discourses during the last two weeks. He indicated that he had opposed any idea of a vote on chapters four and five of the latter schema— the problem of the Jews and of religious liberty—without a thorough discussion of these issues. Hence he did not share the disappointment of the more impatient progressives who felt that the Council had been check-mated by the filibustering tactics of the opposition. Questioned as to the possibility of introducing a truly parliamentary procedure into the Council's debates, he observed that many of the prelates were very sensitive about their freedom to speak, particularly those from Africa and behind the Iron Curtain; and while admitting that the present procedure neither permitted a direct dialogue nor prevented a certain manipulation on the part of a small group who still wielded great influence through two or three well-placed individuals in the Secretary General's entourage, he did not see much to be gained from a tighter control of the speakers by the Moderators, other than an insistence that the individual interventions should be directed to theological issues and principles, while criticism of the conciliar texts should be confined to written communications given to the respective Conciliar committees. He observed that despite provision made in the revised rules for the Council, very few of the Fathers had availed themselves of the right to sit in on the meetings of the commissions preparing the texts for the Council's consideration.

Suenens spoke further about two important matters that both he and the Pope were determined should be affected by the Council: the seminary training of the clergy, and the collegial function of the bishops' office. With regard to the former point, he said that he had conducted a thorough investigation of seminary legislation beginning with Trent and traced its effectiveness over the last four hundred years. Then he had called in ten lay experts to have them analyze present procedures in his own diocesan seminary, and finally polled all the living alumni of that institution. It amazed him to find that Trent's original suggestion that seminary training should be divided into periods based on six months of scholastic training and six months of practical application, seemed to be the formula indicated for modern training. As to collegiality, he alleged it was the Pope's mind that this was now a fact, and it was merely a matter of time and the working out of a proper formula, before such an apostolic college was established. Finally he expressed great satisfaction with the reorganization of the conciliar commissions effected by the Council's election of new members, and the selection of a second vice-president and secretary which had followed immediately.* But he was adamant in asserting that there

* Asked by one of the bishops in the audience if this meant that the presidents of the Commissions were to be seated behind the new vice-presidents as the group of Council presidents were behind the Moderators in the Council itself, he acknowledged the indiscretion of the query, and shrugged it off with a smile.

would be no purge or reprisals for attitudes adopted on either side of the debate, since this would be totally in opposition to the spirit of liberty and charity which it had been Pope John's and now Pope Paul's insistence, was the only possible atmosphere for a Council of the followers of Christ.

There is no sign, moreover, that the Pope has given in on the important issue of collegiality. The vague reference to the topic in his closing speech: "at a time, and in a manner that will seem most opportune to us" merely means that plans will be consummated at the appropriate, Pauline time. In Paul's mind, the collegial government of the Church was an actuality though he had not had time to determine just how or when he would "summon from the episcopate of the whole world and from the religious orders, competent and distinguished brothers . . . who together with the members of the Sacred College [of Cardinals] will assist and counsel us." That this was more than a notional acceptance of the idea of collegiality was certified by a sudden visit he made to the Lateran Palace to inspect the work of reconstruction. Originally the plans formulated under Pope John had called for the transfer to the Vatican of the archeological museum housed in the Lateran, and the location of the Vicariate or administrative offices for the diocese of Rome in the new building. But Paul had cancelled these plans, and he now determined that the new edifice should contain a suite of rooms for himself and offices and quarters for the bishops whom he would summon to Rome for consultation on the Church's world-wide problems. In visiting the site, the Pope had been accompanied by two engineers from Milan, and the radical modifications they had suggested in regard to both the specifications and the costs of the new construction led to a rumor that Cardinal Traglia would be sacked as pro-Vicar in effective charge of running the diocese of Rome for the Pope. But such a change was not in keeping with Pope Paul's manner of handling problems.

As regards the faculties returned to the bishops by the Pope in his Motu Proprio *Pastorale Munus,* communicated to the Fathers on December 3, 1963, in carefully chosen words, the Pope declared that these faculties belong to the bishops by reason of their office, and said that this declaration was a positive result of the Council's debate. Here of course he was cutting across a curial fixation, for the official document bore the title "Concessio facultatum" and in the résumé published in *L'Osservatore Romano,* the author said the Pope had "conceded" these powers to the bishops. But this was merely another minor indication of the fact that the old guard who were still at work could not bring themselves to believe that a revolution was actually in progress. It was this type of act, of course, that gave some justification to the feeling of the critics that nothing had been actually achieved by the Council. What they could not understand was that Pope Paul had his own reasons for not insisting, all down the line, that his viewpoint be scrupulously respected by the curial officials, the most obvious being the fact that he had set his own pace for a thorough reform of the Curia, which he was determined should be brought about by an immediate collaboration between himself and the bishops. Evidently he did not want to anticipate this reformation, or possibly prejudice its direction or thoroughness, by interfering in individual and trifling matters.

It is a reflection on the strange vagaries of group psychology that a large portion of the Pope's audience, both within and outside the Council, should have considered the Pope's closing discourse and the disclosure of his positive plans for the future as somehow inadequate, or even favoring the reactionary tendencies of the intransigents. Not a few of the Fathers and critics felt that somehow or other Pope Paul had let them down. In actual fact, however, a comparison of this talk with Pope John's closing discourse at the end of the first session indicates that the Pauline phase of conciliar thought is not only a positive development in a direct line with John's designs, but is at once more specific and more hopeful. What the critics wanted was for all practical purposes a daily or weekly declaration of revolutionary principles and a series of decapitations or dismissals that would justify progressively enlarged headlines. John's jovial exterior, magnified almost out of proportion, had taken on the lineaments of a myth in the minds of many of the commentators. Hence they could not see that the tremendously complicated project upon which the Church was now embarked in implementing a vast inner renewal, in making an effective effort to bring about the reconstitution of Christian unity, and in approaching the modern and religiously disaffected world, could admit of only one truly revolutionary upheaval, and that this had been experienced in the convocation of the Council. Thereafter, the Church had to settle down to the painful slow labor, first of convincing its own leaders and people of the necessity and feasibility of this startling project, and then of persuading those outside its immediate control to collaborate in the vast spiritual renewal projected on a world scale by the Council. It was part of Paul's genius, as it had been John's gift, to realize that such a revolution could only be affected by the apparently inadequate day to day debate and small-scale but progressive decisions on the part of both the Council and the Pope. If, for example, the actuality of episcopal co-operation in the governance of the Church were to be effectuated by collegial cooperation, the Pope could not be making immediate, Church-shaking decisions on his own, for this would be but a continuation of authoritarian papal rule, the very method that had been the object of the Council's discussions.

Mystery surrounds the release of the Motu Proprio on

January 27th, putting part of the Liturgy Constitution into effect—at least the mystery of how one who is as well acquainted with curial procedures as Paul VI can still tolerate men in positions of power around him, who obviously have no intention of carrying out his desires to the letter. The readiest explanation seems to be that in this matter he probably decided to let the people concerned hang themselves. What happened seems clear enough. The text of the document was prepared by the Congregation of Rites under the guidance of Cardinal Lercaro and Father Antonelli. Evidently the first draft did not meet with full papal approval, although in an article published in the December 6th edition of *L'Osservatore Romano* Father Antonelli had admitted the full implications of the liturgical reform projected by the Constitution. In any case, the document was at least five days late in coming out, and during the interval it is known that Father Antonelli exhibited considerable irritation. When published, the text of the Motu Proprio was castigated as a betrayal of the conciliar Constitution. The text was a terrible disappointment in that it not only said nothing about the changes contemplated for the celebration of Mass, but it contained a phrase that contradicted the Liturgy Constitution itself. Where the latter had authorized regional groups of bishops to select and approve vernacular texts of the liturgy, the Motu Proprio specified that these translations had to be submitted to the Holy See for acceptance. The very next day Cardinal Larraona, Prefect of the Congregation of Rites, let it be known in no uncertain terms that he was not the author of the restriction. "Everyone is blaming me," he confided to a group of associates, "for they know that I was opposed to the original liturgical schema. But once the Constitution was promulgated by the Holy Father and the Council, I accepted it wholeheartedly. That phrase was not in the document when it left my hands." He indicated further that while the document lay on the Pope's desk several members of the Holy Office had had access to the Holy Father's presence. What was even stranger, the next evening, *L'Osservatore Romano* carried an article of explanation signed s.m.,* which said flatly that "The Motu Proprio does not grant very much, particularly for the impatient." This conclusion was preceded by a series of reflections that were bold indeed. The good Benedictine reminded his readers that the Constitution on the Liturgy was not a code of rubrics, but called for a "reformation of mind and mentality in ceremonial matters," and declared that it was based on "new theological perspectives." He said it was useless to look for merely external conformity to the new rules, but that a whole mental attitude had to be developed that would constitute a basis for a reorganization of liturgical prayer. He acknowledged that difficulties would arise over the granting of discretionary power to individuals and bishops. The new Commission would have rough going in its attempt to keep the needs of the whole world in mind while at the same time working out norms that would be suitable for individual areas. He felt many would be disappointed that the bishops had not been authorized at once to continue with experiments already started in these matters on a local level; presumably, the bishops might have been granted authority to begin at once with simplification by dropping the last Gospel, transposing the blessing to before the *Ite missa est,* and abolishing once and for all the prayers said after Mass. But he saw some hope in that the Motu Proprio did not say that the bishops "could not ask for special faculties in particular cases."

The utter frankness of this commentary led observers to believe that it was an "inspired" article; that the author had been asked to write it by someone close to the Holy Father.

* For the Benedictine liturgist, Dom Salvatore Marsili.

Whether this was the case or not, a reaction was immediately evident on the part of certain members of the Curia, particularly the Secretary General of the Council, Archbishop Felici, who seems to take any apparent criticism of things connected with the Council as a personal affront. Father Marsili suddenly found himself literally on the road to banishment. However, as had happened in the case of the Dominican Father Spiazza before the Council, and to Father Bugnini, who was not made secretary of the conciliar Liturgical Commission when Cardinal Larraona succeeded as president, Marsili was rescued: he had the good fortune to run into Cardinal Lercaro in Milan. On learning of his plight, the latter immediately returned him to Rome and had him restored to his former functions.

In early January, on the strength of the Constitution, the German, French and Belgian bishops had authorized vernacular versions of the liturgy, and they immediately protested vehemently to the Holy Father about the Motu Proprio. After considerable infighting between curial officials, a final version of the document was worked out and printed in the official *Acta Apostolicae Sedis*. The new version not only omitted the offending phrase by stating that only the *acta* or final decisions of the bishops should be submitted to the Holy See, but it removed from the text other phrases which had been introduced insisting on the fact that it was the Pope who had been granting privileges rather than the Council's Constitution that had authorized the liturgical reforms.

When the membership of the new Liturgical Commission appointed to oversee the carrying out of the provisions of the Constitution was announced, with Cardinal Lercaro as its president and Father Bugnini as its secretary, and cardinals and bishops as members who were generally known to be in favor of liturgical renewal, most liturgists were satis-

fied. The list contained one enigma, however—the name of
Archbishop Felici. The only conclusion appears to be the
rather uncharitable thought that the vanity and striving for
power of the Secretary General are all too apparent.

In retrospect one may say that two movements interfered
with the efficiency of the Second Session and threatened to
bring the Council to disaster. Both were engineered by the
intransigent curialist party. One was the time-wasting involved in the daily round of certain sacrosanct ritual acts
dear to the Italian ecclesiastical outlook, and particularly
the devotion of whole meetings to the commemoration of
events or anniversaries, for example, the centenary of the
Council of Trent on December 3rd, which could and should
have been handled differently in view of the tight schedule.*
The other was the more important because dangerous challenge to the authority not only of the Moderators, but of the
Council itself, implicit in the questioning of the validity of
the famous five propositions voted on October 30, 1963.
Once the majority has expressed its mind, any effort by a minority to question the Council's decision can only be disrup-
tive. From the behavior of Cardinals Ottaviani, Browne and
Ruffini, and the continued irritating assertions of Bishop
Carli, it almost seemed as if they—aided by the Secretary General—were intent on accomplishing just that. The suspicion is
also strong that this group received the backing of the Secretary of State, Cardinal Cocognani, who, since his return
from the United States seems to have been overinfluenced by
the fear-inspired approach of his old colleagues (e.g. Browne's
"Patres, caveamus"). The Secretary General seemed to be

* Abbé René Laurentin lists specifically the recitation of the *De Profundis*
whenever a council member died, whereas a simple mention of the name, or
names, in the *memento* of the mass would have been sufficient; the Italian
luxuriance of prayers accompanying the *Angelus;* and the enthronement of
the Gospel, which could just as well have taken place during the daily mass
instead of in a special ceremony afterward. *Bilan de la deuxième session,*
Seuil, Paris, 1964, p. 205.

working directly under the Secretary of State, receiving apparently full support from that quarter in the numerous questionable manoeuvres in which he was engaged—one obvious area being his control over the list of speakers; another, the conservative-favoring slant of his announcements and his tactics in closing his eyes to illicit propaganda moves of the conservatives while pouncing on those attempted by the progressives. These human aspects of the conciliar procedure need to be taken into account, for they had a bearing on the course of the Session and almost compromised its success. A comparison with similar procedures and tactics at the Council of Trent would be instructive.

Furthermore, it is known that the board of Presidents was not happy in being supplanted by the four Moderators. Cardinal Tisserant, in particular, felt that not only was his dignity being challenged, but that the Four had not functioned with the efficiency of his own unwieldy group of ten during the first session. It was noticeable that on the first two days of debate, the Moderators, Cardinals Agagianian and Lercaro, had interrupted speakers when they wandered from the topic or went beyond their allotted time, but, on instructions from the Holy Father who was overconscious of not wishing to interfere with the freedom of the speakers, this policy was not pursued again until close to the very end. It has been suggested that this was the result of a lack of confidence in their position on the part of the Moderators, but this is hardly likely. In fact, however, they discovered that their mandate was not clear: when challenged on minor matters, as they were by Cardinal Bacci, for example, they quickly asserted their leadership and control; but when opposed by Archbishop Felici or Cardinal Ottaviani, they found themselves without the backing of the Presidents or the Secretary of State, and eventually had to get the Pope's explicit support. As for the Pope's failure to intervene in the

debates, it can be explained by his unwillingness to interfere on principle, as well as by the large number of issues on
which he received petitions from groups of bishops containing from twenty to more than six hundred signatures, e.g.
he was invited to pronounce on the validity of the five
propositions, to allow the introduction of schemata other
than those proposed by the commissions, to expedite the
solution of the difficulty concerning what to do about the
Virgin Mary, to take a direct hand in getting the chapters
on religious liberty and on the Jews to the floor, to sanction
a conciliar message to priests which in fact came to nothing,
to declare his intention with regard to the episcopal body
which was to advise him—this was the petition with over
six hundred signatures—to interfere in the affair of the
communications decree, to change the formula for promul-
gating conciliar acts, to authorize the immediate application of the Liturgy Constitution, and to allow a concelebra-
tion of all the bishops at the closing ceremony.*

All this must have been somewhat disillusioning to one
who had made up his mind to pursue a policy that would
permit the bishops to enter into their functions as his co-
partners in the government of the universal Church. One can
appreciate his chagrin at finding himself accused of exhibit-
ing a Hamlet-like complex.**

Lacking, in effect, was a concerted effort on the part of
the progressive cardinals to answer in kind the power-play
assertions and moves made by Cardinals Ottaviani and Ruffini, seconded by Browne, Siri, etc. But from the nature of
the problem this seemed to them impossible, without running the risk of disrupting the peace of the assembly. There
was question of some disagreement between the Moderators
themselves, but though as diverse personalities one need not

* List in Laurentin, *Bilan de la deuxième session,* pp. 212-13.
** *Time,* December 6, 1963.

expect unanimity on all questions, it is certain that they were in full agreement on the general policies for conducting the Council and felt that they had the support of the Pope. The rumors regarding disagreement between them were spread mainly by the conservatives, following an old and well-known Roman tactic.

The apprehension felt by a number of the experts and other Council members, as the Second Session came to a close, was based on the not unfounded fear that vengeance would be wreaked on them once the leaders and bishops were out of town. Although several moves were made in this direction, they were on a minor plane and did not go very far. But the possibility of retaliatory action will remain, until a fundamental move is made to reorganize such organs as the Holy Office and the Congregation for Seminaries and Universities, to mention only two of the most important centers. Cardinal Marella is reported to have made this facetious remark about the success of the progressives: "Have no fear, once the talk ceases and the bishops depart, we will change everything back the way it was!"

Nevertheless there are some small signs that the conservatives are perhaps beginning to bend before the wind, convinced as they are that in a "time of troubles" which the Church now seems to be entering, in their view, with the Holy Spirit remaining somewhat inexplicably aloof, their tactic should be to appear to yield on minor matters regarding externals but to hang on at all costs, until the power of God again manifests itself on their side. Thus the head of the Holy Office, in a recent interview (March 19, 1964), acknowledged the *aggiornamento* and the collegiality of the bishops to be important facts, something much more sweeping and meaningful than a mere updating of the Church's rules and regulations. But he was still opposed to a married diaconate as opening the door to a married priesthood.

Recent reports from Rome indicate that Pope Paul's unobtrusive determination that Vatican Council II must speed up work on the remaining schemata has been communicated to the conciliar commissions and has made a great difference in both the tempo and style of their labors.* While considerable secrecy surrounds the meetings of the Coordinating Commission under the chairmanship of Cardinal Cicognani in the offices of the Secretariat of State, the fact that one was held on December 28th in the midst of the Christmas festivities, and two more followed in short order (January 15, 1964 and March 10, 1964) has evidently impressed the commission chairmen with the seriousness of the Pope's intention. In any case, by March 1964, unofficial reports indicated decisive achievements in the commissions dealing with the nature of the Church, with ecumenism, and with the so-called Schema 17, a sort of cover-all document concerned with the Church's attitude toward the modern world. It was a subcommittee of the latter group that seemingly discovered in the principle of a change of venue the secret of breaking the log-jam tactics of the Roman atmosphere. In a meeting at Zurich in mid-January under the auspices of Bishop Charue, this committee outlined the principles that have enabled the secretary to reduce to propositional form the copious material contained in several drafts, the most ambitious of which was a text prepared under the guidance of Cardinal Suenens. This dealt with six principal themes: 1. the dignity of the human person; 2. the rights of man in society; 3. matrimony and the family; 4. cultural progress; 5. economic and social justice; and 6. peace in the community of nations. It thus cut across the work of several commissions and had been hamstrung until the Zurich meeting. Since then its several subcommittees have been empowered to proceed without

---

* In a speech to the Italian episcopate on April 14, 1964 Pope Paul declared that he had set no time limit for the Council.

regard to the sensibilities of vested interests in either the
Curia or other conciliar commissions. An even happier report emanated from the Secretariat for Promoting Christian
Unity, which went into almost solitary confinement for two
weeks at the end of February and produced a revision of all
five chapters of the schema on Ecumenism that was termed
"bolder than the original" by the Paulist Father Stransky.

With regard to the undebated chapters dealing with the
Jews and religious liberty (Chapters IV and V), prelates evidently fearful of what they consider to be a "libertarian"
attitude bound to destroy the Church's authority sent Cardinal Bea a substantial number of cautionary recommendations after the session ended. A hurry call from Rome for
assistance was spread among the American bishops by the
Cardinal of St. Louis and the Archbishop of Baltimore with
gratifying results. The new text will now be sent to the
bishops for study before they report to Rome for the Third
Session, and although, as Archbishop Krol of Philadelphia
remarked in a rather unprecedented address to 400 Jewish
leaders in his archdiocese, it is not certain that chapters IV
and V will remain in the schema, it is certain that they will
be the object of a conciliar vote. This seems to have been
confirmed also by Cardinal Ottaviani in his recent interview.
Archbishop Krol admitted that there was opposition to consideration of Chapter IV on the part of prelates from the
Near East, who felt that the draft condemning anti-Semitism
could not but be construed as a political move by the Arab
nations, but he remarked that such opposition was in keeping with the Council's experience thus far, for it was a fact
that "no schema was free from such discussion, no schema
was spared criticism, and no schema, though accepted, was
without its opposing votes." Statements such as this have
added weight when it is remembered that Archbishop Krol
is one of the six Undersecretaries of the Council, a body con-

sidered to have been unduly influenced by the dominating personality of the Secretary General, Archbishop Felici, during the first two sessions.

Further hints of impending changes seemed to be contained in a speech delivered by Cardinal Tisserant in Paris in January and, significantly, reprinted by *L'Osservatore Romano*. After praising the work of Paul VI, the cardinal took issue with those who were complaining that the course of reforms was too slow, commenting: *"Des transformations ne peuvent se faire qu'avec discernement et dans le calme."* In these remarks the *cognoscenti* found confirmation that major reforms were to come.

Meanwhile, since his return from the Holy Land, Pope Paul has continued with his daily round of herculean tasks, determined to push forward with his plans regardless of the opposition, but in his own good time. A Pauline promise of eventual changes was discerned in his address to the Roman aristocracy on January 14, 1964: "History marches on. The Church is obligated to a realistic view of things, and that view imposes on it—at times painfully—the task of selecting from its heritage of institutions and customs all that is essential and vital so as to reinvigorate its true traditional commitments."

Appendices

✠

Pope Paul VI's address on September 21, 1963 announcing his intention to reform the Roman Curia.

Venerable Brothers and Dearest Sons:

It is easy to understand the motives that have prompted us to call this meeting. We have desired to meet with the Roman Curia, that is to say with the persons of the cardinals, the major and minor officials, the ecclesiastics, the directors and employees who work in the sacred congregations, the tribunals, and the offices, together with the various bodies and institutions of which the Pope makes use for governing the Universal Church, as well as the Diocese of Rome and Vatican City.

We have desired, as we were saying, this meeting at the beginning of our apostolic ministry, above all to give all here present our cordial and reverent greeting in an explicit and collective way. We ourself have had the honor to give our humble service in the Roman Curia for many years. In the ranks that compose it we have had very worthy superiors and teachers, excellent colleagues, collaborators and unforgettable friends. We have shared in the labors, responsibilities, studies, experiences, joys and sorrows of this complex and unique organism. We have followed, for more than 30 years, the development of its life from a privileged observation point—the Secretariat of State, the excellent and dear and faithful office which assists the Pope in his personal activity. We have thus been able to appreciate better the wise composition of the Roman Curia, derived from a coherent and flexible tradition. We have listened to suggestions pertinent to the new needs of this very organism; we have gathered also the criticisms which have been addressed to it, and we have often made them the object of sincere reflection. Finally we have known and appreciated the efficiency of the services that the Roman Curia renders the papacy and the Church.

It has therefore seemed to us a duty from the beginning of our apostolic ministry, to give a sign of our fatherly benevolence to the people who direct and form the Roman Curia, and to make them feel how much we like and how anxious we are to feel in communion with it, not only in the specific activity that engages the whole of it and in the juridical relationship which draws it close to us, but as well in the spirit with which the common service has to be accomplished, for the well being and good example of the whole Church and its mission in the world, and for the glory of Him who is everything to us, the Lord Jesus Christ.

Therefore accept, cardinals, and accept, venerable brothers and beloved sons, the expression of our esteem, our gratitude, our encouragement. Also, maintain for us—in time and in merit the last of the servants of the servants of God—for our very modest person, for our highly difficult mission, the comfort of your constant solidarity, your filial obedience, your worthwhile collaboration; also, as we were saying, of your intimate communion which joins not only hands and minds to our office, but also feelings, prayers, the charity of your hearts to our heart, which if the Lord assists us hopes to be for you all the heart of a friend, a pastor and a father.

Another reason for this meeting has been suggested to us by the extremely beautiful and serious time through which the whole Church, and the Holy See, first of all, and therefore the Roman Curia as well are called to live, certainly by divine design —a historical time, a spiritual time, which in point of fact is the Second Vatican Ecumenical Council, which as is known will re-open its solemn sessions in a few days.

It has seemed opportune to us that the Roman Curia take cognizance together with us of this great event, not because the Curia is unprepared—since on the contrary it awaits it and is busily occupying itself with it; and not because the Curia has neglected to meditate on the enormous importance of the Council during its first session—since its extraordinary and complex dimensions were on the contrary discerned more fully by the Curia than by any other sector of the Church and of public opinion. The Curia's concern was such as to show at times a certain stupor and apprehension about such an unexpected and sudden conciliar convocation and about the gravity of the problems that it would raise. It seemed opportune, therefore, that the Curia and we be aware of this great event in order that such knowledge may be deepened in all of us, may be made uniform and trustful, and may be intimately penetrated by the conviction that a great and mysterious event, guided by the Holy Spirit, is happening at the tomb of the Prince of the Apostles. This event is surrounding this providential center of the Catholic Church in the mighty flow of those hidden powers of God's kingdom which make its functions stand out, which show its cardinal position in the history of redeemed humanity, and which severely and publicly tries its virtues, almost as if to constrain it to be, as it should be, the light of wisdom and of holiness to the whole world.

The hour is great and it is sacred. We, and you before others, members of the Roman Curia, must live it with deep understanding and with magnanimous heart. Let the first expression of this due proportion of our spirit to the greatness of the event be uniformity of will, or rather of fervor, for its worthy celebration. Let it be identity of outlook. He who wanted the Second Vatican Council is a pope to whom truly the spontaneous acclamation of the public voice attributed the Gospel words about the fore-runner of Christ: "There was a man, one sent from God, whose name was John."

We believe history will repeat such words when it registers the salutary consequences of the sudden, splendid decision of the one who called the Catholic Church to the Council and opened doors and heart to the separated brothers for a sincere reconciliation. But whatever the origins of the Council's convocation, it is the Pope who proclaimed it, the Vicar of Christ. It is that successor of St. Peter whom the Roman Curia, second to no one, recognizes as its bishop, its teacher, its head. We are certain that no hesitations regarding the chief desires of the Pontiff will ever come from the Roman Curia; that the Curia will never be suspected of any differences of judgment or of feelings with regard to judgments or feelings of the Pope. If ever such conformity of minds with what the Pope commands or desires must be rigorously univocal on the part of the Roman Curia, if it must be its law and its pride, this is the moment to give it firm and open profession.

And since we know that this is, and is intended to be, the resolution of each and every one making up the Roman Curia, we have in turn desired, with this meeting, to give praise and encouragement to that filial, harmonious, joyous unison of your thoughts and your resolutions with those of the Pope, who today has made his own the heritage of John XXIII, of happy memory, and makes of that heritage a program for the entire Church.

Such accord between the Pope and his Curia is a constant norm. Not only in the great hours of history does such accord reveal its existence and its strength. It is always in force, in every way and in every act of the pontifical ministry, as it is proper for the organ of immediate adherence and of absolute obedience which the Roman Pontiff utilizes to carry out his universal mission. It is this essential relation of the Roman Curia to the exercise of the Pope's apostolic activity which is the justification, or rather the glory, of the Curia itself. From that same relationship arises its necessity, its usefulness, its dignity and its authority. In fact, the Roman Curia is the instrument which the Pope needs and which the Pope utilizes to fulfill his own divine mandate. A most worthy instrument, and it is no wonder that everyone, and we above all, asks so much of it, demands so much of it! Its workings demand the highest ability and virtue, precisely because its office is the highest. Its functions are most delicate, such as that of watching over or echoing divine truth, and of transforming it into a language and dialogue with human minds. Its functions are very vast, such as that which has as its boundaries the whole universe. Its functions are most noble, such as that of hearing and interpreting the voice of the Pope and at the same time not letting him lack any useful and objective information, any filial and well-considered advice.

Because to be worthy of its task the Roman Curia must be very learned and highly expert, as you know—you desire this, and you yourselves have been more eager, even before your critics and even more than they. It must be equal through special virtues to the ever new and growing demands of your office.

We said critics! Yes, because it is known that criticism has been addressed to the Roman Curia, along with much praise and recognition of its indisputable merits. As we have hinted, this phenomenon derives above all from the nature and from the purpose of the Curia itself. The measure of giving is never filled up where it concerns the service of Christ's cause and the cause of souls.

That such a phenomenon appears from time to time along the path of ecclesiastical history is therefore understandable and providential. It is a prod to watchfulness, a recall to observance, an invitation to reform, a ferment to perfection. We must accept the criticisms that surround us, with humility, with reflection, and even with gratitude. Rome has no need to defend itself by making itself deaf to suggestions that come to it from honest voices, especially if these voices are those of friends and of brothers. To accusations, so often groundless, it will reply; it will defend its honor, but without stubbornness, without hurling back charges, without polemics.

Meanwhile, it can be observed today that the resolution to modernize juridical structures and deepen spiritual consciousness not only finds no resistance in the center of the Church, the Roman Curia, it finds, rather, the Curia itself in the advance guard of that perennial reform of which the Church itself, insofar as it is a human and earthly institution, has perpetual need.

It is from Rome that today comes the invitation to the *aggiornamento* (according to the expression used by our venerated predecessor), that is to the perfecting of everything concerning the Church, internal and external.

It is from Rome that has come the announcement of the reform of the Code of Canon Law, of that very law, that is, which solemnly rules the ecclesiastical city and world. It is from Rome that in these last hundred years has come that regular, untiring, coherent, stimulating government which has brought the entire Church to the point not only of external expansion—which all must recognize—but of interior sensitivity and vitality, also of treasures and mysteries with which Christ has endowed it. Today, happily, St. Bernard would no longer write his burning pages on the Roman ecclesiastical world. Nor would the reformers of the 16th century have written theirs.

Papal Rome today is entirely different, and by the grace of God so much more worthy and wise and holy; so much more conscious of its evangelical calling, so much more deeply immersed in its Christian mission, so much more eager for, and therefore susceptible to, perennial renewal.

This we say, venerable brothers and dearest sons of the Roman Curia, with a threefold purpose: to praise you, to bring you peace, and to exhort you.

Praise is in fact owed to the faithful, competent, devoted service that you render the Holy See and the Pope, and therefore to the entire Catholic Church as well. The Roman Curia, as executor of the will of him who has the responsibility and the power to feed the Church of Christ, merits the esteem, trust, and gratitude of the Church itself, and it merits ours.

The peace that we would like on this occasion to infuse in our Curia concerns the possible reforms which should be adopted in its regard. That some reforms should be introduced in the Roman Curia is not only easy to realize but good to desire. As everybody knows this old and complex organization traces back in its current form to Pope Sixtus V's celebrated constitution of 1588, *Immensa Aeterni Dei*. St. Pius X gave it new life with the constitution *Sapienti Consilio* of 1908, and the Code of Canon Law, in 1917, made this substantially its own form.

Many years have passed. It is understandable, therefore, how such an establishment would have grown ponderous with its own venerable age, how it feels the disparity of its organs and of its practices with respect to the needs and customs of new times, how at the same time it feels the need of being simplified and decentralized and the need of being broadened and made fit for new functions.

Therefore various reforms will be needed, They will certainly be weighed. They will be drawn up according to venerable and reasonable traditions on the one hand, and according to the needs of the times on the other. They certainly will be functional and beneficial, because they will have no other purpose than that of dropping what is ephemeral and superfluous in the forms and in the norms that regulate the Roman Curia, and of putting into being what is vital and serviceable for its efficient and proper functioning. They will be formulated and propagated by the Curia itself!

Therefore the Roman Curia will not be afraid of being recruited with a broader supranational vision, or of being educated with a more accurate ecumenical preparation. Did not St. Bernard say, even in his time: "Why not choose from the whole world those who one day will have to judge the whole world?" (*De Consideratione IV*).

The Roman Curia will not be jealous of the temporal prerogatives of former times, of exterior forms no longer suitable for the expression of high religious meanings. Nor will it be miserly of its faculties which the episcopacy, without damaging the universal ecclesiastical order, can today exercise better by itself and locally. Nor will economic purposes and advantages ever carry weight in organs of the Holy See if that is not required by good ecclesiastical order and by the salvation of souls.

It is the sacred rule of the departments of the Roman Curia to question the bishops and to avail themselves of their judgment in handling business. Among the consultors of the sacred congregations are found not a few bishops, coming from various regions. We shall say more: Should the Ecumenical Council evince a desire of seeing some representatives of the episcopacy, particularly among prelates who direct a diocese, associated in a certain way and for certain questions, in conformity with the Church's doctrine and canon law, with the supreme head of the Church in the study and responsibility of ecclesiastical government, the Curia will surely not oppose it. On the contrary it will sense the growth of the honor and the burden of its sublime and indispensable service, which, aside from the due procedure of the ecclesiastical tribunals, both in the Roman Curia and in dioceses, we well know, is specifically administrative, consultative and executive.

Once again the Roman Curia thus will feel, in a stronger way, its calling to good example before the whole Church and the world at large. It is this exhortation that we dare to address to you in a paternal way, at the conclusion of these simple words of ours which seem to us to echo those of the apostle St. Paul addressed to the Roman Church: "Your faith is proclaimed all over the world." (Romans, 1:8).

People everywhere are watching Catholic Rome, the Roman Pontificate, the Roman Curia. The duty of being authentically Christian is especially binding here. We would not remind you of this duty if we did not remind ourself of it every day. Everything in Rome teaches: The letter and the spirit—the way we think, study, speak, feel, act, suffer, pray, serve, love. Every moment, every aspect of our life finds us surrounded by a glow that can be beneficial if we are faithful to what Christ wants from us; that can be harmful if we are unfaithful.

That is why we desire that beyond your specific contribution of qualified service, our Roman Curia—all of you, brothers and sons—give to us, or rather to the Church, to Christ our Lord, the precious offering of your example: of rigorous unselfishness and abnegation, or religious and sincere piety, of loving welcome to as many as have recourse to it, and of attentive service.

The Roman Curia is not an anonymous body, insensible to the great spiritual problems, which dictates law automatically. It is instead a living organ, faithful and docile, of the head of the Church—an organ engrossed in the serious responsibilities of its functions and full of reverence and solicitude toward those prelates whom "the Holy Spirit has placed as bishops to rule the Church of God" (Acts 20:28).

Therefore let the Roman Curia not be a bureaucracy, as some wrongly judge it, pretentious and apathetic, merely legalistic and ritualistic, a jousting field of hidden ambitions and of intractable antagonisms, as others accuse it of being. But let it be a true community of faith and charity, of prayer and action, of the Pope's brothers and sons who do everything, each with respect for the competence of the other and with a sense of collaboration in serving him in his work for the brothers and sons of the Universal Church and of the entire world. We know that this desire of ours expresses yours, sincere and profound. It is this desire that in us and in you becomes prayer, in order that Christ the Lord, through the intercession of Mary Most Holy and of the holy Apostles Peter and Paul, may make shine like the light on the candlelabrum this old and ever new Roman Curia, "so as to give light to all in the house" (Matt. 5:15)—in the house, that is in the Church of God!

Finally, do not be displeased if we ask you all, ecclesiastics and laymen of the Roman Curia, to be willing to add to your labors of office some other spontaneous labors of the ministry and the personal apostolate. Help the Pope to evangelize not only the world, but the City as well, of which you are the foremost faithful and he the Bishop!

Confident in your goodness, and assuring you that all of you are present in our prayers, with all our heart we give you our apostolic blessing.

Address of His Holiness Pope Paul VI at the opening of the Second Session of the Second Vatican Council, September 29, 1963

Greetings to you, most beloved brothers in Christ whom we have called from every part of the world, from wherever the Holy Catholic Church has extended its hierarchical government. Greetings to you, who have accepted our invitation and hastened here to hold with us the second session of the Second Vatican Ecumenical Council, which we have the joy of inaugurating today, under the aegis of St. Michael the Archangel, heavenly protector of the people of God.

Truly it is fitting that this solemn and fraternal assembly, gathered together from the East and West, from the regions of the South and the North, should be designated by the prophetic name of "Ecclesia," that is, a coming together or a meeting. Here, truly, are realized in a new way those words which now come to our mind: "Their voice has gone forth into all the earth, and their words unto the ends of the world" (Rom. 10:18; Ps. 8:5).

Truly, one mystery of unity is joined to another mystery of catholicity; and this spectacle of universality recalls the apostolic origin, here so faithfully reflected and extolled, as well as the sanctifying purpose of our most beloved Church of God. Her characteristic notes shine forth: The countenance of the spouse of Christ is resplendent. Our spirits are elated by a most familiar, yet always secret, experience—that by which we perceive that we are the Mystical Body of Christ and by which we taste the incomparable joy, still unknown to the profane world, of "how good it is, and how pleasant, where brethren dwell at one!" (Ps. 132:1).

It is not futile to realize, right from this first moment, the human and divine phenomenon that we are bringing about. Here we are once more, as if in a new cenacle, which has become confined not by reasons of its vast dimensions but because of the multitude of those who are gathered together within it. Here certainly the Virgin Mother of Christ is helping us from heaven.

Here, around him who is last in time and merit, but identified with the first apostle in authority and mission, the successor of Peter, you are gathered. Venerable Brothers, you too apostles descended from the apostolic college and its authentic successors.

Here, praying together and united together by the same faith and the same charity; here, we shall rejoice in the unfailing grace of the Holy Spirit, who is present, vivifying, teaching, strengthening. Here all tongues will be only one voice and one voice alone will be the message to all the world.

Here, with bold step the Church militant has arrived, after almost 20 centuries of journeying. Here, the apostolic ranks, assembled all together from the world over, are refreshed at the fountain which quenches every thirst and reawakens every new thirst, and from here they will confidently resume their journey in the world and in time towards the goal which is beyond the earth and beyond the ages.

Greetings, Brothers! Thus you are welcomed by the least one among you, the Servant of the Servants of God, even though he bears the keys of supreme office consigned to Peter by Christ the Lord. Thus does he thank you for the proof of obedience and trust which your presence here brings to him. Thus he shows you in act that he wishes to pray with you, to speak with you, to deliberate with you, to work with you.

The Lord is our witness when, at this first moment of the second session of the great synod we declare to you that in our mind there is no intention of human predominance, no jealousy of exclusive power, but only the desire and the will to carry out the divine mandate which makes us, of you and among you, Brothers, the supreme shepherd, and which requires of you that you be his joy and glory, the "communion of saints," offering your fidelity, your loyalty, your collaboration. This same mandate confers on you that which pleases him most to give—his veneration, his esteem, his trust, his charity.

It had been our intention, as hallowed custom prescribes for us to send to all of you our first encyclical letter. But why, we ask ourself, entrust to writing that which, by a singular and happy opportunity—that is, by means of this ecumenical council—we are able to declare by word of mouth?

Certainly we cannot now say by word of mouth all that we

have in our heart and all that more easily could be poured forth in writing. But for this time let this present address be a prelude not only to the council, but also to our pontificate. Let the living word take the place of the encyclical letter, which, if it please God, we hope to address to you once these toilsome days are past.

And now that we have greeted you, we introduce ourself, to you. We are indeed new in the pontifical office which we are fulfilling, or rather, we should wish to say, inaugurating. You know indeed that the Sacred College of Cardinals, whom we here greet again with cordial veneration, in spite of our limitations and insufficiency, on the 21st of June, a day which this year happily coincided with the feast of the Most Sacred Heart of Christ, deigned to elect us to episcopal See of Rome and therefore to the supreme pontificate of the Universal Church.

We cannot recall this event without remembering our predecessor of happy and immortal memory, our most beloved John XXIII. To all of us who had the good fortune to see him seated in this same place, his name brings memories of his lovable and priestly presence as he opened the first session of this Second Vatican Council on October 11th of last year with that speech which to the Church and the world seemed like a prophetic voice for our century. That speech still echoes in our minds, pointing out to the council the path it has to take, thereby freeing us from all doubt and weariness which we may encounter along the difficult road we have undertaken.

O dear and venerated Pope John, may gratitude and praise be rendered to you for having resolved—doubtless under divine inspiration—to convoke this council in order to open to the Church new horizons, and to tap the fresh spring water of the doctrine and grace of Christ our Lord and let it flow over the earth.

Moved by no earthly motives or particular circumstances, but as if by divining heavenly counsels and penetrating into the dark and tormented needs of the modern age, you have picked up the broken thread of the First Vatican Council, and by that very fact you have banished the fear wrongly deduced from that council, as if the supreme powers conferred by Christ on the Roman

Pontiff to govern and vivify the Church, were sufficient, without the assistance of ecumenical councils.

You have summoned your brothers in the episcopate, the successors of the Apostles, not only to continue the interrupted study and suspended legislation, but to feel united with the Pope in a single body, to be comforted and directed by him "that the sacred deposit of Christian doctrine be guarded and taught more effectively."

But to the principal aim of the council you added another which is more urgent and at this time more salutary—the pastoral aim—when you declared: "Nor is the primary purpose of our work to discuss one article or another of the fundamental doctrine of the Church," but rather, "to consider how to expound Church teaching in a manner demanded by the times."

You have awakened in the conscience of the teaching authority of the Church the conviction that Christian doctrine is not merely truth to be investigated by reason illumined by faith, but teaching that can generate life and action; and that the authority of the Church is not limited to condemning contrary errors, but extends to the communication of positive and vital doctrine, the source of its fecundity.

The teaching office of the Church, which is neither wholly theoretical nor wholly negative, must in the council manifest ever more the life-giving power of the message of Christ who said: ". . . The words that I have spoken to you are spirit and life" (John VI: 64). Hence we shall ever keep in mind the norms which you, the first Father of this Council, have wisely laid down and which we may profitably repeat here:

"Our task is not merely to guard the precious treasure, namely our Faith, as if we were only concerned with antiquity, but to dedicate ourselves with an earnest will and without fear to that work which our era demands of us, pursuing thus the path which the Church has followed for nearly 20 centuries. Hence, that method of presenting the truth must be used which is more in conformity with a magisterium prevalently pastoral in character."

We shall have due regard for the great question of the unity in one flock of those who believe in Christ and wish to be members of the Church which, you, John, have called the paternal

home whose doors are open to all. The Council which you have
promoted and inaugurated will proceed faithfully along the
path you pointed out, so that with God's help reach the goal you
have so ardently desired and hoped for.

Let us therefore go forward, Brothers. This clear determination brings to mind another thought. Although you are all well
acquainted with it, because of its importance we nevertheless
feel obliged to treat of it here.

From what point, dear Brethren, do we set out? Bearing in
mind that we should pay attention rather to the divine directives
than to the practical indications referred to above, what is the
road we intend to follow? What is the goal we propose to ourselves? We have a goal which belongs to the realm of earthly
history in that it concerns the time and mode of our present life,
but we do not lose sight of the supreme and final end which, we
know, must be the end of our pilgrimage.

These three very simple and at the same time very important
questions have, as we well know, only one answer, namely that
here and at this very hour we should proclaim Christ to ourselves and to the world around us; Christ our beginning, Christ
our life and our guide, Christ our hope and our end.

O let this council have the full awareness of this relationship
between ourselves and the blessed Jesus—a relationship which is
at once multiple and unique, fixed and stimulating, mysterious
and crystal clear, binding and beatifying—between this holy
Church which we constitute and Christ from whom we come, by
whom we live and towards whom we strive.

Let no other light be shed on this council, but Christ the light
of the World! Let no other truth be of interest to our minds, but
the words of the Lord, our only master! Let no other aspiration
guide us, but the desire to be absolutely faithful to him! Let no
other hope sustain us, but the one that, through the mediation
of his word, strengthens our pitiful weakness: "And behold I
am with you all days, even unto the consummation of the world"
(Mt. 28:20).

Would that we were able at this moment to raise up to our
Lord a voice that is worthy of him! We will say to him in the
words of the sacred liturgy: "Thee, O Christ, alone we know.

Singing even in our woe, with pure hearts to Thee we go: On our senses shine!" (Hymn of Lauds for Wednesdays)

As we thus invoke him, he seems to present himself to our rapt gaze with the majesty proper to the "Pantocrator" [all mighty]—the glorious Christ of your basilicas—O Brothers of the Eastern Churches, as well as those of the West.

We recognize ourself in the figure of our predecessor, Honorius III, who is represented in the splendid mosaic in the apse of the Basilica of St. Paul as a humble worshiper, tiny and prostrate, kissing the feet of a Christ of gigantic dimensions, who as a kingly teacher dominates and blesses the people gathered in the basilica, which symbolizes the Church.

The scene, it seems to us, is reproduced here before us, not as a painted image, but as a historical human reality which acknowledges in Christ the source of redeemed humanity, his Church, as it were, his extension and continuation, both earthly and mysterious. This recalls to our mind the apocalyptic vision of St. John: "He showed me a river of the water of life, clear as crystal, coming forth from the throne of God and of the Lamb" (Apoc. 22:1).

It seems to us opportune that this council should have as its starting point this vision, or mystical celebration, which acknowledges him, our Lord Jesus Christ, to be the Incarnate Word, the Son of God and the Son of Man, the Redeemer of the world, the Hope of humanity and its Supreme Master, the Good Shepherd, the Bread of Life, the High Priest and our Victim, the sole Mediator between God and men, the Saviour of the world, the eternal King of ages; and which declares that we are his chosen ones, his disciples, his apostles, his witnesses, his ministers, his representatives and his living members together with the whole company of the faithful, united in this immense and unique Mystical Body, his Church, which he is forming by means of faith and the sacraments, as generations of mankind succeed one another—a Church which is spiritual and visible, fraternal and hierarchical, temporal today and eternal tomorrow.

If we place before our minds, Venerable Brethren, this sovereign conception that Christ is our Founder, our Head, invisible, but real, and that we receive everything from him so as to constitute together with him that "full Christ" about whom St.

Augustine speaks and who pervades the entire theology of the Church, then we shall be able to understand better the main objectives of this council.

For reasons of brevity and better understanding we enumerate here those objectives in four points: the knowledge, or—if you prefer—the awareness of the Church; its reform; the bringing together of all Christians in unity; the dialogue of the Church with the contemporary world.

There can be no doubt whatever of the Church's desire and need and duty to give a more thorough definition of herself. We are all familiar with the magnificent images by which Holy Scripture describes the nature of the Church: the building raised up by Christ, the house of God, the temple and tabernacle of God, his peoples, his flock, his vine, his field, his city, the pillar of Truth and, finally, the Bride of Christ, his Mystical Body.

In mediating on these revealing images the Church has come to see herself as a historic, visible and hierarchically organized society, animated by a mysterious principle of life. The celebrated encyclical of Pope Pius XII, "Mystici Corporis," has in part answered the Church's longing to express her nature in a full doctrinal form, but has also served to spur her to give herself a more exhaustive definition.

The first Vatican Council treated of the subject and many external influences have caused it to receive attention from students, both within the Church and without. Among these influences are the intensification of social life in temporal matters, the development of communications, the need to judge the various Christian denominations according to the true and univocal conception found in divine Revelation.

It should not come as a surprise that, after 20 centuries in which both the Catholic Church and the other Christian bodies distinguished by the name of church have seen great geographical and historical development, there should still be need to enunciate a more precise definition of the true, profound and complete nature of the Church which Christ founded and the Apostles began to build.

The Church is a mystery; she is a reality imbued with the

divine presence and, for that reason, she is ever susceptible of new and deeper investigation.

Human thought moves forward. Man advances from empirically observed fact to scientific truth, from one truth he derives another by logical deduction, and, confronted by the complexity and permanence of reality, he bends his mind now to one of its aspects, now to another. It is thus that thought evolves. The course of its evolution can be traced in history.

The time has now come, we believe, when the truth regarding the Church of Christ should be examined, coordinated and expressed. The expression should not, perhaps, take the form of a solemn dogmatic definition, but of declarations making known by means of the Church's magisterium, in a more explicit and authoritative form, what the Church considers herself to be.

This self-awareness of the Church is clarified by faithful adherence to the words and thought of Christ, by respectful attention to the teaching of ecclesiastical tradition and by docility to the interior illumination of the Holy Spirit, who seems to be requiring of the Church today that she should do all she can to make known what she really is.

We believe, too, that in this ecumenical council the Spirit of Truth ignites in the teaching body of the Church a brighter light and suggests a more complete Doctrine of the nature of the Church, so that the Bride of Christ may be mirrored in her Lord and discerned in Him with most lively love—her own true likeness and the beauty that He wishes her to have.

For this reason, the principal concern of this session of the council will be to examine the intimate nature of the Church and to express in human language, so far as that is possible, a definition which will best reveal the Church's real, fundamental constitution and manifest its manifold mission of salvation. The theological doctrine has the possibility of magnificent developments which merit the attentive consideration of our separated brethren also and which, as we ardently hope, may make the path towards common agreement easier.

First among the various questions that this consideration will raise, Venerable Brothers, is one which affects all of you as bishops of the Church of God. We have no hesitation in saying that we look forward with great expectations and confidence to this discussion which, taking for granted the dogmatic declarations of the First Vatican Council regarding the Roman pontiff, will go on to develop the doctrine regarding the episcopate, its function and its relationship with Peter.

For us personally it will provide doctrinal and practical standards by which our apostolic office, endowed though it is by Christ with the fulness and sufficiency of power, may receive more help and support, in ways to be determined, from a more effective and responsible collaboration with our beloved and venerable brothers in the episcopate.

Next it will be necessary to elucidate the teaching regarding the different components of the visible and mystical body, the pilgrim, militant Church on earth, that is, priests, religious, the faithful, and also the separated brethren who are also called to adhere to it more fully and completely.

The importance of this doctrinal aspect of the council's work will be obvious to all; from it the Church can draw an illuminating, uplifting and sanctifying self-knowledge.

The same hopes can also be entertained of another chief subject of the council's deliberations, that, namely, of the renewal of the Church. This too, in our opinion, must follow from our awareness of the relationship by which Christ is united to his Church.

We have just spoken of the Bride of Christ looking upon Christ to discern in Him her true likeness; if in doing so she were to discover some shadow, some defect, some stain upon her wedding garment, what should be her instinctive, courageous reaction? There can be no doubt that her primary duty would be to reform, correct and set herself aright in conformity with her divine Model.

Reflect upon the words Christ spoke in His priestly prayer as the hour of His Passion pressed close upon him: ". . . I sanctify myself, that they also may be sanctified in truth" (John 17:19). To our way of thinking, this is the essential attitude, desired by Christ, which the Second Vatican Council must adopt.

It is only after this work of internal sanctification has been accomplished that the Church will be able to show herself to the whole world and say: "Who sees me, sees Christ," as Christ said of himself: "He who sees me sees also the Father" (John 14:9).

In this sense the council is to be a new spring, a reawakening of the mighty spiritual and moral energies which at present lie dormant. The council is evidence of a determination to bring about a rejuvenation both of the interior forces of the Church and of the regulations by which her canonical structure and liturgical forms are governed. The council is striving, that is, to enhance in the Church that beauty of perfection and holiness which imitation of Christ and mystical union with Him in the Holy Spirit can alone confer.

Yes, the council aims at renewal. Note well, however, that in saying and desiring that, we do not imply that the Catholic Church of today can be accused of substantial infidelity to the mind of her Divine Founder. Rather it is the deeper realization of her substantial faithfulness that fills her with gratitude and humility and inspires her with the courage to correct those imperfections which are proper to human weakness.

The reform at which the council aims is not, therefore, a turning upside down of the Church's present way of life or a breaking with what is essential and worthy of veneration in her tradition. It is, rather, an honoring of tradition by stripping it of what is unworthy or defective so that it may be rendered firm and fruitful. Did not Jesus say to His disciples: "I am the true vine, and my Father is the vine-dresser. Every branch in me that bears no fruit he will take away; and every branch that bears fruit he will cleanse, that it may bear more fruit?" (John 15:1-2).

This verse is a good summary of the perfecting process which the Church today desires, above all as regards her interior and exterior vitality. May the living Church be conformed to the living Christ. If faith and charity are the principles of her life, it is clear that no pains must be spared to make faith strong and joyful and to render Christian instruction and teaching methods more effective for the attaining of this vital end.

The first requirement of this reform will certainly be a more diligent study and a more intensive proclamation of the Word of God. Upon this foundation an education of charity will be built up, for we must give the place of honor to charity and strive to construct the "Ecclesia caritatis" if we would have a Church capable of renewing herself and renewing the world around her: there indeed is a tremendous undertaking.

Charity must be fostered because it is the chief and root of the other Christian virtues: humility, poverty, religion, the spirit of sacrifice, fearless truth, love of justice, and every other force by which the new man acts.

At this point the council's program broadens to take in immense fields, one of which, of special importance and fraught with charity, is the sacred liturgy. To this subject the first session of the Council devoted long discussions, which will, we hope, be brought to a happy conclusion in the second.

Other fields, too, will certainly receive the earnest attention of the Fathers of the council, though we fear that the shortness of the time at our disposal will not permit us to treat them all as fully as they deserve and that it will be necessary to deal with them in a future session.

The Council has a third object, one which may be called its spiritual drama. This too was put before us by Pope John XXIII. It is that which concerns "the other Christians"—those who believe in Christ but whom we have not the happiness of numbering among ourselves in the perfect unity of Christ, which only the Catholic Church can offer them.

This unity, objectively speaking, should be theirs by Baptism. It is something which, virtually at least, they already desire. For recent movements, at present in full development in bodies of Christians separated from us, show clearly two things. The first is that the Church of Christ is one alone and therefore must be unique. The second is that this mystic and visible union cannot be attained except in identity of faith and by participation in the same sacraments and in the organic harmony of a single ecclesiastical control, even though this allows for a great variety of verbal expressions, movements, lawful institutions, and preference with regard to modes of acting.

There can be no doubt about the attitude of the council with regard to the great numbers of the separated brethren and of the possibility of multiplicity in the unity of the Church. This too is one of the characteristics of the council.

The council aims at complete and universal ecumenicity— that is at least what it desires, what it prays and prepares for. Today it does so in hope that tomorrow it may see the reality. This council while calling and counting its own those sheep who belong to the fold of Christ in the fullest and truest sense, opens the door and calls out, too, in anxious expectation to the many sheep of Christ who are not at present within the unique fold.

It is a council, therefore, of invitation, of expectation, of confidence, looking forward towards a more widespread, more fraternal participation in its authentic ecumenicity.

We speak now to the representatives of the Christian denominations separated from the Catholic Church, who have nevertheless been invited to take part as observers in this solemn assembly. We greet them from our heart. We thank them for their participation. We transmit through them our message— as father and brother—to the venerable Christian communities they represent.

Our voice trembles and our heart beats the faster both because of the inexpressible consolation and reasonable hope that their presence stirs up within us, as well as because of the deep sadness we feel at their prolonged separation.

If we are in any way to blame for that separation, we humbly beg God's forgiveness and ask pardon too of our brethren who feel themselves to have been injured by us. For our part, we willingly forgive the injuries which the Catholic Church has suffered, and forget the grief endured during the long series of dissensions and separations. May the heavenly Father deign to hear our prayers and grant us true brotherly peace.

We are aware that serious and complicated questions remain to be studied, treated and resolved. We would wish that this could be done immediately on account of the love of Christ that "urges us on." But we also realize that these problems require many conditions before satisfactory solutions can be reached— conditions which are as yet premature. Hence we are not afraid to await patiently the blessed hour of perfect reconciliation.

Meanwhile we wish to affirm before the observers here present some points in our attitude toward reunion with our separated brethren, with a view that they may communicate them with their respective Christian communities.

May our voice also reach those other venerable Christian communities separated from us, that did not accept the invitation freely extended to them to attend the council. We believe these points are well known, but it is useful to repeat them here.

Our manner of speaking toward them is friendly, completely sincere and loyal. We lay no snares. We are not motivated by temporal interests. We owe our Faith—which we believe to be divine—the most candid and firm attachment.

But at the same time we are convinced that this does not constitute an obstacle to the desired understanding with our separated brethren, precisely because it is the truth of the Lord and therefore the principle of union, not of distinction or separation. At any rate we do not wish to make of our Faith an occasion for polemics.

Secondly we look with reverence upon the true religious patrimony we share in common, which has been preserved and in part even well developed among our separated brethren. We are pleased to note the study made by those who seek sincerely to make known and to honor the treasures of truth and of genuine spirituality, in order to improve our relations with them.

We hope that just as they are desirous to know more about our history and our religious life, so also they would wish to make a closer study of our doctrine and its logical derivation from the deposit of Divine Revelation.

Finally we wish to say that, aware of the enormous difficulties still in the way of the desired union, we humbly put our trust in God. We shall continue to pray. We shall try to give better proof of our efforts of leading genuine Christian lives and practicing fraternal charity. And should historical reality tend to weaken our hopes, we shall try to recall the comforting words of Christ: "Things that are impossible with men are possible with God" (Luke 18:27).

Finally the council will build a bridge toward the contemporary world. A singular phenomenon: While the Church seeks to revive her interior life in the Spirit of the Lord—thus distinguishing and separating herself from secular society in which she exists—at the same time she is signalized as the lifegiving ferment and the instrument of the salvation of the world, both revealing and strengthening her missionary vocation, which is to treat mankind, in whatever condition it may be, as the object

360 THE SECOND SESSION

of her dedicated mission of communicating the teachings of the Gospels.

You yourselves, Venerable Brethren, have experienced this remarkable phenomenon. Indeed, you yourselves, when you were undertaking the labors of the first session, aglow with the opening words of Pope John XXIII, instantly felt the need of opening, as it were, the doors of this assembly, and of suddenly shouting to the world a message of greeting, of brotherhood, and of hope.

Singular and remarkable gesture this would be; it could be said that the prophetic gift of holy Church had suddenly burst into expression. And as Peter on the day of Pentecost felt the impulse at once to raise his voice and to speak to the people, so you also have unexpectedly determined to treat no longer of your own limited affairs but rather those of the world, no longer to conduct a dialogue among yourselves but rather to open one with the world.

This means, Venerable Brethren, that the present council is characterized by love, by the most comprehensive and compelling love, by a love which thinks of others even before it thinks of itself—by the universal love of Christ.

This love sustains us now because, as we turn our view to the scene of contemporary human life, we ought to be frightened rather than comforted; saddened rather than gladdened; anxious for defense and condemnation rather than for trust and friendship.

We ought to be realists, not hiding the savagery that from many areas reaches even into this universal synod. Can we be blind and not notice that many seats in this assembly are vacant? Where are our brethren from nations in which the Church is opposed? In what conditions does religion exist in these territories?

At such a reminder our thoughts are aggrieved because of what we know and even more because of what we cannot know about our sacred hierarchy, our men and women religious, our countless children subjected to fear, to persecutions, to privations, to oppression, because of their loyalty to Christ and to the Church.

What sadness we feel in the face of such sufferings! What displeasure to see that in certain countries religious liberty, like other fundamental rights of man, is being crushed by principles and methods of political, racial, or anti-religious intolerance! The heart grieves to have to observe that in the world there are still so many acts of injustice against goodness and the free profession of one's religious faith.

But, rather than in bitter words, our lament must be expressed in a frank and human exhortation to all who may be responsible for these evils to put aside with a noble heart their unjustified hostility toward the Catholic religion, whose followers ought to be considered neither as enemies nor as disloyal citizens, but rather as upright and hard-working members of that civil society to which they belong.

Finally, to the Catholics who are suffering for their Faith we send, also on this occasion, our affectionate greetings, and for them we invoke special divine assistance.

Nor does our sorrow end here. The view of the world fills us with crushing sadness because of so many other evils. Atheism is pervading part of the human race and is bringing in its wake the derangement of the intellectual, moral and social order, the true notion of which the world is losing. While the light of the science of God and in consequence over man's true science of nature is increasing, darkness is spreading over the science of God and in consequence over man's true science. While progress is perfecting in a wondrous way every kind of instrument that man uses, his heart is declining towards emptiness, sadness and despair.

We would have a hundred things to say on these complicated and, for many reasons, sad conditions of modern man. But not now. Now, as we were saying, love is filling our heart and the heart of the Church assembled in council.

We look upon our times and upon their varied and contrasting manifestations with immense tenderness and with an immense desire to offer to men of today the message of friendship, of salvation and of hope which Christ has brought into the world. "For God did not send his Son into the world in order to judge the world, but that the world might be saved through him" (John 3:17).

Let the world know this: The Church looks at the world with

profound understanding, with sincere admiration and with the sincere intention not of conquering it, but of serving it; not of despising it, but of appreciating it; not of condemning it, but of strengthening and saving it.

From the window of the council, opened wide on the world, the Church looks towards some categories of persons with particular solicitude: It looks towards the poor, the needy, the afflicted, the hungry, the suffering and sorrowing. Humanity belongs to the Church, by the right which the Gospel gives her. She likes to repeat to all who make up the human race: "Come to me, all . . ." (Matt. 11:28).

She looks towards men of culture and learning, scientists, artists. For these also she has great esteem and a great desire to receive the fruit of their experiences, to strengthen their intellectual life, to defend their liberty, to provide a space in which their troubled spirits can expand joyously within the luminous sphere of the Divine Word and divine grace.

She looks towards the workers, towards the dignity of their person and their labors, toward the legitimacy of their hopes, towards the need—which still afflicts them so greatly—of social improvement and of interior elevation, to the mission which may be recognized as theirs—if it is good, if it is Christian—to create a new world, of free men and brothers. The Church, mother and teacher, is close to them.

And then the Catholic Church looks further still, beyond the confines of the Christian horizon. For how can she put limits to her love if she would make her own the love of God the Father, who rains down His grace on all men alike (Matt. V:46), and who so loved the world as to give for it His only-begotten Son (John 3:16)?

She looks, then, beyond her own sphere and sees those other religions which preserve the sense and notion of the one supreme, transcendant God, Creator and Sustainer, and which worship Him with acts of sincere piety and base their moral and social life on their beliefs and religious practices.

It is true that the Catholic Church sees in such religions omissions, insufficiencies and errors which cause her sadness. Yet she cannot exclude them from her thoughts and would have them know that she esteems what they contain of truth and goodness and humanity.

For the Catholic Church is in the forefront of those who, as a necessary duty of true civilization, strive to preserve religion and the worship of God in modern society. She is the most vigorous upholder of God's rights over mankind.

Other vast fields of humanity fall under her gaze: the new generations of youth desirous of living and expressing themselves; the new peoples now coming to self-awareness, independence and civil organization; the innumerable men and women who feel isolated in a troubled society that has no message for their spirit. To all without exception she proclaims the good news of salvation and hope. To all she offers the light of truth and life and salvation. For God "wishes all men to be saved and to come to the knowledge of the truth" (I Tim. 2:4).

Venerable Brethren, our mission as ministers of salvation is vast and burdensome. We have come together in this solemn assembly so as to fulfill it better. May the deep, fraternal union of our spirits be to us a source of vigor and guidance.

May our union with the Church in heaven bring us support— the saints of our dioceses and religious orders, the angels and all the saints, especially Saints Peter and Paul, St. John the Baptist and, in a particular way, Saint Joseph, the patron of this council.

May Mary, whom we invoke from our hearts, assist us with her powerful motherly aid.

May Christ preside over us, and may all be to the glory of God in the Holy Trinity, whose blessing we now presume to bestow upon you all, in the name of the Father and of the Son and of the Holy Ghost.

Communiqué of the Secretariat for Promoting Christian Unity, regarding the Chapter on the Jews, issued November 8, 1963.

This morning there was distributed to the Fathers of the Second Vatican Council a draft on "The Attitude of Catholics towards Non-Christians, particularly toward the Jews" (De Catholicorum habitudine ad Non-christianos et maxime ad Iudaeos). This draft was prepared over a period of two years by the Secretariat for Promoting Christian Unity, of which His Eminence Augustine Cardinal Bea is President. It is to form the fourth chapter of the schema on Ecumenism, the first three chapters of which had already been submitted to the bishops.

The document is entirely religious in its content and spiritual in its purpose. It is out of an ever-growing appreciation of the Church's sacred heritage that the Council pays attention to the Jews, not as a race or a nation but as the Chosen People of the Old Testament. The clear and unequivocal language of the text gives the Secretariat confidence that no other motive will be read into it than that of the all-embracing love of the late Pope John who himself had wished that the theme be prepared for the Council Fathers.

The draft deals first with the deep bond that ties the Church to the Chosen People of the Old Testament. According to God's merciful design, the Church has its roots in the covenant made by God with Abraham and his descendants. This plan of salvation for all mankind finds its culmination in the coming of Jesus Christ, Son of David and descendant of Abraham according to the flesh. Through Him the divine call first given to the Chosen People of old is extended through His Church to the entire world.

A second point the draft makes is that the responsibility for Christ's death falls upon sinful mankind. It was to atone for the sins of every man that the Son of God willingly offered Himself on the Cross. The part the Jewish leaders of Christ's day played in bringing about the crucifixion does not exclude the guilt of all mankind. But the personal guilt of these leaders cannot be charged to the whole Jewish people either of His time or today. It is therefore unjust to call this people "deicide" or to consider it "cursed" by God. St. Paul, in his letter to the Romans, assures us that God has not rejected the people whom He has chosen.

The document presented goes on to affirm that the Church can never forget that it was from Abraham's stock that Christ, His Blessed Mother and the Apostles were born.

In keeping with its objectives, the Council document does not propose to deal with the various causes of anti-semitism. However, it does indicate that the sacred events of the Bible and, in particular, its account of the crucifixion, cannot give rise to disdain or hatred or persecution of the Jews. Preachers and catechists, the text states, are admonished never to present a contrary position; furthermore, they are urged to promote mutual understanding and esteem.

It is clear, therefore, that both the contents and purposes of the document are purely religious. It cannot be called pro-Zionist or anti-Zionist since it considers these as political questions and entirely outside of its religious scope. In fact, any use of the text to support partisan discussions or particular political claims or to attack the political claims of others would be completely unjustified and contrary to every intention of those who have composed it and presented it to the Council.

Some recent newspaper accounts have mentioned the immediate possibility of an official observer to the II Vatican Council delegated by the World Jewish Congress. The incident referred to is not a recent one but took place in the summer of 1962. The Secretariat for Promoting Christian Unity did not consider the proposal seriously at that time and is not doing so now.

Address of His Holiness Pope Paul VI at the conclusion of the Second Session of the Second Vatican Council, December 4, 1963.

Venerable Brothers,

We have now reached the end of the Second Session of this great Ecumenical Council.

You have already been long absent from your sees, in which the sacred ministry requires your presence, your guidance and your zealous pastoral labours. Your work here has been heavy, assiduous and protracted by reasons of the ceremonies, studies and meetings of this period of the Council. And now we have just entered upon the sacred season of Advent which prepares us to celebrate worthily the memory of the blessed Nativity of Our Lord Jesus Christ, that yearly recurring feast which never loses its solemnity and wonder and holiness. During this important and aborbing commemoration of the ineffable mystery of the Incarnate Word of God none of us should be occupied with other thoughts, however elevated or holy they may be. None of us should be detained in any other see, however great and venerable, but each of us should celebrate the liturgical mysteries in that place where Providence has entrusted to us his church, his community and his priestly pastoral duty.

We must, therefore, interrupt for a second time the course of this great synod; we must once again bid each other farewell and go our separate ways after these happy days of momentous brotherly conference.

But we must first thank God for the blessings that He has bestowed during this Session and by its means, nor can we withhold our thanks from any of those who have taken part in the Session and have had some positive part in its successful functioning. We thank especially the Presidency of the Council, the Moderators, the Secretariat and also the Commissions and the Periti, the representatives of press and television, those who have fitted out this Basilica, and those who have offered hospitality and assistance to the Fathers of the Council. And we thank

in a particular way those Fathers who have been good enough
to contribute towards the great expense that the organisation
of this great event requires, or have with fraternal charity come
to the aid of their more needy brothers, or have assisted the
Church in her enormous needs and come to the help of the
victims of recent disasters.

Before concluding our labours it would be fitting to sum up
and to consider together the course of the Session and its results.
But to do that would make this address too long, nor indeed
could it be done adequately since so many aspects of this Council
belong to the domain of grace and the inner kingdom of the
soul into which it is not always easy to enter, and since so many
of the Council's results have not yet come to maturity, but are
as grains of wheat cast into the furrows, awaiting their effective
and fruitful development, which will be granted only in the
future through new mysterious manifestations of the divine
goodness.

Nevertheless, lest we seem to leave this holy Council hall without gratitude for the blessings of God, from whom this Council
has here taken its origin, we will remind ourselves above all that
some of the goals that the Council set itself to achieve have been
already at least partially reached. The Church wished to grow
in her consciousness and understanding of herself: see how, on
the very level of her pastors and teachers, she has begun a profound meditation on that mystery from which she draws her
origin and form; the meditation is not finished, but the very
difficulty of concluding it reminds us of the depth and breadth
of this doctrine, and stimulates each of us to strive to understand and to express the doctrine in a way which, on the one
hand, cannot fail to lead our minds, and certainly those of the
faithful who are attentively following our labours, to Christ
Himself from whom all gifts come to us and to whom we wish
to return all, "reconciling everything in Him" (Col. 1:20); on
the other hand, our efforts cannot fail to increase both our happiness in being personally called to form part of this holy
mystical body of Christ, and our mutual charity, the principle
and law of the life of the Church. Let us rejoice, my Brothers,
for when was the Church ever so aware of herself, so in love
with Christ, so blessed, so united, so willing to imitate Him, so

ready to fulfil His mission? Let us rejoice, my Brothers, for we
have learned to understand one another and to deal with one
another, and, though we were almost strangers, through the
process of union we have become friends; have we not profoundly experienced here the words of St. Paul which accurately
define the Church: "Now you are no longer strangers and newcomers, but rather fellow-citizens of the saints and members of
the household of God, built, as you are, upon the foundations
laid by the apostles and the prophets, where the very cornerstone is Christ Jesus" (Eph. 2:19-20), and we do not perhaps
see that if the canon law which governs the Church is developed, its growth will extend in two directions: it will accord to
every person and office in the Church both greater dignity and
greater power of development, and at the same time it will
strengthen, as it were according to the intrinsic demands of love,
of harmony, and of mutual respect—the power which unites
through hierarchical government, the whole community of the
faithful? We must confess that this Council is a great achievement, a great gift of God to His Church, if our minds have been
so resolutely turned toward these thoughts and these proposals.

Moreover, if we ask ourselves about the nature of the
labours of the Council, here again we ought to rejoice that they
have witnessed so widespread, so unflagging, and so lively a
participation by the Council Fathers. Even now the spectacle of
this Basilica, occupied as it is by our revered and thronged
assembly, has filled our hearts with admiration, devotion, and
spiritual joy; even now our hearts are moved by the sight of the
esteemed observers who have been invited to this gathering and
who have so graciously accepted the invitation; and no less
comfort has been brought to a father's heart by the presence of
the auditors who, though silent, have shown the loyalty of true
sons, those dear sons who represent the vast ranks of the Catholic laity working with the hierarchy of the Church for the spread
of the kingdom of God. Everything in this hall and on this
occasion becomes symbolic and speaks to us; everything here is
a sign of heaven-sent thoughts, everything a foreshadowing of
heaven-sent hopes.

Nor does the manner in which the undertakings of this
Council have proceeded cause us any less satisfaction: ought we

not show our debt of gratitude to the Fathers of the Presidency of the Council, to the Moderators, to the Secretariat of the Council, to the Commissions, and to the Periti who have placed at our disposal both their work and their advice?

It would be good to treasure this fruit of our Council as something that should animate and characterize the life of the Church. For the Church is a religious society, a community at prayer. It is composed of people with a flourishing interior life and spirituality that is nourished by faith and grace. If now we wish to simplify our liturgical rites, if we wish to render them more intelligible to the people and accommodated to the language they speak, by so doing we certainly do not wish to lessen the importance of prayer, or to give it less importance than other forms of the sacred ministry or pastoral activity, or to impoverish its expressive force and artistic charm. On the contrary we wish to render the liturgy more pure, more genuine, more in agreement with the source of truth and grace, more suitable to be transformed into a spiritual patrimony of the people.

To attain these ends it is necessary that no attempt should be made to introduce into the official prayer of the Church private changes or singular rites, nor should anyone arrogate to himself the right to interpret arbitrarily the Constitution on the Liturgy which today we promulgate, before opportune and authoritative instructions are given. Furthermore the reforms which will be prepared by postconciliar bodies must first receive official approbation. The nobility of ecclesiastical prayer and its musical expression throughout the world, is something no one would wish to disturb or to damage.

The other fruit, not of small value, that the Council has produced is the Decree on Communications Media—an indication of the capacity of the Church to unite the interior and exterior life, contemplation and action, prayer and active apostolate. We hope that this decree too will help to guide and encourage numerous forms of activity in the exercise of the pastoral ministry and of the Catholic mission in the world.

There are two things to be noted about the Council's work; it has been laborious and, above all, it has enjoyed freedom of expression. This two-fold characteristic which marks this Council and which will set an example for the future, seems to us worthy of emphasis: this is the way that the holy Church works today at the highest and most significant stage of its developmen: it works intensely and it works spontaneously.

Our satisfaction is in no way diminished by the variety, by the multiplicity, or even by the divergence of the opinions which have been expressed in the discussions of the Council; on the contrary, this is a proof of the depth of the subjects investigated, of the interest with which they have been followed, and, as we said before, of the freedom with which they have been discussed.

The arduous and intricate discussions have certainly borne fruit insofar as one of the topics, the first one to be discussed, and, in a certain sense, the first in order of intrinsic excellence and importance for the life of the Church, the schema on Sacred Liturgy, has been brought to a happy conclusion, and today we have solemnly promulgated it. We rejoice at this accomplishment. We may see in this an acknowledgement of a right order of values and duties: God in the first place; prayer our first duty; the liturgy the first school of spirituality, the first gift which we can bestow upon Christians who believe and pray with us. It is the first invitation to the world to break forth in happy and truthful prayer and to feel the ineffable life-giving force that comes from joining us in the song of divine praise and of human hope, through Christ Our Lord and in the Holy Spirit.

We can also include among the fruits of this Council the many faculties which, in order to promote the pastoral ends of the Council itself, we have declared, in the document distributed to all the Fathers, to be within the competence of the bishops, specially those with ordinary jurisdiction.

This is not all. The Council has laboured much. As you all know it has addressed itself to many questions whose solutions are in part virtually formulated in authoritative decisions which will be published in time after the work on the topics to which they belong is completed.

Other questions are still subject to further studies and discussions. We hope that the third Session in the autumn of next year will bring them to completion. It is fitting that we should have more time to reflect on these difficult problems, and that the competent commissions on whose work we place so much hope, will prepare for the future conciliar meetings, in accordance with the mind of the Fathers, as expressed specially in the general congregations, proposals profoundly studied, accurately formulated, suitably còndenesd and abbreviated, so that the discussions, while remaining always free, may be rendered easier and more brief.

Such for example is the question of divine revelation to which the Council will give a reply which while defending the sacred deposit of divine truth against errors, abuses and doubts that endanger its objective validity, at the same time will provide directives to guide biblical, patristic and theological studies which Catholic thought, faithful to ecclesiastical teaching and vitalized by every good modern scientific tool, will want to promote earnestly, prudently and with confidence.

Such also is the great and complex question of the Episcopacy which, in both logical order and importance, is the primary concern of this Second Ecumenical Vatican Council, a Council which, as we shall never forget, is the natural continuation and complement of the First Vatican Council. As a consequence, the aim of our Council is to clarify the divinely instituted nature and function of the Episcopacy not in contrast to, but in confirmation of, the supreme, Christ-given prerogatives, conveying all authority necessary for the universal government of the Church, which are acknowledged as belonging to the Roman Pontiff. Its aim is to set forth the position of the Episcopacy according to the mind of Our Lord and the authentic tradition of the Church, declaring what its powers are and indicating how they should be used, individually and corporately, so as worthily to manifest the eminence of the Episcopacy in the Church of God. The Episcopacy is not an institution independent of, or separated from, or, still less, antagonistic to, the Supreme Pontificate of Peter, but with Peter and under him it strives for the common good and the supreme end of the Church. The coordinated hierarchy will thus be strengthened not undermined, its inner collaboration will be increased not lessened, its apostolic effectiveness enhanced not impeded, its mutual charity stirred up not stifled. We are sure that on a subject of such importance the Council will have much to say that will bring consolation and light.

And likewise, for the schema on the Blessed Virgin Mary, we

hope for the solution most in keeping with the nature of this Council, that is, the unanimous and loving acknowledgement of the place, privileged above all others, which the Mother of God occupies in the Holy Church—in the Church which is the principal subject matter of the present Council; after Christ her place in the Church is the most exalted, and also the one closest to us, so that we can honour her with the title "Mater Ecclesiae," to her glory and to our benefit.

And after these questions, which the Council has already touched upon, there remain many others which it was unable to treat of. But much study has already been accorded them. We will see to it that these questions be subjected to a thorough and deeper re-examinaion so as to be able to present to the next session of the Council schemata which are short and so worded that it will not be difficult to obtain a judgement of the Council on certain fundamental propositions. It will be left to the post-Conciliar Commissions to explain these principles more fully and to work out their practical implications. Among these Commissions, the principal work will certainly fall to the one charged with the compilation of the new Codes, both for the Latin Church and for the Oriental Church. In this work which will follow the Council, the collaboration of the Episcopacy, in new ways required by the need and the organic nature of the Church, will be very precious to us. Naturally it will be a source of joy to us to choose from among the Bishops of the world and from the ranks of the religious orders, as was done for the preparatory Commissions of the Council, distinguished and expert brethren, who, along with qualified members of the Sacred College, will bring us their counsel and help to translate into fitting and specific norms the general decisions of the Council. And so experience will suggest to us how, without prejudice to the prerogatives of the Roman Pontiff defined by the First Vatican Council, the earnest and cordial collaboration of the Bishops can more effectively promote the good of the universal Church.

Let us, therefore, end this Session of the Council by taking stock of all that it has positively achieved: it has worked hard, it has completed some chapters of its enormous task and has made a good beginning on many other chapters of importance, it has shown how divergent opinions can be freely expressed, it has demonstrated the desirability and the possibility of coming to agreement on fundamental questions by discussion and made clear how each and every one holds sincerely and firmly to the dogmatic truths that make up the Church's doctrinal patrimony, it has moreover stirred up in all of us that charity which must always be present in our search for and profession of the truth, it has constantly kept in view the pastoral purpose of the Council, it has always tried to find means and expressions capable of closing the gap between our separated brethren and ourselves, it has accompanied its every act with prayer to God, the source of all hope.

Yet, even so, it leaves us with an even more vivid realisation of what remains to be done and with a more deeply felt sense of our duty of making the Church better fitted to deliver its message of truth and salvation to the modern world. We have not forgotten the conditions of the day nor has our love for the men among whom we live grown less. As each one returns home to his ordinary affairs he will carry in his heart an earnest concern to make that charity more effective. Even before the Council discusses problems of the modern apostolate, we can say that we all of us already know the answers, for the Church's teaching is already clear and profound and the example of the better among our Brethren already point the way. Could we not, here and now, on our return from the Council, give proof of our more ardent pastoral spirit by speaking to our flocks and to all who hear our voices, words of exhortation and encouragement? Could we not, here and now, and by way of preparation for the next, intensify our inner life and be more attentive to the divine word? Could we not take back to our clergy a message of fervour and charity? to our layfolk a word of heartening reassurance? to young people an inspiring invitation? To the world of thought a shaft of truth? to the world of labour a message of hope and affection? to the poor the first of the Gospel's beatitudes?

There cannot be, we believe, a more effective way than that of devoted ministry for disposing us, with God's help, to bring the great Council to a successful end in practical and salutary resolutions.

We are so convinced that, for the final, happy conclusion of this Council, prayers and good works are necessary that, after careful deliberation and much prayer, we have decided to become a pilgrim ourselves to the land of Jesus our Lord.

In fact, if God assists us, we wish to go to Palestine in January to honor personally, in the holy places where Christ was born, lived, died and ascended to heaven after His Resurrection, the first mysteries of our faith, the Incarnaton and the redemption.

We shall see that blessed land whence Peter set forth and where not one of his successors has returned. Most humbly and briefly we shall return there as an expression of prayer, penance and renovation to offer to Christ His church, to summon to this one holy church our separated brethren, to implore divine mercy on behalf of peace among men, that peace which shows in these days how weak and tottering it is, to beseech Christ our Lord for the salvation of the entire human race.

May the most holy Madonna guide our steps, may the Apostles Peter and Paul and all the saints assist us benignly from heaven.

As we will have you all present in spirit during this pious journey, so may you, venerable brethren, accompany us with your prayers so that this Council can come to a good conclusion for the glory of Christ and the good of His church.

Index

�֍